SOUTHERN IMAGINING

Southern Imagining

A LITERARY AND CULTURAL HISTORY OF THE FAR SOUTHERN HEMISPHERE

ELLEKE BOEHMER

PRINCETON UNIVERSITY PRESS
PRINCETON & OXFORD

Published by Princeton University Press
41 William Street, Princeton, New Jersey 08540
99 Banbury Road, Oxford OX2 6JX

press.princeton.edu

GPSR Authorized Representative: Easy Access System Europe - Mustamäe tee 50, 10621 Tallinn, Estonia, gpsr.requests@easproject.com

ISBN 978-0-691- 26204-8
ISBN (e-book) 978-0-691-27420-1

Library of Congress Control Number: 2025940694

British Library Cataloging-in-Publication Data is available

Editorial: Ben Tate and Josh Drake
Production Editorial: Elizabeth Byrd, Kathleen Cioffi
Jacket design: Ben Higgins
Production: Danielle Amatucci
Publicity: William Pagdatoon and Charlotte Coyne
Copyeditor: Norman Ware

Jacket credit: Valerie Loiseleux / iStock; Kitnha / Shutterstock

Printed and bound by CPI Group (UK) Ltd, Croydon, CR0 4YY

10 9 8 7 6 5 4 3 2 1

For John Coetzee

Juegas todos los días con la luz del universo.
Sutil visitadora, llegas en la flor y en el agua.
. . .
Quién escribe tu nombre con letras de humo entre las estrellas del sur?

—PABLO NERUDA, FROM 'POEMA 14', *VEINTE POEMAS DE AMOR Y UNA CANCIÓN DESESPERADA* (1924)

Die aarde sou geen lig gehad het
as die melkweg nie die melkweg
was nie. dit en die sterre

||KABBO, 'DIE MELKWEG EN DIE STERRE', AS RELAYED BY ANTJIE KROG, *DIE STERRE SÊ 'TSAU'* (2004)

All moments in time are the mysterious and powerful companions of fate . . .

—ALEXIS WRIGHT, *CARPENTARIA* (2006)

CONTENTS

List of Images and Map xi

Preface xvii

Acknowledgements xxiii

A Word on Terminology xxix

1 A Hemisphere Awry 1

'All Different, Quite Different' 1

Inhabiting the South in the Mind 4

Where Is the South? 5

Not East: The South as External 11

Thinking from the South with Story 13

The Global South in Theory 16

Outline 18

Southern Curves 22

2 Shared Skies: Speaking and Singing the South 25

Thinking from and through the South 27

Structural Meditation—a Southern Reading 33

Archipelagic Understanding 34

Words 35

Stars 40

Seas 46

3 Reading the South: Camões's 'Audacious Passage' 50

'Laid Down in Some Charts': A Collage of Reading 51

Navigating South, or Worlding in Motion 54

A Very Short History of Mapping the Unknown 58

Reading and Writing Distance 63

The Epic as Portolan: Luís de Camões, The Lusíads *(1572)* 65

Adamastor's Southern Vertex, Camões's Parabola 70

4 Writing Southern Seas: Coleridge, Darwin, Melville, Shelley 76

Turning: Through the Southern Depths 77

Shaping Seascapes 79

Foundational Frames: North into South 82

'The Sun Now Rose upon the Right': Samuel Taylor Coleridge's Rime of the Ancient Mariner 83

Distance and Darwin: The Voyage of the *Beagle* 87

'The White Mass Floating in the Sun': Herman Melville's Moby-Dick 92

Coda—Mary Shelley's Frankenstein, *a Study in Monomania* 98

5 'Silent Vastness': the Farthest South 101

Beset by Ice: Finding the Endurance 102

The Farthest South: An Overview 105

Asymptote 111

South-South Connectivity 116

On Not Articulating the Ice: Orsman, Manhire, Bainbridge, McGregor, Diski 118

6 'Breaking the Solemn Monotony': Settler Cartographies 129

Reading South 130

Writing Elsewhere 132

Latitudinal Links across the South 138

Southern Poetics: Not Far but Here 142

Cartographies and Case Studies 147

7 Keeping South: Writing from Here 163

River, Cliff, and Stars: Jazz Money and Gabeba Baderoon 164

Thinking from the South (Again) 169

Southscapes—Being Here 172

Speaking the Land 177

Connection and Reconnection across the South 184

'You and the Movement of Water' 188

8 Faraway Close 190

On the Farthest Edges of the World 191

And Yet Their Closeness 192

Contrariwise, to the Stars 196

Wheeling across the Sky 199

Turning to Day 200

Within Space-Time 202

A Sound of Southern Space 205

Faraway Close 207

Looping Back to the Distant Edge 208

Notes 215

Bibliography 271

Index 303

Colour insert follows page 114

LIST OF IMAGES AND MAP

Photos are by the author unless otherwise indicated.

xvii The Southern Ocean from Carrickalinga beach, Fleurieu Peninsula, South Australia, October 2024.

1 View onto the Kalahari, 100 kilometres from Askham, December 2024

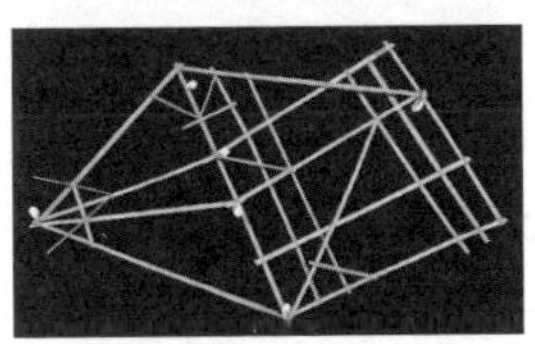

25 Sailing chart from the Marshall Islands. Copyright Pitt Rivers Museum, University of Oxford (1897.1.2).

33 The 77,000-year-old Blombos Cave ochre engraving.
Copyright Iziko Museums of South Africa. Photograph credit: Iziko Museums of South Africa, Conservation, Bradley Mottie/Janene van Wyk. Used with permission.

40 The Milky Way from Namibia, September 2022. Photograph copyright David Clapp. Used with permission.

50 The Sentinels looking out over False Bay, Cape Peninsula, February 2020.

76 An albatross skims over the waves off Otago Peninsula, South Island, Aotearoa New Zealand, December 2019.

105 An iceberg off the Palmer Peninsula, Antarctica, March 2019. Photograph copyright Charne Lavery. Used with permission.

116 A double iceberg formation, Antarctica, January 2025. Photograph copyright Annemie Boehmer. Used with permission.

129 Karoo landscape pictured from the site of Olive Schreiner's grave, Buffelskop, near Cradock, Eastern Cape, South Africa, February 2020.

163 Bird-shaped cloud over False Bay, Western Cape, February 2022.

190 Cape Huay, Tasmania, December 2022.

193 Eucalyptus or lemon-scented gum (*Corymbia citriodora*), Norwood, South Australia, October 2024.

195 Cape Town (33.5°S), March 2022.

196 Adelaide (34.5°S), December 2022.

197 Simon's Town, March 2023.

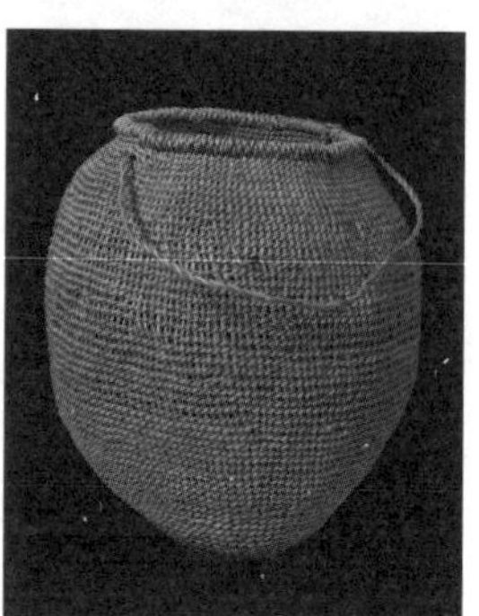

202 Tasmanian dhili basket. Copyright Pitt Rivers Museum, University of Oxford (1893.38.24).

203 Bicornal basket in twined cane weave, Northern Queensland. Pitt Rivers Museum, University of Oxford (1897.1.2).

208 From the rocky breakwater on Mudurup or Cottesloe Beach, Perth, Western Australia, facing south-west, February 2019.

209 From St Clair beach near Dunedin, South Island, Aotearoa New Zealand, December 2019.

210 The Beagle Channel, from above Ushuaia, Tierra del Fuego, April 2019.

211 Cape Point, in a gale, February 2020.

213 Wolwedans Valley, Namibia, September 2022.

271 Pointing due south, Kommetjie lighthouse, December 2024.

Plate 1 Gulumbu Yunupingu, *Ganyu-Stars* (2006). Photo by the author. Art Gallery of South Australia. Reproduction by kind permission of the artist's estate.

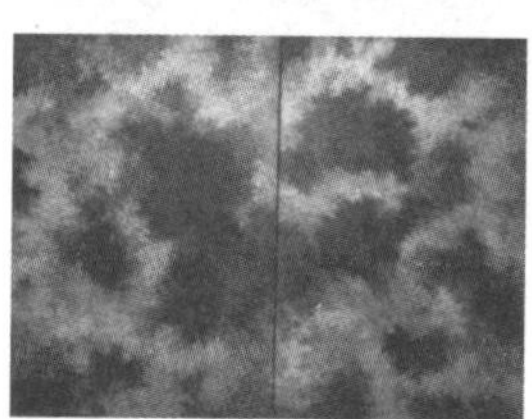

Plate 2 Yatjiki Vicki Cullinan, *Munga Ilkari-Night Sky* (2017). Reproduction by kind permission of the artist.

Plate 3 Lola Frost, *The Edge of the Skirt of the World* (2014). Reproduction by kind permission of the artist.

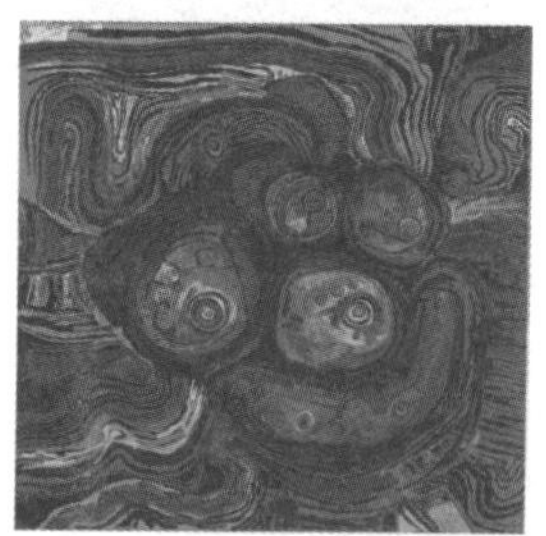

Plate 4 Nyunmiti Burton, *Kungkarangkalpa-Seven Sisters* (2020). Art Gallery of South Australia, Adelaide. Reproduction by kind permission of the artist.

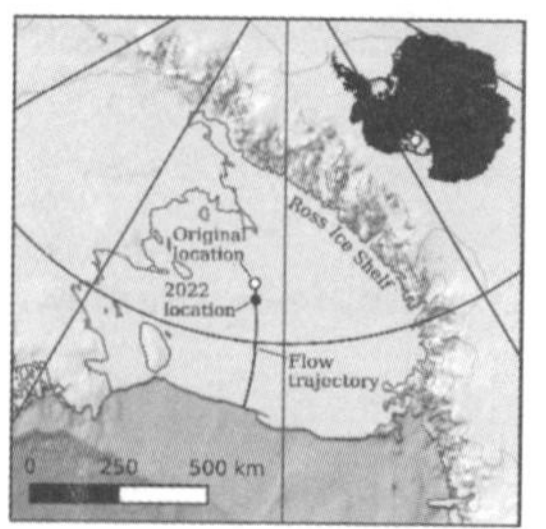

$$\begin{bmatrix} x_{t+\Delta t} \\ y_{t+\Delta t} \end{bmatrix} = \begin{bmatrix} x_t + v_{x_t}\Delta t \\ y_t + v_{y_t}\Delta t \end{bmatrix}$$

101 Robert Law, Calculation to determine the pathway and current location of Robert Scott and his companions' remains through the ice of the Beardmore Glacier, October 2022.

PREFACE

THE SOUTH is the far.

The underside and the upside-down.
It is widdershins and topsy-turvy.
Counter-clockwise.
Contrariwise.
About face.
Antipodal.
Or the wrong way around.
Against the sun.

It is the 'bottom' of our planet. Its verso.

And yet, not.

It depends on where you are looking from. Here, or there.

To the north, the south of the world is contrary. The southern skies are upside down.

But to southerners, the south is plainly *here* and the right way up.

It is itself. In its place.

For centuries, the limits of the known world lay south, at least for Europe and probably also for most of Asia. Beyond, as in Strabo or Ptolemy's descriptions, was empty space. The ultimate *ne plus ultra*.[1]

The geographers of the Ancient World speculated that vast continents lay far south, as counterweights to the northern landmasses.

Their Renaissance successors charted the south as a chimera, an 'amalgamated elsewhere'.[2]

Setting out to discover more, early European explorers found that these spaces were contrary also in their fluidity, their sheer wateriness. Large landmasses far south were, in actuality, few and far between, while oceans were immense, turbulent, and freezing.

To their eyes, everything was the wrong way about.

South of the Tropic of Capricorn, the sun traced its east-west trajectory through the northern and not the southern sky. Sun-cast shadows turned anticlockwise.

And water spirals rotated left-hand-wise, driven like migrating birds by the earth's different spin.

Solar eclipses, too, appeared to move in the reverse direction.

And the seasons were the wrong way about. There was snow in June and spring blossom in October.

Ferdinand Magellan, Abel Tasman, Francis Drake, James Cook, Louis-Antoine de Bougainville, Yves de Kerguélen, and many others—the names of these northern explorers now cover the southern lands they mapped, as if to elide their strangeness.

As late as the 1920s, D. H. Lawrence, on a visit to New South Wales, felt terror at the 'clefts in the atmosphere' that he noticed. Later, again, the science fiction writer Ursula Le Guin described the great southern ice as 'the left hand of darkness'.[3]

But what is clefted or left-hand to whom?

Southern Imagining explores what it is to inhabit the far south of our planet in the mind. The book asks how we see from cardinal points south, as against perceiving the hemisphere through northern lenses, which, till now, most readers of these pages may naturally do.

Northern perspectives are institutionally embedded. While the southern hemisphere makes up one half of the earth's surface, southern geographies, histories, and lives tend to be defined from northern vantage points in northern languages. All of the major world languages have northern roots.

The shelves of most northern hemisphere libraries hold books written on northern subjects by northern writers, yet with this bias (if such it is) invisible to most. Notions of a counterclockwise world remain in the realm of fantasy and oddity for most of the world's readers.

This makes factual sense. Only 10 percent of the world's people live in the southern hemisphere. Eighty-one percent of its surface area is ocean.

The north's geo-linguistic bias is reflected in the many clichéd phrases, like 'down under' or 'the far side of the world', that are used to denote southern hemisphere countries. These phrases assume that the top, the right side up, represents the known and the important. Whereas the south inhabits time past, the time of myth and legend.[4]

In recorded history, the lands of the south have always been perceived as the outside of our planet—spaces too far away, too scattered, too insignificant, to matter fully to the world as a whole.

Yet to those born there, who live here, contrariwise, the south is close and immediate. It is *this* space we are in now (and where I am writing this). The place where we stand. Where we belong.

Where we feel at once on the edge and yet *here*, both on a boundary, yet unbounded. Mindful of our coordinates. Aware of the special thisness or haecceity of our worlds.

Southern Imagining explores these different ways of seeing and imagining south.

Eight chapters trace southern perceptions in a range of myths, stories, legends, and especially literary writings, including poetry, fiction, travel writing, and memoir, extending from the 1500s to the present day. Their southern images and forms are taken to transmit something of the oceanic and light-filled experience of the south itself.

Placing the South Pole at the very heart of its vision, the book endeavours to see the planet differently, from below and in the round. Where no part is insignificant.

The south-centred world map, I suggest, encourages us to think at scale. It makes apparently unimportant southern geographies matter centrally. It destabilises the models of planetary evolution in which the northern human has always been placed at the forefront of history. And it offers imaginative measures that might help to better understand the accelerating climate change worldwide that confronts us all.

But where does the far distant and seemingly unimaginable south in fact lie?

The south of *Southern Imagining* comprises the remoter regions of the hemisphere. The tapering continents, peninsulas and promontories, scattered islands and archipelagos that face the vast Southern Ocean. And, beyond, the great ice of Antarctica itself.

The continents of the southern hemisphere fit into each other like jigsaw pieces, showing that they were all once pieces of one main, the supercontinent of Gondwanaland. The landmasses bear glaciation marks in common. The same vast glaciers once moved across them all.

Southwards, the continental landmasses seem to dwindle, as if thinned and compressed by the rushing southern currents that are, in actuality, pushing them apart.

Other singular features run around and through the hemisphere.

A distinctive sunlight illuminates far southern spaces, both their seaboards and their desert regions.[5] It is a deep blue, ocean-reflected, dryness-distilled light. At night, as the world turns, astounding starry skies reveal themselves hour by passing hour to southern lands and islands. The great arc of the Milky Way appears to blaze. As do the Magellanic Clouds. For, though the solar system finds itself at an outer edge of the galaxy's shining track, the South Pole is oriented towards its centre.

To the first European navigators in the south, the Portuguese, even the stars of the southern hemisphere were alarming and disorienting. The inhabitants of southern lands and islands, however, had long woven legends of journeying, planting, and harvesting into its sidereal shapes. Yet, even today, when southerners look south across the wild ocean to Antarctica, where most weather fronts come from, a sense of mystery and awe hits us, too.

These and other littoral and lateral links will keep surfacing across the length of the book—like the purple flourishing of jacaranda trees in most southern cities in the springtime, September or October. Native to South America, jacarandas thrive in the temperate sub-tropical band between twenty-eight and thirty-six degrees south, where we find most urban centres.

Throughout, *Southern Imagining* insists that thinking laterally, working from the inside out *and* the outside in, making links across the south, is essential for south-centred understanding. And that thinking south, or contrariwise, is vital for our survival on this planet.

Chapter by chapter, the book suggests that the south is something that can perhaps only be known relationally, through a kind of juxtaposition, as in a collage, '*with, through* but also *against* other spaces, places, times, peoples, modes of knowledge and action.'[6]

For most, the northern *here* requires no justification. It is the view from within, and the south is faraway. With *Southern Imagining,* I propose that we reverse these perspectives. We take the south, the southern here, as sufficient to itself. By reading south, we begin to claim a specific sense of southern belonging to this planet—a sense that, finally, may prove crucial for us all, for those of the north as well as of the south.

ACKNOWLEDGEMENTS

A LITERARY-HISTORICAL study of a hemisphere would have been impossible to write, let alone dream of, without the inspiration, encouragement, and help of a great number of people, and the support of several institutions. I am deeply grateful to the British Academy and the Leverhulme Trust for the Senior Research Fellowship 2020–21, SRF19/190028, which allowed me to take research leave and undertake southern travel, both before and after the global pandemic. The Covid-19 extension of the fellowship in the autumn term of 2021 was invaluable, and I am incredibly thankful for it, too. I should also acknowledge the British Academy/Leverhulme Trust's Small Grant award 'Tracing Southern Latitudes: Legends, Languages, Life-Writing', SRG19\190295, that funded the 'Southern Lives' workshops at Wolfson College, 2020–23. I am grateful to the President and Fellows of Wolfson College, Oxford, and the English Faculty at Oxford for granting the periods of leave that allowed me to take up the Senior Research Fellowship.

My gratitude is to the Stellenbosch Institute for Advanced Study in South Africa for the COVID-curtailed fellowship in early 2020 that allowed me to begin the research on chapters 2 and 3 of this book, and for the continuation fellowship in 2025 during which I could present my findings. My thanks to the University of Adelaide's inaugural International Visiting Fellowship 2024, which made it possible to travel to the 'Speaking from the South' cultural event and academic conference during the weeks that I was also assembling the final manuscript of *Southern Imagining* for review. Thank you to Mandy Treagus and Maggie Tonkin, the organisers of 'Speaking from the South', and also to the supremely insightful Meg Samuelson. The Visiting Fellowship further supported a reading group and a workshop, 'Stars, Stardust and Story-Making in the South' at the University of Adelaide on 7 November 2014. Many thanks to my co-convenor, Samuel Jesse Cox, who helped to make it possible.

That *Southern Imagining* has been among the most enjoyable books I have written to date is because its making involved rewarding collaborations and lively conversations with many different people, in many capacities, from across many geographies, south and north. Some of these conversations were with individuals met while travelling, whose names I did not record, or never knew, but I am grateful to them, too—not least, the airline pilots and flight attendants whose ears I bent about southern constellations and feelings of farness, and the fellow admirers of sunsets and seascapes from any number of beaches and rocky outcrops who stopped to chat with me.

It is perhaps bizarre to thank the poets, novelists, and other writers who produce the work that forms the subject of a literary study. However, as literary writing from across the past five hundred years has afforded insights into the far south that were not available elsewhere, I would like to say how grateful I am for the vast and various work discussed in these pages and for the inspiration and joy that they have given. It was always in the first place the literature that showed me how to begin to conceptualise outside the terms and structures of northern knowledge.

Yatjiki Vicki Cullinan and Lola Frost, your paintings of the southern night sky and the 'edges' of the world helped me to orient myself throughout. Thank you. Nyunmiti Burton and Gulumbu Yunupingu's wonderful astral reflections led me through southern worlds within worlds, and I'm deeply grateful for the inspiration.

Special thanks are due to my undergraduate tutor Malvern van Wyk Smith and to the spirit of André Brink for first piquing my interest in early modern conceptions of the African continent and in the work of Luís de Camões and the Adamastor story back in the 1980s and early 1990s. And my warmest thanks to John Coetzee, the dedicatee of this book, for our fruitful conversations on the singular far south for a decade and more, for kindly sharing his hunches and reflections with me, and for his corroborative sense that there were commonalities that engirdled the world 'below' the equator.

Some of the chapters in this book were first drafted, or, in some cases, finished, in welcoming rooms in my homes-from-home in the far south. Lisa Hill, Karina Szczurek, David and Joan Attwell, David Medalie—I can't begin to say how much your hospitality and generosity have meant to me, or the knowledge that I had a bolthole with you in the hemisphere that I call my own. The skies, seas, hills, and mountainsides I have seen from your windows, doors, and stoops were sights that allowed me to say, *here* I write. Warmest thanks also to Charne Lavery, Erica Lombard and Arlyn Culwick, Jane Moss, Sarah Nuttall and Achille Mbembe, and Tamson Pietsch for unforgettable evenings spent on their balconies and verandas, stargazing and talking about southern themes. Karina, where would I be without your books or your dedication to books? Lisa, thanks also for sharing those special southern songs with me, for our extraordinary trip into the Arkaroola in November 2024, and for always knowing where I'm coming from.

I am very grateful to Derek Attridge, Antoinette Burton, and Lyn Innes for their encouragement and support of this project at an early stage. Supriya Chaudhuri helpfully prompted me back in 2018 to further develop the idea of the far south as the exterior of the north. From our conversation, it became clearer to me that the farthest edge of the world is also *a part of* the world. I am grateful to the anonymous readers of the manuscript who helped me to make this a better book.

I would like especially to acknowledge the following for exchanges across the past seven years on southern moods, tones, people and things: David Attwell, Tony Ballantyne, Tom Barron, Danielle Battigelli, Natalie Betts, Maxim Bolt, George Chaplin, Carrol Clarkson, Teju Cole, Sarah Comyn, Samuel Jesse Cox, Dominic Davies, Gillian Dooley, Kai Easton, Riley Faulds, Porscha Fermanis, Eugenia Flynn, Robert Freeman, Kirsty Gunn, Craig Hardner, Isabel Hofmeyr, Lisa Hill, Tom McLean, Nic James-Moore, Nicholas Jose, Ananya Kabir, Charne Lavery, Alan Lester, Jennifer Mahoney, Nelson Mlambo, Stephen Muecke, Ankhi Mukherjee, Lynda Ng, John Noyes, Sarah Nuttall, Emma Parker, Cristóbal Pérez Barra, Tamson Pietsch, Meg Samuelson, Bernhard Schirg, Joe Shaughnessy, Helen Small, Luan Staphorst, Hedley Twidle, Anthony Uhlmann, Paul Walters, Gillian Whitlock, Jon Wood, Robert Young, and Sandra Young. David Clapp, many thanks for sharing your starry pictures from Namibia with me. Annemie Boehmer and Charne Lavery, thank you for the bewitching iceberg photographs.

I was greatly helped by librarians and curators at the Bodleian Library, especially the 'scan and deliver' team, who made it possible to access resources at the time of the pandemic. I should also like to thank the librarians and curators at the National Library of Australia, the Barr Smith Library at the University of Adelaide, the Art Gallery of South Australia, the Alexander Turnbull Collections at the National Library of New Zealand, the Hocken Collections in Dunedin, New Zealand, Iziko Museums of South Africa, and the University of Stellenbosch library. Thank you to the *Oxford English Dictionary* lexicographer James McCracken, and to his colleague Emily Hoyland, for generously sharing their findings on southern-origin words in the *OED* with me in the northern summer of 2019. Thanks to Dan Wakelin and Peter Barber for putting me in touch with the *OED* team. Christine Hobden, thank you for the unforgettable trip to the South African Large Telescope in Sutherland, Northern Cape, in February 2020. Thanks also to Beate Stawarska for being happy to come along for the ride.

Several researchers have given me deeper insights into the physics or linguistics of southern worlds from their particular disciplinary perspectives, and I am enormously grateful to the following. Robert Law, then a glaciologist at the Scott Polar Research Institute in Cambridge in 2022, for talking me through the physics of ice moving over rock, as well as for the calculation that fronts chapter 5. To Tracey Cameron, for allowing me to audit online the 2021 course in Gamilaraay she taught at the University of Sydney, and for generously and patiently sharing her insights, wisdom, and deep cultural and linguistic knowledge with me. Many thanks also to Lynda Ng and Susan Poetsch for letting me know about Tracey's course and for putting us in touch. I was also greatly helped by Menán Du Plessis's extraordinary knowledge and insight into the South African indigenous languages Khoekhoegowab and Khoikhoi. Menán was also serendipitously a fellow at the Stellenbosch Institute for Advanced Study in early 2020 and drew my attention to the 'Nama Praise of the Sea' that is now an epigraph to chapter 2. Muchas gracias to my Spanish teachers Reyes Morlans and Cristina Rodriguez-Oitavén of the marvellous Oxford University Language Centre for your unflagging enthusiasm and encouragement.

I am very grateful to Khadeeja Khaled, Sophie Hardcastle, Joe Shaughnessy, Robert Freeman, and Bhagya Casaba Somashekar, for their valuable research assistance given over different phases of this project, in various capacities—conceptual, empirical, editorial, digital. Robert Freeman's sympathetic understanding of southern parabolic and lateral pathways has been inspired. Bhagya's careful advice on the positioning of the non-Indigenous researcher was invaluable. Joe Shaughnessy's deep book history of twentieth-century New Zealand and South Africa could not be matched anywhere. Thanks also to my then-doctoral students Tom McLean, from Aotearoa New Zealand, and Cristóbal Pérez Barra, from Chile, for their kind interest, and for pointing me to relevant sources and translations. Thank you to Louis Rogers for the lockdown selection of southern hemisphere music and for getting this project from the start. And further heartfelt gratitude to Robert Freeman for heroic help with the index.

Enormous thanks to Katherine Collins, co-organiser with me of the three inspiring 'Southern Lives' workshops that we held online and in hybrid form at the Oxford Centre for Life Writing at Wolfson College between 2020 and 2023. I would like to acknowledge all of the participants in the workshops, spread across fifteen time zones: Elizabeth Chant, Sarah Comyn, Archie

Davies, Porscha Fermanis, Obari Gomba, Charne Lavery, Confidence Joseph, Khutso Eunice Mabokela, Tinashe Mushakavanhu, Isaac Ndlovu, Emma Parker, Cristóbal Pérez Barra, Joanna Price, Carolyn Philpott, Louis Rogers, Priyanka Shivadas, Pablo Wainschenker, and Elizabeth Lewis Williams. They are all now contributors to the essay collection *Life Writing and the Southern Hemisphere* (Bloomsbury, 2024) that Katherine Collins and I edited. Thank you to the Oxford Centre for Life Writing team, in particular Hermione Lee and Kate Kennedy, and also Freya Marshall Payne, Charles Pigeon, and Joe Shaughnessy, for your support of the workshops.

I am grateful to the convenors of and audiences at the following conferences, lecture series and seminars, who gave me opportunities to explore why and how to think south, from different historical, linguistic and literary critical angles: the SC-HASSEG Conference on 'Antarctic Connections at the End of the World', Ushuaia, Argentina, 3–5 April 2019; the 'Southern Circulations' conference, University of Otago, Dunedin, New Zealand, 17–18 December 2019 (special thanks to Tony Ballantyne); the keynote conversation with Professor Carrol Clarkson, at the J. M. Coetzee eightieth birthday celebration conference and cultural event at Amazwi, the South African Museum of Literature, Makhanda/Grahamstown, 10 February 2020 (many thanks, Carrol); the Fellows seminar at STIAS, 5 March 2020; the Oxford English Graduate Conference, English Faculty, University of Oxford, 4 June 2021, where I gave the keynote talk 'The South as Outside: Notes, Explorations' (thanks to Gavin Herbertson); the 'Cosmopolitan Cultures and Oceanic Thought' conference, co-hosted by the Department of English, Jamia Millia Islamia University in India, and the Centre for Indian Studies in Africa, University of Witwatersrand, on 23 November 2020, where my talk was entitled 'Fellowship and Aversion in the South'; the 'Subjectivities of Migration' conference, Barenboim-Said Akademie, Berlin, 13–14 September 2021, where I spoke on 'Migration, Subjectivity and the South in J. M. Coetzee's Post-2013 writing' (thank you, Kai Wiegandt); the English Academy of South Africa conference, 8 October 2021; the *To the Volcano* creative-critical reading and conversation, Liverpool John Moores University research seminar, 19 January 2022 (thanks to Filippo Menozzi); the University of the Western Cape research seminar, 9 March 2022; the HUMA invited lecture at the University of Cape Town, South Africa, 24 March 2022; the 'Writing Lives' forum at the University of Tasmania, 6 December 2022 (thank you very much, Elizabeth Leane and Carolyn Philpott); the 'Antipodean Modernism' conference in the Cambridge English Faculty, 18 November 2023, where it was my pleasure to talk about southness in Katherine Mansfield and D. H. Lawrence under the keynote heading 'Far and Awry'; the University of Essex guest lecture series, 27 February 2024; the English Department at the University of Pretoria for hosting the guest lecture, 'Southern Imagining: Or, Reading From The South', on 14 March 2024 (thank you, Corinne Sandwith and David Medalie). In 'Southern Light in/and Katherine Mansfield', the Katherine Mansfield Birthday Lecture I gave in Fontainebleau on 14 October 2023, I looked at images of veneering light in Mansfield that I also explore in chapter 6 of this book. I would like to acknowledge, in particular, the respondents to the above presentations who asked the far-reaching and always helpful questions that helped to deepen my southern thinking.

Thank you to Nishat Zaidi and Dilip Menon for allowing me further to develop ideas about southern fellowship in the essay, 'Fellowship and Aversion in the South: The Challenges of South-South Collaboration', included in their edited *Cosmopolitan Cultures and Oceanic Thought* (London: Routledge, 2023), 37–46. I enjoyed working with David Attwell on his 'Full Particulars' podcasts, especially 'Where in the World is the South?'. Thanks also to fellow participants Antjie Krog and Carrol Clarkson.

I am grateful to the wonderful postcolonial and world literature research community in Oxford, changing over time, but always stimulating and lively, and especially to my fellow convenors and dear friends, Ankhi Mukherjee and Pablo Mukherjee. Warm thanks also to Michelle Kelly and Graham Riach, and to William Ghosh and Malachi McIntosh.

Ben Tate and Josh Drake at Princeton University Press, it's been great working with you. Thanks for your interest in *Southern Imagining*—and in the significance of southern imagining.

To the Oxford home front, massive thanks for your faith in this project and for never doubting that I would both envision and manage it. And for tolerating this south-centred enthusiast in your midst. Special thanks to Sam for your tireless, always-pertinent questions and for determinedly standing up for the northern world; to Thomas for your extraordinary mythographic imagination and all the amazing books you found and bought for me; and to Steven for your incredible intellectual generosity and for being the best reader bar none in all the hemispheres.

A WORD ON TERMINOLOGY

IN *SOUTHERN IMAGINING* there is frequent reference to the work of Indigenous writers and artists from across the far south. The word 'indigenous' in lower-case is used when the generic meaning is intended, whereas when I capitalise 'Indigenous' in this work, I am making specific reference to Indigenous Australian or Australian Aboriginal people, in line with current usage. In countries other than Australia, the term 'indigenous' is sometimes contested and can be used interchangeably with Māori, Black, or Coloured, depending on the context. 'Coloured' refers to the Western Cape community of mixed Khoi, Dutch, and Malay descent who were historically ascribed an intermediate position in the apartheid race hierarchy before 1994.

SOUTHERN IMAGINING

1

A Hemisphere Awry

'All Different, Quite Different'

About face. Awry. Alien. The farthest far. For many of the world's readers, around nine in ten, the far southern hemisphere is, in every way, out of kilter.[1] The 'edge of the skirt of the world' unsettles the frameworks that most people use to see our planet.[2] Vast and excessive, the south defies everyday comprehension.

Images of the far south as remote, strange, and unbalanced are sedimented into northern perceptions. From ancient legends through to contemporary media, the southern fringes of the world have been perceived as underworlds, obscure and discardable. The first northerners to travel, whether imaginatively or in actuality, beyond the equator and then on to the higher southern latitudes, believed that the hemisphere had a different camber. This oscillation between northern projections onto the south and perceptions of southern difference from within, recurs throughout this framing chapter and continues through the book, so braiding piece by piece a picture of southern imagining as a complex process of entangled diegetic thinking—of conceiving the far south through image, symbol, and story of both northern and (increasingly) southern provenance.[3]

At the turn of the last century, Thomas Hardy, in his 1899 Anglo-Boer War poem 'Drummer Hodge', twice described the constellations of the southern hemisphere as 'strange' or 'strange-eyed'. At the time that Antarctic exploration was gathering momentum, the brilliant southern night sky may have been in the news, though Hardy was never to see it in reality. Some twenty years later, D. H. Lawrence in *Kangaroo*, the novel of his six-month stay in Australia, noticed the 'uncomfortable' tilt of the 'bushy' Milky Way to the south, 'so that you feel all on one side if you look at it'.[4] To his hero Richard Somers, 'things seemed so different. Perhaps everything *was* different from all he had known'. Settler writers across the southern hemisphere might have agreed. The south's geophysics appeared to require an entirely different mode of understanding. To develop the artistry necessary to recalibrate this difference as ordinary would mean remaking thought-worlds from scratch.

No image is more evocative of this apparently unbalanced state than the unusual shape of the kangaroo, captured in northern writing from the time of Captain James Cook's first observations in late April 1770. Even the word 'kangaroo' is an outlier. It is one of only a relatively few words of Aboriginal Australian provenance with widespread currency in the *Oxford English Dictionary*, its other forms being *kanguru*, *gamgarou*, and *Patagaran*. *Bandaarr* was the Gamilaraay word I learned. Along with 'boomerang' (Gamilaroy, *barran*), 'koala', 'bombora', and others, 'kangaroo' assumes a metonymic function. It stands for a land far out of the everyday where duckbilled mammals lay eggs and throwing sticks return to the hand of the thrower.[5]

Within a week of making landfall in Australia, Cook began to note sightings of a 'perplexing' creature, something like a dog and 'less than a deer'; withal unlike 'any Animal I ever saw'. As his ship, the *Endeavour*, groped its way up the eastern Australian coast, the crew repeatedly encountered the out-of-proportion, jumping animal, the thick tail 'nearly as long as the body', the forelegs puny, 'design'd for scratching in the ground &c'.[6] By August, the ship's botanist Joseph Banks had taken note of the local name for the creature, 'Kanguru'. But this was a possible mishearing of *gangurru*, the local Guugu Yimithirr word for a species of large kangaroo.

Some fifty years later, Barron Field in his collection, *First Fruits of Australian Poetry* (1819), introduced the 'not incongruous,/ Repugnant or preposterous creature' into poetry in English.[7] Field spends the greater part of his poem 'Kangaroo' trying to find merit in the animal's anomalies, though, from the start, he has difficulty in distinguishing it from its 'desolate', discordant surroundings. The poem, in this sense, like the creature, lacks proportion. Already the kangaroo has turned into an emblem for the seemingly unpromising country.

D. H. Lawrence, in 1923, incorporated that same contradictory sense of imbalance in the bulky, amazed language of his poem 'Kangaroo', written at the same time as the novel. Once again, the kangaroo, with its contrasting delicate and heavy qualities, its fine facial features, and 'python-stretch of a tail', embodies this 'silent lost' land of the South, 'lost so many centuries on the margins of existence!'[8] Though the poet observed the creature in question in captivity at Sydney Zoo, his poem tries hard to get at its alienness by using repetitive, at times deliberately unpoetic (as if clumsy) diction. The creature's awryness is then reinforced by the visual effects. Its drooping, bottom-heavy shape 'dropping sackwise down towards the earth's centre', if visualised as cartography, resembles the elongated, tapering shape of the southern continents, reversed, so turning the world on its head.

In strong contrast, only six years later, the Australian settler novelist and ethnographer Katharine Susannah Prichard would syncopate her novel *Coonardoo* (1929) with a 'corroboree song' about dancing kangaroos. The titular Aboriginal heroine sings the refrain in her language, Ngarla, at key points in her life:

Towera chinimapodinya
Towera jinner mulbeena
Poodinyoober mulbeena
(Kangaroos coming over the range in the twilight and making a devil dance with their little feet, before they begin to feed.)

The translation, italicised like the song, is built into the text.[9]

At once progressive and distinctively settler colonial, *Coonardoo* is significant for the very different frame of reference Prichard gives a native creature like the kangaroo compared to a European writer like Lawrence—or Field. In the novel, the animals appear to the character Coonardoo not only in reality, trooping over the range, but they also figure, simultaneously, in her song. It seems to us that she is calling them up. The animals are pictured moving together in unison as a mob, awe-inspiring, mysterious, very much of the land, as is Coonardoo herself—fatally so, as it turns out.

For all its intrusive ethnography, Prichard's novel crucially pivots our perspective as readers (whether northern or southern) away from northern representations of awkward, stranded kangaroos, caged or on display. Coonardoo, and her refrain 'sung to the clicking of sticks', recall us (but do not equate) to the view from within. Here, in the south, the kangaroo is but one animal figure among many. The creature features in Indigenous song cycles and legends, for example, as a totemic figure alongside a great crowd of others—cockatoos, dugong, groper fish, crocodiles, and snakes.

Inhabiting the South in the Mind

For northerners, southern spaces for aeons raised questions not only of going beyond the edge of the known world, but quite simply of being *extremely* remote. Even if some features of southern geography—stars, seasons, sun paths—were recognisable, though topsy-turvy, the key element that challenged expectations was the sheer reach of the south.[10] Indicatively, northern versions of world history still deem all the ancient civilisations of the world to have been located north of the equator, bar that of Peru.[11] Till the time of the moon landings, travellers to the Southern Ocean and beyond were as far from the rest of humanity as it was possible to be.

There were seemingly no limits to watery southern worlds, or to the imaginative possibilities they stimulated. For Edgar Allan Poe, and Jules Verne writing in his wake, 'the awful solitudes of the south' presented to the traveller a mysterious 'curtain of vapours' like a 'limitless cataract', and the prospect of powerful polar currents whirling down into bottomless vortices.[12] The 'ancient antipodal trope of the world turned upside down', writes Alfred Hiatt, encouraged utopian ideals of perfect worlds, places of solitary retreat, and contemplation. Yet these alluring spaces also always bore darker connotations of extreme remoteness, danger, threat, and savagery.[13] From the late fifteenth century, with the voyages of Dias and Da Gama, Magellan and de Elcano, Malaspina, Schouten, and many others, the south became code for the long, perilous route to the treasures of the east. The astronaut Michael Collins on Apollo 11 used the metaphor of rounding the Horn to describe his feelings of extreme remoteness when circling around the dark side of the moon.[14]

Yet, for southern peoples, that far-off beyond was home. (Even the word *yet* in that sentence is off-kilter when read 'south'.) They inhabited their spaces inwardly and intimately—as people do. The lands onto which Europe projected its fantasies were where they belonged. Their legends, songs, and stories located them in place from one generation to another and provided conduits for passing their memories on to their descendants within those same familiar southern worlds.

Southern Imagining considers what it is to inhabit the south in the mind, as did these southerners, or, put differently, it looks at how we imagine our planet *otherwise* by counterpointing northern perspectives with southern. Wherever possible, the book keeps in play cartographical concepts (telluric, littoral, oceanic) from southern worlds and northern alongside one another. Throughout, I am mindful that southern geographies have always been encoded in local languages and myth systems—and that these give us powerful tools for deconstructing hemispheric biases. The chapters, therefore, collaborate after their fashion with the 'third archive' project, based in Australia, that juxtaposes western and Indigenous knowledge structures in an intentional fusion.[15] Images and concepts from First Nations legends, star-maps, and mythologies interleave below with ideas from James Cook through Samuel Taylor Coleridge to Olive Schreiner and Joseph Conrad, and on. For austral imagining, singers, poets, storytellers, travellers, and artists and their creations are our primary mapmakers and guides.

Any book commits us to a more or less linear reading experience, yet a study of southern imagining involves destabilising conceptual moves that at once invert space and collapse time. A certain pliability has therefore been built into the design of the book to give the reader, at moments, the vertiginous experience of, as it were, teetering south over the equator, tilting towards the far edge of the world. The elastic figures of the parabola and, in the polar chapter, the asymptote, help me to make these moves, as we will soon see in more detail.[16] As the chapters loop south, across the southern oceans, towards the pole, our latitude of perception as readers, too, will bend, inflect, and sometimes warp. In both the canonical and the lesser-known writings, the curvilinear figures clarify instances that define and sharpen spatial perception and help us to think about and within southern worlds.

Where Is the South?

Across *Southern Imagining*, the south is at once a real and imagined space—a space that bears complex atmospheric, historical, and cultural overlays. Geographically, as in the Preface, 'south' refers to the lands and islands of the far south of the world, facing the Southern Ocean—the distant extremities of the southern hemisphere, its coastlines, tapering continents, wild capes, and peninsular tips, what might be called the verandas or stoops of the world.[17] To use their formal names, southern regions include the far reaches of the two great continents of South America and Africa that run north-south, the island continent of Australia and its icy counterpart, Antarctica, until recently uninhabited, and the various larger and smaller island clusters in the Pacific, and, to a lesser extent, in the Indian, Atlantic, and Southern Oceans. These spaces, on occasion, overlap with the areas comprising the geopolitical entity of the Global South but are distinct from them, as we will see.

The southern landmasses, together with India, formed the southern supercontinent Gondwanaland, which broke up at the start of the Jurassic period between 120 and fifty-five million years ago. Geological features, including basaltic strata and glacial striations observed in southern Africa, South Australia and Antarctica, testify to their prehistoric interconnection. On any world map, the puzzle-piece fit between the continents can easily be discerned and is clearest from the correspondence between the coastlines of South America and Africa. Gondwanaland's fragmentation began with that split, and the final separation was at the Tasmanian hinge that once joined Australia and Antarctica. The break produced the globe-encircling Southern Ocean with its great circumpolar currents and converging wind streams that still impact climates worldwide.[18]

The flora and fauna of the southern landmasses also exhibit family connections despite the long ages that separate them, as part of an extensive Gondwanan biota.[19] Combined, these links provided evidence for the theory of continental drift that began to take shape at the turn of the twentieth century.[20] Scientists noticed that certain distinctive plants feature or featured only across the south, as do flightless birds, including penguins. The Kerguelen cabbage grows on the Indian Ocean island of that name, yet is also found in South America's higher latitudes. The southern hemisphere beech (*calucechinus Antarctica*) grows in Tasmania, New Zealand's South Island, as well as on Tierra del Fuego and Kerguelen, as Joseph Hooker, the palaeobotanist on the 1830s Ross expedition to the South Magnetic Pole, first observed.[21] Fossilised *Glossopteris* specimens have been found on all the southern continents and include the samples from both of Scott's Antarctic expeditions.[22] Penguins, meanwhile, breed naturally only on the south-facing coastlines of Australia, the South American Cone, southern Africa, and the far southern islands, and, of course, on the icy edges of Antarctica.[23]

Portuguese is the predominant language of the south, partly due to the size of Brazil (which, however, lies in both hemispheres), followed by Spanish, Javanese, and then English. The 11 percent of the world's population who live in the hemisphere are concentrated mostly in the higher twenties and lower thirties of latitude, that is, in the novelist J. M. Coetzee's so-called 'one south', where the climate is temperate.[24] Most southern cities lie on the edge of the continental masses within this zone, while hinterlands are 'hollow' demographically. The sparseness of the land—and, for littoral and island dwellers, the immensity of the ocean—impinges constantly on people's awareness. Great winds, southwesterlies and easterlies, batter ocean-facing southern cities—some of which, including humid Wellington, Sydney, and Durban, looking east, are rust prone. The Antarctic convergence powers these huge winds, which roar not only through the forties but also the fifties and sixties of latitude.

In *Prisoners of Geography*, Tim Marshall argues that geography—for him, chiefly, continental location—impacts the interaction between peoples and so shapes societies and economies globally. He observes that the southern tips of South America and Africa lie extremely far away from 'anywhere' and hence are deemed by most people to be of lesser importance (though how 'anywhere' is defined is moot for any southern study on how the south is constructed).[25] Certainly, with respect to the prehistoric migration of peoples, the hemisphere lacks the great east-west land bridge of Eurasia and the further possibilities for cross-continental movement of the once-frozen Bering Sea.[26] For centuries, therefore, major economic, military, and diplomatic activity was concentrated in the north of the globe, with the result that southern lands and seas appeared by most measures to be marginal unless they offered the promise of extractable wealth, as did sealing, whaling, and, later, mining.

Another way of expressing the pervasive sense of southern remoteness is in terms of event density. To speak in intentionally loaded terms, nothing much is perceived to occur in the south, often even by southerners.[27] This relative spatial distance correlates with a lack of expectation on their part of political and cultural importance. Southerners see themselves as if from without, as located far away from where things count. Real stuff does not happen where they live. In effect, they internalise the wider global sense of their relative insignificance. They are seen to inhabit atopias—defined by Siobhan Carroll as intangible, inhospitable, inaccessible spaces that resist conversion into 'places of home and community'.[28] Perhaps the entire south constitutes an atopia—that is, if viewed from the north.

It is indicative that even the two great southern exit points from the Atlantic, the Cape of Good Hope and Cape Horn, though located on historic shipping routes, were nonetheless seen by northern nations as cut off from the wider oceanic world.[29] Traffic passed around here, but key players did not stay. These were the margins where the world's leftovers and detritus accumulated—long out-of-print books in secondhand bookshops; the commodity lists, ledgers, account books, manuals, and other documents piled high in the custom houses of colonial ports; rusting and discarded telescopes; the hull of the Anglo-Polish novelist Joseph Conrad's first command, the *Otago* in the Maritime Museum in Hobart—and greenhouse gases trapped in the Southern Ocean.[30]

As a directional term, 'south' is relative and contingent. Many lands on Earth have their particular south, and many regions, including in the far north, perceive themselves as provincial and out on the edge. In Europe, 'south' immediately bears connotations of the Mediterranean world and the pleasures of its light and warmth but also of temptation and peril, as in John Keats's now-proverbial lines from 'Ode to a Nightingale' (1819) about 'the warm south', or Tennyson's image of the 'warmer sky . . . of the South', in 'You Ask Me, Why, Tho' Ill at Ease' written twenty years later. This south also signifies a quality of character that is more physical yet less industrious. In colonial times, such antiphonal significations deepened with reference to European colonial possessions in the southern tropics and subtropics, where native peoples were labelled lazy and recalcitrant. In North America, till today, as we find in American literature, the violent history of slavery shadows any mention of that South.[31] The American South is an explicitly raced geohistorical entity, tagged as black, oppressed, and minor.

World cartography has understood the planet from a northern vantage point for millennia, relegating the south to realms beyond ken. From the time of Pythagoras, ideas of a great continent in the higher southern latitudes—Terra Australis Incognita, the *alter orbis*—preoccupied seafarers, geographers and thinkers.[32] The great south, a counterbalancing entity to the north, was regarded as world-shaping and 'geographically essential', in the words of John Livingston Lowes, and yet as unimaginable.[33] In Claudius Ptolemy's *Geographia* (c. 150 CE), the Indian Ocean is seen as a lake surrounded by land, including in the south, where an 'arm' of southern Africa stretches east to meet the Indonesian archipelago.[34] Based on information drawn from traders across that same monsoon-swept ocean, Ptolemy's maps laid down models for early modern cartography. By the time Vasco da Gama rounded the Cape of Good Hope to reach India in 1497–98, and the Ferdinand Magellan (and Juan Sebastián de Elcano) expedition circumnavigated the globe around thirty years later, a view of the planet with the North Pole 'uppermost' had become normative, at least from Europe and the Middle East.

Early modern geographers processed the findings from the first Portuguese, Spanish, and later Dutch and British voyages into the southern hemisphere according to this predominant model, establishing relational understandings of the south that persist into the present day: of counterbalancing landmasses, a dichotomous far south, either monstrous or sublime, and distant lands that beckoned northerners to name and claim them.[35] Even representations of the American 'new world' took 'south' as an 'inexact but powerful descriptor' that 'advertised strangeness', in Sandra Young's words. Peter Martyr's *The Decades of the Newe World of West India*, Richard Eden's compilation of Sebastian Münster's *Cosmographiæ vniversalis* based on Ptolemy, and many other sixteenth-century English chronicles of European exploration used a recognisably hierarchical 'language of the global "south"' to encourage colonial ambitions.[36]

Up to the present day, the projection of a European planetary consciousness on the south is reflected in the Linnaean or binomial system of classification through which ecologies from around the natural world were brought under one pyramidical system, beginning from the time of Cook's voyages.[37] Its apex, comprising the most advanced forms of life, was assumed to lie in the north, and the terms cataloguing all life on Earth were taken from Latin. In another telling instance, two centuries later, in 1972, the first pictures of the whole earth as photographed from space, the so-called 'blue marble' image, showed the North Pole 'at the top' when published in the world's newspapers. But the photograph had been inverted for global consumption. Apollo 17's camera had first pictured the globe as bearing the white cap of Antarctica.

Exotic visions of the great southern continent conditioned ideas of what Antarctica might comprise for centuries—and recur in twenty-first-century touristic representations of its glamour and danger.[38] From the 1700s voyages of Wallis, de Bougainville, Cook, and others, the lure of the farthest south drove European exploration into the Antarctic Circle. The British Admiralty famously gave James Cook secret instructions ordering him to seek and, if found, claim this mythic land for the Crown. Arriving in Aotearoa New Zealand on the *Endeavour* in 1769, Cook wondered if he might not have reached the 'Continent we are in search of', but subsequent circumnavigation of the two main islands disabused him of this hope.[39] His finding that the southern continent must lie in the higher southern latitudes harmonised with reports from earlier navigators like Magellan and Drake of open sea beyond the Horn. Within three years Cook had embarked on the *Resolution* on a further quest for the 'southermost land [*sic*]', yet, once again, though his ships lay 'South of Tasmans track', he correctly surmised from the 'high swell' that no land lay within the fifties and sixties of latitude, though there might be some possibility in the 'Meridian of the Mauritius'.

Other late eighteenth- and early nineteenth-century navigators like Jules Dumont D'Urville and Yves-Joseph de Kerguélen-Trémarec were similarly compelled by legends of the far southern continent. They, too, deduced from the evidence of floating ice sheets, prevailing winds, and sea temperatures that there must be a significant icebound landmass to the south. However, till the James Clark Ross and Charles Wilkes expeditions of 1839–43 and 1838–42, respectively, it was mainly whalers and sealers who travelled into the roaring forties and beyond, drawn by reports in Cook and Banks of copious fishing stocks in these waters. An 1831 map of the southern continent, drawn for the Society for the Diffusion of Useful Knowledge, reflects how little known the polar regions were, even then.[40] Right across the nineteenth century, from Coleridge through Melville to Verne and Conrad, the icy austral latitudes goaded the imagination to overleap barriers that humans could not yet physically pierce.[41] The pursuit of the elusive south continued to mark its cartography, and the inscrutable areas of those maps went on encouraging the pursuit. 'The farthest South . . . disappears . . . under the globe', as the poet Elizabeth Lewis Williams writes.[42]

Yet, far south questing was not confined to Europe. Far from it. According to seventh-century Polynesian legends from Rarotonga or Ui-Te-Rangiora in the Cook Islands, as we will see, Pacific Islanders who had migrated eastwards and southwards as far as the Auckland Islands brought back knowledge of bitterly cold waters. They described this ocean as covered in white powder, its powerful currents resembling the hair of a legendary 'woman of the sea'.[43] Twelfth- to fourteenth-century Māori or Polynesian earth ovens on the Aucklands corroborate how far south Pacific navigators came.

All southern lands were, at one point or another in the past five hundred years, colonised by northern powers, and all bear signs of violent incursion, resource exploitation, and cultural marginalisation. Colonisation cut entire populations adrift from their languages, traditions, resources, and industries, producing the uneven networks that shape global geopolitics to this day. Colonial infrastructures—roads, railways, shipping lines—came to dictate that all main routes ran to the capital and from there to the imperial metropolis, while peripheral places were not connected in the same way.[44] North-south unevenness also meant that southern writers and artists were obliged to relocate to northern capitals both imaginatively and in person to forge their careers. Even up to the early twenty-first century, southern authors, including those discussed in this book, have taken pains to situate themselves in a filial relationship to northern metropolitan traditions and write the south as elsewhere, not here.

Southern Imagining takes account of the global expansion of capitalist modernity from the north and the racialised stadial discourses that were used to justify that expansion. Victorian science, for example, placed far-south human beings and animals farther back on a single universal trajectory of development.[45] (Penguins were described as less evolved birds, for example.) Indigenous knowledge was discredited to the point that Europeans declared an entire continent, Australia, to be *terra nullius* for not demonstrating the forms of civilised occupation that they were able to recognise. The remoteness of the south was used to facilitate such occlusion. Abuses of power could thrive here unchecked, far from the eye of the northern law.[46]

Yet, at the same time, *Southern Imagining* strives to keep in suspension the idea of a single, uneven world and allows space for other imagined worlds to thrive.[47] All theories of modernity, at least in English, take Europe as the centre of historicity. Therefore, where possible, my readings sidestep a singular interpretative standpoint located in the northern hemisphere and draw on southern conceptual approaches.[48] I proceed strategically, with care, always maintaining awareness of the limitations of northern theory, drawing in Indigenous interlocutors to cultivate multiple perspectives and question entrenched lines of sight. My readings attend to the links and commonalities across the southern hemisphere that navigators and scientists like Joseph Hooker traced, but that indigenous astral mythologies from around the hemisphere have also recorded. These links become a kind of stimulus for a southern semiotics, a lateral and comparative way of thinking around the Southern Ocean.[49]

Not East: The South as External

The south was not only far, or farther than far; it was also deemed by many would-be observers as a place outside, as early modern maps reflect. For many, the far south still remains a limitless beyond, like outer space, something that can be used without ever being used up. If anything, the seeming externality of the region drove and drives its exploitability. Its unplumbed distances at one and the same time gave exploratory and representational licence and defied policing. New Zealand's fertile plains may have been the last that Europeans found 'before the Earth's supply revealed itself as finite', the historian Michael King writes, but the majority of humanity took several hundred years to compute that finitude.[50]

For Timothy Clark, the concept of 'externality', derived from market economics, implies that within any given system, space for expansion exists. Max Liboiron relatedly discusses how capitalist accumulation ejects its costs to borderlands and edge countries.[51] The idea goes hand-in-hand with the assumption that natural resources are free for the taking, and suffer no damage from processes of extraction. Production is taken to rely on outside or faraway spaces that will absorb excess and contamination, where waste can be dumped without ever seemingly accumulating. Capitalist reasoning along these lines subtends not only most discourses of development but also, specifically for my purposes, historical approaches to southern lands. For, if the earth and its oceans were everywhere taken to be exploitable, this treatment was perhaps particularly severe in the remote southern hemisphere precisely because these edges could be the more ignored, the more occluded. Till only yesterday, the great external of the south has been treated as a dumping ground at the bottom of the world, its lands 'empty' enough to warrant nuclear testing, its seas capacious enough to absorb excess carbon dioxide.[52]

There is probably no more telling example of the perils of treating the south as external than the early nineteenth-century sealing and whaling industries. The oil that lit the burgeoning cities of the industrial age came from rendered whales taken from oceans worldwide. However, the secrecy and anonymity that the high southern latitudes afforded the sealers and whalers efficiently masked the industrial-scale carnage through which they operated. Already by the 1830s, whale and seal numbers in the southern seas had dropped catastrophically to the point that the vast fish stocks that Cook had observed would never again be seen in these waters.[53]

Whaling provides a sobering lesson. Treating the far south as an exploitable outside has had, and continues to have, far-reaching environmental consequences, though the region's remoteness has meant that for over two centuries, this damage went relatively unobserved. In response, *Southern Imagining* invites a more interconnected understanding of southern spaces, a view of the external from the inside, no matter how counterintuitive this perspective might be for most. As in the work of Barry Lopez, the book tries to 'resituate' readers in cultural ecologies that are three-dimensional everywhere, in the south just as in the north.[54] And to do this, it draws out, wherever possible, the geological, meteorological, and atmospheric commonalities that pertain around the hemisphere. Southern poetry and stories serve as astrolabes or mesasuring devices for this purpose, constellating views of the south from across the south, affording relational perspectives on southern worlds.[55] These works remind us, even if only figuratively, that nothing on Earth is so far removed as not to have an impact on somewhere else.

The contrasting relationship of north as against south, or global inside and outside, will inevitably call up associations with Edward Said's influential work on Orientalism as a system of knowledge that Europe used to wield imperial power.[56] Like the east, the lore of the south is a geopolitical construct used to impose cultural values. It, too, may appear to operate according to the polarised dynamic of the west as against the rest that Said theorised. As with the Orient, antipodean myths were projected onto southern lands as ways of organising, managing, and exploiting their resources. The discussion of European centrality and southern marginality in these pages will, therefore, be almost unavoidably indebted to Said's thesis, and his critique assists with any interrogation of western or Global North dominance.

At the same time, however, the remote south does not bear analogy with the fabulous east. It is far from being an austral orient swivelled through ninety degrees, from a north-south to an east-west axis. The south explored in *Southern Imagining* is too amorphous and dispersed to operate as a discourse in the way of Orientalism. Its scatteredness does not conform to the singular idea of an opposite to the western norm. Though northerners assume their perspective is dominant in relation to the south, they are by and large indifferent to it, unlike they have been to the Orient. Post the whaling heyday, the south has always lacked sufficient economic or geopolitical interest. Therefore, if, on western timelines, the east was degenerate and Africa backward, if the former lagged behind and the latter had not yet mounted the scale of civilisation, the south, by contrast, was nowhere on or near this scale. Far distant geographically, it also lay far distant in time, right outside the chronologies of Europe.[57] Where Orientalism had generated an excess of representation, the dubious distinction of the far south was that it appeared to demand new tools of description entirely.

Thinking from the South with Story

If we accept that language informs our sense of being in place, then both writing and reading will be vital to any process of imaginative reorientation south. Though our utterances can never be held to equate to the things they name, still, words that sing or speak the lands, islands, and oceans of the south will, at the very least, make possible a more inward southern understanding. Just as an architectural plan takes a certain vantage point relative to the sun as read, southern texts assume a southern location. They orient south; their sequences parse its spaces. While northern concepts require translation into southern environments, by contrast, south-forged imaginative work conceives of its southern contexts *from within*. 'Down there' is experienced as *right here*.

A starting premise, therefore, is that literature helps to theorise southern space. Far-south poetry and fiction enables us to see the hemisphere differently, whether laterally, from south to south, or from the inside out. While the work of Cook, Darwin, Coleridge, and others first shaped the south in the Anglophone imagination, later creative work generated in the south, itself at times paradoxically moulded by these precursor writers, often makes better sense of southern worlds. It builds our understanding of the hemisphere's differently angled spaces and meets with less conceptual static.[58]

The premise of imaginative inwardness is related to another leading perception of how creative artefacts operate. *Southern Imagining* holds that imaginative work, here embodied primarily but not exclusively in literary writing, itself stimulates and shapes our phenomenological understanding. The approach adapts the idea from reception theory that writing—and also oral narratives, legends, and myths—gives us ways of interpreting our worlds, of thinking from the space we inhabit. Environmental anthropology offers the supporting idea that our surroundings inform our perceptions.[59] Therefore, to read, tell, or hear legends, narratives, songs, and poems from the south is to be located (in the) south, at least for the duration of the reading or telling. It is to experience an otherwise elusive southern haecceity even when dealing in imported tools (languages, genres, technologies of writing). The writings craft ways of understanding *being south*, even in those cases, as with some settler writing, where the dominant sense that is communicated is of being out of place and unhomed.

Putting these two premises together, any attempt to see through southern lenses requires a methodology of attending (reading and listening) south. Close reading, as the Māori scholar Linda Tuhiwai Smith believes, offers a powerful means through which to dismantle established, colonial ways of looking.[60] Across these pages, writers from Olive Schreiner to Judith Wright, from Zoë Wicomb to Alexis Wright, draw links and lines through which southern effects—truths, we might say—become perceptible. Chapters 2 and 3, in particular, work with this heuristic, but it is threaded throughout.[61] Across the book, literary artefacts, including pieces of orature, provide the means through which the far south—its uncomfortableness, its opacity, its difficulty—can be approached and better understood. The epigraphs that head up the chapters, too, set an interpretative course, shedding anticipatory light on the readings to come.

In a realm so vast and fluid, oceanic methodologies offer generative insights, as we find in Edouard Glissant's idea of relationality—of the sea as *the* medium through which worlds are brought into creative exchange with one another. For Glissant, though we cannot strip back colonial history, we can retrieve and filter in understandings from beyond its conceptual range. So, too, Hawaiian Epeli Hau'ofa's concept of the archipelagic draws out writings that are at once discrete and yet interconnected, as in the nature of an archipelago, that highlight the 'mutable relationship between human bodies and the ocean'.[62] The Caribbean poet Kamau Brathwaite relatedly describes the action of the ocean as tidalectic, open-ended, and cyclical, where the local and global exist in a state of continuous contact and interchange. In the far south, glacial striations, atmospheric effects, littoral experiences, and other interrelated geophysical features can be used as alternative prompts for thinking more southerly, allowing us to speak of a certain degree of hemispheric intimacy, as later chapters will explore.[63]

Maintaining hemispheric solidarity, Isabel Hofmeyr's methodological reflections on 'dockside reading' from and through coastal environments offer further helpful protocols for oceanic thinking, always directed from a 'southern latitude'.[64] For Hofmeyr, 'punctuated sequences', stringing together 'a bit of this and a bit of that', provide ways of theorising 'laterally, vertically, and contrapuntally between different water worlds'. This emphasis on affinities and parallels between fluid southern latitudes interleaves with Boaventura de Sousa Santos's precept in *Epistemologies of the South* that 'the understanding of the world is greater than the western understanding of the world'. Or, in Anne Salmond's definition of 'cosmo-diversity', the world is 'a composite of different realities as seen by different peoples'. (Therefore, a song, a chant or indeed a literary text can express 'a world *objectively from inside it*').[65] Such recognitions challenge and disrupt the imperial 'terms and sensibility' of western thought, as Walter Mignolo's work on decoloniality also outlines.[66]

From the layered, collage-like readings that this book gathers together, my hope is that the far south will emerge as a composite space in which different planes of experience—littoral, peninsular, oceanic—may be seen to overlap, diverge, and interconnect again. In this view, in the words of geographer Doreen Massey, the overlooked limits and edges become 'coeval' and 'radically contemporary' with everywhere else.[67]

The Global South in Theory

The south of *Southern Imagining* at certain points intersects but does not coincide with the Global South. 'Global South' is a geopolitical term from development economics referring to lower and middle-income countries, and bears a similar valence to the now-outmoded 'Third World'. As did 'Third World', 'Global South' does work as a geographic metaphor to indicate underdevelopment and peripherality. Yet, while a number of countries in the Global South are in the southern hemisphere, the countries that make up the far southern edge of this book are not all Global South countries. At the same time, most austral countries are primary producers and, therefore, tend to have a client relationship with industrialised economies in the north.[68]

Southern Imagining collaborates with efforts in Global South historiography to recalibrate world thinking in a more southerly direction. It agrees that our efforts to theorise the global mean more than merely expanding the locations where social theory is carried out. Challenging presumptions of universal reach demands that we pay heed to 'counterflows' of knowledge from outside the west, as Gurminder Bhambra also advises.[69] Raewyn Connell's *Southern Theory* (2020) has made one of the more promising responses to this call by drawing Global South theorists, including Raul Prebisch and Paulin Hountondji, into a transnational dialogue with Global North interlocutors about empire, modernity, land and race.[70] For his part, Dilip Menon in *Changing Theory* (2022) develops terms from various African, Asian, and South American languages, including *tarbiyya* (rooftop cultivation, in Arabic) and *dadan* (credit, in Persian), as his contribution to the project of theorising from within nonwestern thought-worlds.[71]

Yet even this important decolonial work does not always question the underlying conceptual patterns in global sociology that keep in place already normative northern vantage points. The unvarying emphasis on binary north-south axes usually takes for granted the methodological predominance of the north. An influential case-in-point is Jean and John Comaroff's apparently south-leaning *Theory from the South* (2012).[72] While the work productively defines the 'global south' as an 'inherently slippery, inchoate, unfixed' sign always in creative flux, it nonetheless sees modernity as singular and hence, paradoxically, as emanating from a still-predominant, technologically superior 'Euro-America'. As also in world-systems theory, this concentrically arranged 'one, uneven' world is conditioned to marginalise southern perspectives.

In historical studies, too, the south tends largely to be taken as a northern projection, defined in relation to Euro-America.[73] Peter Beilharz's *Thinking from the Antipodes* (2015), for example, builds on Australian art historian Bernard Smith's important definition of the antipodes not as a place but 'a spatial and cultural relationship'. Yet Smith's understanding, and Beilharz's after him, nonetheless tacitly privileges the unequal north-south underpinnings to that relationship.[74] Relatedly, David Johnson's *Imagining the Cape Colony* (2012) considers the eighteenth-century concepts of the nation, community, and resistance through which the region was understood.[75] But his account of the Griqua people's resistant appropriation of these ideas does not ultimately contest the predominance of European thinking in local Cape politics.[76]

A comparable, as if involuntary, gravitation shapes even Sujit Sivasundaram's *Waves Across the South* (2021), a history that explicitly sets out to readjust north-south heuristic axes. Sivasundaram emphasises Indigenous creativity and resistance within a broad swathe of revolutionary littoral cultures from across the modern empires of the southwest Indian Ocean, the South Pacific, and the Tasman Sea.[77] Yet the book's fault lines of encounter run between 'Western imperialism' or civilisation and these southern locales. Aspects of imperial experience are forged in the oceanic south, yet the drivers of trade and commerce still operate axially from the north.

As in historical and sociological studies, so, too, literary: critical perspectives from the south tend to lack institutional backing and status. Southern writers are included in global affiliations only to the extent that they conform to outside definitions and expectations.[78] For Pascale Casanova, the process of *littérisation*, the means of achieving visibility in the world republic of letters, assigns a different status to the so-called 'disinherited' provinces, the territories south of the equator.[79] While Jahan Ramazani's *Poetry in a Global Age* (2020) considers how border-crossing poetry theorises its own transnational movement, the book's idea of the global is identified with reference to the Anglo-American north.[80]

This insistent northern focus of literary theory and historiography is, on one level, understandable. The historical biases of language, discipline, and influence are not easily disrupted.[81] Though it was in part written under southern skies, by a southern-born writer, *Southern Imagining*, too, is undeniably located within and shaped by northern conceptual traditions. The study cannot ignore that the main institutions of knowledge about the wider world are located in the northern hemisphere. Moreover, as the new technological and media networks build on those laid down in the colonial era, with every new innovation, the world's unevenness is reproduced and further overdetermined. The online world that many of us now inhabit for much of the time is interpretatively weighted towards the already-dominant hemisphere.

Southern spaces have, without doubt, produced great thinkers, navigators, discoverers, and scholars, yet in the official annals, their names do not feature, and even if they were known or, at least, better known, they would not carry equivalent value. Up to today, southern histories, individuals, techniques, and products gain recognition and comprehensibility only through arriving in the north. Northerners, meanwhile, remain habituated to seeing themselves in the driving seat of world history, commanding the vantage point from which 'the rest' is judged.[82] Or, as Olga Tokarczuk observes in *Flights*, travelling Europeans miss in far-flung places like the green islands of Aotearoa a clear point of geohistorical focus, the sense of a 'real' or recognisable place to arrive at.[83]

All in all, an asymmetric north-south force field continues to shape global vectors of knowledge production and dissemination, including Global South thought. Few to no northern systems are equipped to respect the south's epistemological elusiveness. To address these asymmetries, however inadequately, *Southern Imagining* inclines to the most powerful imaginative resource we have to hand—writing on and from the south that turns northern presumption on its head, for which the so-called margins of the world are consistently present, immediate, and vividly thought and lived.

Outline

As a study in southern perception, *Southern Imagining* might in a previous time have concentrated on bringing the far hemisphere's seeming strangeness into its interpretative purview. It might have begun with northern encounter narratives and 'eventual' responses from southerners.[84] But, in so far as the book also sets about reversing such perspectives, this would not have been a promising way to begin.

Instead, *Southern Imagining* works athwart ideas of singular worlds and crosscuts the northern sightlines that have always been projected onto southern lands. Some chapters follow the parabolic pathways that European travellers took into the south, around the southern capes, routes that went there and back again. Others consider both latitudinal and hemispheric lines of travel that emerge from the south and radiate within its spaces. The readings zoom in on these pathways at their critical turning points and places of resistance, the moments of tension and redirection that some experienced as rebirth and new beginning.

Chapters on Indigenous perceptions of southern environments bracket the book. Empire has meant that the lands, oceans, and living creatures of the south are generally imagined not through local words and ideas but by using concepts from elsewhere that must be adjusted and revised when applied to southern things. Against these northern imports, the framing chapters (2 and 7) prioritise southern ontologies over imperial temporalities, while striving always to respect their difference and separateness. Though at times necessarily brief and provisional, my readings explore how the most vital perspectives on the south are to be found in the artefacts, songs, legends, and, later, written narratives and poetry that Indigenous and southern-born cultures have produced.

This approach does not deny the consequences of colonial history or the fact that any citation of Indigenous knowledge in an unequal world can come across as extractive. Indigenous cultures everywhere have been and remain violently and exploitatively entangled in northern formations. My readings try to recognise this. They understand that any sharing of knowledge under such conditions runs the risk of seeming appropriative. And they attempt to address southern Indigenous cosmologies and languages always in a spirit of quietness and integrity, seeking to listen and to observe. At no point do my assertions of southern hereness intend that the remote south be somehow incorporated or reincorporated into the Global North. Rather, I suggest that the north find ways of acknowledging and learning from the south's simultaneous presentness and remoteness within the planetary spacetime we all share.

Between the bookend chapters, the others build a chronological arc of writing about and of the far south, largely but not only in English. Chapters 3 and 4 engage with northern writings that have been formatively open to the wonder and difference of the south and to perceptions of commonality that link across the hemisphere. Meanwhile, the settler literature covered in chapter 6 and the contemporary Indigenous writing in chapter 7 find ways of capturing the south's distinctiveness, taking pains to stretch imported norms of perception in order to better adjust to its differently tilted environments.

At the heart of the book is a chapter on journeys to Antarctica, so that the South Pole becomes, not inaptly, the centre around which the rest of the book turns.

Chapter 2, 'Shared Skies: Speaking and Singing the South', looks at indigenous southern legends of the skies and the seas that were used to map countries and to navigate the wide ocean. For Indigenous inhabitants of the south, the lands where they lived, whether island or inland, littoral or latitudinal, were *here*. Their perceptual habits fitted the shapes of this world, their languages matched its features and contours. Under the subheadings 'Words', 'Stars', and 'Ocean', the chapter ponders Indigenous words and stories that interact with southern spaces and asks how Indigenous cosmologies might suggest modes of southern reading. The chapter closes with a discussion of Polynesian modes of navigation using the stars, for which southern skies were centred and centring, not other or different.

'Reading the South—Camões's "Audacious Passage"', chapter 3, begins the consideration of the south as the far end of the earth that Europeans began to chart from the fifteenth century onwards. We observe how the work of geographic worlding undertaken by Spanish and Portuguese navigators drew on previous maps and writings to turn the south into a knowable global object. The chapter takes as its case study Luís Vaz de Camões' *Os Lusíadas* (*The Lusíads*), outlining how this 1572 epic about Portuguese navigation around Africa to Asia created and interpreted the other hemisphere for Europe—as, too, Alonso de Ercilla's more or less contemporaneous *Araucana* relayed the history of the conquistadores in South America back to Spain. Even as Camões, for his part, contained the south's strangeness within the shapely ottava rima of his poem, he also captured its uncontrollable spirit in the invented myth of the fearsome Adamastor who presides over the Cape of Storms.

Chapter 4, 'Writing Southern Seas', considers how the early to mid-nineteenth-century writers Samuel Taylor Coleridge, Charles Darwin, Herman Melville, and Mary Shelley, all in one way or another grappled with Camões' challenge of finding a symbolic language through which to give meaningful form to the vast south. Like him, they wrote back through the history of southern exploration, captured most notably in the journals of Captain James Cook (1769–76), while the later writers also took Coleridge's own *The Rime of the Ancient Mariner* as a model. The readings further develop the idea of writing as navigational and cartographic, a way of shaping the beyond by projecting figures upon it, one of which is the parabolic arc that Camões first traced in his epic. Their work begins to build important perceptions of lateral connection across the hemisphere, vividly captured in Charles Darwin's observations of similar patterns of evolutionary change that manifest across the far-flung southern continents.

Outer edge, limit case, the ne plus ultra—the Antarctic continent not only shapes its own climate but has also impinged on all forms of southern imagining. Chapter 5, '"Silent Vastness", the Farthest South', considers imaginings of Antarctica as the definitive south. For Southern Ocean-facing countries, the remote proximity of Antarctica distinguishes their own far distant location and, hence, at least potentially, their interconnection. The chapter opens with the February 2022 discovery of Ernest Shackleton's ship *Endurance* on the bed of the Weddell Sea, a moment that reverberated with connotations of the south as inaccessible and fantastically distant. Similar associations ramify through the responses to the icy continent in the works of Chris Orsman, Bill Manhire, Beryl Bainbridge, and Jon McGregor. In their readings, the truth of the extreme south appears endlessly to recede before the attempt to describe it, in the manner of an asymptote, as a closing reading of Jenny Diski further considers.

From the early decades of the nineteenth century, Europeans in large numbers emigrated to far southern lands. Chapter 6, '"Breaking the Solemn Monotony": Settler Cartographies', explores how settler writers—southern arrivals and the southern-born—experienced the southern lands and landscapes that had become home, yet to which they ambiguously belonged. The featured authors, both novelists and poets—Olive Schreiner, Blanche Baughan, Katherine Mansfield, Judith Wright, and Janet Frame—all articulate an existential unease about inhabiting southern spaces, yet at the same time express a conflicted but intense desire imaginatively to embrace their native land. Their writing seeks ways of expressing centredness, even if with borrowed tools, as Janet Frame perhaps does most successfully. The writers reach beyond the nation for a more mobile and interconnected sense of place, each building in their work a new compass for reading the south.

In counterpoint, the penultimate chapter 7, 'Keeping South', turns to contemporary southern perceptions from within the south, especially Indigenous views of the sky and the land, as expressed in a mosaic of texts from southern Africa, Australia, and Aotearoa New Zealand. The chapter centres how the south is thought and reimagined on its own terms in the present day. Authors like Alexis Wright and Terry-Ann Adams, for example, tune into local and regional cultural vocabularies to address their sometimes dystopian but always symbolically charged southern contexts. The readings amplify the latitudinal, comparative work of previous chapters by surveying the motifs the writers develop for thinking or imagining the south as here and now.

In the closing chapter, 'Southern Tilt', I take personal experiences of southern starscapes and oceanic horizons as frames through which to consider, finally, what these studies from the so-called far edges of the world might teach about reading from the outside in and about understanding our planet in its entirety, as comprising *both* south *and* north. I ask what we are able to see in our imagination when we keep toggling the world's axes and flipping its poles.

Across its length, *Southern Imagining* questions how northern words have named southern things to the exclusion of the south's own indigenous vocabularies and, hence, perspectives and knowledges. Each chapter endeavours to work with, around, and through this overwriting by extending wherever possible the terms of southern linguistic and literary reference.[85] However, that the book's predominant focus is Anglophone is incontrovertible and introduces limitations of which I have been constantly aware. The Anglophone zones of southern Africa, Australasia, and Antarctica make up the main field of concern, in spite of the many interlinguistic and comparative countermeasures I have taken.[86] My awareness of never quite being able to unthink the biases of my disciplinary training has dogged my steps from the moment I first began to parse my way through this project. I have attempted to live with the delimiting consequences by working wherever possible against the grain, drawing insight from some of the writers' own confusion, bafflement, and transport, as we find, for example, when a canonical northern poet like Coleridge considers the south. Time and again, I have found that it is in entanglement and contradiction that a southern aesthetic may suddenly, elusively but vertiginously, like a revolving binary star long ago observed but then forgotten, glimmer back into view.

Southern Curves

As any project of southern imagining means working with a counter-normative polarity, a closing note may be helpful on how *Southern Imagining* sets about doing southern thinking. Throughout, as I anticipated, the readings strive to rotate us around and through curvilinear southern space, making its angles and inclinations dynamic and present. Texts from both the north and the south draw interpretative lines in relation to which more southerly or farther south perceptions of the planet become possible. These lines are the parabola, the asymptote, and the lateral or south-south link-up.

With its rotatory, out-and-back-again movement, the parabola is a predominant figure in the book, one that correlates with how we perceive curving motion through space. As we see in chapters 3 and 4, the boomerang shape of the journey into and back from the south, around the southern capes, not only captures something of the reversal and estrangement that southern travel entailed for northerners but also builds a changing turn into the text and hence into the experience of reading it. The reader arguably becomes involved, through their reading, in the different turn or spin of the hemisphere: the parabolic movement of 'doubling the point' conditions us to a more southerly awareness. It is felicitous that the word 'parabola' shares a root with 'parable', meaning to see and to set side by side. As in *The Rime of the Ancient Mariner* or *Moby-Dick* that trace transformative southern journeys, a parable allows unexpected parallels and surprising new meanings to come to light.

Northern associations of the far south with such parabolic routes date from the early days of European sail, and underpin late eighteenth-century South Seas travelogues, foremost among them the spectral journey of Coleridge's Ancient Mariner. The turning route around the great Capes of Good Hope and Horn encoded a process of thinking into southern space that transferred from travelogues through poetry into fiction, gathering up and interlacing other tropes of extremity and switchback. Joseph Conrad's maritime memoir, *The Mirror of the Sea* (1906), too, is dominated by images of gale-battered ships turning around the two stormy capes.[87] And in his iconic novel of the sea, *The Narcissus* (1897), the parabolic journey 'to the southward', from Bombay to London, with the 'resplendent curve of the Milky Way' overhead, once again takes the ship through a complete metamorphosis, as if retracing that curve. Boarded by 'merciless' seas off the Cape, the crew's fight with the storm transforms them irreversibly from one state to another:

> from that time our life seemed to start afresh as though we had died and had been resuscitated. All the first part of the voyage, the Indian Ocean on the other side of the Cape, all that was lost in a haze, like an ineradicable suspicion of some previous existence. It had ended—then there were blank hours: a livid blurr—and again we lived![88]

In Jules Verne's *Antarctic Mystery*, which appeared in the same year, the shape persists, at least residually. Though the *Halbrane*'s intention is to sail as far south as possible on the trail of Poe's *Narrative of Arthur Gordon Pym*, the crew finds that they have nonetheless turned: 'from the western longitudes . . . into the eastern longitudes': 'we had left the South Pole behind'.[89]

A line that approaches a given curve into infinity—the asymptote gestures at another key feature of southern experience. Especially in chapter 4, on polar journeys, we find not reversal but endless movement towards a limit that is never reached, the traveller (and hence the reader) never quite seeing or locating what they have set out to find. An asymptotic line of infinite and perhaps fatal approach unmistakably begins to intrude upon Verne's same polar adventure tale, for example. This farthest south appears to repel human intrusion: 'it is not permitted to us to venture so far in these latitudes', as the Boatswain says.[90] Mirroring the failed attempts of Cook and others to reach the southern continent, Poe and Verne both relay the awareness that polar adventures bring a new conceptual blur into play, another form of orientation in space, and a new figure through which to emblematise limitlessness.

Returning from the pole, the lateral link-ups in chapters 6 and 7 bring us back to parabolic lines, looping journeys, and transformative turning pathways across and around the hemisphere. But the difference from earlier chapters is that these journeys often begin and sometimes end in the south, and take their bearings from the archipelagic dispersal of the southern lands and islands. Whereas the navigators in the first half of the book, especially those from the north, sometimes found themselves missing the goals with which they embarked, stumbling instead on surprising and wonderful new trajectories of travel, the routes traced now are southern first and last, immersed in southern environments. Accordingly, the readings sweep across austral spaces in wide arcs, bringing different parts of the hemisphere into conjunction and, sometimes, dialogue.

The smaller bounding and jumping curves that surface in particular in chapter 7, show clearly how the continents and even hemispheres might be imagined as side by side, parabolically, rather than as opposites. As in the biographies of Olive Schreiner, Janet Frame, or Witi Ihimaera, among others, though the writers' career trajectories lead away from the south, they eventually curve back there, as is in the nature of the boomerang whose shape they take. Together, these writings weave chains of association between seemingly far-flung spaces, so encouraging the kind of constellated thinking through which the far south might, little by little, emerge under its own lights.

But whether parabolic, asymptotic, or chain-linked, most of the readings that comprise *Southern Imagining* are unmistakably navigational, bearing out their counter-normative purposes with, at times, dizzying effects. Each reading might be imagined as the experience of sailing from a familiar bay, rounding the headland, and then turning south—facing into a dimension where the constellations are upside down, and even the most trusted bearings operate otherwise. The book's extensive footnotes, with the multiple axes of further reading they offer, intentionally intensify this vertiginous quality.[91] But it is at the same time offset and stilled with the inclusion of south-facing photographs at the start of each chapter and throughout the impressionistic closing one. The photographs are offered as points of orientation south, as reminders of where we find ourselves, and where—deeper, lower, higher, farther—we are headed.

2

Shared Skies

SPEAKING AND SINGING THE SOUTH

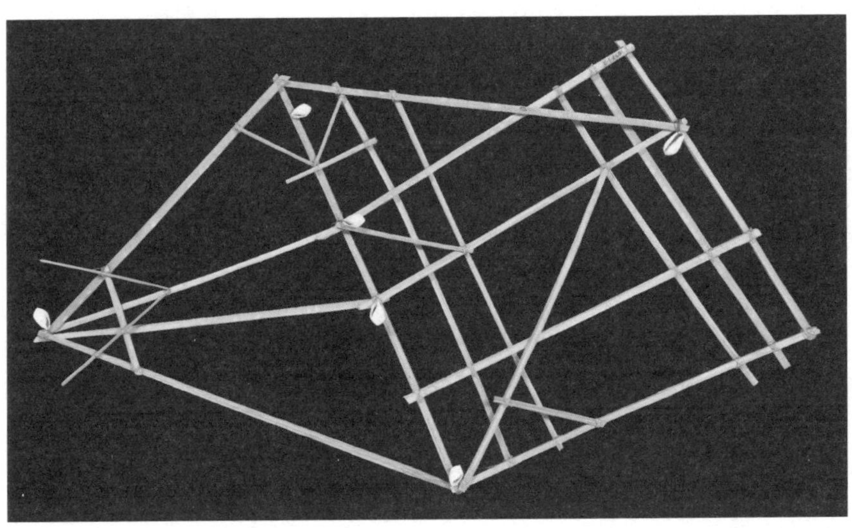

Sea, oh sea,
    you great water
Water of our #Aoni
    people
Praise the sea, you
    #Aoni children
Through him we have
    raised
Sting-rays and
    steenbras
And galjoen

From him we have
  eaten
You great sea, oh
  great water
Water of our #Aoni
  children
Flow, you black
  precipice
Feeder of our children
Please give me the
  stingray
Give me the barbel
Give me the whale
Give me the sand shark
Give me the steenbras
Give me the stockfish
Flow, oh fat
Flow, you flesh-rich water

—'NAMA PRAISE OF THE SEA' (SUNG BEFORE GOING TO FISH)

Back in the beginning, when Baiame, the sky spirit walked the earth, he moulded two men and a woman out of the red earth of the ridges and brought them to life. Before he continued on his way, Baiame showed them all the plants that they could eat to keep life.

For some time, they lived on such plants as had been shown by Baiame and then came a drought and the plants grew scarce. One day the second man killed a kangaroo and he and the woman ate some of its flesh but the first man would not eat this meat although he was very hungry and weak, [and] . . . he walked away angrily towards the sunset. He went over sandhills and ridges until he reached a riverbank near the edge of a coolibah plain. After the second man and woman finished eating, they went searching for their mate and found him lying dead on the other side of the river under a huge white *yaraan*. As he lay there, they saw beside him a black figure, Yowi, the spirit of death with his two large fiery eyes who lifted their mate up and dropped him in the tree's hollow centre.

Then came a terrific burst of thunder as the tree with fiery eyes gleaming was lifted from the earth heading towards the southern sky. Suddenly a loud screeching noise broke the stillness and two yellow crested white cockatoos called Mooyi flew after the spirit tree as this white gum tree was their roosting place on earth. The spirit tree finally planted itself near the Warrnambool that leads to where the sky spirits live.

The second man and woman watched in disbelief as the spirit tree in the sky disappeared from view. They could now only see four fiery eyes shining out. Two were the eyes of Yowi, the spirit of death, and the other two were the eyes of their mate, the first man to die.

Nature then realised that the passing of this man meant that death had come into the world. Much sadness . . . was everywhere. The swamp oak trees sighed incessantly and the gum trees shed tears of blood which crystallised into red gum.

To this day the Southern Cross is known as Yaraan-doo, the place of the white gum-tree, and the pointers are called Mooyi, the white cockatoos. So is the first coming of death remembered by the tribes to whom the Southern Cross is a reminder.

—MICHAEL J. CONNOLLY (MUNDA-GUTTA KULLIWARI PROJECT), 'YARAAN-DOO—SOUTHERN CROSS'

Thinking from and through the South

'Shared Skies' explores pathways towards a southern perspective by considering how southern peoples have been responsive to and centred in their environments across time. The chapter zeroes in on the interpretative devices that selected southern words, legends and heritage stories offer that might help us better to comprehend southern spaces from within. Expanding on the idea that language has a 'shaping power . . . over thought', the different sections conduct an experiment with southern words, especially for star- and seascapes. Southern images variously embodied in names, stories, songs, maps, and night visions offer a means of thinking from and also across the south.[1] Constellating these ideas, the chapter also builds speculations on how interconnected southern perceptions have looped and arced around the hemisphere.

Centredness in the south distinctively marks the utterances above—the Nama praise-chant to the ocean from southern Africa and the Kullilla origin-myth of the southern sky from what is now Queensland in Australia. The utterances approach their surrounding context, ocean, landscape, or starscape, as alive in every element—though to say this is not to overlook the many differences between them or the processes of mediation, including translation, through which they come to us. The fish, the great waves, the ridges, the trees, the stars—are present to the speakers and are also understood in relation to each other. The words bear an unmistakable sense of here-ness or this-ness. And the way in which they invoke their surroundings is immediately valid within the context that they name.

Stories, songs, and other oral forms that develop with reference to the local landscape or seascape and give expression to the lifeways it sustains, have been crucial for the survival and well-being of all cultures. In the far south, where empire has eroded knowledge traditions in especially severe ways, they make up a vital resource. Songs and stories, as well as concept-words and place names, form an integral part of the experience of simultaneously moving through and interpreting the environment. Listening into these forms, therefore, we readers may, even if in a necessarily restricted way, begin to observe something of the south on its own terms.[2] This south, crucially, is not arrived at or entered into. It does not hover elusively beyond the horizon. This south begins in the south and is in place t/here. It has its own near and far horizons, its own many interconnected centres, its own particular haecceity, 'where the sea was alive, waves were alive, currents alive, even the clouds', as the Waanyi writer Alexis Wright puts it.[3]

This idea of fluid yet centred imaginative inhabitation informs the Indigenous Australian idea of *Country*, seen as a living entity where 'Land, Sea and Sky are all connected'—which I draw upon as a guiding idea.[4] The process of singing up Country, of simultaneous chanting and charting, calling your context into your awareness as you move through it, means interrelating with it as with another consciousness. When singing up, Alexis Wright teaches, there is no distinction between internal and external, mind and world, time and geography. At every point, consciousness, nature, and myth interact with and enliven each other. Each part is seen to affect every other part. If remembered and reproduced in the right sequence, the ancient song-cycles bring knowledge of the land and the sky and sea in relation to the land, centrally to the singer's mind. This bringing to mind entails belonging, and the sense of belonging is made actual and intrinsic in the process of being sung. Or, as the elder Joseph Midnight instructs in Wright's novel *Carpentaria* (2006):

> Sing this time. Only that place called such and such. This way, remember. Don't mix it up. Then that place, sing, such and such. Listen to me sing it now and only when the moon is above, like there, bit lower, go on, practice. Remember, don't make mistakes.[5]

It is true that, for those of non-Indigenous and settler backgrounds, the approach to ancient southern knowledge will always involve a necessary encounter with some kind of dissonance. Any attempt to reconstruct linguistic and mythic resources to better discern how southern peoples experienced their surroundings requires the sustained recognition of areas of mystery and otherness.[6] It is not always possible to comprehend what many of these utterances mean, let alone to divine their sacred and secret qualities. Any practice of tapping into chthonic southern knowledge, we must always remind ourselves, exhibits an appropriative, even colonialist tendency to '[seize] upon' Indigenous creations 'for . . . tropes and metaphors', as Goori poet Evelyn Araluen observes—that is, bluntly speaking, to exploit these cultural treasures.[7] It also risks essentialising the local, and seeing the Indigenous and southern as in some simplistic way as 'true'.[8]

With empire—its genocides, epidemics, and many forms of dispossession—any number of Indigenous languages of the southern hemisphere faded or, as it is sometimes said, went to sleep.[9] In the words of Māori theorist Linda Tuhiwai Smith, worlds were materially redefined through the 'renaming and "breaking in"' of the land, and Indigenous peoples were excluded from spatialising and interpreting their worlds.[10] Terms from European languages came officially to categorise and classify southern environments that thereby 'became increasingly disconnected from the songs and chants used . . . to trace their histories'. In the colonial past, Araluen joins Smith and others in reminding us, 'speaking your language was an offence worthy of physical violence or forced removal', with the result that concepts of self and place became blurred.[11] The lands, oceans, and living creatures of the south were now imagined not through local words that grew up in those contexts but via names imposed from outside. To decode heritage texts or fragments of traditional wisdom like the Nama praise-song or the Indigenous 'Yaraan-doo' story above, speakers had themselves to rely on modern translations and adaptations and so grapple with the various challenges of mediation and misrepresentation.

At this point, I introduce more fully an idea that runs throughout this study—that the conceptual and syntactical structures of the languages we speak condition how we understand the world. Different languages open up different ways of seeing that may be partially incommensurable the one with the other but that, when exchanged, nonetheless give insight, however inadequate, into another's world. This understanding relates to Vivieros de Castro and Anne Salmond's concept of cosmo-diversity, introduced earlier, as well as to the Māori notion of words as *kupu*, that bear talismanic properties.[12] In related terms, the mid-twentieth-century American linguists Edward Sapir and Benjamin Whorf proposed that our perception of the world is profoundly shaped by the words and grammatical structures we use to describe it.[13] From this, it follows that, for the purpose of orienting south, words for southern entities, actions, and artefacts can let us into the experience of being in place in southern lands, even if only fleetingly. Language that is shaped by the context to which it refers, in turn, shapes our understanding of that context.

Though we may wish to sidestep as determinist a position as that of Sapir and Whorf, most of us allow that the languages we speak are bound up with our cultural experiences. While our linguistic worlds will not always be mutually intelligible the one to the other, yet the sharing of words may, even so, make some form of communication possible.[14] For example, how spatial information is organised may prime us to pay attention to certain aspects of our surrounding reality over others. Some Indigenous Australian languages like Warlpiri have an antonymic structure whereby naming something also entails naming its opposite. As Nicholas Evans demonstrates, this feature permits Warlpiri speakers to make rapid and efficient scalar adjustments in their perception of space, now focussing in on small details, now zooming out to vast, planetary dimensions.[15] Linda Tuhiwai Smith notes that Māori, too, makes 'no clear or absolute distinction' between the concepts of time and space. As with other Indigenous languages, there exists instead 'a series of very precise terms for parts of these ideas, or for relationships between the idea [of time or space] and something else in the environment.'[16]

This chapter considers elements as small as single words and phrases, as well as longer oral texts, as carriers of spatial knowledge or as expressions of the experience of being *in place* in the south.[17] My reading holds that these devices challenge us to reexamine how our knowledge of the world has been naturalised, especially the way in which northern concepts and orientations have always been seen as prior.[18] Linking across the south, these words and other verbal artefacts also trace out 'networks of cooperation' and lateral juxtapositions, as already configured in the two epigraphs placed together above. Correspondences between stories and voices offer ways, as we will see, of conceptualising synergistically *around* and *across* the hemisphere.[19]

This approach allows that Indigenous cultural objects—including rock art, navigational stick charts, and implements like boomerangs—come to us in mediated forms, their original makers' names and identities often now lost to memory. Yet, even so, I contend, they palpably arise from ways of life long adapted to their environments—fishing practices, modes of navigation, experiences of loss and death—and can be related back to them.[20] The same applies to verbal artefacts: words, chants, songs, and stories articulate perceptions, sensations, and understandings that are woven in with southern spaces, their cycles and seasons, their contours and currents. The artefacts' rhythmic and mnemonic patterns tell us something about the ways in which Indigenous southern peoples lived, perceived, and imagined their environments. By tuning into these patterns, we can better see southern peoples as 'active subjects' of their history, not simply as acted upon.[21] Glancing impressions of being south emerge, though we have always to allow that these are necessarily partial and finite.

An effective way of highlighting how southern knowledge has been buried or suppressed within northern frameworks and yet can make its presence felt is to highlight the southern words embedded in a European-origin, now global language like English. In a 2019 collaboration with lexicographers from the *Oxford English Dictionary* (*OED*), I found that, since the 1700s, upwards of a thousand words for southern referents had been incorporated into versions of English (South African, Australian, or New Zealand English, etc.), and some into global English. These included words for geophysical features (*billabong, vlei*), plants and animals (*buchu*, kangaroo, koala), as well as cultural artefacts and practices (boomerang, biltong, haka).[22] That English was already a creole language shaped by encounter and exchange, to some extent facilitated this take-up, but the presence of the borrowings did not merely demonstrate the global capacity of the language to assimilate words from other, more local languages. The southern loans could also be seen to have an estranging and even disruptive effect, especially words like, say, *Min-Min* (phosphorescent light in the outback, assumed be Aboriginal in origin), *mia-mia* (a temporary shelter, from Wathawurrung) or *eina* (a cry of pain, from Khoikhoi), which have not gained currency beyond a certain region or nation. The words introduce perspectives from distant geographies and wholly different semantic and phonetic systems into a northern language that is often taken as all-enveloping in a simplistic way. The word-lists thereby also underscore the many pathways through which southern knowledge has been adopted within northern sensoria. And they give an impression of important practices and objects of value within these cultures, to the point that they were transferred along colonial communications networks back to the imperial centre and so included in the *OED*.

The chapter now moves to a south-oriented meditation on an ancient stone engraving from southern Africa, which then leads into an account of archipelagic thinking as another powerful means of conceptualising across the south. The three illustrative sections that follow, 'Words', 'Stars', and 'Seas', each offer observations on how selected names, images, and stories might operate as imaginative apparatuses or theories-in-capsule for seeing southern environments from within. The names and artefacts, taken as 'forms of permanence', give some understanding, however fitful, of ancient yet still ongoing southern ways of doing and knowing.[23] In each section, the focus is on cycles and appearances in the natural environment, like star events and the behaviour of the ocean, that would have been widely present to southern peoples.

To further ingrain this southern focus, the chapter initiates the important work of weaving lateral south-south entanglements that recurs across this book—like, for instance, the wild-grape vines 'floating there in the billabong: / Their branches, joint by joint, spreading over the water / . . . [moving] backwards and forwards' that we encounter in the Arnhem Land 'Song Cycle of the Moon-Bone'. For, if concepts of the south from the south can help to challenge perceptions of these areas as minor and marginal, how much more disruptive these challenges may become when souths are imagined in relation to each other, joined up at different points within the hemisphere through etymology, mythic patterns, and astral observation. This objective of working in harmony with the hemisphere's dispersed oceanic and archipelagic viewpoints is pervasive across the chapter.

The sections that follow trace various such south-by-south, or 'joint by joint', movements—with especially striking patterns emerging in 'Stars', which visualises Indigenous myths of the southern constellations that, in fact, arch across the hemisphere. Even before seaways were mapped by Polynesian Islanders, I suggest, southern lands were imaginatively connected through their nightscapes, with the constellations forming southern peoples' one shared point of reference.[24] As we now know, cultures across both the dry and the watery spaces of the southern hemisphere, experiencing the same seasonal cycles and the same kinds of geography, fauna, and some flora, discerned fascinatingly similar patterns in the night sky. Their shared astral canvas allows us to speak with some certainty of southern perceptions rippling around the south, at least in a conceptual or virtual sense. It is within this at once sidereal and archipelagic perception that the most significant contribution of this chapter to what it is to (re)imagine south probably lies.

Structural Meditation—a Southern Reading

The 75,000-year-old Blombos Cave engraving is an ancient southern African carving on ochre that gives clear evidence of the complexity of prehistoric conceptual thought. The carving's network of horizontal and zigzag lines captures, or can be read as capturing, the coeval and interconnected temporalities that this chapter is beginning to sketch. Though it's impossible to say what is 'above' and what 'below' in the engraving, the A-frame suggested by the thicker lines seems to point upward. The top horizontal lines could then be taken as standing for 'sky', and the bottom lines for the earthly or oceanic expanse. The wavier line running horizontally down the middle, equidistant from both, might be the atmosphere or simply that which exists between the top and the bottom.

Tom Phillips suggestively describes the Blombos network as a 'linear maze' or 'structural meditation' that has the power to draw the reflective viewer into a multi-scalar world.[25] While admitting to 'its (finally unknowable) meaning', he wonders, provocatively for my purposes, at the carving's prefigurement of 'the making of maps'. The crisscrossed lines also recall us to the conceptual 'maps' Māori and Pacific Islander informants drew for Europeans to sketch their understanding of their ocean worlds—designs that reflected an intimate knowledge of and attachment to their physical, island-studded surroundings.

I place the Blombos engraving at the head and heart of this chapter, alongside the epigraphs, to draw from it a symbolic yet grounded reading, a graph carved into stone of south-south connection. For, if the sloping lines are taken as sightlines directed from the islands and peninsulas of the nighttime south up to the heavens, to the constellations and galaxies that arch over them all, then the engraving might be read as a correlate for how Earth-to-sky perceptions have zigzagged across the south's scattered spaces for millennia, as southern people on far-apart lands and islands descried similar patterns in the stars, and saw earthly things as reflecting them. The lines dynamically cutting back and forth suggest the reciprocal imagining of sky and sea not in one place only but in many places across the hemisphere—this commonality perhaps signalled, at least to us, by the transverse in-between line that bisects the crisscrossed pattern.

With its triangular arches resembling so many compasses joined point-to-point, the Blombos engraving begins to demonstrate how we might read the south as at once dispersed and yet interconnected. Even as the transverse lines trace the actual and symbolic mirroring of the stars in the ocean and the island clusters in the constellations, the latticework also captures the simultaneous existence of different, if partially overlapping, southern realities. Taking the ochre network as a guide, we can begin to conceive of the south as an assemblage of many different diverging and converging perceptions.[26] The engraving invites us to think connectively through and across the fluid spaces of the south in ways that explode concentric arrangements of (northern) original and (southern) copy.

Archipelagic Understanding

Clusters of stars. Constellations of islands. Song-lines threading through a landscape. Galaxies reflected in ocean currents. Another properly plural way to think from the south is through the concept image of the archipelago—one that the Blombos design already appears to intimate. The idea calls up contrasting notions of the disparate *and* the connected, of 'a number of distinctly different but similar things', a 'menagerie of life-ecologies . . . [that are] subtly related'.[27] These pluri-centric images are true to the character of the blue hemisphere, where oceans predominate, coastlines are long, and the lands and islands attenuated and scattered—strewn puzzle fragments of the ancient supercontinent.[28] They capture, too, the spectacle of blazing stars massed in the night sky and of the stars reflected in nighttime waters as they course around and in between the southern lands and islands.[29]

Though there are many northern as well as southern archipelagos for the Hawaiian historian Epeli Hau'ofa, the archipelago militates against ideas of a world-view imposed from above, encouraging us to see things 'in the totality of their relationships'—the kind of perception that once underpinned Pacific navigational practices.[30] By centring the enveloping ocean that 'sustains us', as Hau'ofa writes in *Our Sea of Islands*, or by locating ourselves in what Alexis Wright calls 'sea country', we are the more stimulated to reimagine the globe from the vantage point of the oceanic hemisphere. The concept of the archipelago also importantly outlines 'inter-island' (and therefore also south-south) movements in Jonathan Pugh's reading.[31] Related tropes 'of assemblages, networks, filaments, connective tissues, mobilities, and multiplicities' highlight island boundaries as shifting, overlapping, and constantly dissolving and recombining. Such archipelagic thinking, with its focus on clusters of things in liquid interrelationship, can properly be termed an 'epistemology of the south', in Boaventura de Sousa Santos's phrase.[32]

Thousands of years before the European voyages into the southern hemisphere, southern peoples lived their lives in relation to both astral and austral archipelagos. They used signs insinuated into the southern constellations to mark seasonal practices, measure life cycles, and navigate the ocean. The Māori writer Witi Ihimaera notes that *purakau*, or ancient creation myths, including those about the stars, enabled his ancestors to amass data on their relationship with the natural world.[33] Polynesian navigators' mnemonic stick charts were crafted to correlate with memorised stars and seascapes, whereby features could be visualised using complexly layered metonyms, with shells standing for islands, for example. This understanding is not unrelated to the Nama praise song to the sea and its fish stocks. The Polynesian charts clearly embody an archipelagic understanding, a south conceived through 'multiple singularities' with the Pacific's 'widely spaced islands' serving as 'a kind of terrestrial mirror for the Milky Way'.[34] Within this vast fluid space, seafarers, map in hand, pictured themselves as stationary with the starry skies revolving overhead, and the islands skimming by on either side, as we will see again at the end of this chapter.[35]

Words

The conceptual role of words in shaping cultural worlds is perhaps especially significant and precious where many languages of the south are no longer widely used, and where northern names now mostly designate southern things. In these situations, in-place southern words work in resonant ways, and include power names, concept words, and even suffixes, those small particles of language that move between presence and absence, between being here and elsewhere.[36] The words capture something, however momentary, of how Indigenous peoples of the south denoted and understood their worlds. For the person or thing's 'true name' invokes their singularity, as the writer Ursula Le Guin wrote. It commits the speaker of the name to that person or thing.[37]

I now take a rough sampling of four Indigenous words from across the southern hemisphere, three unfamiliar, one now widely accepted as a word in English and other European languages. I invite readers to consider them thoughtfully, noticing how these words, when heard or read in context, might have been or might still be especially evocative and powerful.

To begin:

> *Aiagata*—from Yaghan or Yámana, a language of Tierra del Fuego, at the southernmost end of South America, this first word in the missionary Thomas Bridges' 1887 *Yamana-English* dictionary, signifies the particular movement of a whale rising up on end and raising its flukes.

Then:

> *Gogga*—this collective Khoikhoi term for bugs or insects came into South African English through the channel of Afrikaans and arguably retains the guttural quality of the source language, which has also merged with the Dutch creole (*Dictionary of South African English*).

And:

> *Nyamilay*—a greeting in the Australian Indigenous Gamilaraay and some other related Indigenous languages from what is now northern New South Wales, this concept word is interesting for always implying relationship, from the speaker to the listener, and vice versa.

And, finally, by contrast:

> *Boomerang*—also originally from Gamilaraay, this borrowing into English and many other languages denotes the characteristic Australian missile weapon, 'a curved piece of hard wood . . . so made as to describe complex curves in its flight'. According to the *OED* the word first appeared in print in the *Sydney Gazette* of 23 December 1804.

As readers may already have noticed, the feature that links these otherwise very different words from three different parts of the world is how they emerge from and refer back to specialist knowledge, whether of natural surroundings or of context or design. Each in its way captures something of its speakers' intercourse with their environment over time.[38] *Aiagata*'s suggestiveness lies in what it implies about Yaghan culture's close observation of the whale and other sea creatures within a particular oceanic or littoral environment. The word at once points to the whale's watery world, and back to the speaker. So, too, *Nyamilaraay*, the Gamilaraay greeting, implies a relationship between the greeter and the greeted. For its part, the borrowed and creolised *gogga*—guttural, alliterative—may carry some onomatopoeic suggestiveness, its sound sense calling up the visual associations of creeping, crawling, and wriggling of the creatures that are named.

Meanwhile, *boomerang*, among the best known of southern words, both as noun and as verb, has dispersed globally along the tilting pathways that the actual boomerang when in motion itself describes, and that the word designates—pathways of away and back again, of 'complex curves in . . . flight'. In effect, through its transfer first into the English language and then more widely, *boomerang* has looped from having a purely nominative function in its context to becoming a complex transcultural signifier in its own right, even as it always points back to the southern context from which it came. *Boomerang* offers an emblematic instance of how concept words disseminate and creolise back and forth, living anew in different verbal and technical guises.[39]

Crafted verbal artefacts like song-lines, chants, and stories about the earth, sea, and sky communicate how people inhabit their surroundings in an even deeper sense. Like the wild grapevines 'floating there in the billabong,' in the Arnhem Land song cycle, the words are strung into traceable patterns 'invested with precedent'.[40] When repeated in chants or songs, these patterns have the power to bring the environment back to mind. For the Torres Strait Islander Ali Jimmy Drummond, when he set out to learn the Islander language Mabuiag by acquiring knowledge of its songs and stories, a transformative sense of connection with the region's interlaced realities of land, sea, and sky opened up for him:

> If learning single words was like learning about the stars in the sky again, then learning through songs and stories was like connecting the stars and realising full constellations. . . . [Now] I have a more profound understanding about the imperative of harnessing language as a tool to understanding and privileging our ways of knowing and being.'[41]

As Drummond found, just as the environment is impregnated with names, those names, especially when articulated in sequence, call up the land or the sky and tune speakers into it. In the Dreamtime, in the words of David Malouf, 'each totemic ancestor, while travelling through the country, . . . scattered a trail of words and musical notes along the line of his footprints'.[42] Which means, essentially, that space can be traversed in the mind—or travelled in reality—through the mnemonic singing of the right words in the right order. Or, as we remember the elder Joseph Midnight's careful teaching: 'this way, remember. Don't mix it up. Then that place, sing, such and such'.[43]

The concept of the song-line or dreaming-track probably affords as generative a concept of how language speaks space and interacts with context as we find in Whorfian linguistics.[44] For the song-line orients the speaker in space-time along scalar tracks that connect here and there, but also past and present. The approaches come together in the understanding that a language gives access to how its speakers 'see themselves in the fabric of space and time'.[45] In respect of both kinds of thinking, the verbal artefacts afford a palpable sense of how their makers experienced their cultural worlds, even where their languages are no longer widely used.[46] When Indigenous speakers speak the words, stories, and song-lines that relate to their ancestral spaces, they make present how it was (and still is) to live there, however long ago that may have been.

To illustrate, we might look at Khoekhoegowab, a language that was once spoken throughout the South African Cape and now survives in pockets in Namibia. Khoekhoegowab has several words for 'flute' and 'dance' (for example, for the dance releasing a young woman from sequestration after her first menstruation). The prevalence suggests the importance of community ritual to its speakers. Khoekhoegowab also has many words for running (such as for running in fits and starts and for running intermittently), and for different kinds of damp (the dampness of soil as against that of clothes).[47] These sense-realms clearly bore and bear particular significance in a dry region where wheeled transport without roads remains difficult. The names of certain star clusters also feature prominently in many Indigenous word-lists, as we will see again.

The consecutive *and this and then this* pattern of the ancestral song or story entails an especially sophisticated conceptual artefact for plotting both distance and direction—one that is absolutely of the south. The 1870s |xam storyteller ||kabbo gives a correlate for this geographical embeddedness in his image of a San hunter lying on the earth, 'reading' all that is moving on the plain through his body. Recorded by the Cape philologists Wilhelm Bleek and Lucy Lloyd in their *Specimens of Bushman Folklore*, the image has been parsed into contemporary poetry, here by the poet Antjie Krog, first in her language Afrikaans[48]:

dit lyk alsof ons dut
maar ons lees ons liggame
ons voel alles wat daar onder op die vlaktes beweeg
alles wat verby die hutte trek
die holtes agter ons knieë kry 'n gevoel
en dan wag ons
en dan kom al hierdie dinge na ons toe

we read everything which is moving on the plains down below / the backs of our knees tingle / and then we wait / and then everything comes to us

Jump-cut shifts between the skies and the earth, the near and the far, the human and the animal, also characterise the stories of the shape-shifter Mantis|Kaggen, in the same |xam tradition narrated by ||kabbo. In the space of a few moments, Mantis can turn from a dead hartebeest, into a bush bearing hartebeest parts like a clotheshorse, into a flayed hartebeest head. The sensation we get from the |xam stories, in Mattias Guenther's account, is once again of 'dreaming': 'the story one hears takes one as much into the mythic, inchoate, ancestral world of the First Order and First Race as into a vivid dream.'[49]

The interconnection of word and space becomes especially clear in the case of languages where tense is spatially conceived and nonlinear, as, for example, in Indigenous Australian languages like Gamilaraay and Kaurna, as well as Warlpiri. Marnie Hughes-Warrington and Anne Martin observe that, for such languages, 'Country [or place] is the organiser' of the understanding of time, and temporal words denote position and direction.[50] Indigenous place names and names for geographic features, too, carry memories of particular associations with the land. To offer two prominent examples: *Hoerikwaggo*, or Mountain in the Sea, for Cape Town's Table Mountain; *Uluru* for the great red sacred rock at the heart of Australia. These names allow even non-Indigenous listeners and speakers a plastic, embodied sense of what it was to inhabit those geographies before colonisation, no matter how etiolated by modernity these perceptions may now be.[51]

For the South African language activist Denver van Breda, though, 'when you lose land and language you lose identity'. Yet, by reflecting on the Khoi words that live on in Afrikaaps (a version of Afrikaans distinguished by more explicit Khoikhoi overtones), he is able to rebuild cultural memory and '[find his] ancestors'.[52] His work shows once again how a south-centred understanding might be reawakened when southern words are approached as knowledge objects, even if they occur mainly as borrowings into other languages. Backlighting such words in navigators', missionaries', and ethnographers' word-lists represents one important way of approaching the 'perverse' colonial archive slant so as to create an alternative knowledge base. This so-called 'third archive' is captured, too, in anthropological research that finds evidence buried within the settler record of how Indigenous agricultural practices and trade networks were correlated with reference to the night sky.[53]

Stars

For peoples of the southern hemisphere, it seems true to say, the terrestrial was writ large in the heavens, and celestial appearances made to correlate with biological and cultural concerns back on Earth. Archaeological and ethnographic records suggest that across the dispersed lands and islands, stargazers related sidereal rhythms to the seasonal cycles, and wove stories of fishing, planting, and harvesting into the stars. While such observations may be truisms everywhere, they are perhaps especially trenchant in the hemisphere that points into the centre of the Milky Way. For the First Australians, for example, the earthly ancestor spirits reflected in the shape of the constellations provided mnemonics to remember important social laws and lessons.[54] Seagoing peoples such as Polynesian Islanders, meanwhile, used memorised star charts for navigation, as 'Seas' below further explores.

Observing the same bright constellations overhead, responding in synch to the same night-sky happenings, the stargazers of ancient southern societies can be imagined as stitching back together, at least in a virtual way, lands that once formed part of the great supercontinent of Gondwanaland, drawing perceptual zigzag patterns between the earth, the oceans, and the heavens. As in my reading of the Blombos artefact, these story links and songlines radiated from the earth up to the shared sky and back again, all the way between and across southern spaces. The image of reciprocal link-up via the overarching stars is reinforced when we further take into account that southern stargazers often projected homologous shapes drawn from local fauna, especially flightless birds, onto the constellations, as we will see in more detail in a moment.

From the time of the first European voyages into the far south, northerners were struck by the brilliance of its night skies. This was not due to their unfamiliarity alone. How the axis of Earth's rotation is angled relative to the inclination of the Milky Way's plane means that the South Celestial Pole faces a denser or apparently brighter part of the galaxy than the north. As the Milky Way turns through the southern sky, it also exhibits several striking features not visible in northern skies, including the Magellanic Clouds and Alpha Centauri, the closest star to Earth. Interestingly, the first Indigenous words learned and recorded by Europeans were often the names of stars.[55]

By the mid-eighteenth century, the French astronomer Nicolas-Louis de Lacaille's extensive observations from the Cape of Good Hope had already established the town as a 'portal' to the southern skies.[56] Some sixty years later, Joseph Banks, then the President of the Royal Society, once the naturalist on Cook's *Endeavour* voyage, approved the establishment of the Royal Observatory in Cape Town, the first permanent observatory in the hemisphere, offering a parallactic and complementary position to Europe from which to observe sidereal behaviour. Within ten years, the astronomer John Herschel had built a private observatory not far away from which he identified thousands of southern stars and galaxies and developed a theory of the Milky Way's formation and magnitude. The trend for parallactic observation took off. The 1874 and 1882 Transits of Venus were viewed from newly installed telescopes across the south, including in Melbourne, Adelaide, Sydney, Wellington, and Mauritius, as well as Cape Town.[57]

Peoples across the south had, of course, been observing the heavens for aeons, weaving stories emblematising their beliefs and values into astral formations, as in the epigraph story of Yaraan-doo. In a |xam example, ||kabbo's story of !gaunu, or Jupiter, has the bright planet bending to the earth in the springtime to check on the blooming of the desert flowers that come with the rains.[58] Such stories of the southern skies were no doubt stimulated by the geophysics of the hemisphere. Even in ancient times, most far southern populations would have lived at latitudes between zero and thirty-five degrees south, given the terrestrial disposition of the hemisphere, which meant that their nights were never especially short. Year-round, most people would have been able to see thickly clustered stars in the evening and early morning.[59]

In many instances, Indigenous stories feature the constellations of Orion and of the distinctive cluster of the Pleiades (or the Seven Sisters) situated nearby, both of which lie relatively close to the northern horizon and hence serve as prominent seasonal markers, noticeably rising and setting as the earth orbits the sun. Clustered lower in the sky than Orion, for the southern latitudes, the Pleiades generally set in May and rise again in late July or August, then hovering for some time just above the horizon at dawn. In northwest Australia, the reappearance of the constellation in the spring and the beginning of the planting season was explained in Indigenous tales of a group of sisters fleeing together from a rapacious pursuer, the Jampijinpa man. The song tradition appears to have extended east right across the continent, linking different cultures in a kind of geodesic line. Its reemergence in contemporary Indigenous art, as in Nyunmiti Burton's smouldering *Kungkarangkalpa—Seven Sisters*, testifies to its continuing importance for communities today. For Burton, the story signifies the power of women's leadership.[60] Meanwhile, for Māori, the rising of Matariki, the Pleiades, was 'the sign of the first month'.[61] The astronomical systems and celestial myths of South American Indigenous groups, too, associated the 'apparition' of the constellation with the beginning of the new year—the return of the sun, the coming of rain, and the 'renewal of abundance'.[62] And the setting and rising of the constellation also marked the beginning and end of the fertile season in Khoikhoi myth-traditions. For the Khoikhoi, the appearance of the so-called 'hoeing stars' inaugurated the new digging season.[63]

Star patterns were used to guide and orient travellers across far distances, at sea as well as on land. Southern mariners, like their northern counterparts, used the southern constellations as a vital means of navigation, as is more fully outlined in 'Seas' below. Similar to Indigenous travellers moving across deserts and plains like the Nullarbor or the Karoo with the help of story and song, Polynesian navigators were trained astronomers well-versed in the lore of the stars. Rather than working with a flat map showing longitude and latitude as a kind of grid, as did their European counterparts, they held curvilinear star charts in their minds, which they memorised using various mnemonics.[64] In contrast to the movements of sea currents and seabirds, which they also used as measures, star patterns and positions had the advantage of remaining unvaryingly predictable, year on year.

The interconnection of southern lands in relation to star events can be demonstrated using a remarkable night-sky observation from 2017, when, on 18 August, a collision between two dense neutron stars took place 'at the edges of the universe'.[65] As the earth turned, observers tracked the collision's powerful ripple effects across the night sky. The phenomena associated with this 'gravitational tsunami' manifested with particular vividness in the far southern hemisphere, where, as we already saw, the night skies are clearest, darkest, and most silent, and the stars especially numerous and bright. Moreover, August is a winter month in the south, so the night was, relatively speaking, longer, while the location of both radio and optical observatories in Western Australia, the Karoo and the Atacama deserts, meant that perceptions and recordings could be coordinated across the hemisphere.[66] In keeping with this chapter's core symbolism, the 2017 astronomers can be envisaged as collectively creating a curb-chain pattern of celestial-terrestrial observation around the hemisphere—the same kind of reciprocal pattern of sightings that Indigenous stargazers might, in effect, have participated in. They worked not only collaboratively but laterally across the latitudes, synchronising more or less simultaneous findings to create a network of optical and radio soundings from which they could search for further gravitational wave events.

Not unlike the till-then-unprecedented coordinated observations of the 1769 Transit of Venus from points around the world, including Cook's in Tahiti, viewings of the August 2017 neutron star collision represented one of the most intensively coordinated astrophysical studies in the world to date. The synchronised recordings and calculations from multiple vantage points was seen to mark a new phase in so-called multi-messenger astrophysics.[67] Though, in essence, the event simply involved people in different venues observing the night sky and comparing notes, the point is that they were aligning sightings between mainly southern sites. The neutron collision that had cascaded through so many light-years from the far reaches of the universe continued to ripple around the planet through emails, phone calls, and correlated readings.

Such knowing synchronicity between continents would have been physically impossible, let alone imaginable, till very recently. Ancient peoples would obviously not have had the means of cross-checking their night-sky readings. Even so, powerful evidence exists for their having read the sky in similar ways. Shared constellations stimulated forms of visual intersection for millennia, as the Pleiades did most prominently. Ethnoastronomers' comparative examination of 'dark' constellations within the Milky Way also points to mutually relatable 'pattern recognition' among southern peoples around the hemisphere.[68]

Human beings are, by nature, apophenic, seeing shapes within randomness, most notably faces—a special form of apophenia called pareidolia. All cultures have projected designs onto the stars in this entoptic way, throwing orderly nets of meaning over what sometimes looks chaotic, often as a way of predicting the future, as we find in astrology.[69] Yet what is especially striking about premodern observation in the south is that stargazers appear to have identified similar shapes, including in the Milky Way, reading meaning into both light clusters and the dark spaces between them. While cultures worldwide have arranged the stars into patterns, the truly remarkable thing here is that peoples from Patagonia through the Karoo to Australasia drew outlines in parallel. In part, this was, of course, because they shared similar seasons—the same kinds of processes occurred on Earth when certain constellations dominated the sky. But it was also partly because their environments featured creatures from the same species, particularly the flightless bird—the emu, the ostrich, and the rhea. They drew the emu/ostrich shape into the dark spaces within the Milky Way, finding the birds' behaviours of mating and egg-laying mirrored in the galaxy's shift from forward-leaning to vertical between the months of March and July.

Many Indigenous peoples in Australia, including the Gamilaraay (in present-day New South Wales) and the Yamaji (in Western Australia), discerned in *Warrambool* (or *Milnguya*, in Yolngu) the dark shape of a giant elongated emu (*Dhinawan* in Gamilaraay). The changing position of this celestial emu, *Gawarrgay*, they took as a seasonal marker forbidding or licencing certain cultural practices.[70] The dark emu leaning forwards and apparently running in March and April correlated with living emus' mating and egg-laying. Whereas, a few months later, when the great emu was sedentary and seemingly incubating, its head buried in the dark area to the lower 'left' of the Southern Cross (the Coal Sack in English), would be the right time to collect eggs. Or, as Noon and De Napoli write, 'sky knowledge' connects to food knowledge, which 'connects to seasonal knowledge': 'the dhinawan's breeding cycle and its movement across Country [are mirrored in] the movements of Gawarrgay across the sky'.[71]

Similarly, the |xam storytellers of the northern Karoo correlated the tipping forward of the dark ostrich shape in the night sky with actual ostrich behaviour to decide when eggs could be harvested. Further to the west again, peoples of the River Plate basin in South America visualised a rhea resting within or running through starry fields, depending again on the seasons. (South Americans also observed llama shapes in the heavens, as the Khoi peoples did eland and termite, and Indigenous Australians, kangaroos and other marsupials, as well as cockatoos, as above. But these animals were specific to the different southern continents and hence to their different astral projections.)

Further detail only reinforces the remarkable extent of these shared perceptions. The ethnoastronomers Alejandro Martin López and Sixto Benítez observe that the Mocoví peoples of the Gran Chaco basin (an area now straddling northern Argentina, Paraguay, and Brazil) also connected the celestial world with the earthly through the powerful 'connecting thread' of the Milky Way galaxy which served as the spine for an interwoven series of creation stories.[72] The Mocoví astronomical cycle marked two main events: the 'return of the sun' (or mother) at the June or winter solstice, and the rising of the Pleiades constellation (the grandfather or life-giver) in October. Within the galaxy's brightness, the Mocoví further discerned the 'shadow-soul' of the rhea 'master' or totem that, according to tradition, had run away from its human pursuer and, once again, buried its head in the Coal Sack. Its position in the sky reinforced the indications given by the Pleiades of a new season of fruitfulness. The pointer stars of this constellation, Alpha and Beta Centauri, the Mocoví saw as dogs chasing the totem.[73]

In southern African Khoi languages, words for stars give further insight into important seasonal cycles and related cultural priorities. Horizon-hugging star clusters that rise and set with the seasons, like the Pleiades and also Orion, feature predominantly in Khoi word-lists, more so than, say, the always-visible southern constellations like Crux or Cetus. In linguist Menán du Plessis's carefully conserved dictionary of Kora, a faded Khoisan or Bushman language of the Gariep area in the northern Eastern Cape, the group of words for stars is dominated by names for Orion.[74] Of the sixteen words collected, four refer to Orion, including *!xan |'amiros*, the Eland star (referring to four stars near Orion), *||ūs |'amiros*, the Springbok star in Orion, *!omm*, the Tortoise star, likewise, and *!xankukua*, the Eland or Orion itself. The word for the Pleiades is *|hōdi* while the Magellanic clouds are *|'amis ||āub*, the Ostrich Nest. In |xam, the Pleiades are *|xōide* or 'celestial ostrich eggs'.[75] Relatedly, missionary

Thomas Bridges's Yamana-English dictionary records that the Yaghan word for *constellation* is the same as for Orion.[76] Yet the night skies told legends of constancy as well as of cyclical change. In the story 'Yaraan-doo', for example, the Crux shape, the white gum tree in the sky, and the two pairs of shining eyes, signify the unchanging presence of death in human life.[77]

For the ocean-facing Māori, the dark patch of the Milky Way resembles either the 'Long Shark' in the sky or the *waka* or canoe of the ancestor Tama-rereti. Orion and Scorpius outline the front and back of the *waka*, and the Southern Cross and its pointers the anchor or *te punga*, while the blazing clusters on either side represent the foam of parting waves.[78] According to the ancestral legend, one harvest night, the canoeist Tama-rereti scattered shiny stones from the lakeside to light his way through the darkness that was encroaching earlier and more rapidly with the onset of winter. This service delighted the sky god Ranginui to the extent that he placed the dark canoe shape in the Milky Way as a reminder of how the shining stones had traced Tama-rereti's pathway across the water. Torres Strait Islanders, unsurprisingly, also see boat and fish outlines in the sky, scrying the bright stars of Orion as two disobedient boys who defied their elders by fishing in dangerous waters, after which they were dragged up into the heavens.

Though these night-sky stories give only a sampling of the array of southern celestial legends that have survived, when gathered together, they begin clearly to underscore distinctive patterns in common that are by their nature particular to the south. The linked images and storylines are especially salient considering that the storytellers and lawmakers concerned were operating in spaces otherwise so removed the one from the other. Yet they viewed the stars symphonically, their apophenic stories, as it were, linking up and drawing celestial loops around the hemisphere. In rough parallel to how astronomers in 2017 joined up minuscule reverberations relating to a massive cosmic event, Indigenous southern stargazers drew patterns through the southern galaxies and dark spaces that intersected in the skies themselves, within the bright arch of the Milky Way.[79]

Seas

With our eyes still trained on the stars, let us now imagine ourselves setting out from Micronesia sailing east, as the seafaring Polynesians began to do from around the eighth century. They fanned out from island to island across the Pacific, lining up their moving position in relation to the patterns of tides and currents and the pathways of stars and migrating birds.[80] By AD 1200, these open-ocean migrants had reached even the remotest islands, including Rapa Nui or Easter Island in the distant east, and the islands of what is now Aotearoa or New Zealand to the southwest, their voyages proceeding incrementally, expanding from exploratory voyages to making trade connections and settlements. Several centuries before the technologies that made dead reckoning possible for European navigators, the Pacific Islanders had found their way across distances of thousands of miles, without coastlines to hug, in a process of human wayfaring that is now considered 'unparalleled' till the space age.[81]

Early Polynesian *etak* or knowledge of open-water navigation represented a way of living within and between archipelagos that was probably more attuned to the ocean environment or *te moana* than any other on the planet at that time. *Etak* required a remarkable capacity for three-dimensional ideation whereby sophisticated mind-maps were used in conjunction with mnemonic aids like stories but also stick-and-shell structures in a process comparable to how song-lines operate on land. Contrary to European surmise, it would have been impossible to traverse the vast expanses of the Pacific without the help of this stick-map technology—by merely relying, say, on drift and happenstance.[82] Polynesian journeys southwest to Aotearoa New Zealand were especially challenging, taking the wayfarers in a direction against the prevailing winds and currents (in contrast to the monsoon-dependent system used by trading cultures in the Indian Ocean).[83]

To develop a better sense of the skills involved, we might take a closer look at these Polynesian nautical maps, like the Marshall Island stick-and-shell chart I consulted at the Pitt Rivers Museum at the University of Oxford (a reproduction appears at the head of this chapter). The chart comprises a rough parallelogram, the sticks marking the occurrence of tidal patterns, currents, and swells, while the shells indicate the position of islands. We could say that the map makes up, in its way, another southern latticework, not unlike the Blombos carving. Keeping such a chart in hand as they sailed, navigators made constant, shifting projections. They took a running fix on bright stars and prominent constellations, like Canopus or Sirius, or the Pleiades, calibrating these in relation to more fluid oceanic indices, tidal patterns, ocean currents, and the appearance of certain birds, and replacing the guide stars with others as their vessel moved.

But this was not all. Alongside this mnemonic aid, the memorised 'compass' of the constellations that the navigators held in their minds was also vital for determining their changing position. Polynesian *etak* required that navigators memorise from childhood the position of rising and setting stars in relation to surrounding island positions for *every night* of the year. Or, as Vicente Diaz and J. Kehaulani Kauanui note of Carolinian Islanders, to obtain a 'clear and unambiguous sense of one's place' on the moving ocean, *etak* demanded a detailed yet always kinetic awareness of the surrounding 'sea of islands' through which the mariner was travelling.[84] Visualised from the vantage point of a stationary canoe, this fluid picture plotted the exact position of the stars overhead while also seeing them as mirrored in the surrounding ocean.[85]

As Herman Melville observed, in the Pacific cultural world, oceanic and celestial archipelagos were believed not only to reflect one another but to interpenetrate 'far beyond all visible horizons, . . . interflow with the blue heavens; and so form the white breakers of the milky way'.[86] Cosmological chants had 'the ocean on earth mirrored by the sea in the sky', as Salmond shows. And for Pacific writer Alfred Wendt, islands could be sought out by following the 'prophetic stars'.[87] Using both material and mind-maps, Pacific navigators worked constantly between archipelagic worlds, shuttling between different scalar tracks—of the vessel, the ocean's surface and depths, and the night sky. Essentially, they read the ocean as a matrix of unfolding sea paths, including wave patterns and clouds, that they monitored all at once, simultaneously.[88] (Similar shapes outlining reciprocity and tracing movement across great distances group and pattern the readings in the chapters to follow.)

Tupaia, the brilliant Raiatean navigator who sailed with James Cook's *Endeavour* from Tahiti to New Zealand and Australia, was the first to point out to northerners that Polynesian seafaring skills depended on this ability to hold exact astronomical knowledge in the mind. In his native Society Islands or Tōtaiete mā, these skills demanded years of training within professional 'arioi or navigator societies, of which Tupaia had formed a part on Ra'iatea.[89] The chart of the Pacific that Tupaia drew for Cook, centred upon Tahiti, was a two-dimensional representation of this curvilinear mental map, marking out distances in terms of the number of nights it took to sail between the islands. Cook observed that Tupaia could 'shew them at all times during the course of their voyage, to half a point of the compass, the direction in which Otaheite [Tahiti] lay'. He also perceptively believed that a better understanding of this knowledge would help to explain how the Pacific islands 'came to be peopled'.[90]

The 1770 encounter of Tupaia and Cook, two seafaring experts from two very different cultures, represented an eerie conjunction of navigational methods that were in many ways contrapuntal yet were both based on lunar readings. But Tupaia moved between islands and cultures not with the aid of nautical knowledge only. Language, too, proved an important compass—in a way that speaks back to all of the approaches explored in this chapter. A Polynesian speaker, the 'arioi priest became in Aotearoa an extempore translator and interpreter, though by this point the Māori migrations there lay four hundred years in the past. From the very first landfall, Tupaia found he could understand what the Māori were saying: He 'spoke to them in his own language and it was an [a]greeable surprise to [Cook's crew] to find that they perfectly understood him'.[91] Subsequently, everywhere Tupaia went he 'conducted the rituals of greeting with local people', and shared songs and stories.[92]

Tupaia's cultural associations with Māori were reflected in a shared vocabulary, including in the use of Polynesian pronouns implying close relationship. By the time the *Endeavour* had circumnavigated North Island, Tupaia's fame had gone before him, and people called for him to come ashore and act as a broker. When Cook returned to New Zealand on the *Resolution* in 1773, Māori on Te Waipounamu or the South Island called out his name, asked after him and expressed regret to hear that he had died: it would be 'no wonder if at this time [his name] is known all over New Zealand', Cook observed.[93] First bridging between South Seas islands, Tupaia's interlinguistic understanding was thus reproduced within cross-island south-south networks.

The comparative meditations on Indigenous concepts of spaces, stars, and seas in this chapter have necessarily been in part speculative, but I hope they demonstrate, even if at times impressionistically, how it might be possible little by little to retrieve southern perspectives from the knowledge sedimented into words, phrases, word-lists, myths, sailing charts, and other artefacts. This knowledge underpins after its fashion what Raewyn Connell calls 'southern theory', or thinking from outside the north—theory that works with a kind of boomeranging action, swinging from south to north and back again, and so contributing, as Connell writes, to the planet's sum total of thought about the world.[94] When we patch together the half-erased cartographies and cosmologies that these artefacts once plotted, we recompose not only the complicated conceptual tracks that they once projected across the south but also the declarations of hereness and in-placeness that they made possible.

3

Reading the South

CAMÕES'S 'AUDACIOUS PASSAGE'

Nothing could be more dreary than the scene around us. The lofty, bleak, and barren heights that surround the inhospitable shores of this inlet, were covered, even low down their sides, with dense clouds, upon which the fierce squalls that assailed us beat, without causing any change: they seemed as immovable as the mountains where they rested.

. . .

I might use Bulkeley's words in describing the weather in this neighbourhood, and nearly at this season: 'Showers of rain and hail, which beat with such violence against a man's face, that he can hardly withstand it.'

—CAPTAIN PRINGLE STOKES, FIRST CAPTAIN OF THE *BEAGLE*, *NARRATIVE OF THE SURVEYIG VOYAGES OF HIS MAJESTY'S SHIPS* ADVENTURE *AND* BEAGLE, ED. PHILLIP PARKER KING AND ROBERT FITZROY (JUNE 1828/1839).

As when far off at sea a fleet descried
Hangs in the clouds, by equinoctial winds
Close sailing from Bengala, or the isles
Of Ternate and Tidore, whence merchants bring
Their spicy drugs; they on the trading flood,
Through the wide Ethiopian to the Cape,
Ply stemming nightly toward the pole

—JOHN MILTON, *PARADISE LOST*, BOOK 2, LL. 636–43, (1667)

No matter how many vessels attempt
The audacious passage you are plotting,
My cape will be implacably hostile
With gales beyond any you have encountered;

. . .

If what I imagine comes to pass,
Year by year your fleets will meet
Shipwreck, with calamities so combined
That death alone will bring you peace of mind.

—LUÍS VAZ DE CAMÕES, *THE LUSÍADS* 5.42–43, (1572)

'Laid Down in Some Charts': A Collage of Reading

New charts emerge from old—it is a truism in cartography. Maps represent an accumulation of knowledge built up over time. As the gridded map first developed by the Egyptian geographer Ptolemy, began in the early 1500s to gradually replace Medieval *mappaemundi*, European cartographers increasingly relied on a 'geometric armature' combined with accumulated empirical knowledge rather than theological and mythic symbolism to represent the globe. Their grid of latitude and longitude modelled as yet unexplored lands and seas beyond the horizon as 'positive space', an abstract emptiness into which presently unknown geographies might in due course be set.[1] Discursive resources of many different kinds, not least travel notes, journal entries, and letters, combined with earlier cosmographies and itinerary maps, became vital resources underpinning this burgeoning trans-European cartographic project. References to the known helped fill out the blank unknown, turning the wider world into a space that could be held in the mind, as well as claimed and named. The activity was cognitive as well as colonial, investigative as well as possessive.

Sailing from the South Atlantic to the South Pacific, the eighteenth-century commodore John Byron, one of Britain's first circumnavigators of the globe after Francis Drake, referred repeatedly to the charts, logbooks, and observations of previous captains, using these quotations like guiderails. His ship's journal, *An Account of a Voyage around the World in the Years 1764–66*, shows that he often consulted the accounts of earlier navigators like George Anson or John Bulkeley. To establish where the previously observed but persistently elusive 'Peypys island' [*sic*], for example, might lie, Byron noted a 'bank' which 'has not been mentioned by any navigator who has passed the Strait', urging mariners coming after him to check the feature for the benefit of 'future voyages'. In the latitude of what are now the Malvinas or Falklands Islands, he observed small rocky outcrops like 'remarkable hummocks' 'which Bulkeley, from their appearance, has called the Asses Ears, W1/2N'.[2] Pringle Stokes, Robert Fitzroy's predecessor as captain on the *Beagle*, also cites Bulkeley in trying to communicate his experiences surveying off Tierra del Fuego, as in the epigraph above. He found the far southern American coast to lie 'S. S. E. very different from Sir John Narborough's description', even while recommending the Straits of Magellan rather than Cape Horn as the best route for rounding the continent, because of the region's 'abundance of fish'.

'Peypys Island' was also later to frustrate Captain James Cook's attempts to locate its whereabouts despite it being 'laid down in some Charts'. True to character, Cook across his three journeys—especially the first, unsurprisingly—correlated his observations with the sightings, landings and coordinates ('tracks', he called them) noted by Anson, Carteret and Wallis, some years before, as well as Pedro Fernándes de Queirós and Abel Janszoon Tasman, early in the previous century.[3] His readings helped to supplement and strengthen his own predictions. Resolved to 'quit' New Zealand following his figure-of-eight circumnavigation of the North and South Island, Cook recorded in his *Journal* for March 1770 that he would 'steer to the westward until we fall in with the East Coast of New Holland', present-day New South Wales, and then 'endeavour to fall in with the lands or Islands discover'd by Quiros [sic]'.[4] Throughout the time he spent sailing around Aotearoa New Zealand, and later on his second visit, Cook several times noted that 'Tasman [was] here'. In turn, the cartographer Matthew Flinders, who mapped the entire coastline of continental Australia in the early years of the nineteenth century, checked his readings against 'the discoveries and examinations of former navigators', especially Cook, but also Dutch 'manuscript charts', especially of Western Australia drawn by Eessel Gerrits and others.[5]

As these examples begin to suggest, early European voyages into unknown waters, not least the far southern hemisphere, the outer edge of the world, were, to a significant degree, exercises in reading and rereading. This reading unfolded at two primary levels in tandem. First, by constantly taking observations, navigators charted and made legible for those who would follow the ever-changing environment unfolding around them. Then, to best do this, they consulted the ship's logs, journals, and diaries of those who had preceded them, no matter how patchy and inadequate. Their reading of the earlier writings helped to project and plot a way forward.

Eighteenth- and nineteenth-century mariners produced with their charting and notetaking an epistemology of the ocean, as the geographer Philip Steinberg has termed it.[6] Previous observations, often in the form of compilations, served alongside compasses or astrolabes as navigational devices with which to comprehend the unmapped lands and seas. Shipboard journals, in particular, helped incrementally to build an ever more exact and rounded understanding of the wider world outside Europe, and, in particular, in this context, beyond the equator. This dynamic process of knowledge-making at once informs and is reflected in the maritime writing of the south, which, too, is made up of a collation of readings. While routers generated maps and maps more detailed routers, so, too, travelogues and travellers' tales unfolded from earlier travel writing and then informed further journeying—and writing—'for the advantage of future navigators'.[7]

In their turn, therefore, the maritime writers of the far south, linked together in this and the next chapter, like the ship's captains who so interested them, drew upon the imaginative charge and visionary powers of earlier navigators across both real and imaginary seas. They, too, spatialised and interpreted the unknown by drawing upon the known, and their writing contributed to ever-thickening layers of cross-reference about the extremities of the world. Their compilations assumed curvilinear (rather than merely linear) movement and directionality, routes that went *around* the southern continents or looped *back and forth* between distant austral seas. In a word, far south journeys engendered, in the act of being written up, an at once southerly *and* parabolic disposition.

Symbol-rich, ritually invested stories, including religious texts like the Bible, provided the writers with especially fruitful resources for approaching the strange and new.[8] Vasco da Gama and the Roman epic poet Virgil, in their different capacities, furnished Luís de Camões's work with strong narrative underpinnings. So, too, early modern translations of Virgil into Spanish buttressed the number of epics celebrating Spain's expansion into the Americas, like most notably, Alonso de Ercilla's *La Araucana* (1569, 1578, 1589), now seen as the national poem of Chile.[9] Cook's *Voyages, The Arabian Nights,* and Milton's *Paradise Lost* imprint Coleridge's imagination of the far south. (Milton preceded Coleridge in imagining ships plying south 'toward the pole', as in the epigraph quotation from *Paradise Lost,* above.) Charles Darwin reflects on southern geographies with reference once again to Milton, but also Cook, von Humboldt, and the geographer Lyell's *Principles of Geology*.[10] Mary Shelley's polar ice fields are indebted to Coleridge, especially his ballad of the south, *The Rime of the Ancient Mariner*. Melville's *Moby-Dick* is imbued with Coleridge as well as the Book of Job among many other liberally cited sources.[11] These literary and cultural cross-references can be imagined as building an intertextual relay chain that loosely links these works together.

For each one of the writers, the north was taken as the place where knowledge was generated, and the south the material to be processed and so 'worlded'—a term from Eric Hayot's work on literary worlding.[12] This may seem to state the obvious, yet it is an important perception to keep centre stage. For, though vast regions of the south were as yet uncharted, these areas could nonetheless be modelled, encircled, circumscribed, and made safe on the gridded map—and in writing. As might then stand to reason, ships undertaking major voyages increasingly came equipped with substantial libraries. Darwin's cabin on the *Beagle* 'doubled' as the library. The floor-to-ceiling shelves contained 'Byron, Cook, Milton, Humboldt, Lyell, Euclid's geometry, Paley's Evidence of Christianity, all twenty volumes of the 'Cyclopedia Britannica, even Lamarck'.[13]

Navigating South, or Worlding in Motion

European expansion from the early 1500s incrementally created global geographic knowledge, including an in-progress idea of the far south of the world. Pivoting away from southern perceptions of southern lands, this chapter explores how Europe's geostrategic attempts to gather information about routes to India and China came to mould images of the world beyond the equator.

As the ice-bound northwest passage continued to resist European penetration, the apparently inimical but conveniently fluid south became the best way of getting to the east by sea.[14] The discussion considers how maritime writers' observations contributed to the process of transforming the planet into a knowable global object, often led by the hypothesis of the counterbalancing great southern continent. The navigators' various 'scopic' and textual technologies—logbooks, portolan maps, and grids, as well as journals and compilations—helped to project line and form onto the southern welter. And, in an endless relay, these writings and illustrations shaped the observations and further imaginings that emerged in their wake.

From the late fifteenth century, Europeans in small wooden sailing vessels began edging past the equator into the southern Atlantic and west and southwest across to the Americas. Following the terms of the Pope's 1494 Treaty of Tordesillas that divided the entire planet along a line 370 leagues west of Cape Verde, the Spanish were tasked with moving west, the Portuguese south along the West African coastline, and then east around the Cape of Good Hope and into the Indian Ocean.[15] From a southern European point of view, the globe became divided in law as well as conceptually into eastern and western hemispheres, as the Peninsular powers put into action the expansionist agendas of Prince Henry 'the Navigator', and of the Spanish monarchs Ferdinand and Isabella. By 1565, the Spanish had staked their claim to the Pacific Ocean by establishing the shipping route between Manila and Acapulco, undergirded by the rich trade in South American silver with the Ming dynasty in China.[16]

The navigators of both maritime powers, joined in phases across the 1600s by the Dutch, French, and English, proceeded by using charts that were often sketchy through seas they perceived as trackless. Leapfrogging down the African and South American coastlines from river mouth to mouth or, at night, picking their way by following increasingly less familiar star clusters, the crews edged their puny vessels forwards. The navigators missed the affordance of the Pole Star once they had got beyond the line, as noticeably did Luís Vaz de Camões, the poet soon to be in focus. Journeying on past the equator meant forging an uncertain path marked by treacherous straits and sudden, unpredictable, even though anticipated, turns, as for Bartolomeu Dias when rounding Africa: 'driven by storms beyond his predecessors' farthest south, [he] turned east—and lo! There was no land'.[17] The mariners' reliance on earlier intelligence meant that their experience was possibly not that unlike that of the Polynesians proceeding southwest and southeast in their region of the globe, using stick-charts to mark star positions, and gradually evolving their navigational technologies on the basis of what they already knew.

The latter half of the chapter considers how these processes of reading, writing up, and worlding are reflected in a single early modern poem, the epic about a signature southern journey that is Camões's *Os Lusíades*, or *The Lusíads* (1572). Based on the rapacious Vasco da Gama's coastline-hugging voyage around Africa to India in 1497–99, initially following Dias's tracks as far as the Cape, the Portuguese maritime epic lays down some influential early literary templates of southern navigation. As Josiah Blackmore writes, the poem visibly composes a teleology or 'loose code for writing and reading the world under early expansion', even while articulating European ambitions to control and subjugate.[18]

But my concentration on *The Lusíads* should not be to the exclusion of another remarkable sixteenth-century epic set in the far south, which it might be seen to pleasingly counterpoint along a south-by-south axis.[19] Commingling classical and contemporary references, Alonso de Ercilla y Zúñiga's *Araucana*, like *The Lusíads*, recounts the gory history of European penetration into the far south, this time in the territory of what is now Chile. And like *The Lusíads*, the Spanish poem emerges out of a historical Iberian moment when colonial conquest was marked and praised in Virgil-influenced ottava rima. The *Araucana*'s concern with the long-unsubdued titular Mapuche people will merit close attention in studies of southern spatial imaginaries to come. In this chapter, when presented with the difficult question of which poem to discuss in depth, I eventually settled on Camões's epic. The decision was made slightly easier by *The Lusíads* being appropriate to the context—it is a seagoing poem about navigation in the watery hemisphere, in particular the Indian Ocean, that is hyperaware of that ocean's level of littoral interconnection. There is also a remarkable pliability built into the texture of the poem whereby the story it tells of early Portuguese navigation around Africa is at key points enacted within the text, even while we as readers are often proprioceptively centred on deck with the explorer da Gama.

Following on from this reading of Camões, chapter 4 considers the austral writings that emerged some two hundred years later with the rise of British naval dominance in the South Seas and the beginning of the age of whaling: Coleridge's *The Rime of the Ancient Mariner* (1798), Darwin's *The Voyage of the* Beagle (1839), Melville's *Moby-Dick* (1857), and, finally, Mary Shelley's earlier yet intriguingly synoptic *Frankenstein* (1818). These works had a transformative effect on maritime writing in English of the far south and, in turn, stimulated and shaped further southern imagining. In relation to these writers, the poet-navigator Camões is chronologically and linguistically the outlier, yet, as we will see, his work devised important moulds for how the north would continue to perceive the south through the ages of revolution and capital, from the 1760s and into the age of empire, in Eric Hobsbawm's reading.[20]

Camões's *Lusíads* is especially striking for how it appears to chart the unfolding African coastline even as the storyline follows da Gama on his journey, the storyline then bending back on itself around the southern tip of Africa. The poem knowingly tracks how early European navigators into the southern hemisphere depended on those accumulated textual resources of previous travellers—charts and rutters, logbooks and journals. On vivid display in the poem is also the extent to which, in perceptual terms, navigation never involved a simple linear progression or layer-by-layer accretion. Rather, moving into the watery south entailed a kind of oscillation, at once reaching forwards and harking back, looping round and doubling, a feature that the *in medias res* device of classical epic makes possible.

Essentially, as Camões is well aware, seafarers like Dias or da Gama, or, later, John Byron, Wallis, and Cook, built collages of yesterday's notes and calculations to achieve today's horizon. They projected a way forward even while reading back to 'antiquitie', including in their sweep, for example, the influential multivolume 'voyages' of Richard Hakluyt, and the translator Richard Eden's *The Arte of Nauigation* (1509), which 'Englished' and remodelled the Spaniard Martin Cortés's widely-used guide.[21] And their seesawing between imaginative forecasting and diligent retrospection shaped and reshaped the information that they generated.[22]

Cartography thus at once refracted and enabled the project of southern worlding. Maps invited and justified expansion into regions that were brought closer and made visible through these various interlaced processes of projection and erasure. Similar to the making of natural history, early modern cartographic production used 'framing devices and scholarly tools' like 'indices and tables' that iteratively conferred authority on a European frame of reference.[23] These inevitably always represented the south as modularly different. Compilations used images of 'primitive' people derived from the American New World generically to designate 'the southern climates', invariably setting up the peoples of these regions as inferior in relation to Europe and, therefore, as in need of civilising.

The idea from reception theory that informs this discussion is that colonial European journeys into the uncharted southern oceans involved simultaneous exercises in reading *and* translation.[24] Writers drew on the meaning-making mechanisms at their disposal, not least the resources of written language—its syntactic shapes and paratactic structures—which further supplemented their charts and measurements. The translation of the so-called inarticulate came to be a figurative as well as an interpretative undertaking. Treatises of navigation laid down an authoritative 'method of "knowing" the world across the oceans', as Young observes: 'The books do more than recount the voyages . . . ; they help to establish the language, the categories and the representational forms that evolve in the pursuit of knowledge'.[25]

In this sense, early northern cartography operated in a cantilevered way, creating knowledge of 'southern partes' by working from two directions: at once from above, taking a bird's eye view, the 'all-seeing scale of astronomy'; and from the ground or deck, drawing upon age-old seafaring practices, recorded in rutters or routers. (With its origin in Mediterranean coast-based navigation, the *roteiro* or rutter was a handbook of written sailing directions that reiterated information in the foregoing charts and would, in turn, become an invaluable guide for later journeys.)[26] Yet, though layered, this dual process of mapping naturally had a powerful forward vector, as Lisbon and Amsterdam's cartographers turned navigators' readings into ever more distinct images of southern shorelines and islands.[27] While maps at one level expressed mastery, in practical and economic terms, they also laid down the routes to resources that might, in due course, be traded and turned into profit.[28] Such cartographic knowledge could rapidly be commoditised to the point that maps themselves became priceless technologies. The painting *Officer and Laughing Girl* (1657) by the Dutch Golden Age artist Johannes Vermeer, for example, depicts globes and maps alongside other valuable objects like rich fabrics and gold—objects that had been traded along the routes that the maps themselves represented.[29]

A Very Short History of Mapping the Unknown

The pan-European project to develop accurate geographical knowledge of southern lands and oceans was an enormously complex undertaking, involving many powerful players—courtiers, politicians, diplomats, spies, scientists, mapmakers, and native informants and interlocutors, as well as the seafarers themselves. But it was also shaped by happenstance. As for the Dutch captain Abel Tasman or the Portuguese Dias, the early seafarers at times made more significant inroads into discovering the mythical southern continent than they at first knew that they had. In the 1640s, Tasman unwittingly rounded Australia, leaving from the Dutch East Indies colony of Batavia and reaching first Van Diemen's Land, later Tasmania, and then New Zealand's South Island, where a violent skirmish with the local Māori took place. Yet, as Tasman had not touched down on the Australian mainland, the Dutch East India Company was denied the claim to the continent that they might have hoped to have made. Even earlier than Tasman, Dias battling through a storm, as we already saw, unknowingly rounded the southern tip of Africa. Written reports on his journey were lost during the Lisbon earthquake of 1755, but, according to legend, his crew suddenly became aware that they were sailing east and then north, so rightly concluding that they had found their way around the continent.[30]

As also in polar travel, there is something characteristically southern in these experiences of accidental rounding, or of missing a long-sought-after climax. The prize of Terra Australis Incognita, the great southern continent, it seemed, persistently lay always beyond the horizon, whether that was the horizon ahead or the one left behind. In the Dedication to the King prefacing his *Account of the Voyages Undertaken by the Order of His Present Majesty for Making Discoveries in the Southern Hemisphere* (1773), the editor John Hawkesworth noted how strange it was that 'a very considerable part of the globe on which we live should still have remained unknown'. Writing after Cook's first return in 1772, it was to him 'still . . . the subject of speculation, whether a great portion of the Southern Hemisphere is land or water', and therefore what the prospects were for 'the improvement of commerce and the increase and diffusion of knowledge'.[31]

The emphasis on the word *still* in Hawkesworth's prose is significant. After all, it was by then several hundred years since early European voyagers had started to bring back news of those remote southern lands. And yet, as for Dias and other navigators, the far reaches of the southern globe—the South Atlantic, the Southern Ocean, the South Pacific or South Seas—in many ways continued to epitomise trackless immensity. No matter how many new topographical features their logbooks recorded, there was the pervasive sense that the prevailing obscurity and danger of the south would continue to get the better of them. They would reach southern depths without fully understanding what they had achieved—as we see once again in Jules Verne. Camões insightfully records this precise awareness in *The Lusíads*, using the epic machinery he has to hand to review a journey already half-undertaken. For some, it seemed that the key geographic turning points of the far south could only be experienced retrospectively, in the preterit.

Severe peril began at the very point of exit from the wild South Atlantic into the seas beyond, at Cape Horn and the Cape of Storms, later called Good Hope, that marked the southern ends of the two great continents. In respect to the former, expeditions by Magellan, Schouten, Anson, Wallis, Cook, Parker King, Malaspina, and others had, across a period of two hundred years, tried to determine the safest route into the Pacific, whether through the Magellan Strait or around the Horn itself. Many had faced shipwreck. The South Seas that lay beyond appeared to be little more than a great 'watery desert'.[32] Farther south than the Straits lay the Beagle Channel, surveyed by that eponymous vessel on its first voyage between 1826 and 1830 under the melancholic Captain Pringle Stokes and, following his suicide, the often equally depressive Robert Fitzroy. Melville knew about rounding both Capes from experience and hearsay and saw the immensities of the south as '[shadowing] forth the heartless voids . . . of the universe'.[33]

For all the mysteries of the west or the east, voyagers moving in either one of those two cardinal directions found that celestial appearances and some seasonal features at least remained familiar, contained within the same hemisphere, bound by a shared geography and seasonal calendar. Cultures to the east had been known to Europe, at least to some extent, for centuries. Commodities from India and China had arrived along overland trading networks from the time of the Roman Empire. And for hundreds of years, established fishing routes had connected northern Europe to the waters off Newfoundland.[34] To the south, however, no historical links existed. Familiar geographies dwindled into unrecognizability. Even geophysical features like magnetic fields worked in unpredictably opposed ways.

The night skies by which early European mariners had to navigate, too, were frighteningly different. Even while noting the appearance of the (providentially Christian-looking) Southern Cross as the distinguishing marker of the 'new heavens' of the south, Vasco da Gama in *The Lusíads* speaks with his creator's voice when he reports on the disconcerting disappearance of the Bear constellations over the horizon. As the translator Landeg White writes in a note, the 'alien skies cost Camões more disquiet than alien lands or people', especially the skies closer to the South Pole with their constellations of 'Argo, Hydra, Ara, and the Hare'. Here, the Pleiades never dawn', and 'no one comprehends / If a continent begins or the sea ends'. Da Gama's crew are 'Often driven to despair beneath / Heavens with scarcely one familiar star / And hostile to the kind of men we are.'[35] In contrast with maritime navigation west, into regions that would eventually lead to the Indies, as Columbus had confidently believed, leaving the Pole Star behind meant entering radical strangeness. To sail far south was to confront mind-numbing distance, and, for some, like the Ancient Mariner or Captain Ahab, to lose one's sanity.

In their attempt to give far southern coastlines legibility, early fifteenth-century Portuguese charts proceeded by at first small and then incrementally bigger steps. By 1457, they had reached the uninhabited Cape Verde Islands at 16.5° North; in 1488 they got to the Cape of Good Hope at 33.9° South. Hugging the West African coastline, they used a combination of sailing instructions and the gridwork of meridians fundamental to all early European navigation, built on the gathered knowledge and portolan charts of even earlier Mediterranean navigators and pilots like the Greeks and Phoenicians. For this reason, early Dutch navigators like Tasman or Willem Corneliszoon Schouten (the first European to round Cape Horn) called rutters *leeskarten* or reading charts. Whole sections of Book X of *The Lusíads* are unmistakably portolan- or rutter-derived, reflecting the coastal nature of Portuguese exploration down 'toward the pole'.

By the late 1400s, Portuguese maps had started to include the recognisable shape of the African continent based on this accumulated navigational information. Ptolemy's speculations about the existence of a great southern continent were now gradually adapted. No longer did Africa extend into a vast southern continent by way of a strip of land closing off a lake-like Indian Ocean. Sailing down and around had revealed that the continent was lone standing. Portuguese maps of the later 1550s show the coast of South America as far south as Tierra del Fuego, more or less as we know it today, as well as the full coastline of Africa down to the Cape, though the bulge of West Africa is almost as large as the continent's southern extremity. A puny India lies to the east.[36] The Brabantian master cartographer Abraham Ortelius used a contemporary Mercator projection, as well as Ptolemaic theory, to produce in 1579 his *Theatrum Orbis Terrarum*, sometimes called the first modern atlas, which pictured the vast, white South ballooning up to what is now north-western Western Australia, and into the Pacific.[37]

The European states at the forefront of global expansion were, until the mid to late eighteenth century, often at war, which had the effect of differentially inhibiting their activities in some parts, while encouraging them in others. However, the 1763 peace following the Seven Years' War led by Britain and France produced a boom in northern European exploration into the South Seas, inaugurated by John Byron's voyage on the *Dolphin* in 1764. His speedy circumnavigation was immediately followed by the expedition of Samuel Wallis, also on the *Dolphin*, in 1766–7, the journey that brought the first Europeans to Tahiti. Hard on Wallis's heels was Louis-Antoine de Bougainville, a veteran of the Seven Years' War, who reached Tahiti in 1768 and recorded his travels in *Voyage autour du monde* (1771) to sensational effect. His evocative account of the South Seas as an arcadia modelled the ideas of, amongst others, the French *philosophes* about man in the state of nature.[38]

Geographic knowledge of the south, which had previously been so expensively accumulated, now expanded rapidly. British mapmakers processed findings from Royal Navy and merchant voyages as well as information stolen from or traded with other European powers and made this knowledge widely available in the form of commodities like pocket globes and sheet maps. As Katherine Parker writes, the 'nascent' British Empire in the South Pacific was not simply reflected in the workings of print culture, '[but] made within its pages'.[39]

With the gradual shift of Europe's balance of power northwards, the mapmakers, too, became concentrated further north in major trading cities like Amsterdam, London, and Hamburg. Dutch and English cartography became interleaved with earlier Portuguese and Spanish representations, though the maps' proportions remained recognisably indebted to the Iberian cartographers, with Africa still drawn as corpulent and India slender.[40] These already palimpsestic maps were then layered with information in other languages, including African names, that often remained constant across the maps. The 1642 Thornton map, for instance, has the regions of the African continent horizontally labelled, north to south, as Sahid, Barnagaso, Doara, Melinde (or Malindi), Quiloa, Suffalo, and Monomotapa.

This fact importantly reminds us that, from the Portuguese through to the British, maritime notes and charts often depended on the exchange of linguistic, geographical, botanical, and diplomatic knowledge with indigenous peoples, even though local names were later erased. D'Urville compiled a Yaghan word-list from his encounter with the Yamana of Tierra del Fuego. Tupaia, as we saw, conversed in depth with Cook and Joseph Banks as they charted, categorised, and named the antipodes. Samuel Parkinson, the Quaker artist who sailed with the *Endeavour*, collected and translated Tahitian words. Expeditions were increasingly organised as scientific projects that depended on consultations with knowledgeable individuals and local experts en route.

For the Portuguese, intelligence-gathering in an easterly direction was used as preparation for journeys south. As *The Lusíads* shows, da Gama took on board an Arabic speaker from the Middle East, possibly from one of the northeast African ports, operating in the knowledge that Africa was a continent. The assumption was that his expertise might prove useful once settlements on the farther east African coast had been reached. Accordingly, Camões represents the questing da Gama as repeatedly asking the way, disappointed when local people around St Helena Bay, close to present-day Cape Town, cannot understand the Arabic interpreter. They are consequently unable to explain the way to India: 'We were not likely to obtain from them / Any news of the India we desired / Except that it was many moons away' (*L* 5.34). Farther north along the East African littoral, however, Arabic *was* spoken, gunpowder known, and fireworks used. Camões's travellers are back within the intensively traversed, 'historied' spaces of the Indian Ocean.[41]

Reading and Writing Distance

Anne Thell describes the eighteenth-century travelogue as 'an epistemological tool' that afforded a similar function to scientific writing. It created a cognitive space lying beyond or 'outside the habitual', so allowing navigators, travellers, and their readers to speculate about 'what cannot be known for certain'.[42] As we also find with later travellers into the interiors of the western and southern continents, navigators making their first forays into southern seas shaped the distance in the imagination by using preexisting texts as their apparatus. Literary writers about the south, in effect, mimicked these procedures, immersing the reader in the experience of trying to make sense of weltering farness by deploying familiar perceptual frames.

The Lusíads is especially illuminating for how it stimulates in the reader such processes of surrogate navigation, but it is not unique in forging these syntheses. Later writers like Coleridge also matched epistemology to medium, treating the far reaches of the ocean, in Philip Steinberg's words, 'not just as an *experienced* space but as a dynamic field that—through its movement, through our encounters with its movement, and through our efforts to interpret its movement—produces difference even as it unifies'. The watery south emerges as a cognitive space in Coleridge's poetry not because it '*facilitates* movement—the space across which things move—but because it is a space that is *constituted by* and *constitutive of* movement'.[43] As the Polynesians, too, might have said.

In a word, sea-facing and ocean-borne writings—ship's logs, rutters, and, later, memoirs and travelogues—themselves offered crucial technologies for plotting routes towards the unknown horizon.[44] This recourse by mariners to precursor linguistic forms and texts, presents the most persuasive illustration we have of how the diachronic activities of navigation and mapping resembled reading. Like navigation, reading involves a continual making of inferences in the round, and, hence, requires a repeated give-and-take between retrospection and projection. If we objectively imagine ourselves reading, what we observe is a process of constantly tuning and retuning into the meanings of the words on the page as they unfold in relation to each other and, at the same time, in relation to the 'horizon of expectations' that the text lays down.[45]

Relatedly, the navigator moving into unmapped or only partly charted waters balanced the records they carried with them and the measurements they were able to make and then weighed these in relation to the always fluid surrounding context. Tacking between these resources, they plotted their course towards the horizon. As with the reader, so the navigator—their hypotheses as to what lay before them repeatedly modified and adjusted in relation to other stimuli as these flowed in.

Reception theory suggests that reading (or, here, navigating) involves the moment-by-moment processing of new elements (references, implications, assumptions, observations). The reader (or navigator) picks those inferences most relevant to comprehension and, at the same time, steadily discards others.[46] In this way, they bring to mind till-now-unimagined worlds. In essence, then, early European navigation into southern latitudes involved a cognitive balancing act, a seesawing between prolepsis and analepsis, projecting what was to come by relying on past scripts, charting a path forward even while harking back to serially accumulated knowledge. Navigational writing interrelated the two cognitive processes, reading the land or seascape ahead by drawing upon precedence and, at the same time, writing up the journey as a process of reading onward.

As with the mapping of the surmised Terra Australis itself, the southern hemisphere became in the European imagination 'an ancient text' that was however always 'under revision'.[47] Concepts of the strange and the familiar, or of 'full' and 'empty' space, reciprocally impacted one another. These projections perhaps once again resemble modes of Pacific navigation, even though involving the use of very different instruments and processes. Both European and Polynesian navigators used projections in space-time (memorised star charts, longitudinal logs) to give shape to the distance into which they would sail, all the while drawing upon known linguistic and narrative structures. In both contexts, we find a similar syncopation of observation with measurement, a related interleaving of experience, memory, and inference.

The European travelogue, in this way, became itself a catalyst for knowledge-making. Journeys layered up an 'environmental inventory' that, the traveller William Burchell observed about his southern African travels, enabled 'the reader and the author to travel, as it were, the journey over again, and view, in their proper light, the facts in connection, and the impressions made by each event in succession'.[48] And, as journeys were converted into writing, the writing 'tracked' further travel, in turn guiding and feeding into other memoirs and narratives, as Camões's extravagantly referential *Lusíads* demonstrates. The epic immerses the reader in Portuguese navigators' efforts to plot the Africa-to-India route, showing us what the captain sees from the deck of the moving ship.[49]

For the anthropologist Eduardo Kohn, living creatures interact through producing representations. While humans are not alone in responding to their environment with signs, human worlds are all typically semiotic creations. Our thought is continually involved in reaching forwards by testing and retesting existing habits of perception in relation to the surrounding environment. This notion supports the case for southern imagining as a mode at once of spatial orientation and of inference-making and adjustment in relation to the south's particular environmental conditions: 'It is only when the world's habits clash with our expectations that the world in its otherness, and its existent actuality as something other than what we currently are, is revealed'.[50]

To early northern navigators, the far south would have thrown up particularly severe challenges to established procedures of inference gathering. As Kohn further writes, new habits of thought require us to 'remake ourselves, however momentarily, anew, as one with the world around us'. Southern worlds demanded, in effect, a radical modification and transformation of thought-worlds and, indeed, of the self. Camões models such processes when evoking the superhuman climatic forces of the Cape of Storms. First, he shows us the chaos-inducing god Bacchus repeatedly frustrating da Gama's progress. But then he goes a step further, positing the existence of an entirely new god of the south, Adamastor. In effect, he disrupts and extends the classical pantheon itself, as if to suggest that the southern regions of the world require a wholly new mode of understanding—and the rule of a different sort of deity entirely.[51]

The Epic as Portolan: Luís de Camões, *The Lusíads* (1572)

In so far as the Portuguese were the first navigators from Europe to take the search for the wealth of the Orient into the south-east Atlantic, the poet and colonial administrator Luís de Camões was probably the first historiographer of the enterprise—and possibly its most eloquent proselytiser. He was also, as far as we know, the first European artist to cross into far southern waters, the first to see southern Africa and India, in 1553, and, in all probability, the first to write poetry about the experience. His great *Os Lusíadas*, translated into

English as *The Lusíads*, represents a highpoint of Portuguese portolan or roteiro-based nautical writing.[52] Within its scope, Camões developed some of the characteristic narrative procedures that became foundational for later northern writing on the south.[53] More so perhaps than any other literary work discussed in *Southern Imagining*, the poem itself brilliantly presents as a navigational device like a chart or an astrolabe, not only at its close with the world-map tableau it unfolds, but also at many points across its length. Even as it traces a parabolic pathway from the Atlantic into the Indian Ocean, it constantly pivots back to review the way it has come.

The Lusíads' account of the navigator Vasco da Gama's circum-continental journey around Africa to India in 1497–99 gave authoritative embodiment to Portugal's project of maritime expansion, as the *Araucana* did to Spain's continental adventures in South America. Camões based the narrative on his own observations of the exact same journey to India, undertaken fifty years after da Gama. At the time he was fleeing charges arising from a duel that had already landed him in prison. *The Lusíads*, therefore, takes the reader along two interwoven space-timelines, which together, rutter-like and in parallel, trace the African coastline at two distinct points in a rapidly changing history. Camões narrates his own journey on the by-now-established route into the Indian Ocean, even as he at the same time follows the imagined path of his hero da Gama's inaugural voyage.[54] As for de Ercilla in his epic, the national-cum-imperial project underpins the personal history, and the individual story recharges the national myth: 'My own tale in its naked purity / Outdoes all boasting and hyperbole' (*L* 5.89). Within the poem, the histories of the two voyages can be seen as counterpoised, each, as it were, holding the other in balance.[55]

The Lusíads is composed of ten cantos in rhymed ottava rima, most of roughly one hundred stanzas in length. The two longest cantos, three and ten, standing at 143 and 156 stanzas, respectively, undertake the task of recounting Portugal's past and ongoing national story. Canto 3 presents the country's history leading up to the present day—a narrative that, in the story-world of the epic, da Gama tells his East African host, the Sultan of Malindi. In canto 10, the reader encounters a culminating vision of Portugal's imperial future that the goddess Tethys gives da Gama on the return voyage to Lisbon as a reward for successfully reaching the east (*L*10.10). She shows the navigator a crystalline model of the earth suspended in the air, which lays out the full geographic reach of Portuguese expansion and the nation's future deeds of conquest along all the coasts where 'the Indian Ocean sighs'. At this climax of the poem, the voyage transforms into a *máquina do mundo*, a cartographic world tableau that appears to transcend human time.

Across the preceding nine cantos, by contrast, the narrative is forward-moving and dynamic. The trajectory of da Gama's journey is driven by his sense of mission, guided by the gods, interspersed with dramatic, high-action episodes wherever on the coastline he touches down. In key scenes, repeating verbs of movement create a strong sense of this iterative progression along Africa's eastern and western littorals (the order is important): for example, from the account of approaching the Cape of Good Hope in the opening four stanzas of canto 5, 'we passed . . . we crossed . . . we skirted . . . we skirted'. As the Camões critic Josiah Blackmore notes, *how* the history is told plainly recalls 'the oceanic origins of [European] texts on Africa'. The cantos parse the progress of da Gama's ship towards India, the loops and breaks in the voyage reproducing 'the retrospective pauses of maritime journeying'.[56]

The navigational aspect of *The Lusíads* is most clearly demonstrated in the extraordinary tale-within-a-tale episode, a classic *in medias res*, when da Gama narrates his story-so-far to the sultan, laying it out in the characteristic manner of a portolan. First plotting a rutter-type path past what is now the coast of Mozambique, da Gama's storyline then switches back to the beginning of the journey from Portugal, so in effect looping twice more around the continent, back and then again forwards. The oscillating motions outlined earlier, the narrative tilting towards the wished-for Indian Ocean horizon at the same time as it harks back to the Portuguese historical past, are almost palpable. Canto 1 begins with Vasco da Gama's progress: 'In frail timbers on treacherous seas, / By routes never charted, and only / Emboldened by opposing winds' (*L* 1.27). And canto 10's grand sweep through the future, recounting Portugal's colonial history subsequent to his journey, takes a similar shape. In both episodes, Camões appears to be drawing from his own memories of working with *roteiros* while making his way along the same coast.

As is standard for epic, *The Lusíads* celebrates imperial valour in a global sphere while at the same time concerning itself with national consolidation at home. The coming-into-being of the nation—'the famous Portuguese / To whom both Mars and Neptune bowed' (*L* 1.3)—is intimately bound up with the triumphal rise from the thirteenth century of its maritime dominance. The poem insists upon Portuguese control east of the Tordesillas line, a region embracing both 'India's sons and daughters / . . . who yet drink the Ganges' sacred waters', and Brazil in the west where the sun 'casts his last ray' (*L* 1.8).[57] A crusading drive to widen the Christian world southwards and eastwards fuels the expansionist project, most obviously in the form of da Gama's journeys along the East African coastline with its many sultanates.[58] The poem's anti-Islamic sentiment is profound and, to a modern reader, disturbing, captured in scenes of unrestrained pillage and slaughter wherever the Portuguese meet with resistance—a brutality that is consistently represented as heroism. As befits his task as a national poet, Camões uses the vernacular, Portuguese, while situating his epic within a literary genealogy that extends back to classical Rome and, in particular, to Virgil's *Aeneid*, the mythic account of Aeneas's journey that led to the founding of Rome. 'Arms are my theme', the first line of the poem, references the Roman epic, the internal retrospectives resemble Aeneas's account of the Trojan War, and the closing vision of the glorious future, too, is modelled on Virgil (*L* 1.1. line 1).

There are few examples of a European poet more intimately linked with the enterprise of early modern national identity-making than Camões, as Richard Helgerson observes. The poet's own experiences now enlarge and now telescope Portugal's maritime history, to the degree that the poetry at certain points appears to plot causal connections between the two, as if the epic story required the expansion of the empire, and vice versa.[59] Yet for the historical poet himself, the task was racked with contradiction. Camões's anxiety comes through not only in the hostility directed at Muslims but also in the vehement appeals at intervals across the poem to the Portuguese crown for renewed imperial valour. This was not without reason. By the time Camões was writing his epic, the overextended Portuguese empire in the east was in decline.[60] Therefore, even as he issues his repeated calls for the imperial mission to be recharged, *The Lusíads* casts da Gama's great journey in a nostalgic light, etched in shadows of imminent diminishment and the loss of power to Spain.

One of the poem's most distinctive classical devices is the elaborate machinery through which the gods in Camões's poem manipulate Portugal's maritime affairs like puppet masters. Throughout, deities like Venus and Bacchus (associated with India) guide, monitor, and, in some cases, upset (while still monitoring) da Gama's journey. But the captain compares his tale to the ancients' stories to his own particular advantage. While their endeavours amount to no more than 'counterfeit exploits' (*L* 1.11), his, he claims, counts as true history—a history of real-life heroes. The sea of their journeys, the Mediterranean, now appears small and familiar compared to the great oceans that the Portuguese have crossed and charted. Indeed, Camões claims, da Gama's rounding of the Cape is tantamount to Daedalus and Icarus actually learning to fly.

Yet, even as Camões recycles well-known classical myths, he also tacitly acknowledges that the business of comprehending southern worlds requires a different approach, one that expands the Roman pantheon and requires the foundation of a new one. In canto 5, he rises to the challenge in earnest. As da Gama approaches the Cape of Storms, a fearsome shape emerges before the Portuguese ships. The presence introduces himself as Adamastor, a melancholic, rock-imprisoned Titan who presides over the southern Indian Ocean: 'an immense shape / . . . Grotesque and of enormous stature, / With heavy jowls, and an unkempt beard' (*L* 5.35–7). Adamastor tells the crew that following the Titans' wars with Jupiter and his own obsession with the sea nymph Tethys, he was condemned to petrification in these far-distant seas: 'My bones compressed to rock; / . . . The gods moulded my great bulk / Into this remote promontory' (*L* 5.59). The promontory is possibly not only Table Mountain but the entire ridged Cape Peninsula, of which the mountain forms a part. While Camões's model for Adamastor was the cyclops Polyphemus, the son of Poseidon in Homer's *Odyssey*, the craggy giant is also in many ways an original creation—a great force watching over the far-distant and till-recently-uncharted 'Cape of Storms': 'I am . . . the Cape of Storms, / Which neither Ptolemy, Pompey, Strabo, / Pliny, nor any authors knew of'.[61]

For Blackmore, Camões's Adamastor is the expression in godlike form of the peril of the outer edge, an 'affective correlate of the nautical limit or threshold'.[62] Southern African writers and critics have gone further, taking him to be a physical manifestation of Africa's great size—and southern African resistance to incursion, in particular.[63] 'Booming from the ocean's depths', he utters depressed warnings about Portugal's territorial ambitions and condemns their 'dreadful' brutality (*L* 5.40). His dark prophecies are later underwritten by Camões's own pessimistic anticipation of Portugal's retreat. Inhospitable, mighty, threatening, fearsome, the god embodies in every aspect the forbidding far south: 'Here Africa ends. Here its coast / Concludes in this, my vast inviolate / Plateau, extending southwards to the Pole' (*L* 5.50, 27).[64]

Not only the giant's appearance but also its timing within the poem is significant. The 'vast, secret promontory' that the Titan inhabits looms into view in the very middle of canto 5, which is more or less the centrepoint of the poem. It is five months since da Gama's ships began their voyage and five days after their first southern African landfall. They have just reached and rounded the continent's southernmost point (*L* 5.24, 37, 50).[65] Combining these elements, Camões thus has Adamastor inaugurate Portugal's arrival in the far south, and the turning point of the journey around Africa's southernmost tip.

Sailing on into the Indian Ocean, '[c]utting seas no other nation had braved', the Portuguese have at this juncture 'split / Neptune's salty domain in two', passing from the previously unknown, assumed-to-be savage African west coast, or western Ethiopia, as antiquity had it, into the eastern, the unknown (*L* 5.37; 2.2).[66] Further reinforcing the interlocking patterns of five, Adamastor's gravelly warning to da Gama, 'compelled and not by choice' (*L* 5.49), that the Portuguese will be met with 'implacable hostility' in his waters, folds around stanza 50 (beginning at 41 and ending at 59). For the wrong of betraying his hideout to the world, he intones, they will meet with his retribution forever after. As the Ancient Mariner will discover some two hundred years later, nature responds to the rude disruption of its southern seclusion with uncompromising rejection:

> Because you have desecrated nature's
> Secrets and the mysteries of the deep,
> Where no human, however noble
> Or immortal his worth, should trespass,
> Hear from me now what retribution
> Fate prescribes for your insolence,
> Whether ocean-borne, or along the shores
> You will subjugate with your dreadful wars;
> No matter how many vessels attempt
>
> The audacious passage you are plotting,
> My cape will be implacably hostile
> With gales beyond any you have encountered;
> On the next fleet which broaches
> These turbulent waters, I shall impose
> Such retribution and exact such debts
> The destruction will be far worse than my threats. (*L* 5.41–42)[67]

Adamastor's Southern Vertex, Camões's Parabola

Brooding eternally over Africa's stormy southern cape, the god Adamastor manifests Camões's recognition, albeit fitful and inconsistent, that the south's seas and skies required a different form of comprehension, at a different scale of embodiment. This understanding is further complicated and reinforced with the use of a contiguous structural feature—the repeating parabolic turn around which the poem pivots.

In essence, the story that *The Lusíads* tells outlines a parabola that arches around the Cape, with its vertex in the south. By beginning off the coast of Mozambique, some distance beyond this turn, the epic requires that the narrative it traces must loop back in space and time, around the continent, for the early history of the Portuguese nation and of da Gama's journey so far to be filled in. For the reader, this narrative switchback creates an at-once-dynamic and reiterative experience—a device that has the further interesting effect of placing Adamastor at the heart of the poem or, structurally, at the vertex or lowest point of the parabola. In this way, the *how* of the journey narrative becomes a self-reflexive evocation of the *what*, the southern doubling. The loop back and then again forwards around a continent that has already been rounded, recreates the first Portuguese journey through uncharted seas, where 'no human . . . should trespass', *and yet*, at the same time, necessarily recounts the journey as if it had already been accomplished (*L* 5.42). Voyages into the far south seem to be cognitively challenging to the point that they need to be gone over (and over again) in imaginative retrospect.

It is worth pausing a little longer on this interesting manoeuvre. As we saw, the narrated time of *The Lusíads* begins in the middle of da Gama's journey, immediately following the poet's opening address to the Portuguese boy-king, Sebastiao, and *after* the first rounding of the African continent: 'They were midway on the wide ocean / Cleaving the ever-restless waves' (*L* 1.19). Though we do not yet know it, da Gama's ships have *already* passed 'Ancient Africa's southern boundary' into Adamastor's realm, claiming it for their own, and are making their way north up the Madagascar channel: 'There where the south meets the Orient', beyond the former's hazardous 'skies and latitudes' (*L* 1.29, 42). The *in medias res* tellingly situates da Gama the navigator in as-yet-unnavigated waters, or at least, waters till then unnavigated by the Portuguese—though by the time of Camões's narration, they would have come to know this littoral fairly well.

Da Gama then sails into a prosperous harbour on Mozambique Island, the 'safest' in the area, where the Swahili-speaking islanders understand Arabic. These people also have knowledge of 'the Indus and its parched banks', to the 'Lusitanians' relief, as the Africans they have met so far have not been able to enlighten them as to where India lies (*L* 1.55). Da Gama is granted a pilot to 'guide' the ships' course across to Asia (*L* 1.70), but his colonising ambitions arouse the suspicions of the sheikh. After a skirmish, the Portuguese hastily depart, the monsoon winds assisting their exit. The Mozambiquan pilot then takes them past Kilwa, a Swahili city-state, to the harbour of Mombasa, in what is now Kenya, where the local sultan lies in wait to attack them. The trouble-maker god Bacchus has ensured that news of their ferocious behaviour has preceded them up the coast (*L* 2.19). But Venus then moves against Bacchus and summons 'all the forces of the blue ocean' to divert the ships from the Mombasa estuary and guide them to a hospitable reception in Malindi, further north. The 'munificent' sultan, a direct contrast to Mombasa's ruler, is wonder-struck at a voyage 'from so far to India' (*L* 2.55, 101).

In Malindi, the closest East African port to the equator, 'Near to the point where the burning sun / Makes night and day equal', da Gama once again finds himself at the edge of the southern hemisphere, but this time about to reenter that familiar region where 'the Great Pole herds the stars' (*L* 2.63, 105). In response to the sultan's request to 'tell us . . . of your land,/ Clime, and where in the world you dwell', he begins to narrate the history of Portugal from the time of the first king, Afonso I, in the twelfth century (*L* 2.109; 3.30–42; 5.90). This long 'account/ Of exalted and heroic deeds' takes up all of cantos 3 and 4, and canto 5 goes on to tell the story of da Gama's own journey. Thereafter, in canto 6, the real time of the epic story resumes, the ships '[s]et sail once more for the lands of dawn', till at last they see India's 'opulent and spacious land' rise before them (*L* 6.5, 93; 2.80).[68]

Drawing these narrative threads together, in the first Africa-centred half of *The Lusíads*, which is the most salient to my reading, Camões bends da Gama's first chronological tale of 1498 back upon itself as if it were itself a physical rutter. With this temporal switchback, he underlines our sense of the captain's achievement in having overleapt the perils with which his journey so far has confronted him. By the middle of canto 5, the Portuguese are sailing further northeast on a voyage whose arc readers are already acquainted with. Da Gama's ships leave behind lands and islands 'christened' anew, but where the languages were unfamiliar, and no one had heard of India (*L* 5.34, 64, 69, 77). Completing the parabolic path, they sail back into the Arabic-speaking reaches of the Indian Ocean, about which early travellers east had already gathered intelligence.

From the reader's perspective, therefore, by the time we reach the end of da Gama's spoken narrative, towards the middle point of the epic, the first canto's recounting of his progress up the Mozambique coast seems very far away. We are in the future of that now quite distant past, even though in chronological time, it took place but a few months ago. And that near-past was, in turn, the future of the centuries-long history of imperial Portugal that has just been narrated. Da Gama's story moves forwards to join up with the earlier narrative on which canto 1 had already embarked. In short, procedurally, when in canto 5 we again approach and begin to round the continent, we are following a route that the poem's action has already traced. Da Gama could not have attained 'seas beyond all our experience' in the Mozambique Channel had he not already sailed around the continent: 'By now we had made a complete circuit / Of black Africa's coast, pointing / Our prows towards the equator, / Leaving the Antarctic in our wake' (*L* 5.65 and 70).

The Lusíads, in effect, doubles the African continent twice. The epic marks the political and imaginative significance of first Dias and then da Gama's achievement by repeating it—by rounding and re-rounding the Cape, and charting and re-charting the journey: 'We passed Santa Cruz where Dias / Having rounded the Cape of Storms, / And planted a memorial column, / Not knowing of his triumph, turned for home' (*L* 65). Camões must seemingly relive the experience to believe it fully, even while at the same time gloating at his nation's navigational prowess. Canto 10, concluding, then retraces the explorers' journeys all over again, even while the poem elsewhere also executes similar, smaller chronological loops forwards and back. For instance, we are told that the Sultan of Malindi has already received reports of the Portuguese wars, which he then hears about from da Gama in cantos 3 and 4, having perhaps tapped into news passed by word of mouth along the East African littoral. And in canto 3, Jupiter, in conversation with Venus, looks ahead to Portuguese exploits in India that will be narrated in full in canto 10, thanks to Camões's privileged 'foresight' as a later traveller-narrator. In the celestial sphere of the gods, as in Virgil, future and past are held in an eternal present moment, allowing them to prophecy in these ways. Yet the alternating analepsis and prolepsis also allow Camões to cast the Portuguese as the driving force of history, the lords of as-yet-uncharted and yet already navigated space and time.

The Lusíads conveys what it was for the Portuguese, as the first Europeans in the eastern South Atlantic, to move into unknown seas, da Gama following and then extending a route that Bartolomeu Dias had begun to map, to 'discover new seaways' and meet 'the remotest people' (*L* 8, 72). Yet, inventive and courageous though those exploits were, the figures through which Camões narrates that rounding are, in poetic terms, equally as innovative. Cunningly adapting Virgil, the Portuguese poet represents his nation's history with a cartographic eye that magnifies its imperial achievements and looks back at the journey looping the African continent as an already accomplished feat. In this rendition, da Gama, soon to be viceroy in India, has always already rounded the Cape, his journey anticipating and complementing Magellan's navigation westwards through the Straits named for him, doubling South America, some twenty years later. Where da Gama had traced the easterly exit from the South Atlantic, the Portuguese-born explorer who sailed for Spain would trace the westerly.

If the world map with which most western-educated people are familiar widened out from Europe with the first navigations beyond the equator, Camões is unambiguously a poet of that ambitious northern world, and the geography of *The Lusíads* duly expands southwards from the Iberian Peninsula, following da Gama's journey. Yet, at the same time, Camões's linked creation of Adamastor, the southern deity, and of the Portuguese captain's parabolic route through the god's oceanic realm, represents a significant cartographic intervention—one that is symbolically invested in its southern points of reference. Working against his own northern bias (as reflected in his aversion to the southern constellations), Camões tacitly acknowledges that the south may need a different conceptual approach, a complicated switchback and leap forwards that the reader is invited several times to bring to mind. Yet, even so, the region's depth and strangeness may continue to elude our comprehension. In this 'deep, inhospitable' universe, '[e]xposed to gales and tempestuous seas', different laws of movement, spin, and direction apply; a different kind of worlding matters. Here, Adamastor's mysteries alone hold sway—though Camões makes no allowance that those who best understand this world may be African people themselves (*L* 6.97).

The Lusíads holds a headnote place in *Southern Imagining* for its dramatisation of processes of reading and rereading as one of the key means through which the north attempted and often failed to conceive the far southern hemisphere. Camões's epic captures how the south was worlded in and through writing, using techniques such as curvilinear prediction, narrative retrospection, and authoritative citation. Yet the poem also demonstrates that, no matter how sophisticated the literary or cartographical manoeuvres, wherever a northern orientation is taken as the default, the effect each time is to set the actual south—southern geographies and cultures—at a remove. As Lynn Festa suggests, such textual conventions and figures made 'relations with distant others thinkable', yet also maintained 'categorical distinctions'.[69]

Camões was not himself unaware of this paradox—and it impacts some of the writers grouped together in the next chapter also. From this perhaps comes their drive to re-narrate and repeat—to re-round the continent in Camões, or to retell the tale, in Coleridge, or relentlessly to continue the pursuit, whether of the whale, or the monster, or of knowledge, in the other writers. The truth of the south, its strangeness and inhospitality, glimmers through creations such as Adamastor, yet it also recedes behind them. In chapter 4, more than two centuries after Camões, the writers in question continue to grapple with the essential inscrutability of the far south. Their confusion comes through in perverse and frustrated acts, like the Mariner's wanton killing of the albatross, Captain Ahab's self-destructive obsession with Moby Dick, and even Darwin's disturbed, inchoate sense of the earth's longevity. Connecting these writings is an obliqueness that expresses as persistence—a determination to try to make sense, yet a repeated frustration at the continuing perplexity. Again and again, we will be reminded of da Gama's boastful yet uneasy attempts to repeat and redescribe his journey around and through Adamastor's hostile haunts.

4

Writing Southern Seas

COLERIDGE, DARWIN, MELVILLE, SHELLEY

MONDAY 4th [January 1773]. *Winds NE to NNW. Course N 82° E. Dist. Sailed* 112 *Miles. Lat. in South* 58°55′. *Long. in East of Greenwich per Reck.g* 14°43′. *Long. Cape G. Hope* 3°40′. First and middle parts strong gales attended with a thick Fogg Sleet and Snow, all the Rigging covered with Ice and the air excessive cold. . . .

Tuesday 5th. . . . *Latitude in South* 59°51′ . . . Strong gales and Foggy with sleet and snow all the pm.

. . .

Tuesday 12th. . . . Lat in South 64°12′. . . .

Mr Forster shott an Albatross whose plumage was of a Dark grey Colour, its head, uper sides of the Wings rather inkling to black with white Eye brows, we first saw of these Birds about the time of our first falling in with these Ice Islands and they have accompanied us ever sence.

—JAMES COOK, *THE JOURNALS* (*THE SECOND VOYAGE*) (1772–5)

And now there came both mist and snow,
And it grew wondrous cold:
And ice, mast-high, came floating by,
As green as emerald.

And through the drifts the snowy clifts
Did send a dismal sheen:
Nor shapes of men nor beasts we ken—
The ice was all between.

—SAMUEL TAYLOR COLERIDGE, *THE RIME OF THE ANCIENT MARINER*, PART I, LL. 45–59 (1834)

Man has lost that sense of the full awfulness of the sea which aboriginally belongs to it.

—HERMAN MELVILLE, *MOBY-DICK* (1851)

Turning: Through the Southern Depths

My opening comes from Samuel Taylor Coleridge's Romantic ballad-epic *The Rime of the Ancient Mariner* (1798, 1834) that recounts 'how a Ship having passed the Line was driven by Storms to the cold Country towards the South Pole; and how from thence she made her course'.[1] The eponymous Ancient Mariner's story follows a parabolic path arching high into treacherous southern waters, not unlike Camões's, or, some decades later, in a fictional universe, Melville's Captain Ahab. After the killing of the albatross, in the very depths of the south, Coleridge's narrative begins to take an ascending route back towards the equator, 'the tropical Latitude of the Great Pacific Ocean'. Similar to the *Lusíads*, the vertex of the Mariner's journey is reached at a middle point of the poem, in this case, stanzas 7–12 of Part 1. The path drawn around the stormy southern cape, Cape Horn, mirrors the more abstract parabola of the Mariner's leave-taking and homecoming, and conditions the reader to a counterclockwise looping route around the hemisphere.

As we also found in the *Lusíads*, the *Rime* engages the reader in a stage-by-stage deictic process of making sense of the Mariner's journey. Even as the old seaman tells the Wedding Guest, the reader's surrogate, about his painful journey into icy southern seas, and then, eventually, around the world, he invites us to make out the route as if we were standing alongside him. Parts I and II explicitly plot the direction and sweeping spin of the journey, as captured in the changed positions of 'left' and 'right' in the unrhymed *a* and *c* lines. In Part I, stanza 7, once they have left port:

The Sun came up upon the left,
Out of the sea came he!
And he shone bright, and on the right
Went down into the sea. (ll. 25–9)

And then, in Part II, stanza 1, after the Mariner has shot the albatross and rounded the Horn:

The Sun now rose upon the right:
Out of the sea came he,
Still hid in mist, and on the left
Went down into the sea. (ll. 81–5)

Coleridge builds into the rhyme scheme the Mariner's 'mighty loop' around the Horn, 'its apex toward the pole'.[2] We remember the 'vast sweeping curve, cutting the Equator' that Camões traced and retraced in his epic, though moving in the opposite direction.

In the course of Part I, the Mariner's location is further embedded with the triple repetition of the word 'south', occurring twice in only two stanzas just before the southern bird, the 'albatross', appears (Part II, stanzas 11, 12, and 18). The Mariner's ship has now doubled the 'grim promontory' of Cape Horn, a route traced since the 1600s by many European ships.[3] But the rounding of the Horn also represents a break in the action, coinciding with the thundering ice-split that marks the albatross's coming. The achievement of the vertex—this 'turning-post' of the 'huge cosmic race course under the wheeling stars'—brings a change in mood and tenor, after which a series of events begins to work in expiation of the Mariner's crime. The transformational route thus written into the poem will, in subsequent decades, set a compelling precedent for the other writing about far south journeying that this chapter explores, laying down, in effect, a disposition towards thinking south.

Shaping Seascapes

Though 'Writing Southern Seas' pushes the narrative of European seafaring some two hundred years on from Camões, many of the themes we saw emerge in chapter 2 remain in play, at times in heightened form. Once again, we find navigators, poets, and storytellers drawing from the perceptual languages of the north—of distance, limit and sublimity—to write about the experience of moving into the south. However, they also betray a growing awareness that their vocabularies are inadequate and require adaptation for southern conditions. (In the settler writing explored in chapter 6, this awareness will become especially acute.)

Southern journeying is catalytic for each one of the voyagers in question—whether historical (Darwin) or fictitious (the Mariner and Captain Ahab). In each case, it brings reversal and metamorphosis—physical, imaginative, conceptual—which might explain the prevalence of the turning parabolic pathway in all of the texts. Writing itself in all cases performs an at-once instructive and interpretative function, steering the reader about how to approach extremity, first in real life and then in retrospect. Writing up his voyage on the *Beagle*, Darwin perhaps most clearly recognises that southern distances are transformative not merely because of their remoteness but because they *nonetheless* demonstrate interconnection. Collecting and studying specimens in and around the southern tip of South America, and then reviewing his experiences in his journal, he gradually arrives at the core principle of evolution, the idea that 'nothing exists in or for itself, but only in relation to other organisms'.[4]

With its great sweeping curve, Coleridge's *Rime* lays down the blueprint for this phase of southern imagining, which is why I open with it and later swing back to it. The poem is shaped by its creator's extensive reading in maritime literature—Cook, primarily, but also the journals and histories of Magellan, Drake, Le Maire, Roggeveen, Purchas, and many others—and it in turn informs the writing about journeying into the other hemisphere that follows. This is to the point that the *Rime* can be seen as a conduit transferring some key tropes of southern imagining to a new generation, here comprising Charles Darwin and Herman Melville, but also Mary Shelley's meditation in *Frankenstein* (1818) on the perils of trespassing into the polar ice, which appears in the closing section of the chapter.

All the writers are keenly aware that the movement into the far south is not only dangerous but also self-undermining. In Melville, 'the scenery of the Antarctic seas' plunges the reader into an experience of limitless confusion: 'a boundless churchyard . . . with its lean ice monuments and splintered crosses'.[5] Other voyagers entertain comparable apprehensions of derangement and mortal threat. Darwin describes the Magdalen Channel in the Straits of Magellan as a 'gloomy passage' that appears to 'lead to another and worse world'.[6] Travellers like the Mariner and Ahab are haunted by phantoms associated with past wrongs, or a sense of endeavours left unfinished. They approach the far south with curiosity and amazement, yet their experience of its immensity often unmakes them.

Within the chronological frame of the first half of nineteenth century, the chapter responds to three major works in English that take austral journeys and the far south as a subject or theme: Coleridge's *Rime*, Darwin's *The Voyage of the* Beagle (1839), and the American Herman Melville's *Moby-Dick* (1857).[7] More or less following the Mariner's parabolic route, Darwin's travelogue reflects the incremental process by which he moved towards his theory of evolution, using the distances of the south as if as graph paper on which to imagine, till then, unimaginably large-scale change. Like James Cook, another major inspiration, Darwin took the long, layered littorals, multiple bays and inlets, and vast watery spaces of this region of the far south as a canvas across which to theorise, as did Cook about the great southern continent that he had been tasked to locate.

Appearing in 1851, some fifty years after the first publication of the *Rime*, on the opposite side of the northern Atlantic, Melville's great novel of southern circumnavigation takes noticeable pains to acknowledge Coleridge's poem as a precursor. *Moby-Dick* also develops an extended reflection on whaling—the industry that, along with sealing, initiated the process of worlding the far south, opening it up to northern modernity. Yet, even as he tells his story, the narrator Ishmael offers meditations on oceanic vastness that confirm the Mariner's principle of human and creaturely interdependence—and comprehends that vastness by drawing a great parabola through it. The *Pequod*'s looping journey braids together, side by side, the far reaches of the world's great oceans. As in Coleridge's poem, fellowship on the icy wastes of the Southern Ocean is cast both as absolutely necessary and yet as constantly imperilled.

Offsetting these single-minded, heroic pathways is Shelley's *Frankenstein*, whose critique of imaginative excess and irresponsibility furnishes a short coda. This novel's sightlines are directed north, to the Arctic, and upwards, into the Alps, but its nightmarish account of overreaching science set against a polar backdrop is unmistakably informed by Coleridge's *Rime*. In this way, it also neatly complements Darwin's travelogue and Melville's novel, both of which it predates. Yet not Shelley alone, but all of the authors gathered together here are, in their different ways, outliers. Coleridge, like Shelley, did not himself cross the equator into the southern hemisphere, other than in the imagination. Melville wrote from the vantage point of the United States, and *Moby-Dick* is often read as a parable of white American nation formation.[8] *The Voyage of the* Beagle comprises Darwin's field notes of a five-year research trip around the world. Taken together, however, the journeys into the south that the texts describe all bring their protagonists to the point of beginning to view the north from the outside, athwart.

Each one of the books deserves a far lengthier treatment. However, my inductive focus on predominant models and influences has meant that there is not the scope to discuss them in detail. Throughout, my concern is to compare and contrast how these texts operate as heuristic tools; how they calibrate, test, and recalibrate previous readings of the south, always still using the parabola as an interpretative line. The compression that such focussed comparative discussion demands has the compensatory advantage of throwing up patterns in common, even in writings so generically far apart. To illustrate, though Darwin's *Voyage* is a naturalist travelogue, his reflections show fascinating parallels with the more obviously literary works, especially his attempts to think through and with southern space. His reflections on the great age of southern lands, and the biological variety embedded within their geological layers, also lead, as in the case of the other writers, though perhaps even more acutely, to a recognition of their interdependence.

Above all, the element that links the writers to a greater or lesser degree is the recognition that the remote south demands different frameworks of perception—frameworks that may need making up and reinvention, extempore. Coleridge, Darwin, and Melville—and, at a remove, Mary Shelley—all understood, if in part unconsciously, that the hemisphere required, even encouraged, the breaking of old imaginative moulds—essential though these were for making an initial approach. Yet, once this was acknowledged, they also saw, though obliquely, that the special conditions of the south, its contrary spin and reverse angles, might provide the transformative means of getting there—as did the looping pathways that its geography insisted upon. The growling ice of the *Rime*; the counterintuitive geological layering of Darwin's cordillera; the weltering, haunted seas of Melville's *Moby-Dick*—in each case become the media through which southern spaces are interpreted, though never wholly or in their entirety. The writers all tacitly recognise that something of the antipodes must remain forever out of reach, much like Cook's far southern continent.

Foundational Frames: North into South

No less than for Camões in the sixteenth century, literary and mystical frames of reference offered vital cognitive tools to later writer-travellers endeavouring to conceive the always-converse south.[9] Culturally sanctioned myths gave both navigators and writers thematic structures through which the south's 'delusional geography' could be better comprehended.[10] Most obviously, the Christian belief in redemption through confession underpins the Ancient Mariner's tale. To tell his epic story, Melville draws on various 'emblematic discourses', not excepting Coleridge's poem, but also including biblical and Kabbalistic symbolism, and maritime history (*MD* 379–80).[11]

Another major narrative stimulus was the journey of the heroic navigator. Captain George Shelvocke's *A Voyage round the World by Way of the Great South Sea* (1726) supports Coleridge's story, just as Captain Pollard's *The Mariner's Chronicle* (1806) does Melville's.[12] Both texts feature a monomaniacal explorer-hero driven by ambition and obsession to tunnel into the unknown, so endangering human relationship. However, the preeminent model was James Cook's *Journals,* which informed all subsequent northern efforts to comprehend the south—a template consecrated by the captain's great fame.[13] His rounding first of Cape Horn, on the *Endeavour,* and later of Good Hope on the *Resolution,* migrates through the Mariner's story and then into Melville, while the haunting shapes of ice 'clifts' and becalmed ships also filter through Coleridge into *Frankenstein.*[14] At a more mundane level, Cook's daily entries setting down his coordinates (as in the epigraph) gave his readers a useful grid pattern with which to start filling in their understanding of the apparently empty southern oceans.[15]

But readers also perceived that even the most authoritative sources did not always have purchase and that at such moments of breakdown, something of the south's true substance glimmered through. In this, they shared Cook's own growing realisation in the southern summer of 1772–3 that none of his instruments and calculations would allow him to approach the enormous, icy mass that he assumed must exist beyond the 70°S of latitude.[16] As he turned from his farthest point south of 66°37′, beyond the Antarctic Circle, and sailed on to the islands of New Zealand encountered three years previously, on the *Endeavour,* he began tentatively to conclude that the great 'Southern Continent' might in fact comprise two, a land of bluffs and reefs to the west, later called Australia, and an apparently unreachable, frigid land to the extreme south. The following summer he continued to seek 'the great object of [his] researches', this time in the South Pacific, attaining 71°10′ on 30 January (about seventy-five miles from Antarctica), but then deciding that it was not possible to proceed 'one Inch farther South', so numberless and large were the 'Ice Hills' that faced him.

Captured in Cook's phrases, like those above, is his remarkable ability to imagine vividly uncharted space and ideate in the round—something that also stimulated the work of those who wrote in his wake. Coleridge was especially inspired by Cook's imagery, having learned about his journeys at school as well as from his reading. His mathematics teacher at Christ's Hospital had been William Wales, the astronomer on board the *Resolution*, on Cook's second voyage, who was in all likelihood the first person to tell him stories of the 'wondrous' polar sea-ice, 'as green as emerald'.[17]

Cook's—and Coleridge's—capacity for relational thought, toggling between empirical observations drawn from different latitudes, will also have spoken to Darwin, stimulating his interest in the curious parallels that manifested between life-forms despite being separated by thousands of miles of ocean. Looking at crystallised forests in the Andes, for example, Darwin began to understand that this evidence pointed to a history of the earth even more 'incomprehensibly vast' and far more agitated than that plotted by the gradualist Lyell in his *Principles of Geology*, whose first two volumes sailed with the *Beagle*.[18] Darwin's work in its turn duly loomed large over subsequent imaginings of the south, as Cook's had over the writing of previous generations. Another man with a southern mission, Robert Falcon Scott, read Darwin on board the *Terra Nova*, witnessing as he sailed south on his final attempt on the South Pole a ceaseless struggle for creaturely survival play itself out across the formidable icefields that had so alarmed Cook around 150 years before.

'The Sun Now Rose upon the Right': Samuel Taylor Coleridge's *Rime of the Ancient Mariner*

Unlike any other English poem, certainly any not written by a voyager, the Romantic ballad-epic *The Rime of the Ancient Mariner* meditates visually and aurally on what it is to navigate the far south—'the cold Country towards the South Pole', as its 1834 Argument has it. The Mariner narrator takes the reader through and beyond one of the great portals of the Southern Ocean, Cape Horn, transposing older travel accounts of circumnavigating both eastwards and westwards onto this pivotal point. His tale of being 'alone on a wide wide sea', the dead albatross he has slain hanging around his neck, killed at the deepest point of the south, plunges the reader into the existential terrors that northern navigators had experienced on these same deadly waters.[19] Like Camões's Adamastor decrying da Gama's entry into his ocean, Coleridge recognised viscerally that to approach the high southern latitudes was to enter mystery, and so in some sense to trespass.

There are few poems in the English language more cited and recited than *The Rime of the Ancient Mariner*, increasingly so because of its environmental theme of entwinement with the natural world, even in waters seemingly so hostile to human presence.[20] The poem gives far-sighted intimations of the devastating impacts on other living things of human activity—impacts that Darwin later theorised and Melville would sombrely expand upon. The frame narrative with which the poem famously opens sets out in clear terms the core ecological dilemma—how our apparent incapacity to respect nature undermines our need for fellowship with other living things. The Ancient Mariner meets the Wedding Guest within earshot of the church where the wedding ceremony is about to take place—it seems to be as convivial a meeting as one can imagine. But the older man then detains the younger with the tale he cannot quit retelling—about a journey into the threatening icefields where he shot and killed the albatross that showed his crew hospitality.[21]

Avid stargazing and wide reading had 'habituated [Coleridge] to the vast' at a young age.[22] The books that the 'shaping spirit' of his imagination 'transfused' into his poetry, as he himself described the process, embraced both fantastical and nonfictional writing about distant lands, the *Arabian Nights* and *Robinson Crusoe*, as well as the *Philosophical Transactions of the Royal Society* and eighteenth-century 'Equator to Equator round the Horn' travelogues. He also pored over maps of the 'unknown South', including Higden's *Polychronicon* with its depictions of the 'wild chaos of fantastic marvels' that flourished on the world's southern rim.[23] Yet, as much as the 'invisible . . . Natures in the Universe' inspired him, he was aware, too, that his visions of the vast required empirical underpinnings, to capture for the reader the experience of travelling into and through Antarctic waters.[24] Perhaps his most important structural contribution to the writing of the far south, therefore, lies in his poem's architectonics, how he builds the great continent-rounding pathway of the Ancient Mariner's journey into the shape, texture, and movement of the poem.

Coleridge appears to understand intuitively that to write a compelling story of southern navigation requires suspending it from this crucial curvilinear track, so pulling the reader irrevocably into the swirling circumpolar energies of the Antarctic. To begin, as we saw, he recreates perceptually the Mariner's parabolic pathway 'far down beneath the Southern Cross'. As for Camões, so Coleridge, the epic's conventions of climax, resolution, and retrospection allow him to mirror the reflexive motion of falling into and rising out of the south. From the point of crossing the equator, the reader is located on deck with the Mariner, driven by the storm-blast towards the Horn, tacking across the prevailing westerly winds (quickened by the spin of the earth).[25] Then there is an apparent break, a moment of extreme tension. Coleridge understood the physics of the vertex—the still yet unstill point where the parabola changes direction—for it is precisely at this flexing point that the albatross is shot. From now on, the Mariner's state has changed utterly. Directionality is reversed and all norms upended.

But Coleridge goes even further. The old man's compulsive re-narration of his story also draws into the poem a version of the navigational oscillation described in chapter 3—the seesawing between the unknown and the known, that which lies ahead and that which we have left behind. As the old man tells it, he is forced to rebegin his 'ghastly tale' whenever, without warning, its 'agony' overcomes him (Part VI). Pinned down by his story, he must recount his experience in order to move on, passing 'like night, from land to land'. And his audience, the Wedding Guest, and the reader, 'cannot choose but hear' him (I 7 ii). His compulsion, therefore, obliges him to double the Horn not once, but again and again, his story moving along its curving track even as he reflects endlessly upon it, and his listener with him. His tale's reiterative logic commits the reader, too, to a ceaseless oscillation, the *Rime* engaging us in the process of making sense of the parabolic journey both as the story each time moves forwards, and simultaneously in retrospect, if we have heard it before.[26] Stanza by stanza, the forward motion of the narrative is also repetitively withheld by the strophe's recurring pattern, which amplifies the seesawing effect.

Directional markers cooperate in this performative centring and recentring of the reader within the Mariner's tale. Within any given scene (on the icefield, out in the Pacific), we are invited to compare and synthesise mixed familiar and unfamiliar phenomena (wondrous cold, water snakes, electric colours), to make sense of where we are. Even after being becalmed at the equator in Part IV, the poem involves us through the dialogue of the First and Second Voices to try to comprehend the enchantment that eventually brings the Mariner's ship back to his own country. We mobilise its 'mechanics of sense perception', as Anne Thell writes, even as we are confronted with questions about what we are seeing, and from which vantage point—now close-up and immersed, now elevated and distant, with the moon present throughout—full, waning, new.[27]

Derek Attridge observes that reading 'entails a continuous process of prediction' that is repeatedly adjusted as 'expectations are met, intensified, or disappointed'.[28] In the *Rime*, this process is further enhanced with the liberal use of repetition and half-repetition that arrests and thwarts the poem's 'forward energy'. This is especially striking at those points where the ship's progress is stalled, when the ice is 'all around' or the wind drops. The rhythm reinforces the stop-start effects, as do the repeating or half-repeating words and phrases: of 'south', 'silent sea', 'day after day', 'water, water', and so on (to quote from Part II alone).

A key moment of suspension occurs after the crew has been struck down by a mysterious curse, when the Mariner's solitude overwhelms him:

Alone, alone, all, all alone,
Alone on a wide wide sea!
And never a saint took pity on
My soul in agony.

—(PART IV, STANZA 3, LL. 232–35, MY EMPHASIS)

In a traditional close reading, we might have said that the repetition, as in the highlighted line, was for emphasis. The prominent assonantal patterns reinforce the Mariner's solitariness, while the semantics of 'wide wide' invites us to dwell on the idea of expanse. But then we might also notice how we interact with the line somatically and aurally, if we imagine reading it out loud, or speaking it as the Mariner is ostensibly doing. The repetition emphasises the breadth and amplitude of the marine horizon, even as it also works with recursive force, the second 'wide' underlining the image of the blank, cursed sea. As readers, we, too, find ourselves dwarfed in our singleness by that vast and awful expanse of southern water.[29]

Yet, if these repetitive effects operate as a kind of radar, checking and rechecking the surrounding phenomena, then at the same time, steady as an arrow's path, the *Rime*'s four-beat syllabic metre maintains the poem's propulsive move forwards.[30] This constant underlying beat continues with relatively few variations as the Mariner proceeds through the trackless wastes of ice, even despite the reversal of direction around the Horn. It works together with the on-running *abcb* rhyme to underscore the compulsive onward movement of the journey, while also heightening the Mariner's paranoid sense of pursuit (see Part II, stanza 12, ll. 132–4; Part V, stanza 20, ll. 378–9, 402–3, Part VI, stanza 14, l. 467).

Set in regions where the laws of nature appear reversed, *The Rime of the Ancient Mariner* speaks of the need to acknowledge the interdependence of living species. The same recognition of inextricable species entanglement would also come to Charles Darwin as he doubled and redoubled the same far southern continent some thirty-five years after Coleridge's poem was first published. And Melville, too, would note the fatal effects of failing to show hospitality, as the next section but one will show.

Distance and Darwin: *The Voyage of the* Beagle

Setting out in 1831, Charles Darwin circumnavigated the globe for five years on the HMS *Beagle* as the ship's amateur naturalist under the command of the British naval officer, Captain Robert Fitzroy. He wrote up his adventures, observations, and findings, concerned especially with South America, in a three-volume official account, *The Journal of Researches into the Geology and Natural History of the Various Countries Visited by HMS* Beagle (1839). A single volume version soon went into a separate second edition, and, extensively revised, was published again, in 1845, as *The Voyage of the* Beagle that we are familiar with today.

The *Beagle* travelogue tells the by now well-known, though still marvellous, story of the process of ratiocination by which the journeying naturalist Darwin came gradually to his theory of evolution. As layered and expansive as its subject is, his text is impossible to do justice to in a relatively short reading, yet some of its core observations will give a sense of the scope and scale across which the south stimulated him to think. Amassing a huge quantity of evidence on trips into regions like Patagonia and Tierra del Fuego, and on the Chilean fjords, Darwin began to notice changes in geology and biological species that had manifested over aeons—far greater lengths of time than had been conceived in world history up to that point. Building a rutter-like 'itinerary narrative' from his notes, in Nigel Leask's words, Darwin proceeded step by step to draw comparative links, pulling his observations of similar things from different far-flung spaces into one integrative framework. The research eventually allowed him to construe the connections that would produce his theory of natural selection, written up as *The Origin of Species* (1859).

Of the five-year journey to 'carry a chain of chronometrical measurements around the world', three years and one month were spent gathering evidence on land, mainly in South America (*OSVB* 17). Darwin suffered badly from seasickness and so, as Janet Browne writes, he effectively undertook not so much a voyage at sea as a series of 'miscellaneous' travels on land.[31] In April 1832, for example, he came ashore at Rio de Janeiro for three months while the *Beagle* continued on its mission of surveying the southern coastlines of South America. This exercise Captain Fitzroy in his log described as 'trying to do a jig-saw through a keyhole'—an apt simile for the attempt to represent accurately the far south's complex littoral geography.[32] At the time, significantly for Darwin's later analysis of species change, the continent was in a state of political flux, following the end of Spanish control. Everywhere that Darwin travelled, he came across evidence of the brutal campaign that the Argentine army under General Rosas was waging against the 'horse Indians', with the object, he plainly saw, of 'exterminating them' (*OSVB* 82–3). At least at a human level, it was clear that survival meant a fight to the death.

Michael Ghiselin has described Darwin's method of theorising evolution as 'hypothetico-deductive', through which he posited flexible, overarching hypotheses that might be tested comparatively across great distances while drawing upon heterogeneous data-sets.[33] George Levine, for his part, speaks of the naturalist's power of seeing, his capacity for working analytically through careful description, always undergirded by his itinerary narrative and by his reading.[34] Throughout his travels, he constantly weighed what he was finding in the field against the work of earlier navigators, geologists, and botanists like Lamarck, Lamoureux, Cook, and von Humboldt, and in relation to cosmic patterns drawn from, in particular, Milton's *Paradise Lost*, as well as the writing of other scientists working in Chile. This combined methodology allowed him to analyse differences and similarities at scale, not just in southern or equatorial regions as compared to the north, but also, importantly, *across* the south. For Darwin, I suggest, these less populated and yet extraordinarily interrelated reaches of the watery hemisphere provided a particularly fertile conceptual terrain. The layered Patagonian cliffs, or the shells found high up in the Chilean cordillera (later named for him), prompted him to expand his timeline of the earth's history to accommodate evidence of extreme climate change across millions of years. While trying to remain consistent with Lyell's schemas, he developed a logic that might gather such seemingly widely separate phenomena into one long planetary history: 'All these speculations, however, must be vague . . . for we know that along the whole coast of Patagonia, there have certainly been many and long pauses in the upward action of the elevatory forces' (*OSVB* 382–3).

Darwin's theory of natural selection was, in this sense, southern-born, sketched and shaped on a far southern canvas. The vastness of the south conditioned both the theory's scale and its unitary or synthetic nature, whereby myriad differences spread across greater or lesser distances could be processed into one interconnected system. 'An equable climate, evidently due to the large area of sea compared with the land, seems to extend over the greater part of the southern hemisphere; and, as a consequence, the vegetation partakes of a semi-tropical character'—observations such as this are clearly oriented south (*OSVB* 256–7). In Tierra del Fuego, he was also often exercised to note the high latitudes through which he was travelling. Not unlike his rival Alfred Russel Wallace on the Indonesian archipelago, Darwin was thus observing the impacts of remoteness on species change, while at the same time actually working at a great remove from Europe, or, as he described it, in 'one of the most inhospitable countries within the limits of the world': 'the consciousness in what a remote corner of the world you are . . . standing, [comes] so strongly before the mind' (*OSVB* 228–9).[35]

In contrast to the vibrant life of the tropics, the climatic harshness and 'rank decay' evident in this 'extreme part of South America' was often alarming to Darwin.[36] Yet these same conditions, so different from the temperate zones located at comparable latitudes north, exposed in their 'absolute sovereignty' 'the unceasing war' of the 'inanimate works of nature—rock, ice, snow, wind, and water' with each other, and how they were 'combined against man' (*OSVB* 262–4). Everywhere, evolution was writ large in the topography. And whenever links and entanglements were evident, the laws of natural selection, consistent everywhere, could be demonstrated that much more clearly. Observing parallel changes across very different South American geographies, Darwin was also stimulated to think at different scales simultaneously, discerning how in small things lay 'the cipher of the large'.[37] Such consistent patterns of transmutation were simply not as easily discernible in the northern hemisphere, across the far larger and more continuous landmasses of Europe, Asia, and North America.

The same deductive methodology, honed in the south, could in turn also be read back into the south, including by Darwin's successors, as an analytic means of beginning to understand even older processes of the earth's formation. Using Darwin's approach, his disciple, the botanist Joseph Hooker, sailing on the Ross expedition to Antarctica in 1839–43 with a manuscript copy of *The Voyage of the* Beagle to hand, would glean from the evidence of fossilised trees on Kerguelen Island another theory of slow change—a back-projection of evolutionary principles onto the earth's ancient history (though Darwin always disputed it). Hooker was at pains to explain how flora like the Kerguelen cabbage, the southern beech, and its parasitical fungus, could be found in common across far-flung southern islands and archipelagos like Tasmania and Tierra del Fuego. In Darwin's own words:

> Dr. Hooker informs me, that just lately a third species [of fungus] has been discovered on a third species of beech in Van Diernan's Land [*sic*]. How singular is this relationship between parasitical fungi and the trees on which they grow, in distant parts of the world! (*OSVB* 248).

Departing from Darwin, Hooker's response was to propose that the southern landmasses must once have formed part of a single great continent—a biogeographical surmise that laid the ground for the continental drift theory Alfred Wegener and others would develop some eighty years later.[38]

From the very opening pages of the *Voyage,* we find Darwin at once developing and testing his analytic framework, seemingly in the moment, but actually in retrospect, drawing in evidence of similar ecosystems and, though less frequently, human cultural practices from across the south. No curious life form or habit can seemingly be named without it stimulating a memory of related phenomena noticed elsewhere. Observing krill in the waters off Tierra del Fuego, he weaves in memories of finding this 'sea-sawdust' whale food around the Keeling Atoll in the Indian Ocean, and off Cape Leeuwin in Australian waters (*OSVB* 30). A sighting of planaria prompts a quick, panning view across the south: 'I found no less than twelve different species of terrestrial Planariae in different parts of the southern hemisphere'. Or, again, reflecting on whether the plains around Bahia Blanca would in a past era have had sufficiently 'luxuriant vegetation' to support 'great quadrupeds' such as the *Megatherium,* whose remains he had found there, Darwin thinks across to Africa. From his time travelling in the arid 'southern parts of Africa', some days distant from Cape Town, he had noticed that despite the prevailing dryness, the land could support 'a number of large animals' (*OSVB* 96–106). The nesting habits of Patagonian male rhea also recalled to him William Burchell's observations of ostriches in the Cape.

At this point, southern Africa still lay far ahead in the chronology of the voyage, yet, writing up his observations, Darwin was able to move with remarkable deductive facility between the landmasses, also when it came to human behaviour.[39] Dwellings at Ithacaia north of Cape Frio reminded Darwin of drawings of the 'Hottentot habitations' in southern Africa he had seen, again in

Burchell and other travel writing: 'It is curious how similar circumstances produce such similar results in manners' (*OSVB* 34–5). Meanwhile, the ready hospitality extended to travellers by landowners on the Pampas in Argentina took him back (and forwards, through memory) to remembering Boer manners in the Cape: 'At the Cape of Good Hope, the same hospitality, and very nearly the same points of etiquette are universally observed' (*OSVB* 58–9).

On the Tierra del Fuegans or Yaghan people he met, Darwin made predictable comments about their 'lack of improvement', and drew unfavourable likenesses with other 'wretched' people across the south: 'the tribes of Southern Africa prowling about in search of roots, and living concealed on the wild and arid plains', and the 'Australian'—though he had complimentary words for the latter's superior 'acquirement' of the boomerang and throwing spear (*OSVB* 243–64). At the same time, he expressed regard for the Yaghan ability to have migrated this far south, and, uniquely among human communities, to survive below 55° S, within 'a broken mass of wild rocks, lofty hills, and useless forests'. They were enormously assisted, he observed, by their invention of canoes 'which are not used by the tribes of Chile, Peru, and Brazil'. He also noted their remarkable powers of long sight and, as did Fitzroy, facility with language. Within the same terrain, the people spoke 'many different dialects' while 'separated from each other only by a deserted border or neutral territory'. On the Yaghans' notorious powers of mimicry, Darwin speculated in contradictory fashion whether this sophisticated trait might be 'a consequence of the more practised habits of perception and keener senses' common to those not 'civilised' by European standards. The *Beagle* was carrying on board three Yaghan people—Yokcushlu, Orundellico, and El'lelaru, or (the names given by the crew) Fuegia Basket, Jemmy Button, York Minster—whom Fitzroy had picked up on the first voyage and was now returning to the Ponsonby Sound area. Darwin's language about Button is condescending, yet it is evident from several references that he consulted with him on Yaghan culture—their hunting practices and system of belief—as well as on local geography and the distribution of plant species. The 'word of Jeremy Button', he wrote, was always decisive.

A mobile sense of south-south connection continued to serve Darwin's thinking as the *Beagle* journeyed onwards: via the Galapagos, off the coast of Ecuador, now the most famous landing point on the voyage, across the Pacific to New Zealand and New South Wales, effectively following the route of the *Endeavour*, and then through the Southern Ocean, via Hobart, and across the Indian Ocean, tracing *Moby-Dick*'s route in the opposite direction, finally stopping off at the Cape of Good Hope. Everywhere Darwin continued to build comparative links around and across the hemisphere, his written narrative, *Rime*-like, repeatedly roving forwards and back. The 'straight line of yellowish cliff' outside Sydney Harbour 'brought to our minds the coast of Patagonia', while the non-deciduous character of the Australian eucalypt 'appears common to the entire southern hemisphere, namely, South America, Australia, and the Cape of Good Hope' (*OSVB* 444–6). The phrase 'wide extent' is, interestingly, several times used at points of comparison, as when he comments on the 'fossiliferous deposits of wide extent' in Peru, Chile, Tierra del Fuego, Patagonia, and La Plata, which he compares to the coral reefs he has observed (*OSVB* 533–8). But Darwin's most pointed comparative commentary in these later stages of the journey is reserved for what he perceives as the destruction of the indigenous people across the southern lands in the face of the European incursion: 'Wherever the European has trod, death seems to pursue the aboriginal. We may look to the wide extent of the Americas, Polynesia, the Cape of Good Hope, and Australia, and we find the same result' (*OSVB* 446–7).

'The White Mass Floating in the Sun': Herman Melville's *Moby-Dick*

With *Moby-Dick* (1851), his ambitious, rambling tale of the eponymous white whale running before his hellbent hunter, Captain Ahab of the *Pequod*, Herman Melville offered an America still forging an independent cultural tradition, a massive national story that, however, unfolds quirkily on a global, oceanic stage. The episodic, encyclopaedic novel follows the route of the 'grand, ungodly, godlike' Captain Ahab as he pursues his nemesis Moby Dick from the Atlantic through the Southern Ocean, the southern Indian Ocean, and the Indonesian archipelago, into the South Seas (*MD* 176). The southern hemisphere is its primary canvas.

On one level, Captain Ahab's obsessive quest for the whale that he believes once took his leg in a whaling accident situates an expansionist America within a wider, Pacific-facing hemisphere. Intriguingly, however, the circumnavigating *Pequod* approaches the 'interflowing' South Seas from Southeast Asia, not Cape Horn—an apt contrariwise move for a tale of the south. The waters of the hemisphere thereby fuse into a grand optic through which to conceptualise global space. Virtually throughout, the world is viewed 'from below'.[40] For a mid-nineteenth-century novel from the north, this intervention is remarkable.

The many close parallels that *Moby-Dick* traces with other texts explored in this chapter might at a superficial level seem unlikely were it not for the fact of sharing their interests, in at least three areas. First, the novel partakes in related obsessions with distance and extremity; second, in geographic terms, it always tends southerly in its efforts to explore these obsessions; and third, as importantly, it comprehends at every point that its emblematic sources and intertexts be warped and adapted to harmonise with the *Pequod*'s southerly orientation. Though Ishmael declares that he is wary of 'intolerable allegory', and repeatedly makes claims of verisimilitude and accuracy, his crosscutting of ancient and modern mythic sources has the important effect of undermining any authoritative perspective on Ahab's pursuit of the great 'white mass', Moby Dick (*MD* 85, 407). Likewise, the heterotopia of the *Pequod*'s crew, who hail from 'all the isles of the sea', brings together any number of different cultural viewpoints that cut across and complicate northern lines of sight upon the south (*MD* 417–18).

As did *The Lusíads*, *Moby-Dick* operates a little like a rutter, though it paradoxically stops in at no port. Rather, it offers on its looping journey around Africa's southern cape a structural survey of the 'unhooped' southern oceans (*MD* 298, 306)—a space that is represented as forming part of one interconnected system.[41] As Melville claims on more than one occasion, the whale ship is itself an 'explorer', a 'pioneer in ferreting out the remotest and least known parts of the earth. She has explored seas and archipelagos which had no chart, where no Cook or Vancouver had ever sailed' (*MD* 205–6). The first and second mates, Starbuck and Stubb, for example, share a strong sense of a route-encircled world (*MD* 613). They are aware that to sail halfway around the world with the gales will (even if counterintuitively) take them on 'the shortest way [back] to Nantucket'. The same perception informs the Ancient Mariner's account of the wind that 'swiftly, swiftly' flies him from the Pacific back to England. *Moby-Dick*'s interlocking networks of trade and exchange are also neatly captured in Ishmael's image of the 'mysterious, divine' Pacific as comprising 'the midmost waters of the world, the Indian Ocean and Atlantic being but its arms. . . . [It] zones the world's whole bulk about' (*MD* 593–4).[42] Meanwhile, in an extraordinary evocation, Queeqeg, the tattooed 'soothing savage' from the South Seas, is seen in his own person to encompass different time zones. He is 'a man some twenty thousand miles from home, by the way of Cape Horn, that is', and his varicoloured complexion resembles the Andes' western slopes as viewed from far-off in the South Seas where they 'show forth in one array, contrasting climates zone by zone' (*MD* 145, 123).

Moby-Dick opens as the tale of an unlikely friendship between this man of the south, the Pacific Islands harpooner, Queequeg, and a man of the north, the sailor-narrator Ishmael. They meet at the Spouter Inn in the American East Coast whaling port of Nantucket and together sign on to the *Pequod*, a whaler (*MD* 146, 151–2). Yet, once they have set sail, their friendship narrative, combining the hemispheres, morphs quickly into the more equatorial story of Captain Ahab's quest. The skipper's revenge battle begins at Christmas, the northern solstice, the beginning of the 'Season on the Line' (as whales feed in equatorial waters from December to June). Thereafter, the narrative traces a 'three hundred and sixty-five days and nights' journey, the pursuit circling the planet just as the story arcs across a calendar year and the earth rounds the sun (see *MD* 176, 227, 298, 306, 338–40, 566). The *Pequod* meets its final catastrophic end at the following solstice, on the line itself, with the sun directly overhead, shining down on the doubloon from Ecuador fastened on its deck, in 'the sea [the whale] was most known to frequent' (*MD* 541). An equator-to-equator parabolic line familiar from Coleridge's *Rime* has been completed, but in the contrary direction.

A novel all about writing, *Moby-Dick* is self-consciously composed of prior texts and presents as a direct heir of the explorer tradition of navigating by using precursor charts and descriptions.[43] At the same time, it is also a meditation on whale slaughter, self-consciously reflecting the great size and scale of its subject by citing from a vast library of western literature to convey the immensities of the eponymous whale and its habitats. As Ishmael observes, the whale's 'mighty bulk' 'affords a most congenial theme whereon to enlarge, amplify, and generally expatiate. Would you, you could not compress him' (*MD* 471). He duly draws on 'monstrous stories' of whales found in 'books, both ancient and modern', especially in 'Pliny, Purchas, Hackluyt, Harris, Cuvier', as well as 'Colnett's, Huggins's, Frederick Cuvier's, and Beale's' (*MD* 372). Chapter 82, 'The Honor and Glory of Whaling', is typical for its intersplicing of biblical and historical sources about cetaceans. The narrative speculates, for example, whether the whale carrying Jonah might have travelled to Nineveh by the way of the 'great headland' of the Cape of Good Hope, yet concedes that this movement would have wrested the honour of its discovery from Dias.

Its whaling subject does not, of course, automatically associate *Moby-Dick* with the southern hemisphere. Its counterclockwise spin comes primarily from its manipulation of its source texts. Yet the pursuit of the enormous creature across the world's oceans does afford explicitly south-centred reflections upon the uneven global economy of whaling. Though the animals occur throughout the planet's waters, the higher proportion of ocean in the southern hemisphere, and the low population density of humans, not least on the sub-Antarctic islands, always gave whaling an austral focus, as Melville was aware.[44] This insight led him to become probably the first Anglophone author to bring into the open how the seemingly boundless and relatively unpeopled reaches of the Southern Ocean were being used as mass killing fields, the industrial-scale slaughter and rendering conveniently veiled from the eyes of competitor nations and controlling tax officials.[45] Or, as Ishmael observes, the South Seas forms a single 'Southern Fishery' stocked with still-untapped capital (*MD* 407).

Several chapters in *Moby-Dick* offer extended essays on whaling, presented as an ancient pursuit, recorded in myth, not least that of the seagoing hero Perseus, 'the first whaleman' (*MD* 417–4). Yet the killing is carried out using modern technologies of mass production, in order for 'huge hills and mountains of casks on casks' to be piled upon Nantucket's wharves (*MD* 154). Ishmael's prescient point is that modern society relies absolutely upon brutal processes of resource extraction. For the oil taken from the bodies of whales and seals to illuminate the streets of Europe and America and 'light the gay bridals and other merry-makings of men', the whale 'must die the death and be murdered' (*MD* 466–7). By the end of the novel, Melville still stubbornly avers that the oceans form a limitless 'out there', containing an inexhaustible number of whales. However, the scale of slaughter that he represents—'so wide a chase, and so remorseless a havoc'—is gigantic and, by implication, unsustainable. A ruthless lack of respect for species reciprocity, like Ahab's, will lead to the annihilation of all (*MD* 570–74).

As did Coleridge, Melville in *Moby-Dick* pulls us into his watery world by tracing the 'magic pattern' of a parabola extending from one equatorial zone to another, drawn around a tempestuous southern cape.[46] Emulating Camões, the direction of the loop is leftwards, counterclockwise, at least if viewed from the north. Instead of reaching equatorial waters by taking the conventional 'great passage southwards, [doubling] Cape Horn', the shortest route to the Pacific, Ahab turns east. To make sure he will find where it is that Moby Dick '[turns] up his wrinkled brow' (*MD* 301), he follows 'a devious zig-zag world-circle', his pathway hooping through the 'unshored, harbourless immensities' of 'waters hard upon the Antarctic seas' (*MD* 227, 291). Not coincidentally, the transition from Ishmael to Ahab's story takes place at the point of circling around 'Cape Tormentoso', Adamastor's Cape of Storms, notorious for its 'black waters and black air' (*MD* 336–7).

For Melville, then, the south is not simply counterposed to the north. It is also not just a mind-map for analytic speculation, as it is in Darwin. Rather, I would submit, the hemisphere is understood from the perspective of the Pole, always in relation to its distinctive features of wateriness, remoteness, and soul-shrinking solitude. Ishmael consistently views southern climates from a planetary perspective. For him, it is not surprising that June is cold or its days short (*MD* 119). He pointedly observes that 'the 21st June' is 'the longest day in the year *in our hemisphere*'. And, 'It was a short cold Christmas; and as the short northern day merged into night, we found ourselves almost broad upon the wintry ocean' (*MD* 200). The elaborate Andean metaphor describing Queequeg also reflects an intimate view of southern geographies, while the vision of archipelagic starscapes reflected in an archipelagic ocean, cited in chapter one, testifies to an oceanic but also unmistakably south-centred Pacific awareness (*MD* 589). Ishmael several times remarks on the southern night sky bright with 'constellations never seen here at the north', and namechecks distinctive clusters: 'beneath the effulgent Antarctic skies I have boarded the Argo-Navis, and joined the chase against the starry Cetus far beyond the utmost stretch of Hydrus and the Flying Fish' (*MD* 169–70, 378).

Writing about wanton slaughter in far southern waters, Melville was keenly aware of looking through Coleridge's eyes—though he, unlike his precursor, had himself sailed these cold seas. In the same way that the Mariner takes the reader with him on his journey, so that we stand alongside him in the bow, involved in his experience, in *Moby-Dick*, the *Rime* itself turns into a cognitive and navigational device. True, when in the high southern latitudes an albatross appears on deck, Ishmael protests vigorously that 'neither had I then read the Rhyme, nor knew the bird to be an albatross', and so 'by no possibility could Coleridge's wild Rhyme have had aught to do with those mystical impressions which were mine' (*MD* 227). But he protests too much, as the half-rhyme might suggest. From the point in the novel that the albatross appears, the spirit of the Ancient Mariner's tale enters into the prose to the point that many lines echo the poem (*MD* 338–40). The 'black' sea resembles a 'soul in agony'; a whale spout appears as an apparition 'treacherously beckoning us on and on' (*MD* 336–7); tormented souls accompany the *Pequod* in the form of 'homeless' fish and fowl, like 'guilty beings' (*MD* 336–7, 340). And while following the 'demon phantom' that is the whale, the *Pequod* is itself pursued by 'inscrutable sea-ravens', as if it were a 'drifting, uninhabited craft; a thing appointed to desolation' (*MD* 340). Yet the supreme Coleridgean note is perhaps the solitariness of the whale cruisers themselves, 'seldom or never for a whole twelvemonth or more on a stretch, to encounter a single news-telling sail of any sort' (*MD* 277).

The *Pequod*'s haunted isolation comes into starkest relief at the moment when, south-eastward from the Cape of Storms, off the distant Crozett Islands ('a good cruising ground for Right Whalemen'), the ship meets a whaler named the *Goney* (*goney* being the sailor's word for *albatross,* Melville informs us) (*MD* 338–40). For ships to cross paths in these remote, watery immensities is usually not only fortuitous but also fortunate, as Ishmael observes. Meeting up allows the crews to exchange letters and news as they pass, with captains and mates sometimes briefly crossing over from one ship to another.[47] Yet, on this occasion, on the contrary, the two whalers, the *Pequod* and the *Goney,* pass each other without exchanging 'one word'. Ishmael, up at the 'fore-mast-head', observes from a distance that the signs are not auspicious. As the *Rime*-like portents might already have led us to anticipate, the *Goney* has been bleached a 'spectral' white by the elements, and its crew is long-bearded and clad in rags, so long have they been at sea. The *Pequod*'s sailors cry out for news of the white whale, but some force seems to conspire to prevent the *Goney* from giving answer:

> As the strange captain, leaning over the pallid bulwarks, was in the act of putting his trumpet to his mouth [to hail a reply], it somehow fell from his hand into the sea; and the wind now rising amain, he in vain strove to make himself heard without it. Meantime his ship was still increasing the distance between.

At this point, 'the two wakes' cross, and the shoals that had been following the *Pequod* turn and swim away with the *Goney*. Captain Ahab's final word on the matter is that his ship's *poste restante* will be the wide Pacific Ocean.

In the context of the far south, the implications of this strange non-encounter hardly need spelling out. Human exchange out on the stormy southern seas is so transient and risky as not to be worth it, and yet is the more necessary and desired. The *Pequod* is left to continue into perilous waters without company or support, like the Mariner's cursed ship, lacking further guidance as to the pathway ahead, driven on only by the force of Captain Ahab's mania. For Ishmael, the *Pequod*'s crew—human society in microcosm—is consigned to an existential, unhomed loneliness. This condition is reinforced in later non-meetings, first with the *Jeroboam,* a plague ship with a 'malignant epidemic' on board, and then with the *Jungfrau,* a competitor in the hunt for Moby Dick (*MD* 407, 418–25).[48] However, it has already become clear long before this point that Ahab has committed his entire crew to a battle to the death with the whale—a battle from which there can be no escape, such is the grim logic of the fateful loop through the Southern Ocean back to the equator.

Coda—Mary Shelley's *Frankenstein,* a Study in Monomania

In *Moby-Dick,* Melville observes that the wild wastes of the far south test human capacities for survival and insist thereby on a respect for the commons of the natural world, as, too, does Coleridge in the *Rime*. Even so, when ships meet one another on the 'everlasting terra incognita' of the Southern Ocean, in Melville's words, fellowship is as often frustrated as it is sought—perhaps necessarily so, in order that profit can be extracted. Relatedly, Darwin, in *The Voyage of the* Beagle, investigates from his naturalist's perspective long aeons of the struggle for survival as registered within the silt banks of southern America. He finds commonalities across different regions, yet, influentially, little evidence of cooperation between the species.

As inspired by the *Rime* as is *Moby-Dick,* Mary Shelley's cautionary novel, *Frankenstein, or the Modern Prometheus* (1819), rounds out these reflections on the southern imaginings of northern travellers. Shelley takes as her subject Europe's at-once scientific and colonial drive to 'penetrate into the recesses of nature' and divine its secrets. It is the same Promethean ambition that propelled Cook, and, in other domains of activity, Darwin's research, and Melville's whalers—and that from the late 1700s had taken the entire southern hemisphere as its field.[49] Although Frankenstein's ice sheets are alpine or arctic, the novel remarkably shares many of the southern preoccupations that previous sections have traced, not least with the single-minded quest to breach horizons and exploit the earth's resources, and with the fatal consequences of that breaching, when nature's laws are disregarded.

The story of the scientist Victor Frankenstein's making of the Creature, whom misery turns into a murderous monster, is so well-known as not to require summarising here. Its moral about destructive overreaching has entered collective mythology through its many retellings, including influentially in film. In the twenty-first century, at a time when the evidence of anthropogenic climate change has become undeniable, that moral continues to resonate. The novel relates directly to this book's southern preoccupations, therefore, with its representations both of destructive exploratory ambition, and of the signature ground upon which that ambition has been nakedly expressed—the remote outer edges of the planet that are, however, linked by invisible yet binding ties to the centre. This aspect of polar remoteness moulds the frame of Frankenstein's story, where this coda is focussed.

The shell narrative of *Frankenstein* comprises the explorer Robert Walton's letters to his sister about a long-hoped-for journey to the North Pole. Stuck in the Arctic ice, Walton encounters an exhausted and dispirited scientist, Victor Frankenstein, whom he discovers in the act of endlessly pursuing and being pursued by the Creature he has made across the polar icefield—a precursor of Captain Ahab. Walton soon finds that he has met his counterpart in his new friend. Here is a fellow quester after scientific truth, determined to 'unfold to the world the deepest mysteries of creation', and acquire by increase of knowledge 'dominion . . . over the elemental foes of our race' (*F* 28, 48, 59, 60). Yet, as Frankenstein teaches from his own hard experience, the consequences of the quest prove to be deadly to the quester. To pursue 'nature to her hiding-places' is to goad her into taking revenge for the act of exposure (*F* 54). Frankenstein, in his conversation with Walton, interestingly equates his pursuit of knowledge with the discovery of the Americas, and the destruction of the 'empires of Mexico and Peru' (*F* 56). To the Creature, by contrast, 'the vast wilds of South America' represent a potential refuge and retreat (*F* 146).

To describe the polar environment, Mary Shelley draws on *Rime*-like imagery of icy wastes and fiendish pursuit—what she calls 'that production of the most imaginative of modern poets'—thereby immediately couching these northern extremities in the by-now-recognisable symbolism of the far south (*F* 21).[50] Moreover, Walton looks forward in explicit terms to travelling home via the southern capes. While his 'belief in the marvellous' hurries him on to exploring the wild seas of the world, he aims to return, like the Mariner, 'by the southern cape of Africa or America', blown by 'southern gales' through 'vast and irregular plains of ice' (*F* 22–3).

In other words, for Walton, icefields that are Antarctic in appearance correlate with the human desire to penetrate beyond the farthest horizons. However, the same milieu also exposes that overreaching as harmful and perilous. The timing of Walton's journey is significant, too. He sets out on his polar expedition in June, the southern winter solstice, at a time of year when the ice sheets of the North Pole would not have been as extensive as those of the south, even at that time, in the period of the so-called mini-Ice Age when Shelley was writing. The frozen wastes that goad western ambitions to go farther are thus suggestively austral in aspect, and, laid alongside Coleridge's icy 'clifts', bear particular salience also for our times of polar speculation and penetration.[51]

Mary Shelley wrote *Frankenstein* before the expeditions of James Ross and Jules Dumont D'Urville to the great southern ice shelf that now bears the former's name. Yet, channelling both Coleridge and Cook, and anticipating Darwin and Melville, she understood in a deep sense that the far subpolar regions, perhaps in particular the Antarctic, signified an apparently limitless limit that nonetheless formed an intrinsic part of life on earth. The southerly vision of the novel is encapsulated in this holistic understanding. For no matter how extreme or farther-than-human, the outer edge remained bound up with the planet at large.[52] Nothing of it could be outlawed or disregarded, as was the Creature, without fatal consequences for the rest.

In the next chapter, on the frozen heart of the south that is Antarctica, we will encounter human travellers attempting to divine further these icy immensities of the planet, yet finding that wherever they apply their objective measurements, there is always something of the south that eludes their understanding and repels their single-minded quest. For all the writers, both in this chapter and the next, this is the ultimate distinguishing feature of the southern edge: its insistence on our interrelatedness with all other life-forms—albatrosses, water snakes, whales, and marine fossils buried high up in the Andes.

5

'Silent Vastness'

THE FARTHEST SOUTH

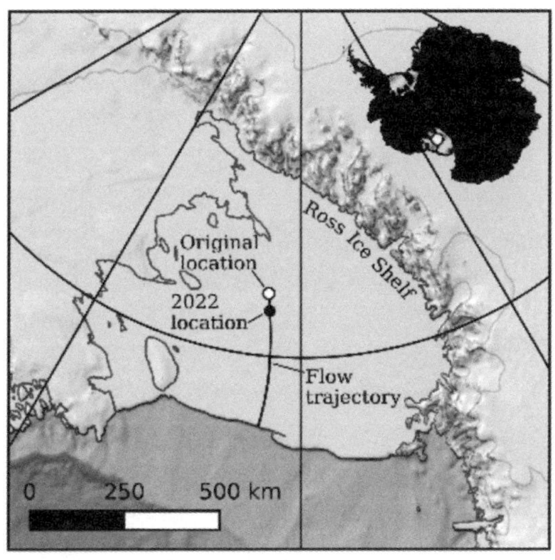

$$\begin{bmatrix} x_{t+\Delta t} \\ y_{t+\Delta t} \end{bmatrix} = \begin{bmatrix} x_t + v_{x_t}\Delta t \\ y_t + v_{y_t}\Delta t \end{bmatrix}$$

What a terrible vast solitude it is, reaching back to the other side of the world, and constantly swept by violent winds and drift.

—CAPTAIN JOHN KING DAVIS OF THE *AURORA*, DOUGLAS MAWSON'S EXPEDITION SHIP, (1911–14)

Ice is the beginning of Antarctica and ice is its end. As one moves from perimeter to interior, the proportion of ice relentlessly increases. Ice creates more ice,

> and ice defines ice. Everything else is suppressed. . . . This is earthscape transfigured into icescape.
>
> —STEPHEN PYNE, *THE ICE* (1986)

> His father had said, looking at the clouds massed on the horizon and not turning: 'That? That must be Antarctica.'
>
> And the boy was seized with enchantment. Antarctica. So near. A land of snow. . . . And yet it was still and always Antarctica. A country of cloud. A land of cloud and snow, a short sail away.
>
> —RANDOLPH STOW, *THE MERRY-GO-ROUND IN THE SEA* (1965)

> She said:
> If Antarctica exists
> And the world is a wobbling wanderer
> Then nothing is straight
> And no one is straight
> Forward.
> If the world is a globe
> Then there is no above
> No below
> No North or South
> No heaven or hell
> No white or . . . black
>
> —MOJISOLA ADEBAYO, *MOJ OF THE ANTARCTIC: AN AFRICAN ODYSSEY* (2006)

Beset by Ice: Finding the *Endurance*

At this middle point in *Southern Imagining*, we meet with ice. *The* ice. Antarctica, the frozen continent—supremely cold, and farther than far. The great bloc of frozen water that tops (or undergirds) our planet represents perhaps the supreme instance of southern imagining. It is the geophysical centre of the southern world, and its extreme climate impacts the entire planet. Over the austral winter, the continental ice cap doubles in size, its 'prodigious' quantity depressing mountains and 'skewing' the earth into a permanent pear shape. The continent's cold deflects the so-called meteorological equator some ten degrees northwards.[1] And the brine ooze extruded from the vast expanses of frozen water drives oceanic circulation worldwide.

As a subject, Antarctica has inspired both fascination and terror. Approaching this crucial central chapter about the icy continent, I have felt both. For any writer, I imagine, the landmass throws up the formidable challenge of how to give it expression. Before the mid-nineteenth century, it had seen no human history. It has no aboriginal language. Antarctic names, including those for ice, are exclusively north-derived.[2] It is the most isolated place on Earth and the most silent (when the wind drops). It lacks flora and fauna, bar the birds, seals, and penguins that inhabit its shores and the surrounding pack ice. Even so, in a book like this, a chapter on imaginative responses to the great ice was unavoidable. And yet I delayed beginning. There were days when I felt like a sailor in a Jules Verne story about the ends of the earth, being swept relentlessly towards some final reckoning. So, my excitement can be imagined when, in early 2022, while reading and thinking about Antarctica, a wonderful true story about human contact and historical rediscovery on the ice burst into the news.

In March 2022, after a years-long search marked by frequent setbacks, Antarctic explorer Ernest Shackleton's ship *Endurance* was found on the bed of the Weddell Sea.[3] It had last been seen on 21 November 1915 when, beset and crushed, the ship finally sank, the sea ice closing over it like a trap. The 2022 recovery project had been mounted by the Falklands Maritime Marine Trust and sailed on the South African icebreaker, *Agulhas II*, captained by the Durban-born Knowledge Bengu. On board were polar geographers, scientists, and marine archaeologists of several nationalities, mainly British and South African, one of whom, the Falklands-born expedition director, Mensun Bound, described the shipwreck as the best-preserved he had ever seen 'by far'. The absence of wood-eating microorganisms in Antarctic waters had left the *Endurance* more or less in the state it was in when it went down, although broken at its stern. There, in the deep, cold seawater, three kilometres down, at 68° 39' S, 52° 26' W, the photography showed history standing suspended. Once felled by an icy 'chaos of churning, tumbling destruction', its rudder torn away, the ship was now upheld by the deep sea itself.[4]

Shackleton's intention in 1914 had been to complete a Trans-Antarctic expedition via the South Pole, in some sense making good yet also overtopping Robert Scott's fateful 1912–13 journey. In the event, however, he and his crew failed to reach even the near coastline. By the year's end, ice had impeded the *Endurance*. The ship then drifted over a hundred miles northwest, rotated by 'the irresistible clockwise sweep' of the Weddell Sea. Yet, though ice floes had ruthlessly squeezed the vessel—in Shackleton's words in his memoir *South*, the oak boards were 'twisted and actually bent by the stresses'—it had remained lying upright on the sandy seabed.[5] The ship's wheel, the porthole to Shackleton's cabin, the library books scattered on the sea floor, the name *Endurance* in raised gold lettering—so many things uncannily resembled the images the expedition photographer Frank Hurley had taken in the days before the ship went down—bar the pale sea creature like an anemone rakishly punctuating the 'a' of *Endurance*. Soon after the sinking, the crew had set out on their now-mythic 850-mile journey, first on foot across the icepack, dragging three lifeboats, then over the wind-torn Southern Ocean to Elephant Island, from where Shackleton and five others sailed on to South Georgia to seek rescue. The 2022 undersea images, laid alongside these, gave Bound an uncanny sense of the past brushing against the present: 'you really do feel the breath of the great man upon the back of your neck'.[6]

For me, following the news from Cape Town, *Agulhas II*'s home harbour, the story said something important about the farthest south—something perverse but true that encouraged me at last to broach the ice and begin this chapter. It was not that the discovery of *Endurance* appeared to have brought the famous tale full circle, to have rounded the unintentional parabola of the Shackleton team's clockwise route, significant as that was. Or that in a world in which stories from the south rarely feature in the world's newspapers, these events told a welcome tale of a southern nation's part in an international achievement. It was rather that, despite everything, *Endurance* remained out of reach. This, to me, was the bottom line. The ship had been located and photographed, yes, but at 3,000 metres, which marine archaeology defines as hyper-depth, that is where she will remain, at least for the foreseeable future.[7] Even if retrieval were possible, Antarctic Treaty protocols insist that monuments like the *Endurance* cannot be removed. Polar history in 2022 may have closed a circle, but we will not be seeing the wheelhouse or the strewn library books up close any time soon. 'Up close' is the experience that Antarctica finally denies.

Shackleton memorably said that 'what the ice takes, the ice keeps', or so the *Endurance*'s navigator, Captain Frank Worsley, a New Zealander, noted in his memoir.[8] In early 2022, the ice seemed to have given back—but only to a degree. The sighting of the ship's name on the hull, visible at last, but actually unreachable, reverberated for me with senses of the far south's ineffability. Of how it ultimately defies and escapes human language. Journals, poetry, and fiction about the Antarctic recognise first and last this difficulty of bringing it into words. No matter how many sentences we craft to get a meaningful fix on it, its true shape still evanesces before us. We strive on to 'one fight more' but

'the power of the night' is in our face, to cite from Robert Browning's 'Prospice', a Shackleton favourite.[9]

As the *Agulhas II*'s crew repeatedly discovered during the time they spent forcing their way across the (unusually thin) Weddell Sea surface, the great ice does not cooperate readily with our efforts to probe its secrets. Their near-miss failure to locate the vessel in 2019 also speaks to that resistance, which had to do not only with equipment breakdown, but also the drift of the ice back in 1915. When Worsley had calculated the coordinates of the *Endurance*'s sinking, he had used longitude tables of temporal reference numbers and the expedition's last reliable chronometer. No one could have done better, but the numbers had been four miles out.[10] The strong push of the sea ice had sabotaged to the very last the attempt to locate the ship.

The Farthest South: An Overview

Many writers on Antarctica draw on a vocabulary of the sublime to capture the seeming alienness of the continent to our human concerns. Writing in the 1980s, the environmental historian Stephen Pyne influentially called the continent a 'wasteland for imaginative literature'.[11] In this century, the countervailing factors of the climate emergency and increased tourism have prompted more writers to respond to the icy immensities. In the high southern latitudes,

Joy McCann observes, 'Ice is the language of the ocean and land'.[12] Even so, for the scholar Elizabeth Leane, the continent is still widely considered an 'underworld': 'it suggests the monstrous, the infernal, the Satanic'.[13] Little seems to have changed since Georg Forster, the scientist who accompanied James Cook on his second voyage, wrote off nature on the 'southern extremities' as gloomy and debased.[14] The attempt to 'achieve the southern continent' filled even Cook's mind 'with horror'. Getting 'in amongst' the ice, he wrote at 71° South, was something that 'no man in [his] situation would have thought of'.[15] The strangeness of the ice world comes through, too, in the Māori legend of the explorer Tama-rereti, who, sailing south from Te Waipounamu (South Island), encountered 'ghostly streamers in the sky' and ice cliffs that defied human footing. (Thereafter, as we saw earlier, he sailed his waka on into the dark constellation of the Coal Sack in the Southern Cross, into the very depths of the south).[16]

Antarctica makes a stark contrast to the images of southern lands and waters in earlier chapters—and this applies whether it is written up by southerners or northerners. Highest, driest, coldest, windiest, remotest continent—however you look at it, contradiction defines it. It is isolated from us yet connected to us; ancient yet endlessly renewing itself; a continuous ice shield that is everywhere crevassed; a constant-seeming blankness yet one perpetually changing.[17] And these metamorphoses are also taking place at many different scales. The time zones converge here, yet physical forces disperse and spread.[18] Katabatic winds drive the solid ice shield off the continent, in all directions, though the interior itself is wind-still. Over the aeons, snow has accumulated and covered the continent, including the mountains, with a thick sheet of ice constantly moving from the pole to the coast. The rocks are unmarked by greenery yet imprinted with fossilised 'plant impressions . . . beautifully traced leaves in layers', in Scott's words.[19] Over-winterers report that time here ceases to have meaning: a day can feel eternal; so, too, an hour.[20]

For centuries, the icy landmass was geographically nowhere—'little but a vague notion'.[21] Though the continent is now inhabited throughout the year, mostly by scientists in research stations, the majority of the world's people do not go there.[22] To the environmental historian Erica Nathan, the place is 'an essentially uninhabitable, geographical outlier' that defies designations.[23] The American novelist Jonathan Franzen has called the landmass 'the end of the end of the earth'.[24] Ursula Le Guin, in her pathbreaking science fiction, *The Left Hand of Darkness* (1969), gave perhaps the starkest description of the ice: 'that silent vastness . . . said in enormous letters of black and white DEATH, DEATH, written right across a continent'.[25] The sense of never quite reaching ultimate south-ness comes to a head on the ice and takes the shape of what I will call asymptotic thinking—a special, degree-zero form of southern imagining that pushes the parabolic figures of previous chapters to the edge of conceivability.

Antarctica is also white—a truism that bears political as well as the more obvious connotations. It is white not only in the sense of being unmarked and pure, 'not yet . . . snared in a [catalogue] of designations and coordinates, of metes and bounds'.[26] It is also tagged white in a colonial and racial sense. In the nineteenth and twentieth centuries, European powers vied to put their expansionist stamp on this last frontier. So-called heroic age white explorers from Britain, France, the United States, and Australia approached the continent as a prize destination through which to define imperial and national honour. It was turned into a place of existential striving and not yielding, to quote the words of Tennyson's 'Ulysses', which feature on the cross erected over the Scott team's cairn.[27] Till the third millennium, Antarctica continued to be a primary ground for what Lisa Bloom describes as a muscular performance of white masculinity. Endeavours on the continent have remained overwhelmingly 'gendered and racialised'—and, it is important to add, north-dominated.[28]

Probes into Antarctica counterpointed the so-called penetration of the dark continent, Africa, in the same period, though the initiatives had very different political outcomes. The quest to reach the South Pole for decades was the ultimate mark of exploratory valour, though admittedly one that was often science-led as well as political in motivation.[29] It may seem obvious but is nonetheless telling that Amundsen and Scott planted their *national* flags at the pole in January 1913. In 1959, these colonialist initiatives were paused with the signing of the Antarctic Treaty, which 'suspended all sovereignty claims', and promoted international cooperation.[30] However, it remains significant that no African nation bar one has a presence in the white—and South Africa's connection dates back to the apartheid era.[31]

Yet, though Antarctica has historically been of interest to a relatively small number of countries, the southern polar region is vital to the survival of us all. To begin, this driest place on Earth contains no less than 95 percent of the earth's frozen water. In less than a century's time, it is likely to be the only year-round ice on Earth. Then there are its links with the climate worldwide. Though the meteorological entity of Antarctica forms a self-enclosed realm, isolated by the vortex of the Southern Ocean, those same mighty currents, even as they insulate the continent, power oceanic circulation around the planet.[32] Should the Antarctic ice sheets begin to degrade at an even more significant rate than at present, the impact on these circulatory pulses would be catastrophic, to say nothing of the knock-on effect for temperatures everywhere. And the physics of ice melt means that the process, once started, would only keep accelerating.[33]

This ultimate geophysical elsewhere is not so external as it might appear, therefore—the more so for the more proximate southern landmasses. South-facing countries perhaps recognise more acutely than most the continent's connections with the wider planet. Fossilised plant impressions and shared glacial striations testify to how it formed a puzzle piece of Gondwanaland alongside the other southern landmasses. Today, from Argentina and Chile, through South Africa, to Australia and New Zealand, Antarctica is a shared horizon. Appreciably affecting weather patterns, especially in winter, the Southern Ocean engirdles as much as separates. In this sense, the Antarctic region gives the measure of the hemisphere. It is a core where southern imaginings converge and crystallise.[34]

The southern lands configure these significations differently, of course. Australia, the closest 'geological cousin', often pictures itself as a counterpart to Antarctica, as a great red desert land balanced against a white.[35] Despite Antarctica's seeming peripherality to Africa, South Africa nonetheless recognises that the white continent is 'determining for its future'. Though till recently the only African country with Antarctic scientific and strategic interests, South Africa may be joined in years to come by Namibia, whose desert valleys, too, the Gondwanaland glaciers have hollowed out.[36] Meanwhile, for the southern cone of South America, the great ice is not so much a world apart as a proximate subsidiary, a kind of next-door. As Leane and Wainschenker observe, national claims go so far as to project primitivist stereotypes onto the region. Hispanophone literatures of the far south often also see the sub-Antarctic islands in archipelagic terms, with the Drake Passage 'acting not as a barrier between two opposed regions, but connecting landscapes with shared features'.[37] The image recalls Epeli Hau'ofa's concept of the archipelago as bracketing dispersed yet interrelated island experiences.

The question of connectivity runs like cracked glass—or ice—through the literary writing about Antarctica that the rest of this chapter is concerned with. These poems, fictions, and other narratives offer ways of understanding its extremity and our relationship to it. The writing accommodates the ice to our human frameworks of perception. For Leane, 'Antarctica's meaning for humans lies in the stories we tell about it'—but the word 'tell' in her sentence is as moot as is the 'we'.[38] For northerners, the challenge of southern inhabitation—how to apply language to unfamiliar space—here becomes absolute. Southerners equally experience this challenge, though the demand of representing the Antarctic without merely giving a 'cartographically inverted version' of the Arctic is perhaps more pressing.[39] Comprehending the cold continent's salience to the rest of the far south is fundamental to shaping a southern heuristic. It also affords a means of imagining *across* the south. But for both southerners and northerners, the truth of the extreme south appears to recede endlessly before any attempt to describe it. The efforts to symbolise forwards, into the unknown, that chapters 2 and 3 considered, are here constantly threatened with nullity and extinction. This evasiveness of the far south will later be captured in the mathematical figure of the asymptote—imagined as a line tending ever closer to the continent, yet without ever touching it.

My readings open with two southern writers, the New Zealand poets Chris Orsman (1996) and Bill Manhire (1999). Though southern hemisphere writing, like that of the north, necessarily emerges from outside the ice, the poets both see the far south as refracted through their own southern landscapes—in Manhire's case, his province of Southland itself. Writing back to failed journeys to the pole, Orsman and Manhire confront experiences of disorientation and absurdity on the ice, and meditate on their meanings. As Manhire observed after a residency in Antarctica, to many New Zealanders, possibly to all South Islanders, 'Antarctica is a sort of psychic territory', 'akin to the desert interior for Australians', an area 'just' beyond the Southern Ocean, and a central part of people's inner geography:

> It's entirely possible that most New Zealanders know or have met someone who has been to the Antarctic—this wouldn't be true in any other country, even Australia or Argentina or Chile. . . . More New Zealanders have died in Antarctica than people of other nationalities.[40]

My perspective then shifts north, to the British writers Beryl Bainbridge and Jon McGregor's novels about researchers on the ice. Bainbridge's *The Birthday Boys* (1991) fictionalises, from the vantage point of the late twentieth century, Scott's second attempt on the pole. McGregor's *Lean Fall Stand* (2021) recounts a disastrous geophysical survey and its aftermath set somewhere in the early new millennium, yet one equally shaped by ambition and miscommunication. In both novels, the continent inflicts scientific visitors whether novices or returnees with crippling feelings of inadequacy and inarticulacy. Indicatively, both Orsman and McGregor consider Antarctic voyagers' attempts to give perspective to the vast landscapes through scale-framing, or by placing figures in the foreground—famously so in the case of Orsman's historical subject, the photographer Herbert Ponting; fatally so for McGregor's fictional group.[41] Such efforts to draw lines around the continent's immensities form another distinguishing mark of Antarctic writing.

Finally, in her compelling travelogue, *Skating to Antarctica* (1997), Jenny Diski meditates on the difficulty not of getting away from the continent but of approaching it, in the opposite direction to McGregor's protagonist, Doc Wright. Contemporary with the New Zealanders' work, Diski's travelogue is consummately asymptotic, tracing the process of sailing to but (possibly) never quite reaching the ice—a trajectory that she develops into a metaphor of partial recovery from childhood abuse. Gathered together, these readings might be imagined as a cluster of intersecting perspectives on the far south embedded at the centre of the book—perspectives that also form a vertex around which the other chapters move. Its arc extends through time from the mythic and still-ongoing past, in chapters 1 and 2, and then on, through the sixteenth and into the nineteenth, twentieth, and twenty-first centuries.

An anticipatory word on the so-called heroic age canon that so obviously moulds many of these writings, northern and southern. The expeditions of Scott (1901–04, 1910–13), Shackleton (1901–04, 1907–09, 1914–17) and Mawson (1911–14, 1929–31), but also James Clark Ross, Roald Amundsen, Richard E. Byrd, and others, undoubtedly comprise an Antarctic master narrative. Many asymptotic associations derive from this dominant story, including from Scott's failure not only to be the first to the pole, but also not to complete the parabola back. Bainbridge and Orsman write within the intertextual warp and weft of his fatal expedition, openly acknowledging their sources, first and foremost, his *Journals*. Manhire's 'Antarctic Field Notes', too, reference the canon, if less faithfully so, while McGregor's protagonist Doc Wright expresses an almost Edwardian pragmatism and commitment to his ice work, both before and after his stroke. And Diski, on her parabolic journey through South Georgia to the Antarctic Peninsula, tips her hat to the 'charmer' Shackleton.[42]

The extent of this deference to the Antarctic master narrative is at times stifling, yet also explicable. In the absence of indigenous representation, it is no surprise that literary writing about the continent draws upon these astonishing tales as models. That travellers in Antarctica have access to a relatively limited range of roles and reference points further reinforces the grounds of comparison, as Leane and Pyne recognise.[43] The Australian Antarctic historian Tom Griffiths remarks that the early explorers 'established the metaphors of language and experience on the ice. One must voyage with them'.[44]

Interestingly, the figures of Shackleton and Amundsen also surface in works of Antarctic fiction from Argentina and Chile, such as Liborio Justo's 'La borrasca' (1932), or Roberto Fontanarrosa's 'La carga de Membrillares' (1985), though these narratives are often inflected away from the tragic dimensions of the Anglophone urtexts.[45]

Asymptote

'Never have I come so near an end; never has anyone more miraculously escaped', was Douglas Mawson's choked comment on surviving for thirty days alone in wind-torn George V land following the deaths of his two travel companions B. E. S. Ninnis and Xavier Mertz as they explored along the far eastern coastline of the continent.[46]

Nearing an end yet narrowly avoiding it, as did Mawson, and so many other early Antarctic travellers—these fatal and near-fatal connotations of the extreme south are illuminated using the figure of the asymptote, which I take from analytic geometry. An asymptote is a hypothetical straight line that constantly nears a given curve but without ever intersecting with it, even into infinity. Conversely put, the curve might also be seen as constantly tending towards the straight line, but without reaching it. The equation for an asymptote (either vertical or horizontal) is expressed as either $\mathbf{y} = \mathbf{f}(\mathbf{x})$ or $\mathbf{x} = \mathbf{f}(\mathbf{y})$, where the value of x or y extends to infinity without meeting the y or x axis (and so equating to zero).

A geometric figure capturing endless approach and ultimate unattainability seems appropriate in the context—an extension into extremity of the parabolic thinking explored in earlier chapters. There, the parabola operated as a heuristic tool that looped the hemispheres together, or allowed travellers to think of them side by side. But, in the supreme south, parabolic pathways are less utile as interpretative tools, being so often interrupted, broken off, blocked. Incomplete journeys that took the pole as a vertex include not only Scott's pathway in 1912–13, but also his 1901–04 *Discovery* attempt, which also involved Shackleton, to 82° South, and Shackleton's own 1907–09 journey that reached 88° S.[47] And Scott, Wilson, and the others' remains are currently tracing another yet-to-be-completed trajectory as they sink with infinitesimal slowness from where they were buried on the Beardmore Glacier, through the ice to the sea, as captured in Robert Law's differential equation and diagram that heads this chapter. In human time, this line, too, might be seen as asymptotic. The bones are still very far from being expelled into the water.

Convergence without ever crossing; a limit that is ever more narrowly approached yet never quite reached—the mathematics of the asymptote pulls together the semiotics of being in Antarctica. The figure encompasses but also exceeds ideas of the sublime—of that which inspires mixed awe and terror.[48] It reminds us that while the polar world invites utopian metaphors of extremes, it also overwhelms such images. Here, claims to haecceity fail. Deixis, the reference to the specificities of here and now, slips. Antarctica's blankness has a way of erasing the vocabulary used to describe it. 'In all the world', writes Alfred Lansing, 'there is no desolation more complete than the polar night. It is a return to the Ice Age—no warmth, no life, no movement'.[49] As a figure of approximation, the asymptote also helps to denote some of these seemingly impossible physical realities of Antarctica—of the massive ice sheet that slides over mountains, of the capricious never-quite-vanishing sea ice at the edge of the ice shelf, 'neither land nor sea, but something else entirely'.[50] Above all, perhaps, the function captures what the Australian writer Helen Garner has called 'the unshowable, the unsayable' of the continent.[51]

Read metaphorically, the asymptote embodies an ambiguity. At this point, we need to remember that there are two main elements at play, the line and the curve, both running to infinity. And two elements are designated, the human observer and the continent. But in any Antarctic situation, and in writing about the far south, it is often unclear who represents what, or what whom. The line might be the human interpreter, endlessly trying to comprehend the continent, which equates to the curve. That is the most obvious reading. But the line might also be the continent itself, always inclining in some way towards us, if only we had the means to comprehend it. The first reading relates to many of the situations we have encountered thus far: the (especially northern) traveller or explorer frantically attempting to reach a southern truth. The reversed reading, by contrast, is more elemental and may recur more frequently later in the book, as writers begin to recognise and reflect on what the far south needs to teach us. It recalls us to Adamastor in chapter 3, resisting the sailors' incursion into his waters, yet sorrowful, too, about being confined to his rock even as he yearns, in spite of his nature, to reach out. He struggles to relay his meaning—a meaning that is at one and the same time about necessity and remoteness, about a vastness that forms an essential part of us that we should not ignore.[52]

The asymptotic line may also be read to signify the conceptual impossibility of death or of conceiving our own end that has frequently confronted

Antarctic travellers, not least Scott's team in their last camp on the Beardmore. In their final journal entries and letters ('preparatory to a possible end'), written with frostbitten hands, Scott and Edward (Bill) Wilson say farewell and consider their legacy, and their handwriting dwindles away emblematically, petering out into parentheses, dashes, stops, starts—and restarts. They cannot quite stop making marks on paper. Wilson to Oriana: 'My own dear wife - goodbye for the present . . . I do not cease to pray for you—to the very last . . .' [parenthesis in text].[53] Or Scott, two days after Oates's death: 'Ill fortune presses but better may come. We have had more wind and drift from ahead yesterday; had to stop marching; wind N.W., force 4, temp. -35. No human being could face it, and we are worn out *nearly* [emphasis in text]'.[54] We might think here of Hamlet's farthest bourn, 'the undiscovered country from whose bourn no traveller returns', widely referenced in nineteenth-century commemorations of Captain John Franklin of the Northwest Passage (*Hamlet* 3.1). Or of Alain Badiou's account of death as radical exteriority, an outside state that the 'programme' of life by definition can never meet.[55] Titus Oates' iconic words before stepping out into the snow—'I am just going outside and may be some time'—assume an asymptotic projection. As he never returned, and his body was never found, he will in one sense always 'be some time'—or, 'In fact, for ever', as the Irish poet Derek Mahon puts it in his villanelle, 'Antarctica' (1985).[56] In some other universe, Oates is always still approaching his icy death, yet never quite reaching it.

From the beginning of Antarctic travel, the weather—the whiteouts, the ice-blindness—produced visionary experiences in travellers already at the end of their tether, experiences that equally signify the almost-here. The sense of the nearly-yet-not-quite slides into Shackleton's experience of the fourth man who appeared to accompany his group, just out of sight, on their walk across mountainous South Georgia on the final leg of rescuing the *Endurance* crew.[57] It also shades through Apsley Cherry-Garrard's sense of haunting while clambering towards Terror Point in *The Worst Journey in the World*: 'I remember having a feeling as of ghosts about'. The sense returns with the strange knocking and tapping he heard at the window of the Cape Evans Hut while waiting with dwindling hope for Scott's South Pole team to return.[58] And it is present, too, in Mawson's description of his solo trek along the Antarctic coastline as 'fighting, always fighting, a terrible unseen force', 'hovering and waiting for a chance to strike'.[59] Having declined to join Scott's team, Mawson went on to lead the Australasian Antarctic Expedition instead

(1911–14), only to find himself, in his turn, facing the death of his companions, and a feeling of encroaching, cosmic threat: 'The winds have a force so terrific as to eclipse anything previously known in the world. We have found the kingdom of blizzards. We have come to an accursed land'.[60] The cursed land image similarly reverberates in the title of Argentine writer Liborio Justo's *La tierra maldita* (1932), set in the archipelagic region of Patagonia, Tierra del Fuego, and the sub-Antarctic islands.

Writing to his wife from Antarctica, Shackleton spoke of sending his 'thoughts over the wasted waters' and willing her to know 'I was thinking of you'.[61] The two central characters in Le Guin's *The Left Hand of Darkness* 'mind-speak' while travelling together across an Antarctica-like ice sheet, though they are of different species: 'intimacy of mind established between us was a bond, indeed, but an obscure and austere one, not so much admitting further light . . . as showing the extent of the darkness'.[62] To a significant number of Antarctic explorers and writers, the white distances of the far south produce such feelings of telepathic, and, again, asymptotic connection—a mode of sympathetic thinking that is sometimes voluntary, and sometimes experienced as a visitation. Telepathy—coordinated imagining together while apart, or thinking in harmony—has been defined by Jacques Derrida as remote proximity—which is how we might also describe how the farthest south signifies to the wider southern hemisphere.[63] Joined-up thinking here affords a way of experiencing the far both directly and indirectly—of being at once remote and yet in touch by synchronisation.

The strong sense of being able to interact with those far away, despite lacking reliable means of communication, is in part a result of the seeming modularity of the Antarctic landscape and weather, and of the feelings of isolation aroused by being there. As Diski writes, everything in the Antarctic region constantly changes, yet remains 'essentially the same, its elements merely rejigged' (*StA* 222–23). For Orsman's Ponting, 'a single image/ of black and white . . . keeps repeating': 'no wonder that he acquires/ a mastery of ice subjects'.[64] Though research teams on Antarctica have had the use of wireless communication since its introduction by the 1912–13 Mawson expedition, magnetic storms constantly threaten these links, and telegraph cables, orbital radio, and sophisticated satellite technology often fail, as they do in McGregor's storm.[65] In this context, ideas of thinking in harmony give comfort. Or, as McCann notices, *bosom* and *heart* are recurring motifs in explorers' diaries.[66]

Antarctic journals and letters are full of their writers' efforts to harmonise their thoughts with loved ones', channelling the other person using shared emotions, activities, and even imagined sightings. Especially when within the same longitudinal zone, individuals try to synchronise using coordinated stargazing, aligning on important days like Christmas and birthdays. Douglas Mawson wrote frequently to his fiancée Paquita Delprat in terms that invited her involvement in a scene or emotion (his 'exultation' at being on the ice), or that imagined warm feelings or words flowing from her 'far distant' world to his: 'It is many days since last writing; though, and you may have felt it too, our verbal chats have been often enough'.[67] Bill and Oriana Wilson fostered a kind of reciprocal thinking in their letters by way of observations on the natural world, especially birds, expanding upon an interest that they already held in common. Wilson's letters to Oriana from the Antarctic, on both of Scott's voyages, were decorated with illustrations of birds, as if to summon her presence through the medium of the images.[68] Bainbridge's fictional Oates says of Oriana that she 'is apparently in accord with [Bill's] soul'.[69]

Connection is also established with the use of shared objects and photographs. Mawson marks a 'spot' in a letter to Paquita, noting that he has kissed it, and 'dreaming that it is near your heart'. The deeply religious Wilson was carrying family mementoes in his pockets when he died, as itemised in a final letter to Oriana:

> Your little books . . . will be in my hand or in my breast pocket whenever the end comes—I have the little silver crucifix tied to the Holland cover—your photos are in these books—they have been well used and a very great joy to me [. . .] Dad's little compass and mother's little comb and looking glass are in my pocket—all is well dear.[70]

These cherished things were for him a channel into the afterlife, where he was sure they would meet again. On occasion, the early explorers felt these moments of connection so intensely, they appeared to produce parallel experiences in the other. In a letter that mentions 'telepathic premonition', Mawson wrote that his father had appeared to him in 'a vivid dream while sledging'. Later correlation revealed that his father may have died at around this same time—a remarkable instance of what he called 'intimacy of mind'. Paquita, in her turn, imagined an answering connection: 'O darling . . . if only nothing is happening to you but I think I should feel it'.[71]

South-South Connectivity

With the meridians converging towards the pole, the great ice is the space where the circles of latitude 'narrow' (to quote Orsman's *South*), and southern meanings concentrate.[72] As the southern lands and islands all share the reference point that is Antarctica, their sense of their own remoteness—and their remote proximity—comes into sharper focus in relation to it. The continent thus becomes a hub through which the different southern landmasses might be said to interrelate, a space where their far south interests intersect. Insofar as these perspectives line up, yet do not always acknowledge their alignment, also bears some reference to asymptotic thinking.

For all of the South-Pole-facing nations, Antarctica is a shared horizon of strategic interest. Five out of the twelve original signatories to the 1959 Antarctic Treaty establishing the use of the continent for peaceful purposes were the southern nations Argentina, Australia, Chile, New Zealand, and South Africa. Not quite 50 percent but a substantial portion nonetheless. All twelve, again including the southern five, had been consultative participants in the International Geophysical Year 1957–8, and in the formation of the Scientific Committee on Antarctic Research in 1948.[73] Closer to the present, the interactive research environment of the continent is daily expressed through communication between these and the other nations' bases, and the scientific collaborations between them. Though many northern nations are involved, all of these links, geographically at least, operate across the south. And the extremities of Antarctic weather mean that the research stations often depend on one another in cases of emergency.

Geological and palaeontological research on the earth's ancient history and the make-up of Gondwanaland has driven Antarctic exploration since the 1890s, and has consistently encouraged scientific exchange within the hemisphere. While Shackleton and Mawson shared thoughts on glaciation and volcanic activity in Antarctica during discussions in Adelaide before the 1907–09 expedition, Mawson and his fellow Australian geologist T. W. Edgeworth David were members of the three-man team who determined the location of the South Magnetic Pole on the same expedition. Both noted the 'intense glacial action' that marked the continent's rocks. It was also Edgeworth David who would draw upon evidence from fossilised penguin bones in Antarctica and New Zealand to suggest that the birds had descended from an ancestor who had inhabited both regions.[74] A trained mineralogist, Mawson was in close communication with geologists in Pretoria, South Africa, about comparative glacial stratigraphy in South Australia and southern Africa. Pre-Cambrian rocks that he had collected in Antarctica were similar to the rocks of the Barrier Ranges. The landmasses had seemingly been scoured by the same glaciers as had Antarctica.[75] Along with other observations, such as of fossilised trees on Kerguelen Island and of the *Glossopteris* fossils Bill Wilson found on the Beardmore, this evidence would help formulate the theory of the Gondwanaland supercontinent. Continuing these south-south links, ozone hole research and investigations into gravity waves across the past five decades or so have also involved intensive transnational collaborations between scientists working on and located in Antarctica.

Everywhere in the far south, Antarctica is a shaping climatic force, the place where the weather comes from. Even from the point of view of southern Africa, the most northern of the southern extremities, the stark, pale sky over the southern horizon in winter is a well-known source of cold fronts. This perception includes Namibia, whose vast coastline is swept by the cold Benguela current from Antarctica, and whose weather is almost entirely determined by it. Or, relatedly, as Douglas Mawson wrote when arguing for the establishment of a wireless base on the white continent: 'The bearing of Antarctic meteorology on Australian weather is apparent to all'.[76] Therefore, it followed that the then British dominions of New Zealand, Australia, and South Africa should collaborate in meteorological research 'for the benefit of the world at large'.[77] Jan Smuts, the 1930s South African Prime Minister, agreed, noting Antarctica's shaping effect on rainfall across the African sub-continent, and hence its special interest to the apartheid state's farming economy. An ecological holist, he lobbied for his country to play a key role in the arena of sub-Antarctic science.

Writers across the south share in this strong sense of Antarctica's relative proximity. Of the 'next stop' being Antarctica. Or, alternatively, of Antarctica as the epitome of southern remoteness, the limit case for understandings of the farthest south. As northern cultures have the pole star, they claim this utterly distant yet shared point of reference, as Randolph Stow already did in the epigraph above. Writing from Western Australia, Tim Winton describes how the southern sky's 'granite clarity' seems to go on forever, all the way to Antarctica.[78] For the New Zealand novelist Janet Frame, her native South Island's 'nowhereness' correlated with her own sense of existential isolation, as we will see again. Her autobiographical first novel, *Owls Do Cry*, and her autobiography *To the Is-land*, take Antarctica with its looming 'snow light' over the ocean as a symbol for this remoteness. The character Chicks reminisces about looking up at the autumn sky, and feeling the sudden chill: 'And then a cloud would cross the sun and we would shiver for the blocked warmth, and it would seem as if there had never been a sun, as if we had lived always in cold'.[79] Hailing from the South Island, like Frame, Bill Manhire, too, takes a view of Antarctica as both neighbourly or at least proximate, and yet alien. In his hometown of Invercargill, New Zealand's southernmost city, he was always aware that 'the next stop across the water is the ice'.[80] Though their sense of 'the tyranny of distance' oppresses all New Zealand writers, he claims, the perception is especially strong for South Islanders, confronted as they are by the cold eye of the continent staring from just over the horizon.

On Not Articulating the Ice: Orsman, Manhire, Bainbridge, McGregor, Diski

The effort by literary writers to capture in language something of a place that has not been originally named by human inhabitants but only had language brought to it bears unmistakable asymptotic features. 'One feels "the dearth of human words, the roughness of mortal speech"'—Shackleton invoked Keats to translate the sense of the 'things intangible' that accompanied him on his thirty-six-hour march across South Georgia.[81] For Cherry-Garrard, his journey to locate Scott's last camp 'had beggared our language: no words could express its horror'.[82] From these canonical voices onwards, Antarctic poetry and prose have been intensely preoccupied with the struggle to express something true about the ice, even while the continent remains elusive. All of the work presented here—the time-bound longer forms of fiction and life-writing, especially, but also the probing lines of the poetry—brings Antarctica to mind by dwelling in its paradoxes of ever-receding farness, and, as Diski writes, of its 'motionless flux' (*StA* 222–3).

Chris Orsman's *South* comprises fifty-one poems divided into five parts, framed by two short prose memoirs, 'The Polar Raffle' and 'The Glory Room'.[83] The poems follow the incomplete parabola of Scott's journey to the pole, from 'Getting There' (Spring 1910) and 'Landing' (Summer 1911), through 'The First Winter' (Autumn and Winter 1911), to 'South' (Spring and Summer 1911–12). The fifth part, 'Heading for Home' (Summer and Autumn 1912), closes with 'The Last Tent', a gathering together of Bill Wilson's final delirious thoughts of 'colonies preserved in beloved capes' and skuas in flight. First published in New Zealand before Orsman's 1998 Antarctic residency, *South* appeared in a revised and expanded edition in 1999, offering a second take on the 'beached light /—polar, clear, stark, white' of that journey ('Forelands', *S* 55).

As Orsman explains in his author's note, *South* is threaded through two main intertexts or 'documentary materials' that made a profound impression on him growing up: one is *Scott's Last Expedition*, which carried a special resonance in his family's history; the other visual, *The Great White South*, by the expedition photographer, Herbert Ponting. Ponting's film *90° South* further amplified for Orsman the 'pristine' images of a 'timeless world in miniature' suggested by these sources—images that several of the poems recreate (*S* 106). Referencing also Shackleton's *South*, Orsman's title locates his work squarely within the genealogy of Antarctic writing. Individual poems have related austral touchstones that we may remember surfaced earlier in this book. *South*'s first epigraph on the 'terrors' of the polar ice is from Livingston Lowes; the poem 'The Polar Lottery' cites *Frankenstein*; and there are noticeable references to Pyne's *Ice* (*S* 18, 72). Meanwhile, lines from the gloss to *The Rime of the Ancient Mariner* preface five poems in the first section, and one in the second, so marking the stages of *Terra Nova*'s journey south towards its ostensible 'native country' of the South Pole (*S* 81).

While the *South* poems, taken as a whole, offer views on the far south mainly as seen from the perspectives of Ponting and Scott, when read sequentially, the collection follows the camera's eye as the party progresses stage-by-stage 'toward the south pole' (Coleridge's gloss is explicitly cited, *S* 16). In

'Getting There', they leave Port Chalmers, meet the 'ocean's turmoil' at the Roaring Forties, approach 'the imaginative boundary / of the South', and cross the Antarctic Circle ('Into the "Fifties"', 'The Terra Nova in a Gale', 'The Ice Navigator', *S* 13–15, 16–17, 20, 23). The Part 2 'Landing' poems record the expedition's various 'autographs' on the snow—the camp's clutter, the 'press' of the men's snow boots. Thereafter, 'The First Winter' forms a mini-series recording the 'descent' into polar darkness broken only by match flares, magic lantern slides, and dreams of home. In 'South', the 'summary horizon' draws the men on, but then, as the references to omens and 'void' ambitions have anticipated, finally arrests their dreams. The 'black dot' of Amundsen's tent cancels the 'reward of priority' ('The Tent', *S* 84–5).

The *South* poems are almost without exception strongly visual, at times explicitly ekphrastic, referencing Frans Hals and J. M. W. Turner, alongside cubist minimalism. Often 'flashlit', scaled by silhouette and vertical lines, the poems explicitly turn around the 'axis' that is 'the fixed eye of the kinematograph' (*S* 28)—as well as of Ponting's camera. Several poems about the southbound ship's journey are closely matched to the graphic imagery in Scott's *Journals*, such as his descriptions of being caught in the icepack.[84] Poems pitched from the viewpoint of the devoutly Christian Bill Wilson are infused with religious feeling, intimations of second comings, and the Resurrection. As if composing marginalia to Scott with the help of Coleridge, the collection is unapologetic about requiring this scaffolding of archival image and script, fore-memory and back-reference, as a way 'to negotiate / the ice savanna's obliterating text' ('The Blizzard', *S* 74–6).

The element that elevates *South* above mere poetic reportage, however, is how the constituent poems themselves work as means to read or, more properly, picture the continent. Instead of attempting to see the ice anew, they rather approximate in line and language the 'new world of enraptured seeing' that Ponting and Scott recorded (*S* 55). All of the poems, bar two, comprise two-line stanzas of variable free verse (mostly ranging between tetrameter and hexameter).[85] These thin, often run-on stanzas serve in ways similar to the various 'long-nosed' instruments that feature in 'Forelands'—the drills, gnomons, and, of course, cameras that the explorers use to 'interpret the visible surface of things' (*S* 53–5). The arterial lines prod the sastrugi here, extend toward the 'magnetic' horizon there, probing 'the architecture of the ice'. When we reach 'The Pole', towards the end of Part 4, Scott's entire body is equated to a 'prosthetic' reaching out to the 'abstraction' of 90° S where the lines of longitude meet, and all directions lie north.

Gradually in 'South', or Part 4, and then definitively in 'Heading for Home', these probes begin to come apart. 'Our rhetoric undoes itself': the poems run up against cliché and set-piece description, or vanish into delirious, dreamlike visions of interplanetary worlds beyond the ice (*S* 91).[86] 'Chums' is no more than a vertically arranged list of the dead dogs' names, a pole-shaped epitaph rather than a probe (*S* 79). 'Akeldama' (a biblical field of blood) pictures the slain ponies' viscera on the ice (*S* 80). There is, predictably, no culmination point to the journey, no moment of final achievement, though 'The Tent', situated at the pole, ends with a brief vision of the pristine polar plateau as 'entirely [the explorers'] own' (*S* 84–5). In 'Turning Back', the faint signs on the snow they encounter are their own dropped belongings, the detritus of the pole-bound journey rising back up to meet them (*S* 91–3). At the last, their sense of vision fails them, their eyelids are 'not adequate to the glare'. The 'light of the south' shrivels and obliterates their bodies, completing the work of frostbite, cold, and 'incessant wind' ('Subtle Dangers', *S* 96–7).[87]

Huts filled with Edwardian foodstuffs; two adjacent poems about skuas eating penguins, unabashed masturbation, exclamations of 'Wow! History! Fantastic!'—Bill Manhire's poetry on Antarctica in 'Antarctic Field Notes', by contrast with Orsman, is informal and personal, at times even irreverent, in keeping with the notational, sometimes offhand style of his other work ('The Hut', 'Evans', 'Some Frames', 'Visiting Mr Shackleton').[88] Yet it is also openly in awe of the white. In response to the 1998 residential trip he took together with his compatriot poet, Manhire produced several works about the ice—*These Rough Notes*, a multimedia collaborative performance, the anthology *The Wide White Page* (2004), and these further 'Antarctic Field Notes' with their titular nod to Scott's phrase from the last sentence of his journal ('these rough notes and our dead bodies must tell the tale').[89] Taken together, Manhire's poems sketch a largely silent soundscape etched here and there by voices on the field phone, a shout going up, the helicopter clattering (*AFN* 265, 267, 269, 271). On the white page, the spare auditory landscape finds its visual complement in the tiny speech acts or 'little shivers of language' that comprise the poems, tenuously linked, here and there, by occasional repeating lines (*AFN* 262, 263, 270, 273, 281).

To address the problem of giving the 'white all the time' expression, 'Antarctic Field Notes' largely avoids the grand frameworks of the well-known heroic legends and their accompanying iconic imagery ('Forecast', *AFN* 273). 'Visiting Mr Shackleton', for example, is made up only of quotations from a presumed Cape Royds visitor's guest book (*AFN* 277). The first line of 'Evans' is 'Another hut filled with food' (*AFN* 278). Manhire elects to mix the banal and the timeless. *Plein air* observations on Antarctica today (the scientific research but also the tourist presence) interleave with quick, glancing reflections on its deep past, not omitting the thick guano layers the penguins roost upon. His description of *The Wide White Page*—that he wanted it to be 'impure and ambiguous and equivocal in all the ways that I enjoy the world being'—also applies to his own ice poetry. Short poems like 'Time Lapse' and 'Song', but also the longer, composite poems like 'Hoosh' or 'Some Frames', themselves made up of fragments, together give an incidental, provisional impression. Yet, by pausing and noticing, these 'field notes' nonetheless let slip something of the wonder and majesty of the icescape—the 'shadowed edge of an iceberg' that captures a second look ('Cape Royds', *AFN* 269–70); 'always the one event of the wind' ('Forecast').

Despite their occasional 'impurity', Manhire's poems converge with Orsman's in their attention to Antarctica's timelessness, especially in 'Hoosh', the longest poem in the collection, and in the repeated references elsewhere to Mt Erebus 'going up' (*AFN* 253–60, 273, 281). 'Hoosh' interleaves three strands of time, 'scientific Antarctica, heroic-age Antarctica, and tourist Antarctica', that are connected through the ice-core drilling of a named scientist, red-haired Emily. As the drill penetrates the polar archive, the layers of summer and winter ice built up across millennia, it releases images like bubbles of ancient air—'samples and traces', endless lists, lines from journals, a mishmash recipe for the titular hoosh or hooch (the explorer's staple of pemmican and fat). The modern vertical probe extracts deep-time spectres, tracing 'ghost of a dog, ghost of a pony, / Oates going deeper and deeper / below the surface'. Yet, as we have come to expect, no matter how deep the drill goes, there is ultimately no 'beneath' to the ice-core—the Antarctic depths have no end, the farthest south lacks an outer edge. As the penultimate stanza observes, Oates and the dogs are still and forever 'gone for some time' (*AFN* 260).

Indeterminacy and open-endedness are also the keynotes of Beryl Bainbridge's Antarctic novel *The Birthday Boys,* a reflection in five testimonial parts on Scott's *Terra Nova* journey and his disastrous attempt on the pole. The novel convenes a forum whereby each of the five men involved in that final push—Birdie Bowers, Taff Evans, Wilson, Oates, Scott himself—narrate a month-long section of the journey. Each traveller notes, as if in passing, their or others' birthdays that fall in the time period, while at the same time recording the many harrowing, near-death experiences that build to the final end on the Beardmore Glacier. The birthday motif clusters the five together in a timeless pattern, connecting them through these life events as well as in their death.

In Elizabeth Leane's reading, Bainbridge's 'prismatic technique' allows different perspectives on the classic story to emerge, without any one reading being favoured.[90] Cumulatively, however, the travellers' missteps and miscalculations along the way expose the crazy hubris and suicidal lack of forethought that marked the expedition. The team's craven mentality of self-sacrifice—Scott to his wife: 'I will reach the South Pole, or I will never come back again'—produces as an almost foregone conclusion the death of all five (*BB* 41). The number five itself—one too many men to survive on the rations that they could man-haul across the ice—encapsulates Scott's unrealistic drive to succeed. In effect, *The Birthday Boys* implies, on the day the pole team set out, their fate was sealed. The compulsion to seek out extremity, no matter the cost, induces a sustained meditation across the five testimonies on the lethal Edwardian and imperialist ethic of heroic self-sacrifice, for which Antarctica served as the supreme testing ground. Scott's belief that 'cowardice is worse than death' is only matched by Wilson's 'delight in annihilation' (*BB* 91, 157).[91] (In other Antarctic explorers, of course—Roald Amundsen, Ernest Shackleton—the ice engenders quite the opposite reaction, the hellbent will to survive, but this mentality does not harmonise in the same way with longings for oblivion that the continent induces in some—the state of mind that also fascinates Diski.)

The ironic motif of the birthday crystallises the team's collective do-or-die ethic. Start-of-life days are noted even as the men move inexorably closer to their end. Oates, who has the final story, walks out of the tent on his birthday—his awareness of the date closes the novel, and circles back to already-recounted memories of his twenty-first birthday party, which was delayed by his time serving in the Anglo-Boer War (*BB* 157). Other birthday moments are more incidental. Wilson remarks on 'an impromptu dance' on the deck of the *Terra Nova* under the stars in celebration of his thirty-eighth birthday. As his story closes, the southern rollers 'sickeningly' lift the ship, jolting Bowers into remembering that it's his birthday, too (*BB* 54, 74).

Though birthdays are 'hardly our first priority', in Scott's words, the motif is unmistakably asymptote-like (*BB* 82). Birth self-evidently represents a reverse trajectory to the deaths to which the men are committed, yet both processes involve the non-convergence of existence and its 'outside', as Badiou reminded us. Relatedly, even as the explorers' determinedly head towards finality, they are caught up in emotions and activities that will ensure their ever-elongating, asymptotic separation from it, at least in the minds of the reading public—through the immortality of writing, in Scott's case; through belief in the afterlife, in Wilson's; and through the undying reputation secured by his final disappearance from the tent, in Oates'.

Other states of 'almost' and 'not-quite' reinforce the novel's—and polar history's—predominant asymptotic thread—Scott's failure to achieve the ultimate prize of reaching the pole first. To give only a sample—the bond between Scott and Evans is soldered during a near-death experience together on the 1902 *Discovery* expedition, when, after falling down a crevasse, they become suspended 'between . . . being there and being gone' (*BB* 4–5). On this trip, the *Terra Nova* is leaky and, from the time the ship leaves England, requires continual pumping, leaving it suspended between floating and sinking (*BB* 18, 90). On South Trinidad Island in the South Atlantic, the crew attempts a near-disastrous landing, almost losing a teammate. Subtending the entire journal is Scott's endless litany of 'infernal bad luck', as also in his journal—his complaints about the foundering of the ponies, the ice breaking up, and 'those blasted motors' that froze soon after they were offloaded (*BB* 75, 82, 97). After this, the devastating sight of Amundsen's flag at the pole reads like something long anticipated. They have reached the southernmost point, yet have been preceded: 'our fearful labours had been for nothing' (*BB* 171).

Jon McGregor's novel *Lean Fall Stand* turns from the heroic past to the more mundane yet still storm-wracked polar present. As the triptych title suggests, the novel is divided into three parts, plus a short coda '/ _ |' that brings together the punctuation marks that have entitled the other three sections. The lines clearly inscribe a broken parabola. 'Lean /' recounts from an omniscient perspective the geophysical survey trip by a British team of three to a remote Antarctic station, 'K', and the stroke suffered by the main character, Robert 'Doc' Wright, a technical assistant, during a violent storm. The storm claims the life of a younger colleague, Thomas Myers, while Wright is left with aphasia, from which he does not fully recover. 'Fall _', the longest section, narrated from the point of view of Anna, Wright's wife, an oceanographic modeller, follows the process of his repatriation and partial recovery, as the demands of caring as well as interpreting for him take over her life. 'Stand |', only a little longer than 'Lean /', covers the work of an aphasia support group, which Robert joins. The section culminates in a drama show in which he is given the opportunity to retell the story of the storm: 'Bang! Bang! Here. My knees. Storm come. Push. Push me. To my knees' (*LFS* 266). This then leads into '/_|', which places Robert back in Antarctica in the immediate aftermath of the storm, understanding that something is wrong, yet unable to articulate it: 'His lack of words was so absolute that he couldn't quite fathom what was lost' (*LFS* 275).

Only the first part of *Lean Fall Stand* is directly about the Antarctic, yet the unending struggle to give the continent expression pervades the novel to the end. As for the New Zealand poets, the work is based on McGregor's experience of visiting Antarctica, in his case as part of a 2004 collaboration between the Arts Council and the British Antarctica Survey. However, it was many years before he was able to find a story to give shape to what he had observed: 'There weren't the words' (*LFS* 60). His sense of the inadequacy of language to deal with the continent became 'the stimulus for an extended investigation of what happens when words go missing', as is evident in the novel from the moment the storm strikes.[92] The men try to establish radio contact, but catch no more than the fragmentary phrases of each other's speech. Wright's increasingly confused stream-of-consciousness then takes over: 'He rawed the rum nubness of his face. No. Rubbed. Rubbed the rum rawness. No. Radio' (*LFS* 64, 65, 73).

Lean Fall Stand ponders our dependence on, yet separation from others, as expressed in the demands of care and the discipline of healing. Above all, though, it is centred in the 'the unsayable' of Antarctica itself, which impacts the lives even of those who have never visited, like Wright's wife. The novel's opening is emblematic of this always-doomed attempt to capture the vastness. To give a sense of 'the way things really were', the three men use photographic scale-framing—the technique of placing a figure in the foreground also used by Ponting—but the attempt leads directly to their fateful separation, the continent as ever resisting human efforts to contain and comprehend it (*LFS* 41, 62).[93] The Research Institute's efforts to develop an accurate account of the double accident is similarly doomed, as Doc can neither fully remember what happened nor describe it. His version of events also fails to correlate with that of the third man in the team, Luke Adebayo, who covers for Doc's failure to establish contact with the base. But the inarticulable qualities of the white come through most powerfully in Robert's struggle to speak after his stroke, in his verbal missteps, his blurted phrases. The long-term devotee of Antarctic work is finally part-claimed by the ice, and the thing it takes from him are the means through which he tried to manage it—by using coherent sentences (*LFS* 275).

'That was the point, for me, of Antarctica', Jenny Diski writes, 'that it was simply there, always had been, always would be, with great tracts of the continent unseen, unwitnessed' (*StA* 162). In *Skating to Antarctica*, her travelogue-cum-memoir, Diski seeks out the continent's whiteness as a salving correlative for her lifelong 'passion for oblivion'—her quest for release from memories of her troubled childhood: 'I wanted to *be* there, in a white, empty, unpeopled, silent landscape' (*StA* 225, 121). Brought up by an unstable mother, with whom she has severed contact, and an indigent but charming father, now dead, Diski herself has a daughter, Chloe, who is trying to find out more about their past, against her mother's inclinations. The journey to Antarctica unfolds in complementary parallel to Chloe's voyage of discovery, which Diski tacitly condones even while seeking to put as much distance as possible between herself and England. It is not so much resolution as a lack of signification that she is searching for, an escape from the interpretations that any reconstruction of the past will impose. Her experience has taught her that signs cause pain: 'I wasn't in search of the drama of life and death, but of what there is or isn't before and after. Changeless stuff. Empty stuff. Oblivion.' Like Orsman, she homes in on the work of a far south navigator, in her case, Herman Melville, to help her understand this blankness—or the 'heartless voids' of the universe, in his phrase (*StA* 49, 162).

Diski's memoir is salient here not so much because of her efforts to write up Antarctic space, as it is an open question whether she lands on the continent, but rather for the opportunity it gives her to reflect on what it is to approach and then comprehend extremity. Her determination to reach the ice means equating herself somehow with its whiteness, even while 'life' in the form of her daughter's bathroom clutter, or the presence of her fellow passengers, or the smells of penguin guano, or even the business of writing itself, keeps intruding (*StA* 57). In the end, she finds, all representation is a form of presence and her writing fails to approximate the continent. It remains, like the 'concentrated' and 'pointless' skating of her title, separate from the 'enigmatic' ice (*StA* 18).

The writer's nihilistic longing, if not for the white and for death, then for near-white and near-death, is counterbalanced by the present-day mother-daughter link at the heart of the story—Jenny's living relationship with Chloe, who persists in her search for her grandmother. To the same degree that Jenny seeks out distance, including distance from any recollection of her mother, her daughter strives to knit the maternal genealogy together. Chloe's ambition propels the memoir, the chapters on travelling to Antarctica alternating with those on memory work. In the first 'At Sea' chapter, for example, as the ship crosses the Drake Passage, the rocking motion produces in Diski vertiginous associations of being in utero. This then leads directly on to the chapter concerned with her father's death and mother's disappearance, and the concomitant vanishing of her younger, more innocent self, 'Jennifer' (*StA* 78–82). Cumulatively, the closer she approaches the continent and the more she writes, the deeper she delves into a state of emotional—and conceptual—whiteness.

It is a fitting complement to Antarctica's seeming indeterminacy that Diski's own touchdown on the continent that has been her goal for so long is, finally, also left uncertain (*StA* 180). She will not or cannot say whether she managed in the end to set foot there. The 'imponderable condition' of the white is respected, as is its asymptote-like unreachability (*StA* 29, 30):

> Did I or didn't I get to Antarctica? At that delicious moment I didn't know what the answer would be. . . . Been there, haven't done that. . . . It's a matter entirely between me and myself. Indeed, I could say, back home, that I did, when I didn't. What difference would it make? Or, come to think of it, I could say that I didn't when I did. And once I'd had this thought, it didn't matter whether I actually did or didn't. (*StA* 219)

Diski's journey is left suspended in the never-ending present continuous of 'skating to', not touching down. The truth of her book doesn't 'depend on arriving at a destination. Nor in failing to arrive' (*StA* 220). This same quality of undecidability winds back through the other texts, surfacing in the challenges of scale and comprehension that Orsman and Manhire confront, in the indeterminacy of Oates's death at the end of *The Birthday Boys*, and in the approximations to coherence of *Lean Fall Stand*'s Doc Wright. In any attempt to reach the farthest south, something always intervenes to frustrate closure. Journeys, tracks, and pathways skirt the line leading towards nothingness, but never quite cross it. On the white continent, human achievement is continually almost. Everlastingly not quite. Ninety degrees south remains an abstraction.

Writers' visions of the far south can be imagined as intersecting like longitudinal lines at the pole, sharing themes and obsessions. But where, in the early 1900s, heroic myths predominated, for both hemispheres, more recently, as in *Lean Fall Stand*, the focus has become distinctly antiheroic and more environmentally aware. Especially for southern writers, the Southern Ocean has grown to be an ever-more-present reality, a space making possible pelagic and archipelagic connections between the southern coastlines—as if redrawing lines of attachment between the still-drifting pieces of Gondwanaland.

Recent South African fictions, both literary and speculative, recognise environmental links between the two continents by retracing the pathways of whales and recording the rise of sea levels, as Charne Lavery and Meg Samuelson explore. A key example—to resurface in chapter 7—is Zakes Mda's *The Whale Caller* (2006) in which an interspecies encounter between the eponymous 'whale caller' and his beloved whale 'extends the geography of the novel (and the continent) . . . towards the far south'.[94] The Southern Ocean comes into view as an important mediating environment between Africa and Antarctica.

Meanwhile, South American writing works against the heroic Anglophone grain by creating archipelagic shapes that align or realign sub-Antarctic environments between Argentina, Chile, and Antarctica, as in Justo's previously cited *La tierra maldita*, or Agustín Graham Nakamura's graphic novel *Terra Australis* (2018). Post-millennium Australian fictions like Robyn Mundy's *The Nature of Ice* (2009) or Sophie Hardcastle's *Below Deck* (2020) feature stories of self-recovery and -transformation set against the mirroring background of the ice. In Mundy, heroic age stories of Mawson and Frank Hurley lay down a script in relation to which the protagonist tracks her own shifting loyalties and commitments.[95]

From the northern hemisphere, Catalan author Alicia Kopf's *Brother in Ice* also uses the classic stories of polar exploration as a model for 'intimate journeying'.[96] In the titular story in Claire Keegan's *Antarctica*, its 'miles of snow' raise visions of a cold eternity for a woman facing a humiliating death.[97] Self-projection onto the blank Antarctic canvas, a standard trope but with a chromatic difference, is a guiding motif in Mojisola Adebayo's *Moj of the Antarctica* (2006)—a one-woman play that reflects on the south's inverted meanings, as in the fourth epigraph above. The Black explorer character, Moj, derives feelings of affirmation from how the blackness of Antarctic rock offsets the physical whiteness of the snow—and the racial whiteness of the continent's history.

From Scott's *Journals* to contemporary writing, human journeys to the white continent in these works approach and perhaps even touch down on the ice, but then, as soon as possible, turn back again. The psychic territory of the distant white attracts and repels at the same time. The farthest south is only ever lightly probed, if at all—the Antarctic asymptote denies too close an approach. For all that it is relatively proximate to the lands facing the Southern Ocean, Antarctica remains forbidding even to them—perhaps the more so to those closer by, who must daily face the freezing gales blowing up from beyond the granite horizon. At the same time, its shared imagined reality presents the supreme test case for how to model global connectivity—to conceive of spaces at once remote and hostile, yet crucial for the survival of all life on Earth.

6

'Breaking the Solemn Monotony'

SETTLER CARTOGRAPHIES

Great Southern Land, in the sleeping sun
You walk alone with the ghost of time

—IVA DAVIES (ICEHOUSE), 'GREAT SOUTHERN LAND' (1982)

Round the Peninsula swept the Southern Sea, pale blue and deep green in fair weather, and black in storms; but always, whether in storm or in fair weather, restless and passionate as no other sea on earth is.

—OLIVE SCHREINER, *FROM MAN TO MAN* (1926)

The sky is a wide black paddock, without any fences.
The Stars are its shining logs;
Here, sparse and single, but yonder, as logg'd-up for burning,
Close in a cluster of light.

—BLANCHE BAUGHAN, 'A BUSH SECTION', *SHINGLE-SHORT AND OTHER VERSES* (1908)

Then the karaka-trees would be hidden. And they were so lovely, with their broad, gleaming leaves, and their clusters of yellow fruit. They were like trees you imagined growing on a desert island, proud, solitary, lifting their leaves and fruits to the sun in a kind of silent splendour.

—KATHERINE MANSFIELD, 'THE GARDEN PARTY', *THE GARDEN PARTY AND OTHER STORIES* (1922)

South of my days' circle
I know it dark against the stars, the high lean country
Full of old stories that still go walking in my sleep

—JUDITH WRIGHT, 'SOUTH OF MY DAYS', *THE MOVING IMAGE* (1946)

Up here at night there is a kind of super daylight, high in the sky, as if the dark were clinging closer to the earth under the whip and strike of the sun.

—JANET FRAME, *OWLS DO CRY* (1957)

Reading South

Bill Manhire's sonnet 'Zoetropes' (1985), a love lyric to his native land 'of the long white cloud', spins this chapter on settler pathways from the high north across to the far south, like the optical animation device it names.[1] Arcing from London to the South Pacific, the poem turns the globe through 180 degrees in the process of our reading it. At the start, we see the poet-speaker 'alarmed' at the chance sighting of a letter *z* that always signifies to him New Zealand. Almost immediately, his yearning attention begins to shift along a parabolic path south and east, first across South Asia and the equator, or latitude degree zero—another *z*. Then, in the final third, his eye comes to rest over the cloudscape of his island, anchored in a far corner of the vast Pacific:

The land itself is only
smoke at anchor, drifting above
Antarctica's white flower,
tied by a thin red line
(5000 miles) to Valparaiso.

Each time they are read, I suggest by way of framing this chapter, the fifteen short lines of the poem incline the reader southwards. The sonnet's south-east vector visualises the planet first from above and then from below, as it swoops 'down' to New Zealand, coming to rest above the South Pole, now positioned at the centre of the map. The last line triangulates this southern anchor point by drawing a long latitudinal link across to Chile. 'Zoetropes' resolves into a moving map not merely for the homesick poet, but also here, at the start of this survey of settler cartographies, which, too, will draw looping and latitudinal links across the planet.

A related navigational device directing the reader's attention southwards emerges in Argentine author Jorge Luis Borges's short story, 'El Sur', translated as 'The South', from *Ficciones* (1953).[2] It, too, traces a southerly arc not unrelated to Manhire's speaker's, forging a route due south to pampas flatlands that are enshrined in both memory and fantasy.[3] And it helps to set the numinous yet unmistakable hemispheric tone that this chapter will explore—one that tends across oceans and open country, away from nations and cities, to places seemingly 'fuera del tiempo' ('outside time'), as Borges writes. Though Borges himself is often aligned with a northern canon, his stories about the 'Pampa' of southern Argentina register a profound attraction to its vastness and seemingly infinite regression of space and light.[4]

In the story, the hero, Dahlmann, is consigned to a sanatorium after a strange encounter on the stairs to his Buenos Aires apartment, the *Arabian Nights* in his hands. After a period of treatment, his physician gives him leave to travel to an archetypal 'country house in the South', surrounded by fragrant eucalypts, that he has not visited for many years. He takes the train, carrying with him the same *Arabian Nights*—a book that gave Borges himself the enchanted sense of infinities embedded within infinities. This copy, however, is lacking a few pages—perhaps pages of as-yet-unwritten far southern literature. The protagonist enters what seems like a different realm, a *llanura* or pampas space of 'elemental' solitude, both 'vast and somehow secret', where the train's shadow appears to extend to the horizon. He feels he is travelling 'not only into the South, but into the past', the only place where, he notes, true gauchos still exist, the lands immortalised in national poet José Hernández's epic *Martín Fierro* (1872, 1879).

The train leaves Dahlmann at an unfamiliar station, penultimate to his destination, and he orders a meal at the *almacén* to which he is directed. At his table, still reading the *Arabian Nights*, he again experiences a strange brush to the head, followed by another. This provokes him to a fight, using the naked dagger an old gaucho throws him. Earlier, significantly, he had identified the gaucho as a pure 'symbol of the South—his very own South', that is ('*una cifra del Sur (del Sur que era suyo)*'). He steps outside to face his opponent, feeling neither hope nor fear, aware that, in the sanatorium, this romantic death under the 'open sky' was the joyful end for which he had longed. The story breaks off with a final shift into the present tense, the outcome of the knife fight undisclosed, the ranch farther south unattained. The south that 'belongs to him' will probably remain forever beyond his grasp.[5]

For Borges as for Manhire, the far southern extremities of the planet from whence they both come, take on the substance of a yearning dream. The southern oceans and the continental plains bring up a longing for something that cannot quite be expressed. The two writers join with the others brought together in this chapter in their use of writing itself as a medium through which to establish, even if intermittently and fleetingly, a far southern orientation, a new inclination to the open sky, a different zoetropic spin.

Writing Elsewhere

From the late eighteenth century, European powers colonised temperate southern hemisphere lands through programmes of mass emigration. As the financial axes of empire shifted southwards from the 1830s, following the abolition of Atlantic Ocean slavery, the southern extremities of the world came to be settled by white emigrants in large numbers. In the view of an ever-more-predominant Britain, settlement was the preferred mechanism through which lands deemed empty or populated by assumed-to-be inferior and dying races might be claimed and controlled.

In 1838, the New Zealand Company, directed by the politician and colonial theorist Edward Gibbon Wakefield, dispatched nine ships of colonists to both the North and the South Island. By 1840, 'over 50,000 Britons had emigrated to the Australian colonies as a whole'.[6] They set out believing that the 'climatically benign, and largely empty lands' of the south were theirs for development: the Eastern Cape and Natal in South Africa, Western and South

Australia, and the islands of New Zealand, especially the South Island, as well as the south of South America.[7] While emigrants' experiences of these lands were inevitably conditioned by local circumstances, most settlers grappled with feelings of separation and unfamiliarity, and the sense, as in 'El Sur', that their new country could never be fully possessed, quite against the promotional rhetoric of the emigration companies. In the evocative words of the cartographer Matthew Flinders, Australia was 'a country where the astonished settler sees nothing, not even the grass under his feet, which is not different to whatever had before met his eye'.[8] Like the other southern lands staked out for settlement, it was also an inhabited country, densely threaded through with other networks of belonging.

This chapter considers how the writers who rose from these settler communities—southern-born, yet educated and conversant in European intellectual and perceptual traditions—conceptualised the southern lands and landscapes to which they ambiguously belonged. In particular, it examines the imaginative means through which they came gradually to understand their location within the vast 'water hemisphere' and to turn elsewhere into here.[9] Olive Schreiner, B. E. Baughan, Katherine Mansfield, Benito Lynch, K. S. Prichard, and, later, Randolph Stow, Robin Hyde, Judith Wright, Janet Frame, Patrick White, Christina Stead, J. M. Coetzee, Peter Carey, Gerald Murnane, and many others, their timelines extending across more than a century and a half, differentially share a sense of cultural and literary dislocation—a 'disturbing consciousness of inner disruption, paradox and contradiction', as Angela Smith writes.[10] And, in response, they all seek imaginatively to make the land their own, often by speaking from within that sense of disturbance and paradox, drawing upon experimental techniques that might look northern and derivative were they not at the same time adapted to address local conditions. By and by, as we will see, their writing itself comes to offer an always-provisional, never-quite-sufficient way of inhabiting, in Baughan's words, 'this God-forsaken last end o' nowhere, right the other side of the world'.[11]

So far, this study has considered two modes of southern imagining that have often existed in tension. The first was concerned with the perception of southern space from within, a haecceity bound up with shared experiences of latitude, geology, starry skies, and the relative proximity of the polar continent, Antarctica. The second involved understandings of the far south as limit and the ultimate beyond. The former was observed—if it was observable at all to northerners—through indigenous myth and story, and more recently, forms of southern writing and storytelling. The latter involved seeing southern worlds through the lens of exile—of 'expulsion from Europe to the bottom of the world', in J. M. Coetzee's phrasing.[12]

It is this latter mode that southern settler communities tended to grapple with, at first, their definitions of self and home deriving from linguistic and cultural traditions now lying at a considerable remove from where they stood. Across the south, we see societies caught up in repeat cycles of self-justification in which writers actively participated, ceaselessly reasserting their right to inhabit the countries they now called home. Yet the writers also recognised that their 'new' austral worlds demanded new modes of perception and representation—what Edward Said called 'a struggle over geography'.[13] They saw that their writing here (and their writing *here*) was up against something intractably spatial for which transplanted traditions were not adequate, even when smashed up and remade in the process of being carried across.[14]

'Breaking the solemn monotony' counters readings of Anglophone settler writing for which the reference point is always either the imperial motherland, Britain, or the settler nation, or both, where the latter is often seen as a reduced version of the former. Most settler literary histories tend first to discuss derivation from Britain, and then the emergence of a colonial nationalism whose foundational ideas are once again European and reductive, no matter how interrogative the movement may be. Certainly, till late into the twentieth century, settler criticism took the transplanted template of the European nation as its point of departure. For many writers themselves, even if native-born, for whom cultural crossings were psychic rather than physical, England or Scotland in many ways remained 'home'. Their imaginative models were northern, their cultural loyalties distantly tethered—their writing 'no longer European, not yet [southern]', to adapt Coetzee's terms.[15] As a symptom of this condition, memorial cairns to the war dead across the Anglophone south were designed to point back to England. (Conversely, houses tended to face south, as in England, and so, as Judith Wright describes, 'let in the coldest winds').[16] Southern homelands, therefore, were always doomed to be seen as lesser or inferior versions of Britain, their cultural landscapes as subsidiary.[17] Tellingly, southern spaces will sometimes appear more distant to the writers in this chapter than they were to northern sea-farers like Melville or Darwin.

From the settler anxiety about being secondary, sometimes called cultural cringe, rose the observation, still voiced in southern lands, of their own social, cultural, or geographical features and achievements being the best, the tallest, the most powerful, at least within the hemisphere. Yet, the unstated assumption was that these things were ultimately minor or lesser when compared to their northern counterparts.[18] So the Cape Colony congratulated itself on having the most important observatory in the hemisphere, following its 1820 selection by the British Admiralty as the site of the Royal Observatory.[19] In the realm of geography, to pick only two of many possible examples, contemporary Tasmanian tourist brochures claim that their Cape Huay features the tallest cliffs of any southern hemisphere cape, while the Andes is said to boast the second tallest peak in the world after Everest, Mount Aconcagua.[20] There are also various claims to having the highest skyscraper, the biggest opera house, and so on. Trollope commented on this phenomenon during his Australasian travels back in the 1870s: 'You are told constantly that colonial meat and colonial wine, colonial fruit and colonial flour, colonial horses and colonial sport, are better than any meat, wine, fruit, flour, horses, or sport to be found elsewhere'.[21]

This disjuncture of culture and geography often created split loyalties for writers and artists.[22] Those whose work circulated internationally, yet were native-born, like Schreiner or Mansfield, articulated or were made to articulate complex identities that were often Greater British before they were local. Later writers like Judith Wright prioritised the local and regional over the international and even the national. Yet all were aware of the difficulty of naming and claiming the environment from which they wrote. All were conscious to some extent of 'double belonging', of having to subscribe to formal protocols—of the colonial pastoral, for example—that derived from the north, yet according to which the south always fell short, exposed as incomplete and supplementary.[23]

Many were ill at ease about this displacement from both Home and new homeland. They longed imaginatively to claim their adopted country, no matter how exotic its geography or malign its aspect. Early on, Blanche Baughan attempted to splice her poetic lens to take in both New Zealand's opalescent vistas and its burnt bush. Wright set about reimagining the Aboriginal songs that might have been sung about her family farm Wallamumbi, songs that had now drifted 'down river' but that her 'great-great-grandfather heard . . . with one part of his mind'.[24] Many writers were interested, not coincidentally, in avant-garde approaches and alternative belief systems that questioned the accepted order of things—modernism, socialism, feminism, and Vedantism among them. My readings will consider some of their searches for other levels of perception, or different ways of tilting their imaginative compass.

By the mid-to-late nineteenth century, the nation came to present a compelling means through which to express cultural singularity and combat feelings of exile or 'elsewhere-ness'. Considerations of place and location were increasingly bound up in national questions—not only among the southern settler colonies. The 'image of a people-nation . . . fashioned by a common history' allowed settler communities worldwide, including also in the Americas, to claim a singular character founded on inherited cultural values and a shared emigrant past.[25] The histories of these new nations told unifying stories of emergence. W. K. Hancock's *Australia* (1930), W. H. Oliver's *The Story of New Zealand* (1960), or C. F. J. Muller's *Five Hundred Years: A History of South Africa* (1969)—were all premised on the idea of a transplanted European heritage held in common that erased Black and Indigenous peoples from the scene. Novelists and poets subscribed to 'a strong (if not overwhelming) sense of community' with 'an overarching British tradition', in the words of New Zealand poet Allen Curnow.[26] But what the Australian Henry Lawson called 'the page of the south'—southern space understood on its own terms—was rarely a point of reference, unless as a curiosity or a provocation.[27]

The clear danger was that the troubling spaces where these writers, historians, and other cultural brokers now found themselves might dislodge an imperial world picture in which Britain stood at the centre. The same fears applied when forging connections *between* southern spaces. Ideas of commonality, solidarity, and seriality threatened national claims to singularity and exclusivity. True, southern tags or emblems sometimes served as a shorthand for national identity, as epitomised in the Southern Cross symbol that features in the flags of Australia, New Zealand, and Brazil (and of Tierra del Fuego, where it stands as an expression of Argentine claims to the Malvinas/Falklands).[28] The constellation paradoxically signalled a southern uniqueness though it was unique to no single nation. All the while, however, the longest cultural roots were perceived to lie in Europe, and the strongest ties were with the imperial motherland. Anglophone settler histories formed chapters in 'the larger story of the British Empire', and of the global spread of the Anglo-Saxon peoples.[29]

Even so, by the nineteenth century's end, some writing, especially that stemming from outside the national mainstream, began gradually to register a different orientation. Poets and novelists came to express a new centredness and sense of belonging, even if with borrowed tools, as Frame would eventually do most successfully. Baughan used dramatic monologue textured by local idiom to reflect the day-to-day struggles of remote settler communities. Mansfield, in her later short stories, distilled what she had learned of light-fall and wind-speed in Wellington to recreate her homeland for European readers. This experience transmits into the powerful ellipsis at the end of her story 'The Wind Blows', for example, in which the force of the wind seems to wrench the narrative perspective about-face, so that the closing image bridges land and ocean, past and present (and perhaps north and south, as well).[30]

To depart from the longitudinal hegemony of north over south, it became increasingly important to consider local, specific and sometimes indigenous detail, the surrounding 'flickers of . . . nativeness', in critic Philip Mead's words; 'the essentials of tree and shrub', in novelist Patrick White's.[31] Introducing his *Book of New Zealand Verse* (1945), Curnow defined national reality as 'local and special at the point where we pick up the traces'.[32] Those same traces had taught the turn-of-the-century poet William Pember Reeves (a favourite of Janet Frame's mother) to see his 'lonely' island homeland as both 'drear' *and* 'a citadel free', washed by the 'earth-girdling' Southern Ocean.[33] Judith Wright closed her autobiography *Half a Lifetime* with childhood memories of seeing, or feeling she had seen, almost, the 'true owners' of her part of New England standing in the shadows of the last remaining trees (*HL* 293-6). As late as this century, Fabián Martínez Siccardi speaks of learning to read the Argentine *meseta*, his native terrain, as much more than just a desert—rather as 'an expansive terrain that entrances the mind'.[34]

The readings later in the chapter consider these simultaneous senses of displacement and hereness in the work of selected southern writers active from the later nineteenth century into the mid-to-late twentieth. It is significant, not accidental, that all are women. Often excluded from, and hence less invested in, national projects, closed out of the male worlds of bush and veld unless as symbols, women writers were in a position to explore other modes of imaginative orientation. They were also often freer to negotiate complicated transnational relationships, as in their different ways did Baughan and Mansfield—and also Robin Hyde, Henry Handel Richardson, Christina Stead, and Doris Lessing after them. Hyde found in migratory birds like the golden plover and especially, the godwit an analogy for New Zealanders' ceaseless yearning north to Europe, as well as their psychic journeys homing back south.[35] A decade on, the poet Charles Brasch in 'The Islands (2)' enshrined the departing godwit as the distinctive emblem of an antipodean autumn, drawing out the great distances separating his islands from the rest of the world.[36] His poem's images of leave-taking, murmuration, and the waiting sea would later give Frame an antenna (and a title) through which to remember back to her beloved South Island.

To circumvent the insistent claims of the settler nation, the readings often proceed by indirection and along several tracks, working athwart conventional north-south sightlines. They pick up on vectors and arcs that loop away from the metropolis and across the ocean, where sky, mountain, and plain become formative presences, as we found earlier in Borges and Manhire. They attend to those glancing moments when the south seems to be intuited from the inside, even if it is at the same time still seen slant, using borrowed techniques. This wide-angle overview highlights where it can aspects of the volumetric thinking from which a southern poetic might begin to unfold—a poetic that syncs with but also expands upon the earlier lateral associations traced across the south.[37]

A representative trans-hemispheric insight is famously distilled into the emblem of the 'towering' aloe in the Karori garden in Mansfield's 'Prelude' (a chiselled-down version of her more obviously colonial *The Aloe*). Kezia, the Mansfield surrogate, bumps into her mother in the garden, standing at the foot of the giant aloe plant with its lower leaves gripping the earth like claws, seemingly embedded yet in fact an alien. Together they consider the plant's mythic presence, impossible age and legendary flowering 'once every hundred years'.[38] The imposing image thrusting up from some prehistoric source seems to arrest the flow of time: 'no wind could ever shake it'. But its complex symbolism also arches across space, recalling Schreiner's Karoo, where the aloe *is* autochthonous. (Mansfield knew, read and identified with Schreiner's 'transplanted' writing and vision.[39]) The implicit lateral reference traces a route she would herself once have taken across the Indian Ocean from Cape Town to Wellington, returning home in 1906 on the SS *Corinthic*.[40] A related south-south floral *and* geographic chain winds through New Zealander Ursula Bethell's Canterbury garden, in her 1920s poem 'Catalogue', of 'Melaleuca, Santoline, Lasiandra, / Cantua, Cassia, Felecia, Luculia, / Daphne'. Most of the named plants in this list are of southern, especially Western Cape, genera.[41]

Latitudinal Links across the South

Perceived latitudinal climacterics and curves across the south—like Manhire's thin red line—hone a southern optic. In settler writing, they serve as the conceptual equivalent of pointing the astrolabe at the northern horizon and working out not only how far south you are, but also who you share the latitude with. Coetzee remarks that isolated southern geographies insist on such lateral connection, so conjuring that 'instant' recognisability of southern spaces to all southerners, regardless of where in the hemisphere's temperate zones they find themselves.[42] Such shared austral awareness produces a sense of collocation, of living and thinking parabolically or side by side with others in the wider south, no matter how far away they may be.[43]

A distinctive instance can be found in the prevalence of coastline imagery in far southern writing. Poets and novelists are noticeably aware of occupying littorals and of the seas that sweep their shores, including the steely waters extending to the Antarctic, as we saw earlier. In *For Love Alone*, Christina Stead calls her fellow Australians 'sea people' who 'look toward the water', know the tides, and reorder the maps so that they no longer appear 'upside-down'.[44] Brasch's poetry resolutely faces out onto wind-pounded, flint-strewn coastlines, as in 'Otago Landscapes', 'Blueskin Bay', or 'Rain over Mitimiti Mountains'. Waking at night in his native Dunedin, he is always aware of 'the epic southern prairies', 'the fathomless ocean breaking about us', an 'icy vigil . . . circling the thunderous poles' that not even the longest summer can warm ('The Clear').[45] The same oceanic forces fill Frame and Baughan with awe. 'Surely it is illimitable?', Baughan asks in her sketch 'The Mountain Walk': 'Before us now there is nothing but sea, sea, sea, one spread, vast moving field, . . . so "out" it stretches, that it seems equally impossible to conceive that anything ever should stop it, or that it should anywhere stop of itself'.[46] Closer to the present day, Terri-ann White describes living in Perth as sitting 'on the edge of this dryness'.[47] Across the water, shifting 'aqueous contours' dominate Mia Couto's 1992 novel *Sleepwalking Land*, set in a civil-war-ravaged Mozambique. As Muidinga, a convalescent boy, and Tuahir, a refugee, make their way through a debris-strewn seascape, land and water intertwine, as do their present and their past: the 'floor of this world is the ceiling of another world below'.[48]

The modular aspects of colonial experience often undergirded such joined-up and merged perceptions. That many regions across the southern imperial world were settled and developed in the same decades meant that features of urban planning and architecture—street-grids, shopfronts, and bungalows—appeared to replicate around the hemisphere. As for the hinterland, at least up to the 1930s, colonial life was confined to isolated homelands and other islanded settlements barricaded against the elements—and the indigenous outsider. These, too, seemed generically related, not least in their sense of peripherality. Henry Lawson's 'The Drover's Wife' gives a powerful instance of such existential isolation, as does Barbara Baynton's 'The Chosen Vessel' or Mansfield's 'The Woman at the Store'.[49] These similarities between cultural worlds produced and reinforced the feelings of colonial sorority that Rudyard Kipling contemporaneously hymned in 'A Song of the English'.

Relational links across the south increasingly had material realisation in new transport and communications technologies, as well as in scientific research. Mass emigration led to speedier travel by steamship between the southern lands. Australians and New Zealanders heading to Europe for work, to complete their studies, or to see more of the world, took journeys that at least in their initial stages were directed south-south, as were Mansfield's. In the twentieth century, the looping routes of new intercontinental air travel also did not always descend from or ascend back to Europe, but might be strung parabolically between southern vertices. While scientific collaboration tended by and large to operate in north-south and top-down ways, the historians Beinart and Dubow point to both competition and collaboration between southern countries in the Anglosphere in the realms of botany, geology, and astronomy. Southern scientists hypothesised together about the Permian pre-history of their 'great south lands', so challenging 'deep-seated feelings of . . . southern hemispheric marginality'.[50] There were cultural, political, and military links, too. Both Lawson and Mansfield had trans-Tasman Sea connections. Lawson lived and wrote in the North Island in the 1890s. Mansfield's first sketches were published in Australian magazines. The 1901 Constitution of Australia made provision for the inclusion of New Zealand, though the possibility was never given political form. And British soldiers sent to fight in the 1870s Māori Wars trained at Port Arthur in Tasmania.

The 1899–1902 Anglo-Boer War contributed several threads to the colonial networks that spanned the hemisphere. The first year of the war saw hundreds of volunteers from the British colonies, including from Australasia, travel across the southern Indian Ocean to join the expeditionary effort. Schreiner threw herself into the debates that preceded the war with exposés like *An English South African's View of the Situation* (1899), which aimed to enlighten both Britain and the wider empire. Blanche Baughan and the *Bulletin* writer Banjo Paterson wrote poetry, and William Satchell a novel, *The Toll of the Bush*, in response to the 'call' from 'Home' to fight for the empire.[51] Baughan's 'Young Hotspur' pictures a young New Zealand volunteer who, 'finished with farming', cheerfully says farewell to his paddock and '*whare*' (the Māori word for house), and sets out for 'a bit of a roam!' in South Africa.[52]

The aftermath of the war made itself felt across the southern seas. Boer prisoners of war were sent to islands like Ceylon and St. Helena, and a community of disillusioned Afrikaners settled in southern Patagonia in the 1900s, in the area of Sarmiento. Seventy years later, Bruce Chatwin crossed their path on his Patagonian travels.[53] The taciturn group he met had followed a southern route, already carved a decade or so before them, in the opposite direction, when William Lane led a group of around 250 Australians to forge an experimental community in Paraguay based on socialist and anti-immigrant principles. Murnane's short story 'The Battle of Acosta Nu' uses this history as the occasion for a series of reflections on identity and internal landscape. Finding himself in Australia when up till now he had thought he was living in Paraguay, the narrator asks what makes the new Australia in Paraguay different from the real Australia: 'I stood on a hill northeast of Melbourne and looked across the folds of suburbs towards the Kinglake Ranges and almost believed I was in Australia after all'.[54] Australia, real or imagined, most clearly comes into focus with reference to another southern place. In a further link, in Prichard's *Coonardoo*, the young Phyllis Watt briefly considers going to 'the Argentine' to set up a cattle ranch with her new husband.[55]

Different kinds of imaginative identification, including exchanges of letters and postcards, embedded these cross-ocean connections and provided means of spinning the geo-imaginary zoetrope. Later antipodean writers of many stripes discussed together what it was to be a 'writer from the South . . . published in the North' and therefore '[following] norms and [conforming] to standards set in the North', as Coetzee wrote of his own southern status in 2017.[56] In the 1930s, the Auckland short-story writer Frank Sargeson began a correspondence with the South African poet Roy Campbell—one of whose collections was *Adamastor* (1930)—about his decision to write in Europe, far away from 'the terrible spaciousness of the African veldt and the too-bright colours of African oceans.'[57] The journalist and academic James Bertram looked out from New Zealand in the reverse direction, upon the 'green Pacific, with her waiting eyes', and saw 'an empty ocean [stretching] all the way to Chile', the homeland of Pablo Neruda, 'a poet of the *southern* hemisphere', who he, as a progressive writer, named as a climatic or spiritual '*companion*' (his emphasis).[58] Meanwhile, Curnow's 'An Abominable Temper' has his settler great-grandfather facing both ways during the 1840s depression. With 'Australia bankrupt, New Zealand fallen to zero', he plans to export 'Maori-felled' kauri spars to Chile.[59]

Later, again, in the 1990s, Australian writer-critic Peter Read in *Belonging* could still relate to the fraught belonging of 'African-born intellectuals like Doris Lessing and Olive Schreiner' who, he found, had to learn to be migrants in their own country, as he had done.[60] Meanwhile, Tim Winton in *Island Home* claims the terrifying Westralian sky 'going on forever' both for his state and for the south: 'In our hemisphere the sky stops you in your tracks, derails your thoughts'.[61] It is the same sky—'the roof of a vast room'—that arches over the shifting sands of Randolph Stow's littoral childhood world in *The Merry-Go-Round in the Sea*, while the sky makes 'one great loop' of the wide horizon in South African Dan Sleigh's *The Islands*, a historical novel about the early Dutch Cape.[62] For Brasch, again,

> It is all the sky
> Looks down on this one spot,
> All the mountains that gather
> In these rough bleak small hills
>
> —'THE CLEAR'

Southern Poetics: Not Far but Here

Reflecting on the Canadian settler imagination, the mythographer Northrop Frye proposed in the 1970s that for the settler, the question 'Who am I?' depended on another, 'Where is here?'[63] The second question was relational, resting on the assumption that another place existed in respect of which the unknown here might be plotted. But for settler writers on the far side of the world, in lands always understood as 'there' or 'out there', further removed again than Frye's Canada, the second question begged yet another, one that sought even greater specificity: 'Where is *this* here?' or 'What here is this?' A similar distinction emerges, ironically, from the propagandist Wakefield's observation in *A Letter from Sydney* (in fact written from an English prison): 'There is a great difference, in short, between looking *to* a place and looking *from* it'. Literary writing about the south has not always been *from* the south, Philip Steer points out.[64] Till well into the twentieth century, it was neither psychically nor emotionally located in the hemisphere.

According to Paul Carter's still-persuasive *The Road to Botany Bay* (1987), settlement was always as much a rhetorical as it was a physical act. 'Transforming space into place' meant shaping the environment by writing it, or composing a southern poetic with which to interpret it.[65] Allen Curnow captures the idea in 'To Introduce the Landscape', where he speaks of bringing 'the landscape to the language' (1957). Or, in 'Landfall in Unknown Seas', of giving 'seas to history' (1943).[66] N. P. van Wyk Louw, one of the South African 'Dertigers' or poets of the thirties, expresses a related insight in lines now carved onto the Afrikaans Language monument in Paarl. He believed that the changes of landscape endured by the Dutch settlers at the Cape had turned their new language of Afrikaans into an instrument for giving expression to the country: '*En so het Afrikaans in staat geword om hierdie nuwe land uit te sê*'.[67] To join land and words had required the indigenisation of language itself, as in the case of the creole, Afrikaans.

The question 'Where is *this* here?' emerges from a simultaneous perception of farness and hereness, a kind of space-time compression of being both in place and yet, inevitably, at distance, at least in the envisaged mind of the wider world. In much early settler writing, the aspect of distance features strongly; less so, the second, of being *nonetheless* in place, though strenuous efforts are made to bridge the gap. To cite Curnow again: inhabiting his south imaginatively meant 'just living here', as the cowman in 'House and Land' asserts.[68] But it also meant *writing* here. Or recognising that the task of the writer was to craft figures of speech that knit the faraway (sign) and the nearby (geography) together—or, Borges's gaucho and the *llanura*.[69] As also in Manhire's 'Zoetropes', writing fulfilled a cartographic purpose. Genres and forms, even sentences and phrases, supplied tools with which to shape and comprehend the southern environment, pinpointing its edges, inclining to its angles. For Murnane, finding 'apt words' for the 'peculiar qualities' of the 'very southern edge', never written about (at least in English) before, entails a kind of sacred responsibility:

> We were at the very southern edge of an enormous land whose fund of poetic inspiration had barely been tapped. . . . our little zone of bare hills lying between the emptiness of the Southern Ocean and the hazy plains inland. It was our responsibility to preserve in poetry what no one else had written about. And it was our right to be free to search for the most apt words unhindered by history or tradition.[70]

But, at the same time, no amount of poetic inspiration could blot out entirely the foundational trauma of being in spatial and spiritual exile—out of place, and even outside time. The new land remained at a visceral level an atopia that resisted what the New Zealand critic John Newton calls 'affective habitation'.[71] Artists in Argentina found that 'la pampa' offered nothing to see, nothing to paint.[72] For Lawson, the bush was 'the home of the weird'.[73] William Satchell in *The Land of the Lost* (1902) describes a deforested Northland (in New Zealand) as 'the stranding-ground of the dead-beats of the world'.[74] Three decades on, Curnow wrote, notoriously, of a 'great gloom' pervading 'a land of settlers / With never a soul at home' ('House and Land'). His fellow-countryman Brasch concurred, speaking of a 'land of uneducated hearts—with its barbarously ugly towns and cities and its barbarous treatment of its great natural beauty'.[75] By the mid-twentieth century, the poet A. D. Hope in

'Australia' was no more sanguine about his homeland. The country was 'without songs, architecture, history':

> a vast parasite robber-state
> Where second-hand Europeans pullulate
> Timidly on the edge of alien shores.[76]

Amidst their southern 'stranding-grounds', narratives of nation-building helped writers to give shape to new temporalities. Allegories of arrival and stories of settlement—land clearing, homemaking—faded out the regional and linguistic differences that the emigrants' long sea voyage had not yet erased.[77] Ballads of drovers, trekkers, and stockmen, adventurers' stories of journeys into the interior, as emblematised in Paterson's work, and, later, White's *Voss* (1957), or Randolph Stow's *To the Islands* (1958), or Percy Fitzpatrick's *Jock of the Bushveld* (1907), provided durable materials for national mythmaking.[78] These homogenising stories helped resolve the tension that all nations face between the claims exerted by historical origins and the need to found a common future, at one and the same time.[79] Ideas of a rooted national identity legitimised what often felt like usurpation, no matter the persuasiveness of the rhetoric. The condition of being out on the edge could be framed as a special national problem, though it was shared across the colonised south. The history of colonial dispossession was rewritten as 'geographical destiny', as Newton writes.[80]

From the late nineteenth century, magazines like *The Bulletin* in Australia, or the *South African Literary Quarterly*, later Roy Campbell's *The Purple Renoster*, or Charles Brasch's *Landfall*, or keynote anthologies like Frank Sargeson's *Speaking for Ourselves* (1945), or Guy Butler's *A Book of South African Verse* (1959), became prominent outlets through which to assert and develop a distinctive national character and literary voice.[81] Manifesto-like editorials and introductions urged the importance of 'realising' the 'real culture' of the new country in the mind and avoiding imitations of Europe.[82] Frank Sargeson felt able to reject Mansfield as a model for the combined reasons of her 'suspension between two hemispheres', and modernistic divorce from a 'sense of social tradition.'[83] Yet, as his disapproval indicates, distinctive national character was usually understood to be exclusive, insular, and, invariably, masculine. Stories of nation formation favoured independent-spirited male heroes, like Paterson's Australian bushman or Hernández's Argentine gaucho.

Culturally-adrift settler writers across the south turned early on to Indigenous myths, symbols, and other vernacular reference points with which to embed and authenticate their writing. These borrowings recognised, even if partially, the recalcitrant details in the environment that did not fit into a northern perceptual framework. The nineteenth-century poet Eliza Dunlop depicted her Hunter River environment by using distinctive Indigenous names, like the 'gibber-gunyah' (or sheltering cave-formation) in her well-known 'The Aboriginal Mother'.[84] Mary Gilmore's 1932 poem 'Australia' figures ancient Arunta voices speaking through different creatures from the core of the Australian earth, as in the frogs' trumpeted (and heavily primitivised) 'Gobbagumbalin!' refrain.[85] Patrick White was sensitive to the Indigenous presence in the Australian interior, most obviously so in *Voss*, though his Aboriginal characters remain largely static and two-dimensional.[86] In *To the Is-land*, Frame refers to 'Maori' step-relatives as part of her extended family, but Māori characters are otherwise in the background. Singing the Māori anthem 'E Pari Ra' at school floods the young Janet with apprehensions of grief and loss.

Right across the south, the terrible cost of settler indigenisation was the violent displacement and dispossession of Indigenous peoples themselves. What Terry Goldie calls 'the impossible necessity [for the settler] of becoming indigenous', essentially involved building a relationship with the land by extracting local myth while simultaneously excluding the presence of the mythmakers.[87] Indigenous people, including artists and cultural brokers, were reduced to ciphers standing at the margins of their own landscape and history, as in the work of the 1930s Jindyworobak movement, to cite only one of a host of possible examples.[88] In many contexts, the Social Darwinist belief that native races, being 'less developed', would eventually become extinct, fuelled both genocidal military and police actions, and ethnographic and linguistic retrieval projects.[89] '[M]ost is dead', one of Baughan's settler grandmothers opines.[90] Prichard's complicated novel *Coonardoo* signs up to primitivist readings of 'the blacks' of north-west Australia as fatally impacted by the white incursion, while at the same time representing them as more integrated with the land, standing nearer to 'the source of things', like the titular heroine herself.[91]

Two nineteenth-century ethnographic endeavours stand out for their extensive impact on settler efforts to indigenise both in their time and across subsequent generations. First is the vast quantity of material on local cultures that the intellectual imperialist George Grey, the 'Patron of the Southern Hemisphere', amassed while serving as Governor of South Australia (1841–45), New Zealand (1845–53, 1861–68), and the Cape Colony (1854–61). His compilations extend from a *Vocabulary of the Dialects Spoken by the Aboriginal Races of S. W. Australia* (1839) to the translated Māori and Polynesian narratives he collected together with authorities like Wiremu Te Ranhikaheke, as in *Polynesian Mythology* (1855) or *Nga Tipuna* (1857). They also include the 'native literature' he gathered in South Africa, including missionaries' word-lists and grammars. In the 1860s he bequeathed over five thousand manuscripts to the Cape Town library. The collection of papers he later gave to New Zealand contained the largest known number of Māori cultural materials in the world and provided a resource from which turn-of-the-century 'Maoriland' writers like Baughan would borrow.[92] The second endeavour is the Cape linguist Wilhelm Bleek's collaboration with his sister-in-law Lucy Lloyd and narrators like Diä!kwain (David Hoesar), |han‡kass'o (Klein Jantje), and, especially, ||kabbo (Oud Jantje Tooren), to collect Khoikhoi beliefs and stories, published as *Specimens of Bushman Folklore* in 1911.[93] Himself the curator of Grey's South African collection, Bleek had devised an orthography that allowed him to transcribe and record with Lloyd the |xam and !kung languages.

Anthropological and philological citation continued to vivify settler art and letters across the south till deep into the twentieth century, while also powering the global spread of exploratory modernist writing.[94] European modernism, with its commitment to making new, would always represent an ambiguous affordance for settler poets and novelists. As they were already deforming convention to give shape to new psychogeographies, experimentation in a modernist manner risked reducing their rule-breaking to seeming (once again) merely borrowed and derivative. Many writers would come to find that homegrown formal innovation—such as unexpected elisions, scale-shifts, startling juxtapositions—provided more useful tools for tilting perceptual frameworks and flipping cultural biases—or for capturing that frisson when, suddenly, and irrefutably, 'distance looks our way' (Brasch one more time).

Many of these devices, including indigenous borrowing and scalar innovation, come together in Australian Les Murray's 'The Buladelah-Taree Holiday Song Cycle', with which I close this section on writing *here*. The poem adapts the Wonguri Mandjigai 'Song Cycle of the Moon-Bone' (encountered in chapter 2), to celebrate the practice of going home for Christmas, in this case to Murray's country around Bunyah in northern New South Wales. The thirteen free-verse stanzas trace journeys from the city back to family homes 'At the place of the Plough Handles, of the Apple Trees Bending Over, and of the Cattlecamp', orientating with reference to the hot solstice weather and the Pleiades 'pinned up high on the darkness' to register feelings of plenitude and ordinariness—of *this* life on *this* land as sufficient to itself. Though Murray's use of the song cycle is undeniably appropriative, the telling feature is how he labours to inhabit the form, honouring the age-old land by holding it in mind using distinctive local toponymic practice. The recursive flow of his long lines and coursing stanzas lift us through worlds, scaling from contemporary cars and barbecues up to the overarching sky made significant in ancient song and story: 'The Cross hangs head-downward, out there over Markwell; / it turns upon the Still Place, the pivot of the Seasons, with one shoulder rising'.[95] It is an endorsement of Murray's work of cultural embedding that Coetzee includes the poem as one of the final entries in his Argentine *Biblioteca Personal*, alongside two extracts from 'The Song Cycle of the Moon-Bone' itself.

Cartographies and Case Studies

Schreiner, Baughan, Mansfield, Judith Wright, and Frame—the writers in focus in this second half are in their different ways all concerned with the matter of where they stand—with delineating *here* in contrast to there. They articulate what might read as an existential unease about inhabiting southern space, yet seek ways of expressing centredness, even if with borrowed tools. Whether they are writing about land clearances or indigenous haunting or family divisions, they all detect insufficiencies in the fabric of colonial representation and take the risk of working aslant inherited vocabularies to address them. All write from outside positions of colonial male privilege and national authority and hence are more willing to interrogate the status quo, more open to exploring solidarities other than what the nation affords, and more hospitable to plotting connections across southern space, as earlier in Mansfield's aloe scene, or the switch-back in 'The Wind Blows'. Strong parabolic rhythms also emerge from the oscillating patterns that their writing describes—the swooping views across worlds in Schreiner, the scalar shifts and sudden close-ups in all five.

OLIVE SCHREINER—'WEIRD BEAUTY.' Olive Schreiner's fiction gives a forensic account of power and powerlessness on the colonial frontier, specifically, in the semi-desert Karoo region where she grew up.[96] She saw clearly that literary writing played a cartographic role in the process of interpreting that seemingly alien space, but she also understood that inherited tools had to be remade to give it expression in English prose.

To write as a settler, Schreiner (1855–1920) knew, was to bear witness to a seemingly irresolvable condition of cultural dislocation, and yet, nonetheless, to create new work from that process of witnessing. Her efforts across four decades to finish her third novel, *From Man to Man* (1927), testify viscerally to the difficulty she encountered in coming to any final reckoning with her native ironstone landscape.[97] Both in her better-known feminist novel *The Story of an African Farm* (1883), and in *From Man to Man*, my focus here, her narrative eye deictically places and locates: here is the lone kopje in the midst of the dry sandy plain 'with its coating of stunted karoo bushes'; there is the spur of the mountain 'to the left of the farmhouse where the long waving grass grew'. However, she is not alone among early settler writers in resorting to realistic detail and precise pointing to relay her perceptions. There are interesting parallels, for example, between her work and the Australian Joseph Furphy, as well as with the Argentine novelist Benito Lynch's accounts of the tough, down-at-heel life of the gauchos on the South American pampas. Like other Argentine *criollists* and like Schreiner, Lynch (1885–1957) was concerned to identify his country not only as other than Europe, but as autochthonous—a space in and of itself. His pampas settings are represented in harsh, uncompromising terms, as at once tamed and taxing to inhabit—very far removed from the paradisical scene-painting of the more widely read Argentine-British author W. H. Hudson.[98]

Schreiner began *From Man to Man* in the late 1870s, before *African Farm* was published, and, by 1884, often commented that the writing had entirely possessed her, that she did not exist, only her work existed. The novel's double portrait of two sisters, Rebekah, the long-suffering wife, and Bertie, the eventual prostitute, pushes further her debut novel's primary lines of investigation—into what it is to be a settler in Africa, and what it is to bear a woman's body. In *African Farm*, the central characters all fail to thrive, and in *From Man to Man*, the storyline similarly frays, with both sisters at the close facing uncertain futures. It is as if the plot structure, such as it is, defied Schreiner's ability satisfactorily to resolve its central dilemmas, at least within the confines of its Cape context.[99]

Schreiner developed socialist and liberal ideas on human freedom and development from her wide reading as a young woman, borrowing books by John Stuart Mill, Herbert Spencer, and many others from the public library in her native Craddock, the dusty 'town' in *From Man to Man*. But she also understood early on that she formed part of a remote world that these thinkers' perceptual frameworks could not adequately encompass. Though she articulated the racial thoughts associated with her milieu, the more so in *African Farm* than in the later novel, she was keenly aware, too, of the violence and fragility of white imposition on the land.[100] Both novels picture white colonial characters, especially men, as rootless drifters who appear out of nowhere, wreak emotional havoc, and then disappear again into the vastness.

From Man to Man's loose-knit structure afforded Schreiner a particularly fertile space within which to consider the 'representational challenges' of the Karoo and its relationship to the world beyond.[101] Rebekah's chapters-long meditations on evolution weave between earthly and creaturely timescales that extend globally.[102] Though she is frustrated that the geology and botany books she has to hand say nothing about Africa, her studies nevertheless draw 'close internetted lines of interaction' 'between the most distant planet and the ground we tread on, between man, plant, bird, beast and clod of earth'. Darwin's ideas about entangled life allow her to understand better human fellowship and the closeness of the races:

> Between the spirit that beats within me and the body through which it acts, between mind and matter, between man and beast, between beast and plant and plant and earth, between the life that has been and the life that is, I am able to see nowhere a sharp line of severance, but a great, pulsating, always interacting whole (*FMtM* 180–181).

Rebekah's holistic vision anticipates Thomas Hardy's understanding of the Universal Will that motivates all life on earth. But it also resonates with, and provides a model for, the trans-oceanic, cross-continental geophysical connections that make southern imagining possible, as we saw with Darwin. Or as Rebekah says: 'all life seems to be knit together even across boundless time' (*FMtM* 475). This same vision of boundlessness prompts her to adopt and bring up the mixed-race Sartje as her own daughter—her husband's illegitimate child with the servant girl.

The kloof on the farm in *From Man to Man* is a primeval space, fecund and exotic, pregnant with threat and promise. Here, the young Rebekah likes to go and dance by herself, and Bertie is fatally courted. But the land is also imprinted with indigenous belonging. The 'narrow upward footpath' that the sisters take along the mountain spur above the farm has, Schreiner takes pains to observe, been made by the 'maidservants' 'when they went to fetch wood'. Other routes up the spur are carved by the African goatherd, and a tall precipice is known as the suicide point of a young African mother driven to despair by her husband. The writing is persistent in marking both the living presence and the long history of black people on the land. Similarly, in *African Farm*, Waldo traces in the 'Bushman-paintings' drawn on the Karoo rocks evidence of age-old Black custodianship—evidence that Schreiner may have derived in part from research like Bleek and Lloyd's, which Rebekah's work on fossils, too, appears to reference. Among her treasured possessions are a 'Bush-man stone' with a hole in the middle and a fossilised leaf. As significantly, the place in the garden where, as a child, she likes to play house comprises a great 'circular floor of smooth and unbroken stone' like a kraal or threshing-floor.

In both novels, though the black servants are marginal figures, they are ubiquitous as interpreters and translators, and often as dealmakers and defenders, presiding with authority over the white characters' exchanges. Their vernacular—'Old Dutch' or Afrikaans, and Khoi or Nama—is insinuated into both the dialogue and the scenic descriptions using code-switching and loanwords: *ting-ting-kies*, '*kunee trees*', '*gorra-gorra*'. 'Old Ayah, the Hottentot woman' is present at the birth (and death of one) of the twins. The observant servant Griet is always aware of comings and goings on the farm, not least of Bertie's suitors' misbehaviour, and sabotages the domestic projects of her love rival. As significantly, Rebekah's evolutionary musing twice feature African women as innovative artists and makers, and single out also the inspiring story of a Xhosa woman-warrior fighting at the head of her troops, her arms full of assegais, in one of the Frontier Wars (*FMtM* 435–7).

Coetzee observes in *White Writing* that Schreiner's topography is vast, desolate, and unreadable. Yet his emphasis on its featurelessness may be overstated.[103] Schreiner is keenly interested not only in landscape detail—its extent and granularity—but also in *how* we see it.[104] Bridging far and near, the familiar and the unfamiliar, her scene-painting resembles layered impasto. She grounds us in a 'bare patch of sand', piles on detail, and then steps back to allow our vision to range across the veld and up to the sky. Individual sentences set the very small against the very large; in Coetzee's own words, 'the infinitesimal' against 'the infinite'. These techniques are in play from the moment *African Farm* begins—the sentences busy with scale, toggling between levels, constantly adjusting focus.[105] The opening scene alone counterposes the great full moon with the wide monotonous plain, and then the 'kopje' with the homestead. In between, the narrator fills in clusters of things, 'karoo bushes', 'small succulent plants', 'ironstones', 'roofs'. And then zooms back to draw lines and positions, 'here and there', 'at the foot', 'before the house', interspersing these with abstractions—'solemn monotony', 'oppressive beauty', 'peculiar brightness'—that pan back and consider the scene as a whole.

In *From Man to Man*, the spatial axes of *African Farm* shift dramatically again. The characters' activities, and news about those activities, connect the farm and the town with, at a far broader level, the city of Cape Town, and the 'noisy, babbling, worried, worrying world' beyond—in short, the imperial margins and the metropolis (*FMtM* 85–6). At first, the scene-setting shunts as before between the minuscule and the gigantic, the tiny flowers ('the nam-nams and jasmine shrubs'), and the great mountain spur. But soon it also begins to move horizontally between very different yet connected geographies within the wider world-system, the narrative lens again continually recalibrating focus. Now our attention is directed to the farm with its 'great dam' and overshadowing spur, now to the town with its market square and great coaches passing through from the Diamond Fields. Now we look at Cape Town with its ocean-swept peninsula and 'tree-lined avenues', now at rainy London, the vivid scenes flashing out of the surrounding emptiness (*FMtM* 238–9).

In the final long chapter, Schreiner builds paragraphs of self-reflection on her own narrative approach into a conversation between Rebekah and her new interlocutor, Drummond. Just as Drummond's attempts to write up the African 'scenery' give the sense of something bursting into consciousness, as he says, so Schreiner challenges the reader to compose the African settings in their mind by working from one 'flash' or 'burst' to another, the different pictures coming out 'one after the other in a moment', just as the exposed fossil (in Rebekah's analogy) emerges into the sunshine, springing into life, 'here, on the opposite side of the earth, after all those ages' (*FMtM* 475–6).

B. E. BAUGHAN—SHINGLES SHORT. If Schreiner began to point to the gaps in the 'long miles of rolling karroo' that required new descriptive terms, Blanche Baughan's 1900s verse sharpens this awareness of representational difficulty still further, in a specific direction. A New Zealand immigrant, Baughan (1870–1958) inventively used the aural textures of her favoured poetic form, the dramatic monologue, repeatedly to disrupt readers' expectations of finding beauty and composure in the South Pacific. In poems like 'Shingle-Short' and 'A Bush Section' from her 1908 collection *Shingle-Short and Other Verses*, she abandoned the language of the picturesque that distinguished her travel writing, for the insistent rhythms of local speaking voices who witness to the loss and waste that colonial development has inflicted.[106] All around them lie burnt bush and denuded ground—'raw devastation'—with idyllic seascapes restricted to the far horizon. In Baughan's view, the colonial Eden is everywhere a 'shingle-short'—an 'Australasian term' denoting insufficiency or incompleteness, as she glosses, which she uses to striking effect in the title poem. (Frame takes the same phrase in *Owls Do Cry* to capture the local view of her brother's epilepsy.) Even in the early 'The Old Place', from *Reuben, and Other Poems* (1903), the reality of building a homestead amidst the 'glossy karakas . . . twinkling to the big blue twinkling sea', is unforgiving. The speaker, a homesteader, has been driven by fire and bankruptcy to leave this 'brute of a place' 'that's broken my heart—the place where I've lived all my life!'[107]

Born and educated in Britain, travelling to New Zealand only as an adult, Baughan was a spiritual quester from an early age.[108] A generation older than Mansfield, she appears before her in this line-up, sandwiched between two better-known southern fellows, the imaginative and geographic contours of her work both complementing and counterpointing theirs in suggestive ways. As her biographer writes, she 'revered' her adopted landscape to the point that she could both lament its being stripped and quarried, yet retain a sense of its transformative powers, how it made one 'lose sight of oneself . . . [and] gain a new world, because a new view of the world'. The parallel with Mansfield's 1910s vision of making her new Pacific world leap into the eyes of the old is unmissable.[109]

As well as poetry, Baughan published *Brown Bread from a Colonial Oven* (1912), a collection of prose sketches of life in the turn-of-the-century colony where spring occurs 'in autumn'. The best-known sketch is 'Pipi on the Prowl' featuring a would-be cunning older Māori, Pipi, who contrives to trick a pakeha woman she meets on the road to give her clothing and tobacco, but is herself outmanoeuvred—referencing a time when government land schemes favoured white settlers. Here, too, the lavish scene-painting—'the little long, low spits, emerald-turfed and darkly crowned with trees'—also takes in the desolate swamp with its 'withered *raupo*'. 'The Mountain Track', too, observes the impact of colonial development in the form of blackened bush, the 'stumps [that] stand everywhere mouldering'. Similarly, in 'An Early Morning Walk', 'for inches of such verdure there were acres and acres of barren devastation'.[110] Together, the sketches call up landscapes that are lush and open, but also harsh and battered by the elements and by development. The wind blows 'furiously', communities are isolated, and ever-present on the horizon is the 'old cold' 'adventurous' ocean, a 'sea-mirror too bright to be looked at for long'.

But it is in *Shingle-Short* that Baughan is most intent on showing the reader loss as well as fullness, sometimes within the same frame, and her verses cast an unrelenting light on all that is awry about colonial life. Lighter poems like 'Maui's Fish' based on Māori myth, or 'The Eternal Children' with its strange Edwardian dream vision of pink-white children sea-swimming, interleave with far darker monologues bent on exposing imperfection and damage, while the long closing poem 'The Paddock' presents a 'cantata' of voices from both before and after settlement. In the title poem, 'Shingle-Short', the speaker, Barney, a simple-minded farmhand, works through the night to fashion a ship from a piece of *totara* wood he has found, destroying a cottage clock and an umbrella in the process. His eventual creation, incomplete and mismatched just as he is represented as being, draws an analogy also with the colony where 'Everything slops, or else comes short'.[111]

'A Bush Section' paints the bleakest picture of a landscape laid to waste by burning and logging: 'all the tawny, tumultuous landscape / Is stuck, and prickled, and spiked with the standing black and grey splinters'.[112] The opening lines bristle with synonyms for 'the long, prone, grey-black logs', reflected also in the abruptly varying line lengths, the acute angles cutting up the flowing lines of the New Zealand landscape we remember from the prose sketches. The sharp shifts in scale hark back to Schreiner's scenic textures, as does the use throughout of local idioms, including 'Maori words' 'with pronunciation indicated'. But Baughan's language with its startling similes and accumulations of negatives—'no life to be seen, nothing stirs'—is at times even more defamiliarising than her South African counterpart's. A run of extraordinary images compares the fallen logs that litter the landscape first to a 'dead disconsolate ocean', and then to stars, as if the waste were so all-consuming as to be repeated in the sky (as also in the epigraph):

> The sky is a wide black paddock, without any fences.
> The Stars are its shining logs;
> Here, sparse and single, but yonder, as logg'd-up for burning,
> Close in a cluster of light.

While critics have dismissed the 'star-logs' metaphor as hopelessly unpoetic, this reading would rather highlight the reverberations that it sets up between the earth and the night sky. The 'sparkling constellations overhead, infinite in number, each one a world' are aligned with the dense scatterings across the landscape, in an evocation of at once plenitude and disorder, that is unmistakably located *here*, in this landscape, under this bright astral array.[113]

The central consciousness in 'A Bush Section' is the boy Thor Rayden, 'twice-orphaned', his only companion the river, 'jammed-up' with logs. The stark opening scenes erode from the start the assertion of his youthful, pioneering will on which the poem ends. Here, as elsewhere in her work, Baughan demonstrates a keen sensitivity to the fact that cultural reference-points taken from England must be mixed and broken to communicate the stark contrasts of her new homeland. The sidereal is brought down to earth to capture at one and the same time the 'tenfold illumination' of the southern skies, and the environmental wastage that settlement here requires:

> 'Tis a silent, skeleton world;
> Dead, and not yet re-born,
> Made, unmade, and scarcely as yet in the making:
> Ruin'd, forlorn, and blank.[114]

KATHERINE MANSFIELD—'NOTHING TO MARK WHICH.' Her Wellington birth aside, Katherine Mansfield (1888–1923) might seem, at least at a superficial glance, to lie outside the frame of specifically south-centred writing.[115] From her late teens, after her return from school in England, she wrote off New Zealand cultural life as restrictive and provincial. Like many others of her generation, and since, she signed up to the idea that Europe set the pace of artistic innovation, and that, to write as a modernist, she should sync with its rhythms.[116] By contrast with Schreiner, who also travelled from the colonial periphery for her education, and whose later pathways oscillated between the north and the south, Mansfield left New Zealand for good in 1908, at the age of twenty, to forge a career as an artist in London. To nationalist writers of a later generation, her restless quest after modernity compromised claims to count her as a socially embedded New Zealand writer.

Yet the landscapes of her youth pervaded her writing, and alchemised her later short stories, which unmistakably yearn south, and establish a distinctive southern climate. Especially after the death of her brother on the Western Front, she induced in her work a 'willed haunting', a nostalgic determination to recreate scenes from their childhood together and, as she wrote, to make 'our undiscovered country leap' into the eyes of the 'old world'.[117] Even early on, as in her most characteristic colonial story, 'The Woman at the Store', or the disconcerting 'How Pearl Button was Kidnapped', she used subtle local detail to distil the blue oceanic light and capture a sense of the lush environment. But it is in the memorialising later work with its vivid use of colour and sharply focused outlines that she places us centrally in a South Pacific landscape, so that the vegetation and flowers seem to shine out, as if newly wetted by the dew.

Far from merely applying modernist techniques from Europe to recreate New Zealand, I suggest that Mansfield also took antipodean points of reference to unsettle and refresh her acquired avant-garde aesthetic.[118] Her writing brings out a disorientating parallax between near and far, here or there, that allows her to give her recollections from childhood 'solidity and substance', as critics acknowledge, but at the same time to collapse the distance on which the exotic depends.[119] The far south's sun-bright perspectives helped her to hone the prismatic shapes with which she transformed the short story, removing plot in favour of filmic flashbacks and jump-cuts that often catch and refract the remembered piercing light. Gardens, roadsides, and seascapes that on one level appear ordinary, on inspection are filled with 'a sense of mystery, a radiance, an after glow'.[120] Like Schreiner writing of the desert stones 'throwing up a red reflection', Mansfield paints 'colour . . . so intense' that it is reflected in her characters' faces and 'in their hair. The very rock on which they climb is hot with the colour'.[121] Her aim, as she wrote, was to intensify 'so-called small things, so that truly everything [became] significant', and to make her images as 'familiar' to the reader as to herself, distant and strange though they might otherwise seem.[122]

Mansfield's ability to merge and mutually defamiliarise contrasting worlds is prominently on show in some of her best-known longer short stories, 'At the Bay', 'The Garden Party', and 'Prelude'.[123] Senses of the south come through interstitially yet insistently in the images of the drenching dew, or the shining karaka plants, or the pervasive fog blurring the borderline between land and sea. In 'The Garden Party', the marquee, band, lace dresses, and ices call up an English Edwardian world, yet the expected associations are thrown together with a wholly other set of references that build to a point of concentration in the 'far, far away' sleep of the dead workman. In 'At the Bay', the writing conjures up scenes even as the mist blurs them, so that we see double:

> The sandy road was gone and the paddocks and bungalows the other side of it; there were no white dunes covered with reddish grass beyond them; there was nothing to mark which was beach and where was the sea. A heavy dew had fallen. The grass was blue.

Mansfield might here be describing her own poetic which, as she wrote, aimed at once to smother and disclose: 'And just as on those mornings white milky mists rise and uncover some beauty, then smother it again and then again disclose it[,] I tried to lift that mist from my people and let them be seen and then to hide them again'.[124]

For the Cape Town-born New Zealander Robin Hyde, Mansfield was a writer 'permanently out of place'.[125] Yet the uncompromising mix of the familiar and the unfamiliar in her work suggests rather that her imagination remained in important ways grounded in the South Pacific. Her writing sprang from its collisions between worlds—of town and bush, bright daylight and bewitching twilight, the marquee and the karakas behind them, growing 'as if on a desert island'. Like Baughan, she took the measure of the absences and silences of the colony, the repressive and claustrophobic 'pockets of colonial intruders, [and] the silence of the vast sea-desert that encircled them'.[126]

JUDITH WRIGHT: 'NOT MINE, BUT ME.' For Judith Wright (1915–2000), the history of colonial violence in Australia condemned settler poets like her to a state of self-division.[127] They yearned to gain a better knowledge of the land and to give it expression, but, constrained by guilt and fear, were unable to achieve reconciliation with those who had been harmed and to fully take the country into their heart. She opened her memoir *Half a Lifetime* with the question, 'In Australia, who am I?', responding: 'The place to find clues is not in the present, it lies in the past: a shallow past. . . . It begins in another hemisphere' (*HL* 3). In *this* hemisphere, on the beloved family farm Wallamumbi, her sense of belonging was trammelled by glimpses of displaced Aborigines hovering like shadows 'on the fringes of our lives', despite the fact that on this 'eastern side of the tableland' their gathering places appeared to have been erased (*HL* 34, 67). As she vividly records, she awakened only gradually to the awareness not only that the country was haunted, 'wet' with Aboriginal blood, but also that Aborigines remained present, living on the land (*HL* 74). They were not mere ghosts. Though 'only the grass' might mark their ancient dancing-ring, she could, growing up, discern dark faces moving among the trees, 'dispossessed and silent' ('Bora Ring', *CP* 8; *HL* 296).[128]

Wright's feelings of alienation impacted on her understanding of her role as an Australian poet: 'I remember those rocks of the valley as clearly as I remember any part of my childhood, but with a sense of my own exclusion from their meaning. I was born within their influence, but I do not have any right to their story' (*HL* 67).[129] Settler writers, she believed, were condemned to a perpetual struggle to keep their attention on the foreground of what they were trying to describe, as the 'background [kept] intruding'.[130] Her poetry stemmed at once and the same time from two sources, the rocks of her 'New England' landscape, and the feelings of trespass and exclusion that blocked her view of them. She was determined to 'create a heartland from which she could speak', as A. D. Hope recognised, even as she understood that the history of Australia's colonisation meant that she was not entitled to do so.[131] Forswearing possession, declaring belonging, she recognised: 'These hills and valleys were—not mine, but me. . . . I felt it under my own ribs' (*HL* 158). And, in the signature poem 'For New England':

> Many roads meet here
> in me, the traveller and the ways I travel.
> All the hills' gathered waters feed my seas
> who am the swimmer and the mountain river;
> and the long slopes' concurrence is my flesh
> who am the gazer and the land I stare on;
> and dogwood blooms within my winter blood
> and orchards fruit in me and need no season
> —CP 22–3

Her 'double consciousness' as a poet was further complicated by her gender. As she found from her experience of trying to make it as a poet after the war, she was excluded from claiming a national voice on par with those of her male compatriots, such as Ken Slessor. Even so, writing offered a route to greater independence, as modelled for her by Miles Franklin's novel *My Brilliant Career*. Poetry, in particular, was a tensile power she felt she could 'command' in a society where men dominated (*HL* 53–54, 148–9). Like her contemporary Janet Frame, Wright understood that the world was divided between inside and outside, where inside represented domestic confinement, and outside, the world beyond the house, a territory of freedom and magic, of 'mustering trips' and 'timber-clearing'—'the clean, lean, hungry country' of her early poetry ('South of my Days', *CP* 44). As also for Frame, writing provided ways of drawing these divided spaces together, tapping into a deeper reality that both might have called mythic. Wright drew images from the natural environment, like the red blossoming may-tree, and built them to bear a greater symbolic significance—though one that is often again discarded, but never irrevocably: 'break and beckon, change and elude, go away, and never go away' ('The Child', *CP* 34).

Wright mobilised her haunted understanding of white trespass in Australia in service of her life-long environmentalism—and her perceptions of the inescapable contradictions of settler belonging constantly filter back into her poetry. She tirelessly interrogated the premise of limitlessness on which the colonial nation of Australia 'born of the conquerors', was founded, with its visions of boundless horizons to explore, and bottomless wealth to mine. In her efforts to 'rethink the development of the west which had brought us to this present state', she always returned to Indigenous ideas of Country as a repository of spirit. But she did so in a way that honoured this understanding, without using it merely to extract symbols for her poetry, as previous poets had done (*HL* 191). As in 'At Cooloolah', her vision that 'earth is spirit', meant walking thoughtfully among past and present footprints on the 'clean sand': 'Those dark-skinned people who once named Cooloolah / knew that no land is won or lost by wars' (*CP* 140–1). She tried to see Country as an overlapping array of life-worlds, believing that this vision might eventually undo her sense of trespass and allow her partial entry. There are recollections here of Schreiner's understanding, through Rebekah, of lives past and present as forming a 'pulsating, always interacting whole'.

JANET FRAME: 'SUPER DAYLIGHT.' Of the five writers featured here, Janet Frame (1924–2004) most fully embraces the far south as her existential focal point. From her first novel *Owls Do Cry* (1957), through her autobiographical trilogy, *An Angel at My Table* (1982–5, 1989), to her posthumously published novel, *Towards Another Summer* (2007), the South Island remained the unquestioned centre of her world, Oamaru, where she grew up (Waimaru in *Owls Do Cry*), 'her kingdom by the sea'.[132] *To the Is-land* (1982), the first volume of the autobiography, illuminates how her early years in Southland, the southernmost region of New Zealand, and later Otago, only a few degrees further north, laid the foundation stones of her southern vision. From the beginning, she had the sense of inhabiting a dreamlike expanse tinged with snow light from Antarctica, 'in the embrace of weather that existed of itself without reference to people or creatures and their everyday lives' (*TtI* 22, 29, 66, 182–3). That weather continued to condition and channel her creative energies throughout her career, as did her impassioned reading in New Zealand literature. In the 1930s nationalist poets Baxter, Brasch, Curnow, and Sargeson (who would become her mentor), she found 'a fact of belonging' that, she said, 'overwhelmed me'.[133]

Frame's full-hearted acceptance of her South Island coordinates freed her to a degree from fretful preoccupations with questions of identity as a New Zealand settler writer, differently from some of her peers. Even as she adapted narrative personae, as the self-conscious modernist she also was, she always placed these within distinct, fully realised southern worlds.[134] Her work contrasts with the other writers profiled here, as her imaginative compass points are very rarely, if ever, external to the South Island. (Even the North Island seemed to her for many years exotic and distant.) Her settings tend not to require the adjustments of scale that we find in Schreiner or betray the anxieties about possession that beset Wright. At the same time, her far south is an often difficult and threatening place to inhabit. As the mother Amy in *Owls* says, the Aurora Australis is frequently visible if you know where to look. Her daughter Chicks, too, observes:

> Down in the south you feel all the time a kind of formidable background, like a block of grey shadow, of a continent of ice, Antarctica in the wings. The dark there is more frightening and less friendly, you are trapped in it as in a tomb, and the stone of ice will not roll away. (*Owls* 173)

So close was Frame's identification with this formidable region that she would later relate her own lifelong sense of aloneness to its far southern isolation: 'I have got to learn that I am alone for ever . . . I will never have anybody close to me. The rest of the world is miles away over desert and snowfield and sea.'[135] The feeling comes through also in the island metaphors that pervade her work, with the word *island* seen and heard as *is-land*, the silent 's' pronounced, as she had said it as a child (*TtI* 17, 59, 207).

The recognisably autobiographical *Owls Do Cry* begins Frame's lifelong work of mapping the world from the Oamaru shoreline, and tells the story of the Withers family, Bob and Amy, and their children Francie, Toby, Daphne, and Chicks. The first part of the novel covers their growing up and Francie's death, and the second, 'twenty years later', Daphne's incarceration in a mental institution. In a notable early passage, the narrative locates itself south, or *here*, 'halfway between the South Pole and the equator':

> Their town, called Waimaru, was small as the world and halfway between the South Pole and the equator, that is, forty-five degrees exactly. There was a stone monument just north of the town to mark the spot in gold lettering. Traveller, the writing said, Stop here. You are now standing halfway between the South Pole and the equator. What did it feel like to be standing at forty-five degrees? It felt no different. (*Owls* 20)

The many references to books and places elsewhere—including hymns, the Bible, English poetry, Shakespeare—are all placed relative to this precise southern coordinate (one that correlates with an actual monument on the highway leading north out of Oamaru). Daphne imagines the mountain from which Jesus ascends as a 'Southern Alp' (*Owls* 33). And Ariel's song from *The Tempest*, which gives the novel its title, sung by Francie in a school production, is threaded into a chain of association with the local owl, the morepork, crying in the 'macrocarpa and cabbage trees' (*Owls* 29).

The far southern location of Frame's writing is confirmed and expanded in the autobiography of her childhood, *To the Is-land*, again set in this 'familiar kingdom', 'listening to the waves crashing over the breakwater' (*TtL* 185, 207, 232). As before, literature from other places seems to wash naturally into Oamaru, flowing 'like an array of beautiful ribbons through the branches of a green, growing tree'. Frame transplants flora from across New Zealand and the wider world into her fantasy land, Ardenue, giving substance and certainty to 'a new inner "My Place"' (*TtI* 207, 211, 243). In a striking scene, when a teacher reads from *The Rime of the Ancient Mariner*, the young Janet seems to recognise in the poem her own particular geography, 'feeling the nearness of a sea-scape that was part of Oamaru' (*TtI* 182–3). Coleridge's poem of the far south thrusts upon her an 'inescapable dream' that is at the same time a fundamental reality—'a "pure" dream of that time on the sea in the embrace of weather that existed of itself'.

Towards Another Summer, Frame's last novel, unpublished in her lifetime, pairs with *Owls* not only chronologically, as last against first, but also thematically. Many images from *To the Is-land* surface here, too, including of the roaring sea 'so near', bringing visions of a land 'swallowed by waves' (*TAS* 154). Whereas *Owls* looked out at the world from Oamaru, *Towards Another Summer* is set in London, yet feels the magnetic pull of the south, the narrative yearning back along the same curving track drawn in Manhire's 'Zoetropes'. The writing repeatedly ponders the driving Coriolis forces created by the turning planet—forces to which migrating creatures like godwits and Frame herself are attuned, and which spin counterclockwise in the south. While the two novels are in this sense cantilevered, one set north, the other south, in both, the south is the pivot around which the imagined world spins. The lines from Brasch's poem about godwits syncopate the narrative.

The action of *Towards Another Summer* is minimal. In the depths of an English winter, a New Zealand novelist, Grace Cleave, who is trying to make her way in London, yet missing 'her country', is invited to spend the weekend with magazine editor Philip Thirkettle and his family in his home outside London. The temperature in the fictional Relham is said to be 'a degree warmer' than in the capital. The distress Grace feels at having to spend time with other people provokes her in the second half of the novel to retreat early to her London flat and write 'the story of the weekend'. While reflecting on her homesickness—that way in which the 'Southern Cross cuts through my heart instead of through the sky'—she comes to realise that her solitude is ultimately easier to bear than company and also that her geographic displacement has somehow denatured her: 'Here I live in a perpetual other season unable to read in the sky, the sun, the temperature, the signs for returning' (TAS 7, 9–10, 18–19, 55–59). Imagining herself as a migratory bird, or a capsule projected south, releases in Grace an extraordinary series of meditations on 'true identity', '*my* place', and gravitation that run through the novel to the end: 'How can I ever contain within me so much of one land?' 'How had she ever been able to exchange the sun, the beach, the shimmering tent of light . . . for [this] brick bleeding wound'? (*TAS* 56, 58, 103).

In her work, Frame tried to better understand the make-up of a higher reality that she sometimes saw as the imagination, and sometimes 'the manifold', a term she took from Kant.[136] The image calls up associations of plurality and difficulty—as might relate to the granularity of sand and ice plant in Schreiner, or of log-like stars in Baughan, or blends of sea and shore in Mansfield, or the 'blue caves of the south' in Wright (*CP* 53). The manifold held out for her a 'terrible everlasting substantiality', as she explores in explicit terms in *Living in the Maniototo* (1979), a substantiality that connected back to the icy edges of her childhood world, the 'constant roaring of the sea on the foreshore', and to the magic of words (*TtI* 91). That the physical correlate for the manifold is evidently the South Island means that her imagination, too, always remained south-directed, seeing distance and closeness as conflated, the land possessing the writer even as her writing called up the land. As she wrote in *The Carpathians,* her island became her 'gravity star' whereby galaxies very far away could also seem, through a kind of diffraction, very bright and close.[137]

The south often retreats before southern settler writers' attempts to describe it. Whether the region is the burning Australian interior, or the rolling southern African semi-desert, or Patagonia, evoked by Borges as a region of the mind, southern space demands ceaseless imaginative effort. Yet, from the writers' sense of inadequacy and outsideness eventually also come new modes of orientating to the far south, and a growing interest in the shaping effects that might be created from its detail, scale, and depth. The young protagonist's ignorance of living in a place called Australia in Randolph Stow's *The Merry-Go-Round in the Sea* modulates in Frame to the idea of containing the land *within* herself. She takes to perhaps its farthest extent the attempt to imagine the hemisphere from the ground (or the pole) up, though all of the featured writers make significant contributions to this endeavour. From their different angles, they speak to the power and importance of being both *south* and *here*. And, to do so, they develop ways of challenging a dominant northern aesthetic, and of seeking connection with contiguous southern worlds, not least the Indigenous, which forms the next chapter's focus.[138]

7

Keeping South

WRITING FROM HERE

Stars shone all around him. A splash, and half the sky exploded.

. . .

what was in the glittering sky: the origins of different stars, the stories of dark spaces between, the way the sky and its slowly shifting constellations signalled that rain was due, whales would be appearing, emus nesting inland. . . . He told sky stories of how things became the truths they are.

—KIM SCOTT, *THAT DEADMAN DANCE* (2010)

It was first told by the San People, that in the blackness of night, a girl took roasting roots and ashes from a fire and threw them into the sky. Thus the stars were born. A path was made in the sky, and hunters who were lost followed it home.

The San were an old people. They might have been the first people. And so, when the wind took their tale through the summers, its whisperings intoned new factors into the story. It was thus told by the Basotho that the children of the first Gods had walked the path in the sky to reach the place of the rising sun, where Molalatladie, the Lightning Bird, rested in eternity.

That was long ago. It was when people sat around fires to recall the world's past with each other. There was no time for that anymore. People now told stories while passing each other.

—RESOKETSWE MANENZHE, 'CHILDREN OF THE FIRST GODS', *SCATTERLINGS* (2020)

When he talked about the stars, they said he knew as much about the sky as he did about water. The . . . mob said he had always chased the constellations: We watched him as a little boy running off into the night trying to catch stars. They were certain he knew the secret of getting there. They thought he must go right up to the stars in the company of groper fish when it stormed at sea, when the sea and the sky became one, because, otherwise, how could he have come back?

—ALEXIS WRIGHT, *CARPENTARIA* (2006)

I watch the stars in an ink-blue sky. The Milky Way is a smudged white on the dark canvas; the Three Kings flicker, but the Southern Cross drills her four points into the night. I find the long axis and extend it two and a half times, then drop a perpendicular down onto the tip of the Gifberge, down onto the lights of the Soeterus Winery. Due South.

—ZOË WICOMB, 'A TRIP TO THE GIFBERGE', *YOU CAN'T GET LOST IN CAPE TOWN* (1987)

River, Cliff, and Stars: Jazz Money and Gabeba Baderoon

The Indigenous Australian poet Jazz Money's 'bila, a river cycle' (2021) meditates on the sacred wisdom that rivers transmit as they wind through the land to the sea before again returning to the sky as water vapour.[1] In a comparable series of reflections on buried ancestral knowledge, the South African poet

Gabeba Baderoon in *The History of Intimacy* (2018) labours to restore silenced human histories to utterance. The poets' projects correspond to what Toni Morrison terms truth inventions—imaginative acts that work against dominant histories and ontologies to 'yield up a kind of truth'. As such, they craft a correlative opening for this chapter on Indigenous writing from within the south.[2] Not insignificantly, Money is of Indigenous Wiradjuri and Irish descent, Baderoon Cape Malay. With their use of vivid natural images and vernacular words, the two poets weave cyclical and ramifying shapes that bridge across rifts in the present-day understanding of their southern worlds—the New South Wales three rivers area for Money, the Cape Peninsula for Baderoon. In both cases their musings and meanderings also plot sightlines up to the stars, and so counterpoint the astral and oceanic connections that chapter 2 first outlined.

> to dive into a world known as kin but always one hard to hold
> to flow out and out to be reimagined as rain
> and rejoin the lands of all rivers
> of all stars
> welcomed again into bilabang

Beginning in 'snow melt' and 'well-spring', the Murrumbidjee bila or river of Money's poem seeks to know itself as a timeless flowing force that has always interacted with humans, yet has also (increasingly) been disrespected by them. The bila takes in on its journey both 'smooth worn stones along their ribs', and dams and pollutants that interrupt and poison its natural course, and turn it into 'a sludge of gasping fish'.[3] 'Redirected', it becomes a subterranean water course, yet at the same moment rises up from the land as an ancestral form, at once human-seeming yet aqueous: 'a river is always a river ey even when submerged'. With fish suspended within its flesh, the bila then moves across to the delta region where mangroves clear its silt and 'all is fertility and possibility'. Its human sense of itself (or 'themselves') and riverine 'curiosity' connects with Alexis Wright's blended sky and seascapes in *Carpentaria* later in this chapter. It will also recall the Murrumby of Tara June Winch's *The Yield* that was once clear 'twenty feet down', but now, with 'Dam Built' and 'Rain Gone', no longer flows, though its course persists.[4] Despite everything, bila finds its way through like the 'songlines of our ancestors [that] continue to follow water like markers on a highway'. It holds within its shape, flow and direction the age-old memory of its capillary routes—'just so with cause of course'.

The poet-speaker in 'bila' raises the vision of a fluid, cyclical world, onward-flowing though trammelled. The song cycle form develops a recitative cadence, even as the river's dendritic spread also guides and shapes the open-field or bio-mimetic form of the poem on the page. Ancient totemic presences, '*ngarradan, bilbi, dinggu*', speak advice and warning ('*don't drink from here no more no good*'), while following the irrepressible movement of the water: '*and so*' '*and so*' repeats like a partial refrain. The lines simultaneously lead on and make digressive sideways sweeps, the words sometimes pooling as does river water into *bilabangs*. The interplay of the poem's English with the Wiradjuri words reflects something of this merging and winding, with the unfamiliar names translated by the context, and the English meanings at the same time infiltrated and reshaped.

Though 'bila' is a lamentation, it finally records a kind of transcendence. The poem's governing idea of return is beautifully captured in the meanings of *bilabang* as they recur across the poem, signifying water cut off from the main river, and also the Milky Way or the universe. As Money remarks, poetry matters for paying attention to such dual meanings and their reciprocities. The Milky Way, 'our home in the vastest sense', as she observes, is captured in the changing pattern of clustered asterisks and numbers from 1 to 9 that first appears in the poem between the first and second stanzas, and then repeats three more times, mirroring the movements of the circuitous but clogged river as it proceeds. 'all bila survive, even if degraded'—the 'on-going, endless regenerative cycles of the world' that emerged in the early chapters of this book, persist through the poem, too. And as with ancient song cycles, so here: each time we read or hear the poem we recompose in our mind bila's winding course that reaches beyond and presses through 'settled boundaries and limitations of beginnings, middles and end'.[5]

While in Jazz Money the *bilabang*'s currents disperse through the atmosphere and come back as rain, in Gabeba Baderoon Cape histories converge, break apart, and re-entwine, mingling with the tides that wash the Peninsula's shores.[6] Baderoon's lyrics listen closely to the many stories of southern islands and isthmuses that impact each other at the stormy Cape. Trade routes connecting Europe and Asia converge here in experiences of displacement, dispossession, and silencing for both Indigenous Africans and transported Asians: 'Nothing tells us/ what pulls apart our centre'.[7] Baderoon's poetic project is to restore these lives to memory. Her retrieval work with its pointed use of Afrikaans, the vernacular of the wider Cape community, relates to the creative work of other 20th- and 21st-century Cape poets in the language, such as Diana Ferrus, Lynthia Julius, Ronelda Kamfer or Nathan Trantaal, some of whom use the creolised version of Afrikaans sometimes called Afrikaaps. She shares community memory also with writers like Alex La Guma, and, more recently, the novelist and playwright Nadia Davids. Davids's memoir *An Imperfect Blessing* is a lamentation for communities destroyed by the 1960s apartheid state policy of forced removal, yet also a celebration of attachment to place and to people, beneath Table Mountain.[8]

Of Baderoon's collections, including *The Dream in the Next Body* (2005) and *A Hundred Silences* (2006), it is the late 2010s *The History of Intimacy* that is in play in this section for its keen awareness of the entangled presence of hidden pasts—or of how the air 'thickens with history' ('A Prospect of Beauty', and 'Axis and Revolution', *H* 15, 22). The collection's often quietly pitched lyrics tune into the silenced spaces of history to sense the bodies no longer physically there, and to compose and recompose the voices of Camissa, the place of sweet waters—the name for the Cape in the Indigenous language 'Khoe', in Baderoon's spelling (*H* 66–8, 26–7). So, for example, 'The Flats', which reflects on her parents' experience of forced removal, registers their perceptions of the strange distances that have opened up within the once-familiar spaces of their old neighbourhood. They have tried to turn their loss 'into an ordinary tragedy' but remain many decades later unable to look in the direction of where they once belonged (*H* 44–45).

Baderoon's occasional reliance on her community's vernacular, Afrikaans, forms a resonant part of her giving voice. In the Glossary to *The Dream in the Next Body*, she defines Afrikaans as a creole 'developed among slaves and others . . . drawn from Indigenous Khoi Khoi and San languages, Malay, Arabic, English, Dutch, German and Portuguese'—in other words, from all the points of the compass.[9] She also emphasises the importance of having one's own name. The prose poem 'No Name' about her family's reliance on cheap 'no name' supermarket brands, puts it clearly: to name yourself, especially in your own tongue, is to refuse negativity. When apartheid ends: 'At last we are not nothing, we are a name, we exist' (*H* 57–59). Similar to Money's Wiradjuri, or Wright's Waanji in their contexts, her colloquial Afrikaans and Malay words properly texture the remembrance of the community to which they belong. Hinge phrases and end-words are often in Afrikaans: for example, the word 'bodem' in 'Hangklip', or her mother's comment in 'No Name', 'daai is doenya se goete' (these are only earthly things) (*H* 67). In *History* as in other of her collections, Baderoon experiments with the double negative that is a grammatical feature of Afrikaans and the 'double erasures' that it permits, such as the powerful assertion of 'not nothingness' in the titular 'The History of Intimacy' (*H* 67–8).[10] As she urges in 'Everything We've Said', a language is only 'beautiful if we remember everything / we've said in it' (*H* 30).

Perhaps the most haunting—and haunted—of the poems in a collection crowded with ghosts of memory, is the poem 'Hangklip' (*H* 52–3), or Hanging Rock. The toponym designates the promontory beetling over the sea at the far end of False Bay from Cape Town, topographically counterpointing Cape Point (which was captured in the Schreiner epigraph to chapter 6, and of course in *The Lusíads*). The cliff faces due south, seemingly onto infinity, and is the 'place to which slaves at the Cape ran away', as Baderoon's note has it. Any further escape meant jumping to their death. In the poem, the sea is the repository of memory, the medium through which the poet, a dream-swimmer, imagines herself weaving 'like a sea snake' along the long parabolic littoral, 'through the pull and pulse of current'. The run-on lines echo the flowing movement of the water, as in 'bila'. In the first line, she sinks to the seabed, the 'bodem', the hard, plosive Afrikaans word marking the depth. From 'Diving', we already know that water is her element, if often a hostile one (*H* 31–2). Then, retracing the runaways' 'almost' circular route around False Bay, she pulls herself along a 'cord of names', past Strandfontein, Monwabisi, Khayelitsha or 'New Home' (mixing Afrikaans and Xhosa), then moves further past river-mouths named for 'endlessness', opening on wide southern horizons, to the point at Hangklip where the runaways returned to the waves that had brought them from Macassar, 'the place across the ocean'. With the word 'endlessness' repeating across the final stanzas, it is as if the great blue infinity of the Southern Ocean were dissolving into the poem even as slave memories endlessly wash the cliffs.

The catalogue of place-names in 'Hangklip' restores historical distinctness to the 'sky of water'. For Baderoon, writing takes us inside the experience being described; language is imbued with attachment. Names are important enough that even the strand 'with no name' is marked. The poet's route takes in 'Kogelbaai' or Bullet Bay, which harks back to an earlier poem 'Koggelbaai', spelled the Afrikaans rather than the Dutch way (*H* 38), which again confronts the ghosts of the slave past. An uncle 'born with the helm', gifted with second sight, accompanies the family on camping trips to the titular bay, also watched over by a mountain. Able to 'look through the door of time', he sees the presences of fleeing slaves who used the kloofs for shelter. Perhaps they 'live here still', the poet observes, a cryptic acknowledgement that the caves remain occupied by their present-day vagrant descendants as well as by ghosts.[11]

The History of Intimacy ends on a dream vision in 'Cardinal Points' of once again swimming out from False Bay into the Southern Ocean (*H* 73–4). The poet and her friend float spreadeagled, making 'five-pointed figures' like stars, or the Southern Cross constellation, the night 'endless/ in all directions', the cardinal points turning around them. As they lose their bearings in 'gravity's centrifuge', south becomes east, where the poet's ancestors came from. Like 'Hangklip', the poem draws long fluid lines in all directions, so that the floating forms themselves become turning compass roses, reflecting, as in Jazz Money, the stars overhead, and the endless water-cycle connecting sea, sky and land.

Thinking from the South (Again)

The writings clustered in this chapter are not only centred in but also centre southern lands. The writers speak from within southern locations about long southern histories in language that is of the south—referencing *bilabang* and *bodem*, *yurali* and *ngurru-mirgang*, *ghoera* and *ghanna*, hunters' pathways and summer winds, but also rapacious mines, toxic swamps and whale death—intrinsic features of where they belong.[12] Their work articulates an intimate understanding of the land or country, its fragility and its resistances, its cycles and seasons, its declivities and inclinations, as do the above re-imaginings as rain and sea snake of Jazz Money and Gabeba Baderoon. Poets and novelists testify to great loss as well as to powerful memories and associations. And they invite their readers, Indigenous and (at times) non-Indigenous, imaginatively to recreate and rebuild lost worlds together.

Circling round to where this book began, 'Keeping south' returns to southern perceptions cast from within the south. The readings dwell in Indigenous writing and wording, branching out to other writing where it relates to and learns from these perspectives. This work deeply inhabits distance (at least as constructed from the outside), which means that nothing here is regarded as 'about-face' or on the edge, nor is *here* positioned in relation to elsewhere.[13] Where settler writing took the south as antithesis, this work names the land-, sea-, and skyscape as the primary reality, sufficient unto itself.[14] This *here* is where imaginative compasses are centred.

For all of the writers, literature has the power of revising history and retheorising space, or, in the terms of Wiradjuri poet and critic Jeanine Leane, of interrogating gaps and tears in the historical memory of Country.[15] For Waanyi author Alexis Wright, fiction helps to gather and keep 'stories and knowledge and secrets of Aboriginal land'. Her novels *Carpentaria* (2008) and *The Swan Book* (2013) express 'something . . . of ourselves[,] of what has been unwritten, so as to affirm our existence on our own terms'. Exploring these subjunctive realities creates 'alternative narratives and places to visit from time to time, or live in, or believe in, if given the space'.[16] Literary writing also provides a vital means of (re)making sense of southern space, or, to stay with Wright's terms, of examining places of 'enormous energy', like her Gulf Country, or Winch's Ngurambang.[17] This is perhaps especially clear in how lyric poetry makes possible 'planetary enmeshments' and places 'contrary or divergent realities in relationship', as we saw in 'bila'.[18] Linguistic retrieval thus forms an intrinsic part of this work. Wright joins with Tara June Winch, Baderoon, Zoë Wicomb, Terry-Ann Adams and others in their efforts to retrace etymologies and requicken spatial memory by tuning into idiolects, dialects, slang, and other local vocabularies. Where colonial place-names once disconnected Indigenous peoples' songs and stories from the landscape, reviving the first toponyms allows buried memory and ceremony to be retrieved.[19]

From their different standpoints, the writers all work with ideas of space-time or what Doreen Massey called the 'radical contemporaneity' of different histories, as when Kim Scott or Alexis Wright emphasise the hereness and nowness of Indigenous history.[20] 'Deep time . . . is a big, big story', Winch's Albert Gondiwindi comments towards the end of his life, 'The big stuff goes on forever, time ropes and loops and is never straight, that's the real story of time' (*Y* 3). Goori author Melissa Lukashenko's *Too Much Lip* offers a comparable image for space-time change. Contemplating the lands and water around the family home, protagonist Kerry Salter observes the flow of the red dust down from the Great Dividing Range and eventually out to sea: 'It goes on and on in a dizzying loop. . . . It never ends. The beginnings, which are endings, which are beginnings again. . . . *everything is connected up*'. The land shifts, changes, remains the same, the river flows on around sacred Ava's Island, 'the borrogura calls us all back in the end': 'everything is always pulling at everything else whether we know it or not'.[21]

The three sections that follow consider, from the perspectives of landscape, language, and interlinkage, how writers imagine and reimagine from the south and for the south, in the present day, though often through ancient frames. In each case, the discussion continues and amplifies the latitudinal, south-south work of previous chapters by comparatively surveying the patterns writers have developed for thinking the south, at times in resonant parallel.

'Southscapes—Being Here' explores fiction that is self-consciously located in southern land- and seascapes, most notably *Carpentaria* which, with novels like *The Yield*, responds in exemplary ways to the 1992 'Mabo turn' in Australian Indigenous fiction, and the renewed attention to issues of sovereignty it brought.[22] From there, I move in 'Speaking the Land' to considering how southern languages help to centre the fictions in southern space-time, even as the fictions in some cases reciprocally work to revitalise language. Alongside *The Yield*, South African texts referencing or engaging with the creole that is Afrikaans, and its further hybridised version Afrikaaps, or Kaaps, supply a case study of how creative adaptations of a language that has bridged between communities, itself forges and renews interrelationships.

The final section, 'Connection and Reconnection across the South', expands upon a leading theme of *Southern Imagining*. I consider how Indigenous and related texts draw links across and through southern worlds. Juxtaposed and intercalated, the writings plot lines and parallels between different regions of the south, and different southern skies, often shuttling between the microcosmic and the macrocosmic, as did Money and Baderoon.[23] They operate volumetrically, in multi-scalar ways, always questioning concepts of the far and the marginal. They recognise that small shifts can produce seismic events. And they insist not only on the interrelationship of the world's so-called edges, but on the importance for better planetary understanding of recognising that interdependence.

Reading between and across several very different skeins of southern writing, 'Keeping South' avoids imposing a uniform or overarching reading. Rather, I work with an assemblage of quotation and observation, linking and interspersing texts that share energies and images. Together, these selected writings and readings make possible a kind of constellated thinking from which a more south-centred understanding of the planet might crystallise. The responses bear in mind the guidance of Indigenous critic Marcia Langton on Aboriginal 'intersubjectivity' as something 'remade over and over again in a process of dialogue, of imagination, of representation and interpretation'.[24]

The chapter marks a drift away from the singular parabolic journeys traced earlier and considers instead repeat patterns, nonlinear sequences, and looping, spiral trajectories. The move stands to reason where the writers are often located at the vertices of north-south travel, as it were, looking back along former lines of arrival and departure. Trajectories of travel and desire sometimes now move towards the north, as in the work of South African novelist Zoë Wicomb or Aotearoa New Zealand writer Paula Morris, or, more often, they trace complicated twists, looping back to places of beginning while also moving on in time, as in the stories of whale callers, whale riders, and whale spotters featured in the final section.[25] Journeys along littorals, across oceans, and among islands trace complex lattices, zigzags, and other interlaced patterns—what Indigenous theorist Nerida Blair calls 'zones of colliding trajectories' that mix flows and currents.[26] The image is derived from the Yolngu metaphor of Ganma that describes the behaviour of foam and water in an Arnhem Land mangrove lagoon. If there is a common thread that runs through all the work, as we shall see, it is of the felt need for reciprocity with the natural world, that Witi Ihimaera calls the power of interlock or partnership.

Southscapes—Being Here

A striking feature of post-2000 south-centred writing is how frequently the different elements, water and air, land and sea, the human and the more-than-human, merge and intersect. The continuous cycles and minglings of scale we find in Money and in Baderoon, recur, amplified, enlarged, insistent, in the overlapping biospheres in Manenzhe's *Scatterlings*, in Ihimaera's *The Whale Caller*, in Winch's *The Yield*. The 'Desperanians' of *Carpentaria*, their minds a treasure chest of story, 'forever have all seas in their sights', yet they are also at home within the constellations, by which they navigate (*C* 50). As with Polynesian star charts, the circulatory heuristic that these works sketch, zigzags between the blues above and the blues below, between the stars up in the night sky and those reflected in the ocean. Explosive, multidimensional sea- and landscapes stimulate visions of planetary interrelationship, of the earth as a matrix of different depths, centre points and axes, like Menak's 'vast beneath and beyond . . . Far as the horizon, further' in *This Deadman Dance* (244). Or, in Albert Gondiwindi's definition of *manhang* or soil:

> Once you find a piece of something you know about, afterward you end up getting given more and more pieces of the puzzle everywhere you go. . . . *Manhang*—that's where the body goes eventually, and everything else from the *manhang* to the stars is eternally alive with our spirits'. (*Y* 76–7)

Resoketswe Manenzhe's historical novel *Scatterlings* (2020) initiates such volumetric imagining from its first page, opening with a San myth, 'children of the first gods', quoted in the first epigraph above, in which human dispersal is reflected in the stars, and where the stars give a constant measure of that scattering. The novel proceeds to tell in two parts the story of a diasporic Cape family of wanderers or scatterlings impacted across several generations by slavery and apartheid, and so binds together divergent perspectives on southern African history in the twentieth century. Though the story is indigenous to the subcontinent, the West Indian mother, Alisa, knows and carries it, too, as if in her body. The outlines of vast marine horizons intersected by deep slave history that she brings into the narrative—'the sky, merging its endlessness with that sea, looked bluer than ordinary'—link with Baderoon's 'Hangklip' and Diana Ferrus's work.[27] Farther afield, the mythic frame also recalls the stirring section openings of Ihimaera's *The Whale Rider*, 'In the old days, in the years that have gone before us', which tell the story of the 'long sought' coming of the first whale rider.[28]

Scatterlings plots links between different, ramifying African histories, as though by analogy with the path of the Milky Way through the sky. The first part of the novel is set in 1927, the year that Act No. 5, the first law against mixed marriage, came into force in South Africa, and charts the devastating impact of the legislation on the mixed-race Van Zijl family living on a wine farm close to Cape Town. The second part comprises the wife and mother Alisa's diary, which has been salvaged from the fire that consumes the farm. The adaptation of the star myth and the routing of slave stories through the southern tip of Africa powerfully suggests reconnection, even as the family falls apart. The scatterlings are connected through generational patterns, as is the fabric of the novel itself, with the Afrikaans-speaking Nanny Gloria serving as a catalyst for the process of reassembling. Currents from the Atlantic world and Basotho and San cultures mix in the unlikely hub that is southern tip of Africa, but its seeming remoteness from the rest of the world is relativised first and last in relation to the constant presence of the stars.

Like *Scatterlings*, Alexis Wright's visionary epic *Carpentaria* (2006)—a 'contemporary continuation of the Dreaming story', in her own account—sets the predatory activity of modern-day mining against the backdrop of 'the great ancient sagas that defined the laws, customs and values of our culture'.[29] The narrative interlaces past and present, starscapes and seascapes, land and ocean, switching between and often fusing 'real and imagined worlds', in Wright's phrase. Different time frames, human, earthly, climatic, wind through one another, as they do in myth and oral history, to create 'a spinning multistranded helix of stories'. The reader is kept in mind of the complex links between people and other living entities, not excluding the river, the sea, and the sky, and the relations of guardianship connecting them.[30] The novel's key contribution both to this chapter, and *Southern Imagining* as a whole, lies in how Wright 'renovates' Aboriginal literary sensibility, in her terms, to mount a devastating critique of mining, or 'the new war' on Country 'for money' that is changing the nature of time itself. The critique plays out at multiple levels, overland, underground, and at sea (*C* 379, 387).[31]

Carpentaria is set in the Gulf region of northwestern Queensland, in the mining town of Desperance, with at its edges the warring Pricklebush Indigenous community, at a time that is both the late twentieth century and all time. Desperance was intended as a port for shipping goods and raw materials from the 'hinterland' of northern Australia, but the tidal river shifted its course, leaving the harbour dry. The action follows, in particular, the fortunes of the Phantom family with, at its head, Normal or Norm, a fisherman, taxidermist of fish, and lawman of the sea, and Angel Day, his distanced partner, an artist of recycled materials that she finds on the town rubbish dump. In the course of the novel, their activist son Will works with others to sabotage the Gufurrit International mine, which is contaminating the surrounding land and ocean environments, and turning the community against itself (*C* 44). Will's lover, Hope, is the granddaughter of Norm's rival, Joseph Midnight, another traditional owner and a lawman of the land.

Working on a vast, often dystopian canvas, *Carpentaria* opens with a declaration of the 'serpent's covenant', a foundational 'Aboriginal Law' that correlates with the knowledge the elders Phantom and Midnight hold, competitors though they may be (*C* 1, 10, 217–18). The serpent is said to have made all rivers, including the town's tidal river with its swirling motions: 'its being is porous; it permeates everything. It is all around in the atmosphere and is attached to the lives of the river people like skin' (*C* 1–2). With the chapters beginning 'Once upon a time' or 'One evening', this novel of 'ancient times' is framed by a communal narrative voice that shuttles between second and third person, marked by interjections and colloquialisms: 'Well!', 'Shh!', 'And so on and so forth' (*C* 50, 407).[32] Even as we are never unaware of the serpent's dreaming tracks running across the 'stolen continent', out into the Gulf, and up through the skies (*C* 50, 407), so, too, we are repeatedly reminded of the old people's knowledge 'churning' constantly through the present day (*C* 375). Or, as Joseph Midnight notes when laying down guidance for Will's rescue of Hope towards the novel's close, there is nothing new about the contemporary world: 'It's the same world as I live in, and before that, and before that. No such thing as a contemporary world' (*C* 379). And, 'history could be obliterated when the Gods move the country' (*C* 492).[33]

Mobilising their knowledge of Country, the warring elders are eventually able, after their fashion, to conspire with the bonds of sea, sky, desert, and kinship to support Will in his mission of sabotaging the mine. Sparking the novel's huge, orchestral unravelling, he begins by blowing up Gurfurrit's slurry pipelines, but then is apprehended by its paramilitary security force. Local guru Mozzie Fishman comes to the rescue by starting fires that wipe out not only the mine but the surrounding environment, too. From what we know of the watchful presence of the serpent, the immense cyclonic storm and tidal wave that follow are part of a cosmic revenge plan. Will is washed out to sea afloat on a junk island, still learning how to read the ancient navigational routes that Joseph Midnight has taught him: 'Will, remember, you will only travel where the sea country will let you through.' (*C* 376)

Norm Phantom himself sails back inland after the storm, walking away from a flattened Pricklebush hand-in-hand with Bala, Will and Hope's son, to sing the watery country 'afresh.' Once again 'remembering the journey of the heavens, all of the stars, breezes', he navigates by Crux Australis and Kudawedangire, or the Pleiades, following 'the star of navigators' as he did as a child (*C* 494, 504, 519). Like Midnight, he has kept listening to 'the ghosts in the memories of the old folk', their assurance that 'anyone can find hope in the stories: the big stories and the little ones in between, so . . .' (*C* 12). Both remember the sacred sequences in which 'moments in time are the mysterious and powerful companions of fate.' It is worth quoting again, in full, the lesson Midnight gives Will (first cited in chapter 2):

> 'Sing this time. Only that place called such and such. This way, remember. Don't mix it up. Then next place, sing, such and such. Listen to me sing it now and only when the moon is above, like there, bit lower, go on, practice. Remember, don't make mistakes . . .' The song was so long and complicated and had to be remembered in the right sequence where the sea was alive, waves were alive, currents alive, even the clouds. (*C* 390, 375–6)

The advice folds back into the novel as a whole, offering a final retrospective meditation on the 'continuation of the dreaming story' we have just experienced, how it ramifies out 'between different spaces of time', to transcend 'an unacceptable history', and so 'explore the possibilities of other worlds.'[34]

Wright's novel after *Carpentaria*, the dystopian *The Swan Book* (2013), lacks its cathartic energy, yet is worth drawing in here for how the action interweaves space-time and telescopes cosmologies. The novel profiles a situation of internal migration and exile set within the heart of the Australian continent, a century into the future. Climate change and mining have forced a group of Indigenous people, as well as other asylum-seekers and refugees from history, including a crowd of black swans, into an 'oasis of abandonment', an apartheid-type reserve in a Northern Territory swamp. Their situation resembles a refugee internment camp, enclosed behind 'a high, razor-edged fence from the decent people of mainstream civilization'.[35] The second half of the novel, set in a flooded and lawless southern Australian city, continues the work of exposing how Indigenous dispossession in Australia has intersected with environmental devastation—or what Evelyn Araluen calls the settler 'logic of elimination'.[36] The final pages present a qualified release when the protagonist Oblivia Ethylene helps the black swans to escape from a second oasis of abandonment, this time a city tower block, and scatter back into Country. However, what homecoming they might ultimately find there is left uncertain.

Melissa Lukashenko, in her novel *Too Much Lip*, gives the terrible logic of settler development a contemporary setting in the story of the damaged and dispersed Salter family, of Bundjalung, European, and Chinese heritage, living on the outskirts of the fictional Queensland town of Durrongo. The family reunites around an elder's final illness to resist the commercial development of Ava's Island, a sacred river island where the graves of their ancestors lie. Led by their daughter, Kerry, the family draws on knowledge both ancestral and New Age to successfully stop the development while also coming together after twenty years of separation (*TML* 32). In their everyday lives, too, different states of being intersect. Kerry is able to tune into animal communication, the crows instructing her to 'Gulganelehla Bundjalung' her Indigenous language (*TML* 9, 60). And her nephew Donny, whose totem is whale and shark, communes with the marine creatures to the point of drawing a shark upstream of the tidal river. Before, 'he might have learned to call them in off some coastal headland . . . [using] special whale ways'. Today, he is able to summon the shark to play a part in the final showdown with the developers (*TML* 51).

Oceanic symbiosis also distinguishes Noongar novelist Kim Scott's *That Deadman Dance* which undertakes to counter stereotypes of Indigenous people as 'continental in a narrow sense' (*TDD* 5, 242, 312, 399). Set in nineteenth-century colonial Albany, then King George Town, the Western Australian whaling port, the novel mingles Indigenous whale lore with a global whaling imaginary filtered through Herman Melville, to show the extent of Noongar involvement in the shore-based whaling force. The Noongar hero Bobby Wabalanginy's totem—like Donny's—is whale, and he aptly works on the European whaleboats as a steersman and lookout. His strong affinity with the creatures who come in close to the land each winter is emblematised in a story of diving into the heart of the whale that the elder Menak bequeaths him when he is very young (*TDD* 1–3, 160–1). Though the Noongar community's relations with the colonials becomes exploitative as in-shore whale stocks diminish, Bobby's story resists a trajectory of decline at least in terms of how it is told. The four-part narrative repeatedly builds up to moments of seeing farther, inspired by feelings of intimacy with the sea creatures, as when Menak draws a whale into the bay, or, in Bobby's whaling heyday, when he 'sang and danced on a whale's back and the inside of the sea spilled all around him' (*TDD* 160–1, 244–5).[37]

Speaking the Land

For many writers of Indigenous backgrounds, language holds the past and embodies the land. This means that any act of speaking or singing far southern experience using southern words involves a powerful form of repossession. Speakers, writers, reciters, singers are able to 'let go' of 'the moral, symbolic, discursive and psychological significance of the coloniser that occupies their minds', as Linda Tuhiwai Smith urges, so that Indigenous knowledge and values can wash back in.[38] Revived grammars can also give a profound sense of space-time relationality—an especially key benefit given that, for many indigenous southern languages, time and space do not entail separate categories of thought.[39] In Wiradjuri or Gamilaraay, for example, the emplacement of time is reflected in interchangeable prepositions of directionality and position. Or, as Winch's Albert Gondiwindi explains the word *yandu*—'yet, if, then, when, at the time'. Therefore, *yandu* is also 'the glue' of stories (*Y* 24).

This section considers not only how indigenous language transmits local perception but also how fiction can help to revive language, with a special focus first on the work of Tara June Winch, and then on the South African writers Zoë Wicomb and Terry-Ann Adams's varying engagements with Afrikaans. In these cases, as also earlier in Lukashenko, the characters' dialogue, in particular, taps into colloquial and indigenous rhythms and resources. In Winch's *The Yield*, the combined processes of word storing and storying together become the driving force of the narrative. While Wright extensively references Indigenous concepts and locutions in her fiction, Winch moves a stage further. As if in response to the grandfather Albert Gondiwindi's question '*dhuganhu naurambang?*', or 'where is your country?', Winch turns her novel into a breathtaking language-revival project (*C* 470).[40]

The Yield shuttles between three perspectives: August Gondiwindi's, who has returned to the banks of the Murrumby River for her grandfather's funeral; the epistolary testimony of the New South Wales ethnographer, Ferdinand Greenleaf, reporting on the treatment of Aboriginal people on his Prosperous Mission; and the elder Gondiwindi's, an amateur lexicographer resident at present-day Prosperous and August's Poppy. To write Albert Gondiwindi's character, Winch took as her leading premise, as she has said, the idea that 'nothing is ever gone', which also underpins Aboriginal dreaming. In this, she was guided by a 2010s West African linguistic initiative mentored by Wole Soyinka, to revitalise Indigenous arts in Indigenous languages. The project showed her more clearly than she had seen before how a language is an archive, or a handbook of culture. This language handbook explains how kinship works, which feelings count, and how to read the stars. Geo-historical memory is buried in the constituent words and phrases (*Y* 337–41).[41] Language thus also compresses space-time—reaching across 'impossible distances', and 'singing mountains into existence'—effectively reimagining landscapes that were thought to be lost (*Y* 34).

In the novel, Albert Gondiwindi, the lexical change-agent, sets out to relearn and make a dictionary list of 'the old language, the first language—because that is the way to time travel. You can go all the way back' (*Y* 1). This project undergirds his mission to establish Native Title to the Prosperous land, despite the incipient coming of a tin mine—a mission that August eventually helps to complete (*Y* 201). He compiles the Wiradjiri word-list that eventually closes the book, a mechanism that commits him to telling anecdotes, mini-tales and pieces of personal history about the words. On the principle that the whitefella world is 'backward', the word-list runs from *y* down to *b*. There is no *z* or *a*, no conventional beginning or end. Albert's poetic definitions of, for example, *dharrang-dharrang* (messenger, but also librarian), or *murru* (marks or tracks, also lifeways), or *gibirrban* (the Southern Cross constellation), revitalise Wiradjuri within the pages of the novel itself: 'The dictionary is not just words—there are little stories in those pages too' (*Y* 11, 101–2, 125–6). A personal backstory is also attached to many of the words, such as about Albert's time in the Aboriginal boys' home, or his relationship with his wife and family—a backdrop that then threads the individual stories into the wider group's. The words are often viscerally experienced, especially by hungry or *ngarran* August (as blood, as bumps in the mouth). At one and the same time, they speak the history of violence in her region, and yet allow the past to be reclaimed and reconceived (*Y* 24, 29, 33).

In the southern African context, the weave between European and Indigenous roots that Winch mobilises in her fiction is already live within Afrikaans, a creole that served as a *brugtaal* or bridge language between |Xam, Nama, and Dutch communities on the nineteenth-century Northern Cape Frontier. It now forms the lingua franca of the Coloured community concentrated in the wider Cape ('Coloured' in the South African sense).[42] Or, as Manenzhe writes, the 'brew' of Afrikaans allows 'a dozen or so' different cultures to recognise 'parts of themselves in it' (*S* 40). In the Northern and Western Cape, and in southern Namibia, former |Xam and Nama identities are now 'articulated in Afrikaans', and are marked by strong feelings of attachment to the landscape viewed as a living resource. South African writers with access to the language therefore have at hand a rich resource for code-switching and wordplay. Nearly a century ago, author and translator Sol Plaatje's 1930 novel *Mhudi* laid down an early blueprint for such linguistic borrowing, stirring Tswana, Dutch, and Afrikaans into English prose to tell the story of his intrepid heroine and stargazer Mhudi's overland search for her people.[43] For his part, the South African novelist André Brink in *Die eerste lewe van Adamastor* (1988) (translated as *The First Life of Adamastor*), uses Afrikaans wordplay interleaved with Khoi to unfold the tale of the Khoikhoi patriarch who is presented as the original Adamastor.[44] At those points where the prose mixes Khoi with Afrikaans, the sonic blur between the languages is heightened, most noticeably the guttural *k* and *gg* sounds that are common to them both: as in, 'the monotonous drone of the *gurah*', the 'glowing embers of *Tsoab*' (the Milky Way). Brink's sense of affinity with the language may rise from a phenomenon that the poet Antjie Krog also observed when translating extracts from the Bleek and Lloyd archive: she felt that she was translating 'back into the original Afrikaans'.[45]

In so far as any creole describes a continuum of greater and lesser degrees of mixing, the writers in English who draw on Afrikaans line up relative to the degree of their borrowing and adaptation. On one end of this spectrum lies Scotland-based South African author Zoë Wicomb, whose fiction takes standard South African English as its narrative medium, yet marks conversation in domestic settings, as between family and close friends, by using the Coloured home language of Afrikaans. My reading here focuses on Wicomb's short fiction, in which conversations are noticeably textured in this way. On the other end of the spectrum, not treated in this chapter, we find the work of poets like Nathan Trantaal and Ronelda Kamfer, whose writing, though syntactically Afrikaans, is characterised by a high level of code-switching and the use of English chiefly for imported abstractions.[46] The 2020s writer Terry-Ann

Adams's remarkable work sits at a lively median point within this spectrum, in which not only conversation between the characters but also the narrative voices shuttle energetically between Afrikaans and English. The writers, all with Coloured roots, to a greater or lesser extent all create with their use of the language associations of domestic intimacy and a sense of embeddedness in community.[47]

Wicomb's *You Can't Get Lost in Cape Town* (1987) and *The One That Got Away* (2008) are linked story collections in which the same characters appear in different stories, trading minor and major roles.[48] These links underline the feelings of unexpected relationship that the stories at times feature, such as the sense of connection Grant Fotheringay in *The One* develops in relation to his long-time research interest, the Scottish abolitionist Thomas Pringle, 'Father of Colonial South African Poetry' (later the subject of Wicomb's multi-voiced 2020 novel *Still Life*). Or that the young South African Jane experiences on honeymoon in Glasgow when she catches her own 'unmistakably coloured', 'distinctly Khoi' features in the face of the female statue representing South Africa in the Doulton Fountain (*One* 189, 71, 76–77).[49]

As also in her novels about the wider Cape where she was raised, Zoë Wi-comb asserts through her characters' memory work as well as in their dialogue an uncompromising creolised perspective that identifies with the term Khoi to denote the original inhabitants of the Cape, and obliquely embraces their language in so far as it is now mixed into Afrikaans. In the stories 'There's the bird that never flew' and 'Another Story' from *The One*, Wicomb's Coloured characters alternate between justified annoyance and grudging recognition at finding Khoi representations in western art as well as in museum displays closer to home: 'Hottentots in a big glass box' in 'shameful loincloths of animal skin' ('Another Story', *One* 189).[50] The most subtle and evocative of these instances comes with Jane's moment of recognition in 'There's the bird that never flew'. The Doulton fountain, built for the 1888 International Exhibition, represents the colony of South Africa with a group of three figures, a male Boer figure, the titular form of the ostrich, and the non-stereotyped woman who comes across for Jane in a way that celebrates ordinary 'miscegenation': 'South Africa, then, comes to offer a different kind of knowledge' (*One* 65–79).

Wicomb's fictions often trace a north-south axis between Scotland, her place of residence for over four decades, and the Cape, and she has spoken of feeling permanently out of place in the former, and no longer at home where she grew up. Even so, as she puts it, her 'whole intellectual and emotional life is in South Africa', and it forms the setting for much of her fiction.[51] Her narrative perspective is, correspondingly, attuned to its settings, the 'tie-dye' sea colours and 'blinding southern light', as well as to its speaking voices (*One* 15, 24, 35, 108, 117). Wicomb frequently spotlights the Cape's distinctive 'flora', its rhythms and seasons, picking out, for example, March lilies, prickly pears, fig trees rubbing against the window, and Namaqua daisies that flower with the early spring rains (see 'Nothing like the wind', *One* 139). In 'A Trip to the Gifberge', the self-described 'Griqua' Mrs Shenton several times stoops down in the veld to identify and enumerate medical and culinary uses of indigenous plants, like ysterbos and *ghanna* (*Can't* 176, 180). South African flora is poignantly showcased in 'In the Botanic Gardens', set in the domed Kibble Palace hothouse in Glasgow. Dorothy Brink most strongly feels the presence of her missing son Arthur amidst the brilliant display of 'nerine, strelitzia, agapanthus' (*One* 169). South Africa is located on the outer circle of the hothouse, not insignificantly, along with 'Australia, New Zealand, a South American jungle . . . : how quickly it took to tread the entire world'. When Dorothy collapses in front of Papua New Guinea, she believes that the man who helps her is speaking Afrikaans (*One* 169, 171).

This is far from being the only instance in the short stories where Afrikaans offers 'a different kind of knowledge'—a knowledge of community and hence of the heart. Close beneath the surface of Wicomb's narrative prose run the rhythms of spoken Afrikaans, which is signalled using borrowings, interjections, and wordplay. Much of the conversation between friends and within families is conducted in the language, mixed in with Khoikhoi words, as syntactic order and in-group reference suggest. The glossary at the end of *You Can't Get Lost in Cape Town* interleaves Khoikhoi, Malay (bobotie), and Afrikaans, with 'Khoi-khoi' defined as 'Cape aboriginals' (*Can't* 183). And while house-proud Coloured matriarchs associate English speaking, or 'speaking nicely', with social respectability and class elevation, 'comfortable Afrikaans' is their chosen medium, as is again evident in Terry-Ann Adams's work (*One* 87, 173–190). In 'A Trip to the Gifberge', Mrs Shenton, who has 'stubbed' her tongue teaching her daughter English, now feels disrespected by her in it (in that she addresses her in the blunt English second-person of 'You and Your', *Can't* 171). The wordplay on 'hoity-toity' or 'khoity-toity' in 'There's the bird', highlights the fine line drawn between social propriety and linguistic identity. As Grace observes: 'no matter how toity, there's no getting away from the Hotnot, or Khoi, as you youngsters say these days' (*One* 66).

Wicomb pointedly signalled her southern and Indigenous, or Khoi and Kaaps, coordinates early on in her work. The story 'A Trip to the Gifberge' that closes *You Can't Get Lost in Cape Town*, itself closes with the narrator and Wicomb surrogate Frieda Shenton locating her position relative to the 'Due South' by using the Southern Cross constellation, in the classic folk way, as quoted in the epigraph above. The story shows Frieda and her mother coming back together after the former's long absence in Europe and the death of her beloved father. Slowly negotiating the differences that have widened between them, the two take a trip into the Matsikamma mountains, at the mother's suggestion (*Can't* 173). The indigenous name is used in the story; the title references the Afrikaans Gifberge or 'poison mountains'. Yet the plants they find on the trip are anything but poisonous to their relationship, as ancestral logic would indeed dictate. Mrs Shenton twice reminds her daughter of her 'ancestors who roamed these hills', and adds that the protea plants belong to the veld, they are not merely a nationalist or Boer emblem:

> A bush is a bush; it doesn't become what people think they inject into it. We know who lived in these mountains when the Europeans were still shivering in their own country. What they think of the veld and its flowers is of no interest to me. (*Can't* 172, 181)

The story's intensifying southern inclination, captured first in the references to local comfort foods like 'stamp-en-stoot', then to indigenous plants, described in detail, each with its known uses (the mother hailing the proteas with an Afrikaans song), builds to the point where mother and daughter take an afternoon nap together in the veld. They gather grey Khoikhoi bush-bedding to lie on, the plant seeming to drug them both while bringing them closer. On leaving the spot, the mother asks Frieda to take up a white protea bush for her, so replacing the shop-bought flowers she has brought from the airport. Finally, on their way home, Frieda's sightline moves up once again to the 'huge stars burning' into the darkness that she had already noticed on her first night. The moment is preparatory to the assertion of her southern compass, the curiously feminised Southern Cross with 'her four points', in the story's final lines (*Can't* 174, 181–2).[52] Though Mrs Shenton has not achieved her aim of looking back at her home in the 'Klein Namaqualand' from the mountain edge, she accepts 'with interest' Frieda's closing thought about possibly returning home to Cape Town, and, implicitly, re-entering the world of her Griqua ancestors.

Terry-Ann Adams's novel *those who live in cages* (2020) tunes into the interlinked lives of five Coloured women, Kaylynn, Bertha, Janice, Laverne, and Raquel, each trying to 'survive another day' of domestic violence, marital fallout, teenage pregnancy and other rites of passage in Eldorado Park or Eldos in the south of Johannesburg.[53] In this formerly Coloureds-only area, according to apartheid's distinctions, the vernacular is Afrikaans: 'Everything was built with a purpose . . . to keep the Coloured people locked in and occupied' (*Cages* 37). The women's phone calls, diary entries, and conversation make immediate Eldos's sounds and flavours—the street games like 'drie blikkies' and dice, the speakers blasting on street corners, 'the smell of Cobra polish and new paint after Christmas bonuses get paid in'—as, too, does the fully hybridised Afrikaans-English narrative prose. Relayed exclusively via the women's speaking voices, the storylines about coping with their demanding men, having children, and getting, or not, an education, switch continually between Afrikaans and English. The energetic transactions propel the action, such as when Bertha makes clear that she wants a divorce. Her intentions would be opaque to a reader without Afrikaans (*Cages* 77).

those who live in cages is told in four parts, each prefaced with a view on Eldos as if from the perspective of the community, and the concentration of Afrikaans shifts between the characters depending on their age and status. At one extreme is Bertha Louw, a cleaner, the mother of Raquel or Kela, Keagan and Janice, whose medium is an earthy street Afrikaans, with occasional code-switching into English for emphasis ('baby' rather than 'baba', ''n rubbish', ''n injustice', *Cages* 47). A distinctive sample: 'Ek gaan eers next week werk toe maar ek het nog so baie om te doen hier by die huis.' ('I will go back to work next week but I still have so much to do here at home') (*Cages* 18). At the other extreme stands the socially aspirant Kaylynn Abrahams, the daughter of Bertha's neighbour and Janice's friend, who hopes to study design in Cape Town. Kaylynn duly uses mostly English laced with Americanisms ('Holy Shit', 'she puts so much pressure', *Cages* 22, 43), and mixes registers for effect, as do her peers or near-peers Janice and Raquel. Religious Laverne, a Louw cousin and single mother visiting from provincial De Aar, tells her story in diary form using a more composed, reflective prose. Cape relatives' 'brei' pronunciation in Afrikaans introduces another linguistic strain again, that Janice lightly mocks: 'want djy moet van jou kop af wies' (*Cages* 147–8).

But to unpick the different voices is to parse too precisely this 'profound imagining' of present-day Coloured realities, and belies the griefs and aggravation the women suffer, in particular Bertha.[54] Her son Keagan, 're-found' by drugs, dies after rehab, 'verlei' by 'tjommies', led astray by his mates. Bertha's frustration about his situation builds from an early stage: 'Keagan maar hoe kon jy so careless wees?' (*Cages* 28, 47). Raquel, married to Black media-star

Sandile, 'a well-off man with connections', unable to have children, empathises: 'When will my mother ever have peace?' (*Cages* 80). But Raquel also betrays a deep-seated prejudice about her own community. Her further comment, 'The bastard behaviour is kamstig hereditary', reflects prejudice about her own mixed origins. As Kaylynn observes, the apartheid-made township is divided into the titular cages within cages that extend into people's minds: 'You are not an individual here; you are a part of something bigger' (*Cages* 97). Relatives and friends perpetually snoop into each other's business, condemning family members roundly for child murder and selfishness, as Bertha and Laverne do to Janice after her abortion. The night is full of the cries of 'broken women, the wounded women and the women scorned' (*Cages* 91). Though their verbal vibrancy brings the characters little lasting relief, their ability linguistically to mingle 'footsteps from all over South Africa', makes their lives survivable, and gives day-to-day existence a sometimes joyous performative charge (*Cages* 136).

Connection and Reconnection across the South

For Alexis Wright, Indigenous lore and law have a supra-continental reach extending back to ancient Palaeozoic times. The mighty ur-ancestor's tracks radiate so far and wide through and beyond the Australian continent that they inscribe 'a book of another kind covering thousands of kilometres', a story drawn down from 'thousands of creation stories for the guardians of Gondwanaland' (*C* 124). A related geo-mythic idea emerges in *The Swan Book* with its complex symbol of the swamp oasis that knits together swan myths and legends from around the world. Oblivia Ethylene's guardian, the storyteller Bella Donna, sets the tone, telling stories of migration that have themselves been carried across from other continents. *Praiseworthy* further amplifies the preoccupation with Australia as a space of multiple migrations, including of donkeys and butterflies.

This final section draws inspiration from Wright's complex images of migrating and radiating stories, and Adams's of mingled linguistic footsteps, to return to the patterns of latitudinal lines and lattices that we earlier imagined running around the hemispheric south. Though the texts gathered together in this chapter emerge largely from the continental landmasses of Australia and southern Africa, they nonetheless register the 'pressure of geography' in the far south at large. The condition of being out on the edge, on 'the periphery of the periphery', reverberates through them, and sea-facing views and littoral aspects predominate.[55] These commonalities of experience encourage the reader to weave some of the 'joint by joint' metaphoric connections that chapter 2 began to explore, with perspectives from peninsulas, islands, and desert coastlines repeating around and across the hemisphere.

Money and Baderoon's poetry raised visions of riverine, littoral, and sidereal interconnection. Relatedly, Australian-South African Yvette Christiansë's fragmentary poems about exile and displacement in the southern oceans address remote and yet entwined islandic conditions. As does Baderoon, Christiansë in *Castaway* (1999) and *Imprendehora* (2009) follows 'a southern-hemispheric set of itineraries', that connect Indian and Atlantic waters through the Cape's 'deadly inflection point', and then thread these links further to St. Helena in the southern Atlantic, the island of those 'shipwrecked by history', like Napoleon, and like her enslaved grandmother.[56] Throughout *Castaway*, in particular, Christiansë is aware of this grandmother's spectral presence summoning her to write the poems in order to retrieve the memory of things lost—to produce 'geographies of connection' out of experiences of 'displacement and dispersal', as Meg Samuelson writes.[57]

Elsewhere, too, islands abound. Staying within the South Atlantic's inclement waters, Karen Jennings' fable-like novel *An Island* (2021) describes the predicament of a lighthouse keeper on an outcrop resembling Robben Island somewhere off the southern African coast, a place 'ravaged by the elements' and choked up with 'smotherweed'.[58] Farther afield, to the east, New Zealander Eleanor Catton's historical thriller *The Luminaries* (2013) circles around the South Island, repeating and amplifying many of the commonplace motifs of Southern Ocean fiction—of gold mining and smuggling, whaling and whalebones, coasteering and star-gazing.[59] Ava's Island in Lukashenko's *Too Much Lip*, too, formed a centre of spiritual gravity, while islands cluster just beyond the horizon in *That Deadman Dance*, marking the rim of Albany's coastal whaling grounds. Oblivia's oasis of abandonment in *The Swan Book* was a hellish but sovereign island in the midst of the desert. Meanwhile, out at sea, in *Carpentaria* and in *The Whale Rider*, toxic islands of junk and radioactive waste float like 'roaming armadas' (*C* 386, *WR* 67).

These island perspectives can be imagined as serially repeating across the southern oceans, mirroring Nerida Blair's zones of colliding trajectories. Writers speak of occupying ledges and verandas of land, coastlines where the desert meets the ocean, places of 'inhuman scale' and 'earthly mystery', swept by southwesterly gales, and flooded with bright, white southern light.[60] Bobby Wabalanginy in Kim Scott has been 'over the horizon . . . [and] sailed away and back from between the islands, from where the sun rises and the whales also come' (*TDD* 61, 103, 178). Brink's T'kama takes his bearings from the wind, which blows from the south. The restless New Zealand swimmer Jacob in Avi Duckor-Jones's *Swim* comes to terms with the loss of his father by striking out on ambitious ocean swims to an island just beyond the horizon, a 'little shadow . . . scalloped out of cloud'.[61] Ihimaera in *The Whale Rider* describes the ocean extending to Antarctica as 'the well at the bottom of the world': 'when you looked into it you felt you could see to the end of forever' (*WR* 13, 108). Many south-facing bays and sea cliffs that 'give depth and protection' not unexpectedly form whale nurseries. *The Whale Rider* describes these as 'Te Whiti Te Ra. The nursery, the cetacean crib . . . within the Antarctic feeding range' (*WR* 19).[62]

As for overland routes, most obviously water courses, these, too, move shorewards, as we saw with Money and Baderoon, with Wright and Winch. Māori poet Robert Sullivan's 'Hello Great North Road' imagines going west towards the sunset along the road north from Auckland, to take the surf at 'Karekare, . . . Muriwai, . . . Bethells, . . . Piha'.[63] Muidinga and Tuahir in Mia Couto's *Sleepwalking Land* experience the littoral as both littered with civil war debris and layered with mythic histories.[64] And, as if continuing into the present day the Nama praise song to the sea that headed chapter 2 above, the 'poesía del agua' of the Chilean poet Pablo Neruda (in the words of Octavio Paz), habitually looks out to sea from the edge of his longitudinally-disposed homeland. Its littoral, like Namibia's, like Western Australia's, faces west. Neruda's long poem 'Cuándo de Chile' or 'When from Chile' (from *Las uvas y el viento*), addresses the question implied by its title with perspectives from both within and without the country. Describing Chile as a 'largo pétalo de mar', he imagines himself from exile as a river running out to the ocean, and as engirdled with foam. These sightlines once again outline an archipelagic logic of intersecting pathways, working with and against the magnetism of the horizon.[65]

Further out from the shore, sea creatures' flight paths and swim tracks create reticulations of kinship between different living beings across the southern and south-facing oceans. The complicated migratory pathways of seals, whales, and sharks augment the patterns that, elsewhere, legend and language describe. Deep-swimming groper fish shape Norm Phantom's sea- and sky-routes (*C* 6–7). Kindzu in *Sleepwalking Land* suffers from 'the whale's illness', a cross-species hypersensitivity to 'their great sighing that causes the ocean to fill and ebb', for which the cure is to travel the shoreline and seek remote frontiers. And 'the Doctor', the shark protagonist in Lukashenko's *Too Much Lip*, while swimming into the open Pacific, feels a 'sudden tug' and heads back upriver to Ava's Island to keep a cross-species appointment with Donny. She beats a rhythm into the water 'as though she was playing a watery instrument, her entire body the bow' (*TML* 258–59).

Some of the closest and most striking interactions across the species divide manifest in Witi Ihimaera's haunting, parable-like *The Whale Rider* (1987) and Zakes Mda's equally ambitious *The Whale Caller* (2005). Facing each other across the Southern Ocean, the two novels stereophonically challenge readers to think about ourselves in interrelationship with other creatures across far southern waters, 'inextricably intertwined' like the bull whale and the girl rider, Kahu (*WR* 156). Yet they also both consider the consequences of when that relationship becomes unbalanced under social and environmental pressures, which include, in the case of the former novel, the resistance of cultural elders to change.

The Whale Rider takes as its reference point the Māori origin story about the arrival in Aotearoa of human beings from the Pacific led by the first whale rider, Paikea, who brought life to the islands by casting spears onto the shore from the back of a whale (*WR* 173). Though the human narrator of the modern sections of the novel is Rawiri, uncle to the gifted child Kahu, iterations of the legend open each of the novel's four parts, told from the perspective of a whale pod migrating through the Pacific from Antarctic waters. The citations track the changing seasons from spring through to late winter, the time when the whales come closer to the shore near Whangara on the east coast of the North Island to breed. In the present of the novel, the current whale rider, the elder Koro Apirana, is on a mission to preserve the ancient traditions by finding and appointing a male successor. To this end, he runs a Māori cultural school exclusively for boys, all the while overlooking his great-grandchild, Kahu, who has been symbolically anointed by Paikea's last spear. While the boys fail to accomplish the tests that Koro sets for them, Kahu excels at them all.

Resolution comes on the day when Kahu establishes an affinity with a beached old bull whale, Koro's cetacean counterpart, who, however, unlike her grandfather, recognises her as Paikea's successor. Anthropogenic changes in his underwater world—including from nuclear testing—have disoriented him, as they did a large pod fatally stranded on a nearby coast the night before (*WR* 134). Kahu senses his need and swims out to him, and he, in turn, modifies his body surface to give her handles and a breathing space to be able to ride high on his head and guide him back out to sea. This sacrificial act nearly costs Kahu her life—the whale mothers must intervene on her behalf—but its outcome is that she at last gains acceptance from Koro Apirana. The novel closes with the whales' breathing chant 'Let it be' which has sounded throughout, reconfirming the interlock between the 'threads of Paikea'—between both the species and the generations.

Set around the coastline of Hermanus close to Africa's southernmost promontory, Mda's *The Whale Caller* intertextually expands Ihimaera's migratory whale maps into African waters.[66] The titular Whale Caller is besotted with a southern right whale he names Sharisha, and the whale appears to reciprocate his interest. Returning each spring from her deep south feeding grounds, she swims close into shore in response to the call of his homemade kelp horn, cavorting to the sounds that penetrate 'deep into every aperture of [her] body', tail-slapping and flashing a 'surf-white smile' (*WC* 36, 57–9). The intensity of the feeling the two share is set against the Whale Caller's relationship with his human girlfriend, Saluni, which is acrimonious and humdrum by contrast (*WC* 97).

The sexual charge between the human and the whale—his high-pitched wails and deep breathing, her lobtailing and groaning—actualises their interspecies affinity but with fatal consequences. The Whale Caller becomes hooked to the practice of summoning Sharisha, believing that their 'intimate moments' give her joy, even when she has a calf (*WC* 11–12, 117). One day, during a storm, Sharisha succeeds in beaching herself, and, by the time the Whale Caller reaches the scene, she has been killed. None of the ties he has built have helped her; in fact, the contrary. As in *The Whale Rider*, human affinity with the cetaceans is impacted by disharmonies in the wider oceanic world, though the implication in both novels is that the potential exists for the breach to be restored, that ancient lore and legend can be revised and adapted for present-day needs.

'You and the Movement of Water'

The southern, largely Indigenous writers gathered together in this chapter, trace and retrace mythic, social, linguistic and migratory lines across the south. 'Bila' and 'Hangklip', *Carpentaria* and *The Yield*, create a stickiness between different contexts and challenge readers to connect across divides. The writing approaches southern environments not as prey, victim, or exploitable resource, as does the Gurfurrit mine, or, further back, Captain Ahab, but rather as complex, entangled zones in ceaseless motion. Whale riders and callers, stargazers and word-list makers, outline an at-once-southern and planetary poetics that is both experimental, tapping into alternative linguistic and mythic resources, and co-lateral, rising out of interchange across the south.

Collectively, these works offer an alternative vision of the global—alternative not only because their perspective is from the south, but also because they recognise the philosophical and ethical implications of seeing otherwise and about face. Together they can be seen to build 'an interconnected frame of analysis' that conceives of the planet simultaneously from local, regional, Indigenous, and oceanic positions, and sidesteps the northern paradigms that still persistently shape theory, including theory from the south.[67] The writings recognise not only that the globe as seen and experienced from austral vantage points spins differently, but also that this spin can help to adjust historical imbalances, to find new hope in ancient stories, and stimulate 'alternative modes of conceiving planetary co-existence'.[68]

Connectivity between lands and longitudes is a keynote everywhere. Speakers and characters, by interacting with their surroundings, allow themselves to be impacted by the interaction. There is 'no difference between you and the movement of water as it seasonally shifts its tracks according to its own mood', in Alexis Wright's words (*C* 3). The texts' multi-layered spaces—like *Carpentaria*'s underground caves extending to mangrove mudflats abutting oceanic depths—express what the Indian author Amitav Ghosh in his environmental work highlights as the vital continuities of experience that we all need better to observe: the 'dense web of mutual sustenance and symbolism' that connects nature and culture.[69] We see that the seemingly remote in time and space is, in fact, proximate, impacting us here, now. The far away, so often labelled external and not worth thinking about, has repercussions wherever in the world we stand.[70]

8

Faraway Close

time weaves a horizon of many strands

—JAZZ MONEY, 'HOW TO MAKE A BASKET' (2021)

Southland . . . where each day and night could be felt in its existence, and the grass and the insects in the grass could speak and be heard.

—JANET FRAME, *TO THE ISLAND* (1982)

When you see the Southern Cross for the first time
You understand now why you came this way.

—CROSBY, STILLS, NASH, 'SOUTHERN CROSS', *DAYLIGHT AGAIN* (1982)

On the Farthest Edges of the World

Southern Imagining has explored ideas of southern lands and oceans as the quintessential beyond, the farthest far. Yet, throughout, these distant edges and seascapes have also taught us about their pressing hereness and nowness—everywhere. How they form an integral part of life on Earth. How their existence and their wellbeing are fundamental to our sustaining and even conceiving our planetary being in its fullness.[1]

In closing, I take the arcing routes through and around the far southern hemisphere that the previous chapters have traced, to mould a kind of convex lens through which to reflect back on the path I have come. I want to look at some of the things that this distinctive southern optic may have clarified, and to consider once again how its curving lines can condition readers to a more southerly disposition. In this task, I take my inspiration from the ways in which my own southern experiences have informed the senses of the south that the book has explored. So, whereas I previously read the far south through literary writing, I now think back through my readings, and try to see in sharper focus the degree to which they were illuminated by the austral perceptions that have always shaped my understanding.

Flying over the folded red landscape of Namibia in the southern spring of 2022, or, in early 2019, breaching the orange-brown Australian coast, dotted with saltpans, I follow with my eyes the spread of age-old watercourses across these now bone-dry desert lands. I see the shadow of the plane race over vast glacial valleys carved out by Palaeolithic ice. I watch the long cloud-streamers that wash up with the cold ocean currents from the icy south—the Benguela, the West Australian. I think of the signs made long ago on those same rocks by the inhabitants of these lands as they situated themselves, in their time, in their surroundings—marks that in some places remain to this day. I am swept by senses not so much of limitlessness as of almost-inconceivable expanse, ancientness, and aloneness.[2] And yet, wherever I touch down, strong feelings of recognition sweep through me. I raise my face to the incomparable light and feel the air seethe around my body. And, no matter where this is, I know that, somehow, I am home.[3] My being, my writing, is in its place again. My mood compass, always yearning south, has come to rest.[4]

Born at 29.8587° S, in November, in Durban, South Africa, the thermometer standing at over 40°C, I am always still at ease when I find the sun in the northern sky. Here, in the south, where I am writing this sentence, I understand not only the fall of the light, but also its 'oceanic edge-of-the-world' quality.[5] I trust that after sunset, the night sky, too, will blaze. The unparalleled clarity of both southern daylight and starlight explains why I have written this book as far as it was possible under southern skies. And where it was not possible, I have written, nonetheless, with southern skies in mind. At the end of a day's writing, I have gone out and looked up. I have squinted into the orange setting sun. I have pinpointed the Southern Cross in the southern sky and the Pleiades in the northern. I have gazed up, up, up, into the blue overhead, till it was as if I was diving into it. Seeing with this light, I have understood clearly that the concepts and models that arise from these spaces are in all cases best placed to respond to them.

In what follows, I take my bearings from the southern writers featured in the previous chapters, from their attempts to use images of light, cloud, oceans, horizons, stars, to afford views on the south from the south. Photographs I have taken in the far south throughout the writing of this book, and that also feature at the beginning of the chapters, highlight and extend these reflections. These juxtaposed fillets of southern perception will, I hope, reilluminate once more the connectedness of the very far with the seeming centre. Rocky promontories, curling waves, and, above all, the singular blue-blue-white light, will reassert the importance of what I call the remote proximate—the far-but-here southern awareness that, though counter-intuitive to many, may need to become second-nature to all.

And Yet Their Closeness

For many cultural practitioners, including southerners, the south remains the supreme correlate of the far, the ultimate *ne plus ultra*. The idea persists both in film and in literary writing. End-of-world remoteness pervades the signature

landscapes of New Zealander Jane Campion's films and television series. *Top of the Lake* (2017) extends and deepens the earlier atmospheric engagements of *An Angel at My Table* (1990) and *The Piano* (1993).[6] The plot of compatriot Eleanor Catton's apocalyptic novel *Birnam Wood* (2023), set in the South Island, in the Southern Alps, revolves around the idea of being remote—out on a far promontory, beyond a cut-off mountain pass, away from the sight of the world, though not of a supra-survivalist's drone surveillance.[7]

And yet, no matter how remote and inaccessible the far south may seem in these works, they simultaneously acknowledge a perception that has recurred across *Southern Imagining*. From Coleridge's *The Rime of the Ancient Mariner* right the way through to Jazz Money's 'bila', the writings have made observations on atmospheric, hemispheric, and wider planetary connectivity. They have recognised the interaction of southern lands and oceans, both with each other and with everywhere else. Some have offered object lessons on what happens when we treat these interrelations with contempt, or when we privilege the northern human at the cost of other creaturely flourishing.[8] Others, including J. M. Coetzee, Witi Ihimaera and the many following their imaginative prompt, have taken the further step of consciously angling their philosophical and environmental perspectives in a more southerly direction, as Coetzee explicitly does in 'The Novel in Africa', from *Elizabeth Costello*, for example.[9] Together, they have underscored that the planetary 'edge' is anything but marginal, anything but out there on its own.

As we now know all too well, northern peoples have long been habituated to seeing themselves at the epicentre of world history, commanding the vantage point from which the visibility of everything beyond is registered. Distant southern spaces in particular have been bracketed from northern consideration, though it was here that many of the raw materials that fuelled capitalist development originated, as Herman Melville memorably showed. Under the modern empires, southern sites of extraction lay at the end of long shipboard journeys, down single-lane, purpose-built roads, and one-track railway lines. Later, as these resources ran out, or fell out of use, so did the communication lines, and the memory of these 'outside' places, already partially erased, proportionately faded still further.[10] For northerners it has long been at once supererogatory and demanding to try to see the world from the south.

In his 2023 book *Sensational*, Ashley Ward explains how sensation is processed in the brain, suggesting that human perception makes up a far more complex 'weave' than the well-described categories of the five senses are able to capture.[11] According to Ward, the fifty and more extra possible senses include magnetoreception, or the ability to detect Earth's polarity, and proprioception, the sense of our body's position in space. Both senses surely inform what I have outlined in these pages as a southerly disposition, responsive as it is to the opposite tilt of the earth, the different inclination of the sun. Both suggest routes into a keener understanding of southness as a matrix of feeling, of being here yet still far—an approach that northerners, too, can tune into. For, as Melville also taught, these other ways of looking at the world—south-side-up, counterclockwise—bear better witness not only to southern interrelationship, but also to the importance of noticing and acknowledging it.

As I understand it, the feeling of the far south is so singular and suggestive as to constitute an independent slice of the sensorium, one moulded at one and the same time by light, spin, pull, and inclination. This complex challenges us to conceive of the world through a wider, cross-planetary range of models, to respond to southern environments in ways appropriate to their uniqueness, their own particular haecceity.[12] Lola Frost's *The Edge of the Skirt of the World* (2014) represents this feeling in painting (see colour insert, image 3). The reduced, desolate-looking 'southern tips of Australasia, Africa and South America', a bleak, brownish cluster of rocky outcrops, face back up to the rest of the world, taking 'a pot shot' at the dominant northern (or western) vantage point that has moulded our views not only of the world, but of what most counts in it.[13]

This afterword partakes in that abashed yet defiant gaze 'back up', and responds to fragments of that sensorium, as my epigraphs, too, have done throughout.

Contrariwise, to the Stars

At nighttime, a defining feature of the far south—to dark-sky astronomers perhaps *the* defining feature—comes spectacularly into view, the 'fierce field' of the southern stars.[14] Most prominently, the great white sheet of the Milky Way with its dark median gash arcing across the sky. Further to the south and west, the two spiral dwarf galaxies of the Magellanic Clouds, like silver

smudges from a Titanic finger. And the focal point due south, the array of Crux or the Southern Cross, five-pointed, windmilling, *gibirrban* in Tara June Winch and Albert Gondiwindi's Wiradjuri dictionary, with the two brilliant pointer stars, Alpha and Beta Centauri, on a line extending to the asterism's 'left'. This nighttime brilliance is an objective physical fact, as we saw, rising from the orientation of the South Pole to the centre of our galaxy. Moreover, some stars, including Alpha Centauri, are actually closer by and so appear to blaze. It is, perhaps, another kind of remote proximity, on a universal scale.

Across time, writers and artists have often noticed that the southern darkness is never purely dark. On clear nights in the desert or on the pampas, it is said that you can read by starlight. In Schreiner's description in *From Man to Man*, 'ten thousand stars . . . [throw] down their points of light brighter than any diamonds'.[15] For maritime voyagers, the extent of ocean in the hemisphere has always amplified the effect, with the astral array reflected in what Joseph Conrad called the mirror of the sea.[16]

The images above of the southern night sky I took with my iPhone in Cape Town (33.5°S), Adelaide (34.5°S), and again Cape Town, in March 2022, December 2022, and March 2023. The sky in the first photograph is greenish-white, in the last two light-grey, in all three cases light-polluted, but the Crux pattern is still clearly discernible. All southern cities lie within the same broad band of latitude, so that even from large conurbations like Johannesburg or Buenos Aires, the Southern Cross and its pointer stars tend to be unmissable, including on partly cloudy nights. The constellation is circumpolar, making a full revolution through the sky in any twenty-four-hour cycle. South of 35°, the full cycle is visible at all times of the year. Which means that the asterism's position from one city to another around the hemisphere is always comparable, depending on the hour and the time of year. Farther south, Crux lies higher overhead. In Dunedin (45.8°S) in December, I saw the Cross from the Brackens lookout, leaning at an angle of ten o'clock over Signal Hill. From Ushuaia in Tierra Del Fuego, the southernmost city in the world (55°S), in the southern autumn, it was almost directly overhead.

I remember, growing up, how the Southern Cross constellation stood high over the roofs of the neighbours' houses, especially in the wintertime. The more lopsided False Cross leaned 'above' it, closer to the zenith. I remember listening to the British astronomer Patrick Moore's weekly programmes on the radio. A self-confessed fan of the arresting southern skies, Moore guided listeners in identifying features like the Triangulum Australe, close to the celestial pole, or the Coal Sack, the dark nebula near Crux, the place where the Dark Emu lays its beak. On clear, dry evenings, I would run back outside after listening to the programme, the Milky Way almost implausibly bright overhead. I would stand and pick out the stars and constellations Moore had discussed. There was Gamma Crucis or Gacrux, the 'top' star of Crux, ninety light-years away, and Ginan, the more indistinct fifth star, and Beta Mimosa, leftmost, four times as far again, and yet shining just there, here, over the nearby roofs.

Whenever I arrive back in the south, I go out as night falls to see the stars begin to emerge. They come in at first gradually, then in radiant bursts and clusters—pink, blue, white. And, though I am back in place, I am sometimes also filled with deep, cavernous feelings of remoteness and isolation—that sense of what D. H. Lawrence described as the southern 'underdark'.[17] I hear a car crunch down the road, and then the noise fading. Suddenly, it feels very still and quiet. The darkness between the stars is deep. I am aware that it would take many hours of driving to reach the borders of this night. Or, as Samanta Schweblin writes in her novel *Distancia de Rescate*, translated as *Fever Dream* (2017):

> The sound of the trees, the cars on the road every once in a while, and the barking of a dog confirmed that the country spread out immensely to either side, and that everything was miles away.[18]

This 'solitude reinforced by remoteness', in Eduardo Fernando Varela's account in *Patagonia, Route 203*, creates an 'opaque melancholy' that invades the body, as I acknowledge.[19] For this, too, is something of the south—feeling the desolation of its great distances from within.

Wheeling across the Sky

For southern stargazers, the hemisphere's constellations might be imagined as knitting the world's margins together. The five bright stars of the Southern Cross have guided me in understanding how.

Northern cultural lore takes the Pole star as the fixed point in the heavens in relation to which travellers orient themselves. The southern night sky, Luís de Camões jibed, lacks this steady point of reference.[20] Yet, I would riposte, what the southern night sky has instead is a kind of astral stick map, the frame of the Crux asterism itself. Working with its parallelogram shape, it is relatively easy to pinpoint due south, as does Frieda in Wicomb's 'A Trip to the Gifberge'. First, draw a line from Gacrux through Acrux. Triangulate the line with the perpendicular from Alpha and Beta Centauri. Then, from the point where they intersect, at the Southern Celestial Pole, drop a third line down to the southern horizon.

Watching the Southern Cross as a child turn slow somersaults across the night sky, I imagined its rotations tracing a pathway west. Though my geographic imagination at that stage probably reached no farther than Cape Point, the sense began gradually to creep over me, even then, that the revolving constellation operated in the manner of a celestial tracing wheel. Later, the turning asterism afforded me a means of linking southern worlds in my mind, sewing them into one interwoven band.

Whenever I have flown across the south, within the hemisphere, this idea has each time grown clearer. Travelling west or east from any point beyond 32° South at nighttime, the Crux is always there in the southern sky. I have watched it on overnight flights from Cape Town to Rio, from Sydney to Auckland, from Adelaide across to Western Australia, a steady marker over the wing. I have peered out at it from a plane window over Melbourne in 2009, over the Cape Peninsula in 2022, right above Hoerikwaggo in 2024. Following its turns, a sense of lateral connection increasingly crept upon me that I have built into this book as a structuring idea. I began to see the links that in premodern times manifested, at least virtually, in the interlaced myths and stories with which cultures explained seasonal change and their own life cycles.

My first intercontinental journey across the south was as a scholarship student in 1979, flying from South Africa to South America, Cape Town to Rio. As the plane travelled west, I remember watching Table Mountain, tinged gold by the setting sun, sinking slowly below the darkening horizon, the dying light turning to rose, then purple-blue, and the stars coming out. I remember the Southern Cross standing over the wing, how it seemed to stay with us and track our path, how it emphasised that were moving *through*, and not leaving, the hemisphere. *This* hemisphere. That we were travelling within the south. Many years later, on a cross-south flight from Johannesburg to Melbourne, looping over Kerguelen Island, the sensation returned. The experience of travelling hour by hour with Crux lying over the wing, inaugurated once again the expansive yet contained feeling of being within the south, and of this being sufficient. There was no need to go further. It is the kind of feeling that northerners must have about their hemisphere all the time.

I thought during that later flight, and have many times since, of the Indigenous Australian artist Yatjiki Vicki Cullinan's huge starscape *Munga Ilkari*, or *Night Sky*, reproduced earlier in this book, that I first saw in December 2017, in the Art Gallery of South Australia. The painting shows a conglomeration of blazing constellations, coronae clustering in upon coronae, nebulae overlapping nebulae, exactly as we find in our galaxy. The stars crowd out the blue-red darkness blotched roughly at the zenith, at the centre of the painting, the dense impasto dots heightening the massed effect so that the entire sky seems to be filled with starlight, in every direction. Lacking an earthly vantage point, immersed in the night sky, viewers share, perhaps, the eyeshot of stargazers across the south, across the ages—their perspective trained on far-distant deep time that they at the same time wove into their understanding of life-rhythms here on earth.[21]

Turning to Day

But if astral light in the south is distinctive, austral daylight is perhaps even more so, though also more indefinable—blue-blue-white, incandescent. Wherever in the hemisphere south of around 20° latitude we travel, this is the light that pours down. It is recognisable in most photographs of the south, whether of cities or deserts, whether in colour or black-and-white. Horacio Coppola's 1930s photographs of his native Buenos Aires with their sunstruck streets and sharp shadows reflect intensively on this light.[22] The 2010 Chilean documentary *Nostalgia de la Luz* takes the *luz* as both its subject and its medium of investigation.[23] Radiant austral light with its laminating or veneering effects probably gives the nearest physical correlate for what in this book I present as southern perception. It gives us a primary affordance for seeing the south up close, as *here*.

In *An Imperfect Blessing*, Nadia Davids speaks of the southern sky as 'duck-egg blue', the 'too bright' light illuminating the edges of things 'as only the Cape sun can [do]'.[24] Melissa Lukashenko in *Too Much Lip* resorts to metonym to capture the effect of a blast to the eye from 'late December bouncing straight back up . . . off the tar'.[25] The northerner D. H. Lawrence in *Kangaroo*, too, remarks on 'the unspeakable beauty' of southern sunlight over the sea, the 'pure blue sky, so light and absolutely unsullied, it was always a wonder'.[26] Katherine Mansfield had preceded him in noticing the sunlight's silver sheen on the ocean in her stories set around Wellington harbour. For the South African novelist Christopher Hope, this 'smoky blue' light has a kind of presence, floating above the 'red earth gardens and over the sandy roads' of the Pretoria suburbs where he grew up.[27] To Eleanor Catton in the Southern Alps, the sky takes on a 'perfect watercolour fade from azure down to baby blue'.[28] In the desert context of Botswana, Elizabeth in Bessie Head's *A Question of Power* watches the sunlight 'flying in all directions' off the hero Sello's face. The light appears to move and have substance, perhaps also to bear a spiritual power.[29]

This vast light drenches my southern memory. I remember flying into South Australia one December, though it could also have been the South Island or South Africa or perhaps even South Georgia, and it could have been October, or April, or even May. The light blazing off the corrugated roofs opposite struck the corner of my eye and, at the same instant, I knew, I know, I am in the south. I look away, blink, look back, and, yes, it is true, I am *here*. I have my bearings.[30]

That southern light radiates in this distinct way makes physical sense in a hemisphere that is more oceanic and atmospherically 'bluer' than the northern, the sea-stranded southern peninsulas and islands forming an archipelago that is as big as half the world.[31] The sun's perihelion, when it is closest to the Earth, also occurs during the austral summer, around the fifth of January each year. Therefore, the light bears everywhere, perhaps, a tinge of the sun-soaked ocean. The relative proximity of Antarctica, too, may filter the light, as Janet Frame saw, giving it an icy quality quite unlike the warm Mediterranean light with which it is sometimes compared.

The white-blue blaze of southern light forms an intrinsic part of the hemisphere's sensory matrix. I also like to think that it may be epistemologically significant. It operates in the opposite direction to scale framing, in Timothy Clark's definition. As we find in climate-change fiction, scale framing allows large-scale issues like global warming to be metonymically captured and controlled within human-sized scenarios.[32] By contrast, southern light always assumes a vaster frame beyond the frame. It bursts open our senses of proportion and dimensionality. The Buenos Aires city streets in Coppola's photographs gape like canyons. The light on the Southern Ocean in Verne or Stow or Frame strikes the fear of annihilation into the heart.

Within Space-Time

But southern identifications can manifest at a closer range also. I discovered this for myself at a small exhibition of south-crafted objects held in the Pitt Rivers Museum in Oxford, England, in the depths of the global pandemic. I

found that the act of looking closely at these objects—for me, in particular, two woven baskets—communicated a tactile sense of southern life-worlds, even though it was not possible to touch them.

The two objects in question were Indigenous Australian baskets: a 'bicornual' bag in twined weave from what is now Northern Queensland, decorated in a broad, red zigzag pattern, and a plainer dilly or *dhili* basket in white-iris plant fibre from Lutruwita or Tasmania.[33] The baskets had been collected in the later decades of the nineteenth century and so were probably made in the 1860s. Though the curators had asked us to avoid handling the objects, some of which were fragile, we were encouraged to study them up close—close enough to be able to follow with our eyes the wind and weave of the fibre used in their making and to develop a near-tactile sense of their shape.

The baskets had been made by skilled craftspeople, that was immediately clear. They were visibly shaped for use, the twist and turn of the fibres adapted to be hooked over a shoulder, or hunched up on a hip, such as, say, after walking home from foraging in rock pools. The Queensland bag, for example, was unmistakably made to take the shape of the fish that it had been designed to carry, with the creatures' dorsal curves mirrored in the basket's bellied bottom. The round Tasmanian *dhili* bag, too, had room for several layers of shellfish, or seedpods, which I could imagine as stacked up in rows against the firm, high sides. Or, as Jazz Money writes in 'how to make a basket', a poem about 'making the land right': 'everything worth holding in two hands/ has a basket to respond.'[34]

I looked so closely at the *dhili* basket, the tight weave, the binding that reinforced the rim, that it must somehow have become imprinted on my memory. This was to the point that, when I next encountered similar objects two years later, in the Tasmanian Museum and Art Gallery in Hobart—now so much closer to where they had been made and used—it was with a jolt of recognition. Past the foyer, in the first room on the right, which was about Indigenous Lutruwita, the display case of about five *dhili* bags, all with the same bucket-like shape, immediately leapt into focus.

The nearby information boards filled in details of the bags' use and the craft that had gone into their making. I learned that they were indeed used as fish baskets, that their strong, bendable size afforded compact and efficient transport for seafood. I read that the local Bruni cultural leader Trukanini (1812–76) had probably used fish baskets just like these. I discovered that the white-flag iris or Tasman flax-lily fibre (*Dianella tasmanica*) offers flexibility in weaving, and strength and durability over time. I enjoyed the story of a contemporary Tasmanian educator, Colleen Mundy, who has continued her community's traditional practice of *dhili*-making. She has learned from 'respected weavers' in her family, studying the design of baskets passed down the generations, from mother to mother. In her daily life, too, Mundy has tried to live 'off the land' and has 'collected plants and lichens for bush dyeing and fibre crafts', always inspired by the 'love of the land and the sea and what they give to us.'

Taking all this in, I saw suddenly that a crafted object like a *dhili* bag had woven into its form a recognition of stewardship, a respect for the interrelations that exist between humans and the surrounding land and sea. Even while looking from behind glass, I felt that bags, the marks and textures of their making, had not only embedded skills but also held temporal depth—in essence, the dimensions of space-time. I understood that they made proximate certain southern practices that are, however, important everywhere—processes of tending, carrying, cleansing, caring, in which humans work together with their environment. Or, as Jazz Money closes 'how to make a basket':

> First you must begin
> With the grasses
> First you must tend the blades
> The sweet small shoots
> First you must make healthy the soil
> Care for this place
> Tend with fire
> Carry the seeds
>
> . . .
>
> What you care for will care for you

A Sound of Southern Space

If southern farness has a sound, it might be the ringing, shirring sound of a device like a high-frequency radio, perhaps from a shipping vessel, trying and sometimes failing to communicate across the miles. In the nineteenth century, the technologies of the telegraph and the wireless brought the reaches of the southern hemisphere closer to the northern, yet the sound of a radio whining and beeping still conveys, at least to me, the sense of hearing remoteness.

Sometimes, when I find myself in the south, I twiddle the tuner on the radio simply in order to listen to those 'metallic' bleeps and whistles, to dwell in the feelings of distance they call up.[35] Quite other than this, however, was one of the most striking southern sounds I have ever encountered. It was not a ping or a beep but a human sentence that I picked up in a Zoom room in the far north that is southwest England, though it was spoken half a world away in Sydney, Australia, on Gadigal land, by my Gamilaraay teacher, Tracey Cameron. The sound was remarkable not only because it was *of* southern space, but also because it was *about* it. The sentence was offered as an example of a certain grammatical feature, but when Tracey spoke and explained it, its potency seemed to unfurl in the virtual space between us like a water plant. It joined her context to mine.

My Gamilaraay class ran for five months from late February 2021, through a Covid-19 lockdown. Though the pandemic had closed borders, it had also made permissible something special. It had made it possible to teach the Indigenous language Gamilaraay online at the University of Sydney for the first time. For several years, as part of my efforts to confront northern linguistic bias, I had been searching around for an Australian Indigenous language course. I had found out that only seven universities in Australia teach Aboriginal languages, in some cases only as part of one- or two-week summer schools, and that many of them were now suspended by the pandemic. Then, at the beginning of the year, a friend's tip-off hooked me up with Tracey Cameron. Hailing from southern Gamilaraay Country in New South Wales, Tracey was a teacher of Gamilaraay at Sydney and had made the decision to deliver the course online rather than not to offer it at all. She began the first meeting by saying that she was guided in everything by her belief that the language provided 'a unique window through to the worlds of our ancestors and to our Country'.[36] For her, it was worth it to keep that window open. Whereas losing our language puts knowledge systems in danger, she also explained, learning and even relearning it reconnects with those systems, even when the language has been damaged. *Takan-di*, she would sometimes add. Not everyone needs to have the whole story, but it's fine for you to know part of it.[37]

The time I am especially remembering must have been during our fourth or fifth lesson, 2 p.m. in Sydney, early in the morning for me, the pale spring sunshine leaking into the conservatory at the back of our house. There were eight of us in the group. The topic that day was space-time marking, how, in Gamilaraay, temporal words can be used to show direction and position. First, Tracey led us through the customary acknowledgement to the custodians of the land, then we sang the greeting *ngaadi nginda* to the tune of 'Frere Jacques'. After that, she launched in. She began by explaining how suffixes of position in Gamilaraay change depending on the ending of the noun they mark. Otherwise, however, these parts of speech are interchangeable. *on, near, at, around, about*—all might be indicated by the endings *-ga* or *-dha*, all marked a certain spatial aura of 'aroundness'.[38]

And then Tracey used a phrase by way of illustration. *Ngandanganda gunagala-**ga***, she said, or 'star in the sky'. But also, *ngandanganda buluuy-**dha***, she glossed, 'star in the darkness'. (I have used bold to capture the shift.) She said the words clearly, speaking directly to the camera so that we could all follow, and it was as if the concept came straight at me along with the sound she spoke. This spatial idea of here *and* all around. Of nothing being excluded. Of everything being relative to everything else. That under the overarching sky, there is no margin or edge—no over *t*/here in England, nor right t/*here* in the Gamilaraay classroom, but the two together, *here*, as if side by side.

Faraway Close

The frames of perception I have run through so far will have begun to suggest some of the yield that comes from seeing south, or, more conventionally put, from looking back from extremity.

The south has always represented the ultimate edge, the spaces that many people—northerners as well as southerners—have occluded because they are too difficult and overwhelming to keep thinking about at any length. Yet there are consequences to this shutting out, especially now, in the face of global heating. For it is often on the margins of the planet that the future first manifests that will later confront us all.

From Southern Ocean studies we know that climate change is accelerating in far southern regions at a greater rate than in most places, other than in the vicinity of the North Pole. The ocean is warming faster, the winds are speeding up, the phytoplankton supplies decreasing. The Antarctic Convergence that powers the planet's continent-cooling and warming currents, like the Gulf Stream, is slowing down. In the southern winter of 2023, which was the warmest ever on the Antarctic continent, the surrounding sea ice thinned to unprecedented levels. Even the great Ross Ice Shelf turned soft and pulpy.[39] And so we could go on. Unheeded and disregarded, the far south's warming and thinning have continued unabated for decades, at greater volumes and intensities than we can easily comprehend. Indeed, we might further say that these accelerations have been left to escalate and have thus been exacerbated precisely because they have been so ignored.

Yet, whereas conventional or northern-produced patterns of thought have struggled to imagine such magnitude, on the contrary, thinking from the south, with the support of south-centred metaphors, may help to build a more comparative, at-once-austral-and-planetary understanding. So, as we saw earlier, Charles Darwin developed a model for thinking south, theorising evolutionary time by working laterally between and across southern continental geologies. This century, scientists like Cape oceanographer Sarah Fawcett draw on data taken from across the circumpolar swoop of the Southern Ocean and its interconnected biosphere to conceptualise the rushing waters' complex responses to rising CO_2 emissions.

In this book, the poems, travel writings and fictions selected from across five hundred years and more have, after their fashion, helped to produce a southern heuristic, especially where the texts have worked dialogically and stereophonically, Coleridge alongside Melville, Money beside Baderoon, Mda along with Ihimaera. Bonnie Roos and Alex Hunt call such a heuristic an 'ecosocial imaginary', an aesthetic form that helps us see how 'larger, seemingly invisible structures' operate—or, in this case, how we might better understand the planet 'from below'.[40] The image of the faraway close or the proximate remote stands out as one such form, as 'alive to turbulence, drift, refraction' as the Southern Ocean, one that encourages us to think oxymoronically, and at different coeval scales.[41]

The heuristic of the far-flung south teaches that there is no way of contemplating our earthly life from the outside. It allows no outside—and yet it also refuses incorporation.[42] It makes possible a view that brings the little and the great, the near and the far, into one frame. It shows that the remotest edges have impact on everywhere else but retain their necessary opacity. It compels us to see assemblage and interrelationship, including with other life-forms, across great distances. It encourages us to recognise that everywhere is part of us, close by even when it seems far away.[43]

Looping Back to the Distant Edge

I offer four snapshots in closing, each from a different southern landmass.

My first photograph was taken from the rocky breakwater on Mudurup or Cottesloe Beach in Perth, Australia, facing southwest, about an hour before sunset. I am finding it difficult to keep my foothold on the slippery rocks, to keep the camera steady. My companion offers to take a photograph instead. The water lapping just below is inky blue, Indian Ocean blue, a comfortably familiar colour. These are the same waters that wash my birthplace, Durban, six time zones away, over that horizon. I imagine the intervening curve of the waters, like a clear lens. The light is level, golden, warm. Teenagers are playing a ball game on the sand. Just out of sight is Rottnest Island, the destination of an annual open-water swim, when the human swimmers plough their course alongside the sharks that also like to ply the channel. A brisk wind blows just as the camera shutter opens. At the same moment, a seagull flies past and leaves its blurred shape printed on the sky.

The photograph I hang up next brings us eastwards, to St Clair beach close to Dunedin, New Zealand. It is mid-morning. The sea is jade-green, and small foamy waves curl onto the white sand. Janet Frame's final home, a small bungalow, lies only a few streets away. It is high summer, just a few days off the solstice, but the temperature is no more than 14°C. I take off my shoes, and the sand is cold and clammy underfoot. A passing dog walker sees me shiver. 'Enjoy the summer', he laughs. 'Summer?' I say. 'That's due south', he points to White Island on the horizon, a rocky outcrop. 'What can you expect? There's nothing between there and Antarctica'. Even so, I paddle into the waves, the cold like a vice around my toes. I remember the albatross I saw yesterday, from a boat off the Otago Peninsula. I remember the incredible size of the bird as it banked and dipped silently over the slate-grey waves. And I remember thinking, as it swooped, how the mighty wind channels of the Antarctic Convergence that it had soared along had intersected, just for that moment, with the pathway of our vessel.[44]

My third picture is from high up, a cliffside above Ushuaia, in Tierra del Fuego, on the southern edge of this southernmost province of Argentina. It is noon and I am looking due south over the Beagle Channel, across to Chile and last of the Andes, where they begin to taper down to Cape Horn. Later, I will find out that it is unusually bright and clear. Cloud shadows slide over the water and the shoreline. I have never seen mountains looking this raw and serrated, as if they had only recently erupted from the seabed. The chasing clouds enhance the effect of upheaval. I want to think about Darwin seeing exactly this view, about Fitzroy mapping and remapping

these intricate coastlines, but my eye keeps being led away, across the mountains, to the blue distances beyond. I have the same vertiginous sense that I had on St Clair beach, of the icy blueness stretching up and up, all the way to Antarctica.

To complete the gallery of photographs, I circle, finally, to a picture grabbed in a gale at Cape Point, one of Africa's southernmost tips. It is February, a windy month in these parts, and today the gusts are so strong that they would blow the phone from your hand if you ever relaxed your grip. Below, the Atlantic is churned up, the waves creating white nimbus shapes around the rocks. Though it is a bright, sunny day, the blue line of the horizon is blurred by spray. These weather conditions might explain why my companion and I are, for over half an hour, the only people out here on this craggy sandstone point at what is a popular tourist destination. We watch a small boat rounding the point, battling hard. We hear the wind shriek around the old lighthouse on the higher peak of the point behind us. 'I'm imagining this air blasting over from Queen Maud Land', my companion says. 'What would it take, five hours or so to get here? After all, there's nothing in the way.' A gust pushes us back across the viewing platform. I turn around, raise my arms, lean into its force. I feel that I am flying. The photographs we take are fuzzy from the wind battering our hands.

It is perhaps no accident that so many of the photographs of the southern hemisphere that I cherish, like these four, are of marine horizons taken from the land veranda that is the beach or the cliff, the promontory or the cape. Because here is where I always loop back. To reflect on the far, the farthest far, I bring to mind the immensity of southern oceans when seen from the land's edge. I remember again Chris Orsman's *South* wherein the south was not edge but depth, his poems sinking by degrees through the high southern latitudes, down to the Antarctic ice sheet. I turn to Mxolisi Nyezwa's *Bhlawa's Inconsolable Spirits* (2023) in which the isiXhosa poet pent-up in his township home at the edge of the ocean ponders 'the agony of the sea', 'forced' like the fishermen he obsessively watches 'to invent [every day] new ways of escaping death'.[45]

Writing this book, I have often faced the question of how we bridge great distances in our imagination. How we take in farness. Or, more precisely put, how we approach it in our thoughts, while always acknowledging its irreducible distance from us. Or, again, how we might think of ourselves as present to Antarctica without the icy continent being immediate and knowable to us. The question became especially pertinent during the global lockdowns in 2020–21, with the bans on air travel and the closing of national borders around the world. The beginning of the pandemic found me in South Africa, queueing to take one of the last flights back to my family in Britain before travel became impossible. I did not return to the southern hemisphere till 2022. Like many people around the world, I was separated for what became the longest time in my life from some of the places that mattered to me the most.

Yet in this experience of separation lay a kind of answer to my question. My southern frameworks of reference had been reinforced in their absence because I had had to make do. The answer lay in the idea, the process, the activity (all of these) of southern imagining. Of holding distance in mind and at the same time considering it up close. I took figures like those featured in this final chapter to imagine my way back to the far south. To think its haecceity. And I read, and reread. I read Melville, Mansfield, Money, Mda. Their writings became navigational tools. They traced the contours of southern affinity.[46] Reading, I came to detect a more demanding southern disposition in the writing that I had not fully noticed before. I saw over and over again how austral stories are not merely metonyms for larger and seemingly more important histories. And I reflected on geographic paradoxes—on the experience of being beyond, yet centred. On the writing of the edge being anything but marginal.

'Time weaves a horizon of many strands'.[47] I came, finally, to crafting an interpretative device—the far southern imaginary that I have outlined in these pages. I saw how the writers' images of the south and my own photographs might coalesce into an optic through which I could look back at the rest of the planet, a device that merged 'strange-eyed constellations' and 'enormous flashing seas', that looped together Bass Strait and Magellan. Spanning 'the immediate and the far-distant, the intimate and the general', this southern imaginary gave the means to mobilise the kind of interconnected thinking now required against the climate catastrophe that confronts our planet.[48]

These are the southern lights I have been vouchsafed. That the far is never far enough away for us to forget about it. That the remote is not a supplement. That the south lies at the heart of our definition of the human—and the non-human. That the southern beyond, the undervalued end of the earth with its vast polar icecap, is as important as everywhere else when it comes to our planetary survival—perhaps more so.

For from beyond the southern horizon comes the weather, not just to southerners, but to us all.

NOTES

Preface

1. See Sarah Pothecary, trans., *Strabo's Geography* (Princeton and Oxford: Princeton UP, 2024); D. Graham J. Shipley and contributors, *Geographers of the Ancient Greek World* (Cambridge: Cambridge University Press, 2024).

2. The speculation about counterbalancing landmasses was adopted by early modern geographers, including Alexander Dalrymple's *Historical Collection of the Several Voyages and Discoveries in the South Pacific Ocean* (1770–71), an influential compilation James Cook used on board the *Endeavour* (1768–71). See Sandra Young, *The Early Modern Global South in Print: Textual Form and the Production of Human Difference as Knowledge* (Farnham, Surrey: Ashgate, 2015), pp. 7, 25, 51.

3. D. H. Lawrence, *Kangaroo*, ed. Bruce Steele (London: Penguin, 1997), 83–91; Ursula Le Guin, *The Left Hand of Darkness* (London: Penguin, 2016).

4. Johannes Fabian, *Time and the Other: How Anthropology Makes its Object* (New York: Columbia University Press, 1983). Meanwhile, for Global South theorist Boaventura de Sousa Santos, *Epistemologies of the South* (London: Routledge, 2016), southern spaces lie within or beyond an epistemological abyss. Even this view assumes a dominant northern perspective, however.

5. James Halford, 'Southern Conversations: J. M. Coetzee in Buenos Aires', *Sydney Review of Books*, 28 February 2017, https://sydneyreviewofbooks.com/essay/southern-conversations-j-m-coetzee-in-buenos-aires/. To give only one of myriad instances where this blue light slants into southern literature, here is Richard Flanagan, *The Narrow Road to the Deep North* (London: Chatto and Windus, 2013), 5, 57, on 'the great blue sky', a repeated phrase, as we will notice again—it is a light that, to his hero, is associated with 'the lost freedom of his childhood'. Many other examples are found across this book.

6. Elena Fiddian-Qasmiyeh and Patricia Daley, Introduction to *Routledge Handbook of South-South Relations* (London: Routledge, 2020), 4.

Chapter One

1. As in the Preface. Ninety percent of the world's population lives in the northern hemisphere and mostly will not have reason to visit the south.

2. Lola Frost, 'Going South: Traversal and Attunement in Painting', *GeoHumanities* (2015): 1–11, especially 1, http://dx.doi.org/10.1080/2373566X.2015.109505.

3. Maurice Godelier, *The Imagined, the Imaginary and the Symbolic* (London: Verso, 2020), avers that what we imagine is not separate from our experience and understanding of the real but part and parcel of it. It is a view that this book shares.

4. Thomas Hardy, 'Drummer Hodge', in *Selected Poems*, ed. David Wright (London: Penguin, 1978), 257. D. H. Lawrence, *Kangaroo* (1923; London: Penguin, 1950), 20. The subheading quotation above is from the same passage.

5. And, moreover, where 'this word, supposed to be Australian, is not to be found as the name of this singular marsupial animal in any language of Australia' (*OED*).

6. James Cook, *The Journals*, ed. J. C. Beaglehole for the Hakluyt Society, and Philip Edwards (London: Penguin Classics, 1999), 126, 145, 153, 157.

7. Barron Field, *First Fruits of Australian Poetry* (Sydney: George Howe, 1819); and *Kangaroo and Other Poems* (Sydney: University of Sydney, 1998).

8. This 'weird, big country', as Lawrence also wrote in a letter. See D. H. Lawrence, Letter to Else Jaffe (13 June 1922), in *Collected Letters*, vol. 4, ed. Warren Roberts et al. (Cambridge: Cambridge University Press, 2002), 263.

9. Katharine Susannah Prichard, *Coonardoo* (1929; Angus and Robertson, 1956), 1, 85–6, 111.

10. 'Topsy-turvy' was the word used by Roald Amundsen's translator A. G. Chater to describe his experience at the South Pole: 'I cannot say . . . that the object of my life was obtained. . . . I have never known a man to be placed in such a diametrically opposite position to the goal of his desires at that moment. The regions around the North Pole . . . had attracted me from childhood, and here I was at the South Pole. Can anything more topsy-turvy be imagined?' Roald Amundsen, *The South Pole* (1913), quoted in Emma McEwin, *An Antarctic Affair* (Bowden, South Australia: East Street Publications, 2008), 55.

11. A case in point is Naoise Mac Sweeney, *The West: A New History of an Old Idea* (London: W.H. Allen, 2023), an account of non-Greco-Roman histories of civilisation, which nominates as the world's ancient civilisations outside the west, Bolivia, India, China, Egypt, Mexico, and Peru. Only Peru lies (just) south of the Equator, with its southern-most point at 18°S.

12. Edgar Allan Poe, *The Narrative of Arthur Gordon Pym of Nantucket, and Related Tales*, ed. J. Gerald Kennedy (1837; Oxford: Oxford University Press, 2008), 123, 172, 289, 292; Jules Verne, *An Antarctic Mystery*, trans. Cashel Hoey (1897; Orinda, CA: Seawolf Press, 2020), 182, 183, 188.

13. Alfred Hiatt, *Terra Incognita: Mapping the Antipodes Before 1600* (Chicago: University of Chicago Press, 2008); Anne M. Scott, et al., eds., *European Perceptions of Terra Australis* (Abingdon: Routledge, 2017). See also Kate Fullagar, *The Savage Visit: New World People and Popular Imperial Culture in Britain 1710–1795* (Berkeley: University of California Press, 2012). Edgar Allan Poe's Tsalal island, imagined as lying beyond the Antarctic ice barrier, is inhabited by dark-skinned peoples who plot to entrap the exploring ship's crew.

14. Elleke Boehmer, 'Time and Distance', *Agenda* 35, no. 4 (2021): 99–104.

15. See Margo Neale, 'On the Spot', *History Today* (November 2021): 112; and 'First Knowledges: An Introduction', in Karlie Noon and Krystal De Napoli, *Sky Country* (Melbourne: Thames and Hudson, 2023), 1–9, especially 4.

16. If we wish, their shapes might be taken to mirror the attenuated (kangaroo) shapes of at least two of the southern continents themselves, especially when they are viewed 'upside down'.

17. See Joy McCann, *Wild Sea: A History of the Southern Ocean* (Chicago and London: Chicago University Press, 2018), 127; Tim Winton, *Island Home: A Landscape Memoir* (Sydney: Penguin Random House, 2015), 9–27. The formal names for the continents, as listed in this

paragraph, are largely northern appellations. Alternatives do exist, however. Abya-Yala, for example, is an indigenous Panamanian term for South America meaning 'land of life-blood'.

18. Gillen D'Arcy Wood, *Land of Wondrous Cold: The Race to Discover Antarctica and Unlock the Secrets of Its Ice* (Princeton: Princeton University Press), 100–102, 135, 145, 154–7. See also David Abulafia's great 'human history' of the 'interconnected oceans': *The Boundless Sea: A Human History of the Oceans* (Oxford: Oxford University Press, 2019); and David Armitage, Alison Bashford, and Sujit Sivasundaram, *Oceanic Histories* (Cambridge: Cambridge University Press, 2017).

19. Thomas Halliday, *Otherlands: A World in the Making* (London: Allen Lane, 2022), 85–7.

20. Evidence for continental drift began accumulating from the time of Kerguelen and Hooker's research in the Southern Ocean area in the 1830s and led, in 1895, to the sixth International Geographical Congress that gave official endorsement to research on Antarctica and to the 1901–4 and 1907–8 British expeditions. The German geologist Alfred Wegener published his theory of continental drift in *The Origins of Continents and Oceans* (1915), which plate tectonic theory refined in the 1960s. Wegener's *Origins* was probably the first south-born planetary theory of modern times.

21. D'Arcy Wood, *Land of Wondrous Cold*, 53–4, 174–5; Kate Teltscher, *Palace of Palms: Tropical Dreams and the Making of Kew* (London: Picador, 2020), 84. Hooker assembled botanical evidence from across the hemisphere, from Tierra del Fuego to Tasmania, to think about continental shift. See also Nicholas Shakespeare, *In Tasmania* (New York: Overlook Press, 2004).

22. Julian Dowdeswell and Michael Hambrey, *The Continent of Antarctica* (Winterbourne, Berkshire: Papadakis, 2018), 43, 203; Barry Lopez, *Horizon* (London: Vintage, 2019), 462; McEwin, *Antarctic Affair*, 1–2. On the fatal 1911–12 Scott expedition, Edward Wilson found on the Beardmore Glacier a 'beautifully traced' fern fossil embedded in a piece of coal. Scientists have observed the fossilised markings of the Dicroidium fern and Nothofagus, the southern beech, in rocks of similar age in South Africa, Australia, India, South America, and Antarctica.

23. The islands include the Galapagos, penguins' northernmost island location. In our century, penguin populations across the south are plummeting as a result of ocean warming. To take another example, fossilised remains of the Lystrosaurus reptile found in the Transantarctic Mountains in the 1960s, correspond to those also located on the African continent and other southern landmasses. There are also rumours of echidna-type fossils found in Patagonia. Tom Griffiths, *Slicing the Silence: Voyaging to Antarctica* (Boston: Harvard University Press, 2007), 79–82.

24. Halford, 'Southern Conversations'.

25. Tim Marshall, *Prisoners of Geography* (London: Elliot and Thompson, 2015), iii, vi, vii, xiii-xiv, 120, 245, 247. Marshall's conservative reading of shaping geography—'the land on which we live shapes us'—is symptomatic of the default of northern strategic thinking, as he briefly concedes. His thesis overlooks other forms of inter-linkage—for example, the possibilities of south-south imaginative connectivity that this introduction and subsequent chapters explore.

26. See Barry Lopez, *Arctic Dreams* (1986; London: Vintage, 2014), with its speculations about travel across great distances (258). Open-water journeys on rafts, canoes and catamarans, meanwhile, were often one-way and extremely dangerous.

27. On 'life as elsewhere', see, for example, Benedict Anderson, *Imagined Communities: Reflections on the Origin and Spread of Nationalism*, 2nd ed. (London: Verso, 1993); Edwin Ardener, 'Remote Areas: Some Theoretical Considerations', *HAU: Journal of Ethnographic Theory* 2.1 (Spring 2012): 519–533. The feeling is not confined to southern regions, however. Nayanika Mathur, *Paper Tiger: Law, Bureaucracy and the Developmental State in Himalayan India*

(Cambridge: Cambridge University Press, 2015), spotlights the sense of provincial remoteness that can characterise life in a Himalayan town. Dipesh Chakrabarty, *Provincializing Europe* (Princeton: Princeton University Press, 2000), famously used the historiographic metaphor of the waiting room to describe and question how European representations consigned colonised peoples to the margins of history.

28. Siobhan Carroll, *An Empire of Air and Water: Uncolonizable Space in the British Imagination, 1750–1850* (Philadelphia: University of Pennsylvania Press, 2015), 12–14.

29. Meg Samuelson, 'Yvette Christiansë's Oceanic Genealogies and the Colonial Archive', *Eastern African Literary and Cultural Studies* 1, no. 1–2 (2014): 27–38, https://doi.org/10.1080/23277408.2014.941751.

30. Isabel Hofmeyr, *Dockside Reading* (Johannesburg: Wits University Press, 2022), 4–8. The *Otago* hull I viewed on an 8 December 2022 visit to the Hobart Maritime Museum, Tasmania. Consider also the expression 'to go south' which means to fail or plummet in value.

31. Zandria F. Robinson, ed., 'The Imaginary South', special issue, *Southern Cultures* 26, no. 4 (Winter 2020).

32. See Avan Judd Stallard, *Antipodes: In Search of the Southern Continent* (Melbourne: Monash University Publishing, 2016). William Eisler, *The Furthest Shore: Images of Terra Australis from the Middle Ages to Captain Cook* (Cambridge: Cambridge University Press, 1995), traces the concept of a southern continent back to Pythagoras.

33. John Livingston Lowes, *The Road to Xanadu: A Study in the Ways of the Imagination* (1927, 2nd ed.; London: John Constable, 1951).

34. Claudius Ptolemy, *Geographia* (New York: NY Public Library, 1932).

35. Due south of Europe, the African continent was sometimes seen as divided into civilised and barbaric eastern and western halves. See Malvern van Wyk Smith, *The First Ethiopians: The Image of Africa and Africans in the Early Mediterranean World* (Johannesburg: Wits University Press, 2009). See also Malvern van Wyk Smith, 'Ptolemy, Paradise and Purgatory', *T'Kama—Adamastor: Inventions of Africa in a South African painting*, ed. Ivan Vladislavic (Johannesburg: University of the Witwatersrand Press, 2000), 83–97.

36. Young, *Early Modern Global South*, 6, 11, 25, 154, 183–4.

37. Mary Louise Pratt, *Imperial Eyes: Travel Writing and Transculturation* (London: Routledge, 1992), 15, 29–31. To illustrate, the names of southern (and northern) birds within the Linnaean taxonomy are overwhelmingly derived from the last names of the male European scientists who first described 'new' southern species. See Christopher H. Trisos, Jess Auerbach, and Madhusudan Katti, 'Decoloniality and Anti-Oppressive Practices', *Nature, Ecology and Environment* (2021): 1–8, https://doi.org/10.1038/s41559-021-01460-w. European explorers' names and those of their sponsors also disproportionately name southern geographical features, as the map of Australia, for example, reflects. This was to the point that properly new names became ever harder to think up. Cook's *Endeavour* journal betrays some effort in finding names for the features of the eastern Australian coast that he and his crew encountered. See James Cook, *Journals*, 119–174, especially 136 (April to August 1770). The Swedish naturalist Daniel Solander, trained by Carl Linnaeus, worked with Joseph Banks cataloguing flora and fauna on Cook's first journey. He was the first to bring reports of the kangaroo to the *Endeavour*. See also chapter 2, note 52.

38. Elizabeth Leane, *Antarctica in Fiction: Imaginative Narratives of the Far South* (Cambridge: Cambridge University Press, 2012).

39. Cook, *The Journals*, 111–12, 254. See also Peter Moore, Endeavour: *The Ship and the Attitude that Changed the World* (London: Penguin Random House, 2018), 92–104, in particular; James C. Hamilton, *Captain James Cook and the Search for Antarctica* (Huddersfield, UK: Pen and Sword Books, 2020); Hampton Sides, *The Wide Wide Sea: Imperial Ambition, First Contact and the Fateful Final Voyage of Captain James Cook* (New York: Doubleday, 2024).

40. D'Arcy Wood, *Land of Wondrous Cold*, 132.

41. Lowes, *Road to Xanadu*, 116–17, 122–3; Joseph Conrad, *The Mirror of the Sea* (1906; London: J. M. Dent and Sons, 1949), ch. 23.

42. Elizabeth Lewis Williams, 'Remote Imag(in)ing the Antarctic: Life-writing and the Resonant Page', *Life Writing and the Southern Hemisphere*, ed. Elleke Boehmer and Katherine Collins (London: Bloomsbury, 2024), 215–37.

43. McCann, *Wild Sea*, xi, 87–88. As chapter 2 explores further, some eight hundred years ago, the Polynesians appear also to have had contact with indigenous Americans. See Agence-France Press, 'Indigenous Americans Had Contact with Polynesians 800 Years Ago, DNA Reveals', *The Guardian*, July 8, 2020, https://www.theguardian.com/world/2020/jul/08/indigenous-americans-polynesians-dna-800-years-ago?CMP=fb_gu&utm_medium=Social&utm_source=Facebook#Echobox=1594245866. In respect of Asian knowledge of the far south of Africa, fourteenth- and fifteenth-century Chinese cartographers Zhu Siben and, later, Ch'uan Chin showed the wedge-like shape of the continent's southern tip in their world maps, decades before the first Portuguese journeys. The Ming-era explorer Zheng He made several expeditions into the southern Indian Ocean and along the African coast. See Melanie Yap and Dianne Leong Man, *Colour, Confusion and Concessions: The History of the Chinese in South Africa* (Hong Kong: Hong Kong University Press, 1996), 2–3.

44. The operation of these infrastructures offers a further explanation for the apparent event sparseness of the south. Remote southern spaces could be used as 'laboratories of modernity' where different modes of 'progress' could be tested at a safe distance from Europe and then reimported, following the 'boomerang' movement that both Hannah Arendt and Aimé Césaire have outlined. See Hannah Arendt, *The Origins of Totalitarianism* (1951; London: Penguin, 2017); Aimé Césaire, *Discourse on Colonialism*, trans. Joan Pinkham (1950: New York: Monthly Review Press, 2000). See also Frederick Cooper and A. Laura Stoler, eds., *Tensions of Empire: Colonial Cultures in a Bourgeois World* (Oakland CA: University of California Press, 1997), especially 1–5; L. Elena Delgado and Rolando J. Romero, 'Local Histories and Global Designs: An Interview with Walter Mignolo', *Imperial Discourses* 22, no. 3 (2000): 7–33. On continuities into the present day, see Kojo Koram, *Uncommon Wealth: Britain and the Aftermath of Empire* (London: John Murray, 2022).

45. McCann, *Wild Sea*, 87 88, 99.

46. As Richard Flanagan's *Gould's Book of Fish* (London: Atlantic, 2002), captures in its account of the conflagration of violence that colonialism unleashed in early nineteenth-century Tasmania.

47. Immanuel Wallerstein develops the concept of the 'one, uneven world' of capitalist globalisation in, amongst other works, *Historical Capitalism with Capitalist Civilization* (London: Verso, 1996).

48. An interrogation of northern dominance through northern frameworks alone, no matter how decolonial, interrelational, etc., tends eventually to throw up a contradiction in terms. As Meg Samuelson notes concerning the critical writing of the Anthropocene, wherever this is

directed from a northern perspective, 'more than half of the world' is cast into shadow: 'the very totality that the Anthropocene is expected to represent' is obscured. See Meg Samuelson, 'Thinking the Anthropocene South', *Contemporary Literature* 61, no. 4 (2020): 537–49.

49. Eric Hayot, *On Literary Worlds* (Oxford: Oxford University Press, 2012), describes as 'trans-periodising' such comparative work across clusters of cultural texts to discern shared tendencies and motifs. Trans-periodic reading helps to question the ideas of 'derivativeness and belatedness that all too often accompany studies of non-European literary culture' (4, 6, 149, 156).

50. Michael King, *The Penguin History of New Zealand* (Auckland: Penguin, 2003), 8. King is citing from Geoff Park.

51. Timothy Clark, *Ecocriticism on the Edge: The Anthropocene as a Threshold Concept* (New York: Bloomsbury, 2015); Timothy Clark, 'Towards a Deconstructive Environmental Criticism', *Oxford Literary Review* 30, no. 1 (2008): 45–68; Max Liboiron, *Pollution is Colonialism* (Durham, NC: Duke University Press, 2021). Quoting la paperson, Liboiron discusses how the primitive accumulation of capitalism involves using natural resources like land and water as 'a sink, a site of storage for waste', so ejecting or 'externalising the "cost" of the accumulation' in the form of contamination (39–40). In effect, for this study, the entire Southern Ocean has been used as a sink for the waste rising from nineteenth- to twentieth-first-century capitalist development.

52. For example, during the 1950s, the British Government used Maralinga and Emu Field in the remote desert country north of the Nullarbor in Australia for nuclear tests, deeming these lands to be sufficiently remote and sparsely inhabited—a belated and terrible form of *terra nullius* thinking.

53. James Cook's accounts of large seal and whale populations stimulated exploration of the Southern Ocean in quest of their valuable skins and oil. See McCann, *Wild Sea*, 111, 179, 183; D'Arcy Wood, *Land of Wondrous Cold*, 148.

54. Lopez, *Horizon*, 303.

55. George B. Handley, 'Derek Walcott's Poetics of the Environment in *The Bounty*', *Callaloo* 28, no. 1 (Winter 2005): 201–215.

56. Edward Said, *Orientalism* (London: Pantheon, 1978), *Culture and Imperialism* (London: Jonathan Cape, 1993).

57. Johannes Fabian, *Time and the Other: How Anthropology Makes Its Object* (New York: Columbia University Press, 2002).

58. Anne M. Thell, *Minds in Motion: Imagining Empiricism in Eighteenth-Century British Travel Literature* (Lewisburg: Bucknell University Press, 2017), argues that eighteenth-century travel writing evolved as an at-once aesthetic and scientific discourse of the wider world.

59. See, for example, Elleke Boehmer, *Postcolonial Poetics: 21st-Century Critical Readings* (Basingstoke: Palgrave, 2018); Terence Cave and Deirdre Wilson, eds., *Reading beyond the Code* (Oxford: Oxford University Press. 2018); Terence Cave, *Thinking with Literature: Towards a Cognitive Criticism* (Oxford: Oxford University Press, 2016); Dan Sperber and Deirdre Wilson, *Relevance: Communication and Cognition* (Oxford: Blackwell, 1995). On environmental anthropology, see Eduardo Kohn, *How Forests Think: Toward an Anthropology Beyond the Human* (Berkeley: University of California Press, 2013).

60. Reading operates, in essence, as a decolonial technique. See Linda Tuhiwai Smith, *Decolonising Methodologies: Research and Indigenous Peoples* (Auckland: Zed, 1999). Smith prefers

a decolonial over a postcolonial approach, as the postcolonial suggests that the colonial project has drawn to a close, whereas Indigenous writers are keenly aware of operating in still-colonial space. Stephen Clingman, *The Grammar of Identity* (Oxford: Oxford University Press, 2009), 31–33, observes that the transitive operations of fiction model 'our very forms of understanding'. In this book, this powerful idea of the transitive applies to all literary writing, poetry, and prose, as well as travel writing. See also Jo-Ann Archibald, Jenny Lee-Morgan, and Jason De Santolo, eds, *Decolonizing Research: Indigenous Storywork as Methodology* (London: Zed Books, 2019); Selina Tusitala Marsh and Jeanine Leane, 'A Trans-Indigenous Scholarly Dialogue', South Pacific ACLALS Speaker Series (online, 14 February 2021).

61. Édouard Glissant, *Poetics of Relation*, trans. Betsy Wing (Ann Arbor, MI: Michigan University Press, 1997). Other important interventions from postcolonial thought include Simon Gikandi and Sarah Nuttall's writing on complex entanglement, often between contrasting realities. See Simon Gikandi, *Maps of Englishness: Writing Identity in the Culture of Colonialism* (New York: Columbia University Press, 1996); Sarah Nuttall, *Entanglement: Literary and Cultural Reflections on Post-Apartheid* (Johannesburg: Wits University Press, 2008).

62. Epeli Hau'ofa, *We Are the Ocean: Selected Works* (Honolulu: University of Hawai'i Press, 2008); Elizabeth DeLoughrey and Tatiana Flores, 'Submerged Bodies: The Tidalectics of Representability and the Sea in Caribbean Art', *Environmental Humanities* 12, no. 1 (2020): 132–166, https://doi.org/10.1215/22011919-8142242. See also Peter Brunt and Nicholas Thomas, *Oceania* (London: Royal Academy of the Arts, 2018), focused on Oceania's complex modernity. By contrast, *Southern Imagining* is more concerned with sightlines, journeys, and approaches from and within the south, which may be modern but are not necessarily framed in response to the north.

63. By analogy with the 'planetary intimacy' Olga Tokarczuk evokes in *Flights*, trans. Jennifer Croft (London: Fitzcarraldo, 2006), 103, 230, 267, 276–7, 280–314. Reflecting on the experience of remoteness, Tokarczuk allows for the strange sense of proximity it can generate, as when spaces geographically far away from each other nonetheless bear similarities. Cook expresses a notable planetary intimacy in his *Endeavour* journal when he thinks of his native Yorkshire, even while mapping Aotearoa in collaboration with Tupaia. So, too, does Thomas Hardy, in an extraordinary moment from *A Pair of Blue Eyes*, ed. Tim Dolin and Alan Manford (Oxford: Oxford World's Classics, 2009), 305, when the narrator observes that if a wedding were performed at the altar of heroine Elfride's Devon church, 'it might be witnessed from the deck of a ship on a voyage to the South Seas, with a good glass'. Though he did not travel south of the equator, Hardy's reading must have given him insight into new astronomical discoveries concerning the magnitude of the universe and the dispositions of its energies, including black holes. In his novel *Two on a Tower: A Romance* (London: Sampson Low, 1882), in chapter 2, he describes these as the 'inter-spaces' or 'pieces of darkness' between the stars, like the Coal Sack in the Southern Cross, which he namechecks. Mark Ford, *Thomas Hardy: Half a Londoner* (London: The Belknap Press of Harvard University Press, 2016), 68–9, speculates that Hardy must have come across John Herschel's *General Catalogue of Nebulae and Clusters of Stars* (1864), which expanded his father William Herschel's similarly titled *Catalogue*. John Hershel's *Catalogue* was based on observations taken at the Cape of Good Hope (see Ford, *Thomas Hardy,* chapter 2, section 05).

64. Isabel Hofmeyr, 'Southern by Degrees: Islands and Empires in the South Atlantic, the Indian Ocean, and the Subantarctic World', in *The Global South Atlantic*, ed. Kerry Bystrom and

Joseph R. Slaughter (New York: Fordham University Press, 2018), 82. Hofmeyr's essay focuses on the southern Atlantic and the Indian Oceans. Her emphasis on ocean life as central to the imaginaries of the global south is highlighted in Antoinette Burton, 'The Sea's Watery Volume', in *Reading from the South: African Print Cultures and Oceanic Turns in Isabel Hofmeyr's Work*, ed. Charne Lavery and Sarah Nuttall (Johannesburg: Wits University Press, 2023), 148–58. For American hemispheric studies, see Bianet Castellanos, Lourdes Gutiérrez Nájera, and Arturo Aldama, eds, *Comparative Indigeneities of the Américas: Toward a Hemispheric Approach* (Tucson: University of Arizona Press, 2012). See also the Southern Conceptualisms Network, http://www.museoreinasofia.es/en/southern-conceptualisms-network.

65. Boaventura de Sousa Santos, *Epistemologies of the South: Justice against Epistemicide* (Abingdon: Routledge, 2016), 19–41, offers models of language reclamation and carbon sequestration in Latin America, amongst others, as a means of tuning into local knowledge sources, or worlds that people are living in 'at the time'. See also Anne Salmond, *Tears of Rangi: Experiments Across Worlds* (Auckland: Auckland University Press, 2017), 1–3, 18, 54. Salmon's idea is derived from Vivieros de Castro's ontological determinism. James Clifford, *Returns: Becoming Indigenous in the Twenty-First Century* (Cambridge, MA: Harvard University Press, 2013), 64, relatedly speaks of 'composite [cultural] worlds'. See also Sugata Bose, *A Hundred Horizons: The Indian Ocean in the Age of Global Empire* (Cambridge, MA: Harvard University Press, 2006); Anne Salmond, *Two Worlds: First Meetings between Māori and Europeans, 1642–1772* (Auckland: Viking Press, 1991).

66. Walter D. Mignolo and Catherine E. Walsh, *On Decoloniality: Concepts, Analytics, Praxis* (Durham and London: Duke University Press, 2018).

67. Doreen Massey, *For Space* (London: Sage, 2005), 6–9. See also Sophie Bond and David Featherstone, 'The Possibilities of a Politics of Place Beyond Place? A Conversation with Doreen Massey', *Scottish Geographical Journal* (2009): 401–20. https://doi.org/10.1080/14702540903364443.

68. For the history of the Brandt line dividing Global South and Global North, see Willy Brandt, *North-South: A Programme for Survival* (Cambridge, MA: MIT Press, 1980). Eduardo Galeano, *Open Veins of Latin America: Five Centuries of the Pillage of a Continent*, trans. Cedric Belfrage (New York: Monthly Review Press, 1997), influentially contended that the dominant flow northwards of resources, artefacts, and bodies produces the massive disparities of development between the hemispheres. The Prebisch–Singer thesis explains that the price of primary commodities will always decline relative to the price of manufactured goods. See Raúl Prebisch, *Towards a Dynamic Development Policy for Latin America* (New York: United Nations, 1963). On the northward flow of food energy, see also Archie Davies, 'Unwrapping the OXO Cube: Josué de Castro and the Intellectual History of Metabolism', *Annals of the American Association of Geographers* 109, no. 3 (2019): 837–856. Charles Dickens, *Dombey and Son* (London: Penguin, 2008), is keenly aware of northern economic predominance: 'The earth was made for Dombey and Son to trade in, and the sun and moon were made to give them light' (2).

69. Gurminder Bhambra et al., eds, *The Sage Handbook of Global Sociology* (Thousand Oaks, CA: Sage Publishing, 2024). See also Ross White, Sumeet Jain, and Catalina Giurgi-Oncu, eds, *Counterflows for Mental Well-being: What High-Income Countries Can Learn from Low and Middle-Income Countries* (London: Informa Healthcare, 2014).

70. Raewyn Connell, *Southern Theory: The Global Dynamics of Knowledge in Social Science* (London: Routledge, 2020).

71. Dilip Menon, *Changing Theory: Concepts from the Global South* (New York: Routledge, 2022).

72. Jean Comaroff and John Comaroff, *Theory from the South: Or, How Euro-America Is Evolving toward Africa* (Boulder: Paradigm Publishers, 2012), for example, 45, 47.

73. Sarah Comyn and Porscha Fermanis, 'Introduction: Southern Worlds, Globes and Spheres', in *Worlding the South: Nineteenth-Century Literary Culture and the Southern Settler Colonies* (Manchester: Manchester University Press, 2021), 1–36.

74. See Peter Beilharz, *Thinking the Antipodes: Australian Essays* (Clayton, Victoria: Monash University Publishing, 2015); Bernard Smith, *Imagining the Pacific in the Wake of the Cook Voyages* (Carlton, Victoria: Melbourne University Press/Miegunyah Press, 1992). Moreover, Beilharz's focus is exclusively on Australia and New Zealand. See also Matthew Boyd Goldie, *The Idea of the Antipodes: Place, People and Voices* (London: Routledge, 2010).

75. David Johnson, *Imagining the Cape Colony* (Edinburgh: Edinburgh University Press, 2012).

76. Even Jared Diamond's counterintuitive historiography *Guns, Germs, and Steel: The Fates of Human Society* (London: Vintage, 1998), while distributing agency across a range of non-European and non-human actors, questions but still accepts predominant influence from the north.

77. Sujit Sivasundaram, *Waves Across the South: A New History of Revolution and Empire* (Chicago: University of Chicago Press, 2021).

78. As in David Damrosch, *What is World Literature?* (Princeton: Princeton University Press, 2003), 5–6. Martin Puchner, *Literature for a Changing Planet* (Oxford and Princeton: Princeton University Press, 2022), agreeably observes that one of the constructive affordances of world literature is to help us imagine the world at scale, which is to say at the dimensions larger than the national that are so crucial for ecocritical reading.

79. Pascale Casanova, *The World Republic of Letters*, trans. M. B. Debevoise (1999; Cambridge, MA: Harvard University Press, 2004), 95, 101.

80. Jahan Ramazani, *Poetry in a Global Age* (Chicago: Chicago University Press, 2020).

81. Richard Shelton, 'Littorally Speaking: A Folk History of the West Coasts of Britain', *TLS*, no. 6083 (1 November 2019): 29.

82. Maps visualizing the world in proportion to internet users unsurprisingly inflate India, China and North America relative to the rest of the shrivelled world, especially Africa and South America. See, for example, 'This is What the World Would Look Like If the Map Depicted Each Country's Internet Users,' Scroll.in, December 23, 2016, https://scroll.in/article/751799/this-is-what-the-world-would-look-like-if-the-map-depicted-each-countrys-internet-users. Such views reflect how the dominant northern powers, most notably the United States of America, view the rest of the world as an exploitable source of raw materials and as a marketplace. See Noam Chomsky, *Hegemony or Survival: America's Quest for Global Dominance* (2003; London: Penguin, 2023).

83. Tokarczuk, *Flights*, 280–314. The unnamed protagonist reflects that for the traveller, the concept of distance requires a point of reference against which to relativise the space traversed. We might also recall from Australian Peter Carey's *Theft* (London: Faber, 2006): 'If you are American, you will never understand what it is to be an artist on the edge of the world' (144).

84. Salmond, *Tears of Rangi*, 54; Massey, *For Space*, 7–11.

85. Indigenous Australian writer and theorist Eugenia Flynn in her paper 'Beyond Cultural Difference: Australian Indigenous Literary and Creative Writing Practices as Sites of Knowledge

Production', Postcolonial and World literature seminar, English Faculty, Oxford (29 November 2024), discussed insightfully how Indigenous writers might advance their claims by working 'in, of and through' settler colonial discourse.

86. As will again become apparent in later chapters, I have learned Spanish to read Spanish American works in the original (2019–24) and took classes in Gamilaraay (2021) to better understand the conception of distance and relationality in at least one Indigenous language of the many hundreds that existed in Australia at the time of European arrival.

87. Conrad, *The Mirror of the Sea*, chs. 23 and 24; Lowes, *Road to Xanadu*, 122–3.

88. Joseph Conrad, *The N—of the 'Narcissus'* (1897; London: Penguin, 1987), 6, 35–6, 73, 84. The novel was published in the United States as *The Children of the Sea*.

89. Verne, *Antarctic Mystery*, 192, 194. By contrast, Poe's 'MS Found in a Bottle', often considered a companion text to *The Narrative of Arthur Gordon Pym of Nantucket*, represents the Pole as an immense roaring whirlpool (Poe, *Narrative*, 179–189).

90. Verne, *Antarctic Mystery*, 169.

91. In this my practice aligns with the work of Katherine McKittrick on alternative referencing such as when she writes that 'the function of communication, referencing, citation, is not to master knowing and centralize our knowingness, but to share how we know'. To demonstrate our pathways of alternative knowing is to chip away at authoritative edifices of knowledge creation. See Katherine McKittrick, *Dear Science and Other Stories* (Durham, NC: Duke University Press, 2021), 17–19.

Chapter Two

Note to first epigraph: Anonymous, 'Nama Praise of the Sea (sung before going to fish)', in Kuno F. R. Budack, 'The ǂAonin or Topnaar of the Lower !Khuseib Valley and the Sea', *Khoisan Linguistic Studies* 3 (1977): 1–42. Many thanks to Menán Du Plessis for drawing my attention to this article. The # sign signifies a click sound. Confidence Joseph, 'The Representation of Water Spirits in Southern African Literature', in *Life Writing and the Southern Hemisphere*, ed. Elleke Boehmer and Katherine Collins (London: Bloomsbury Academic, 2024), 145–56, points to the fact that, to this day, littoral communities from both the eastern and western seaboards of the African sub-continent propitiate ocean spirits with offerings and entreaties.

Note to second epigraph: Michael J. Connolly, 'Munda-gutta Kulliwari project,' Yaraan-doo—*Southern Cross*, 2024, https://www.kullillaart.com.au/dreamtime-stories/The-Southern-Cross-Yaraan-doo-The-place-of-the-white-gum-tree. Accessed 12 April 2021. *Warrambool* is the Milky Way, and *yaraan* the white gum. I have made small alterations to the online text for a more fluid reading, using names for place numbers. I have also reversed the order of Indigenous and English names.

1. Nicholas Evans, *Dying Words: Endangered Languages and What They Have to Tell Us* (Oxford: Blackwell, 2010), 163. See also Ann McGrath, Laura Rademaker, and Jakeline Troy, eds, *Everywhen: Australia and the Language of Deep History* (Lincoln: University of Nebraska Press, 2023); and the 'Rediscovering Indigenous Languages' website, an online resource at the New South Wales State Library. https://indigenous.sl.nsw.gov.au. Accessed 19 March 2024.

2. And hence dislodge, even if momentarily, northern 'cognitive empires'. The term is from de Sousa Santos, *Epistemologies of the South*, who observes that southern oral histories reflecting

indigenous worldviews are by their very nature disruptive of the universalizing history of the west.

3. Alexis Wright, *Carpentaria* (Sydney: Giramondo Press, 2006), 375.

4. Bawaka Country, quoted in Karlie Noon and Krystal De Napoli, *Astronomy: Sky Country* (Melbourne: Thames and Hudson Australia, 2023), 23.

5. Wright, *Carpentaria*, 375. See also Anonymous, 'The Song Cycle of the Moon-Bone', in *The Thunder Mutters—101 Poems for the Planet*, ed. Alice Oswald, trans. R. M. Berndt (London: Faber, 2006), 201–209. And 'Alexis Wright in conversation with Nicholas Jose', *Signposts* 1 (2020), https://www.slv.vic.gov.au/signposts. Accessed 11 April 2021. In 'The Song Cycle of the Moon-Bone', Wright observes, the counterposed stories of the waxing and waning of the moon, and the rising and setting of the Evening Star, 'tell of the on-going, endless regenerative cycles of the world in which we live'.

6. Wright, *Carpentaria*, 6–7, 375. See also Deborah Bird Rose, *Nourishing Terrains: Australian Aboriginal Views of Landscape and Wilderness* (Canberra: Australian Heritage Commission, 1996); Amos Rapoport, *The Meaning of the Built Environment: A Nonverbal Communication Approach* (London: Sage, 1982).

7. See Evelyn Araluen, 'Resisting the Institution', *Overland* 227 (Winter 2017): n. p., https://overland.org.au/previous-issues/issue-227/feature-evelyn-araluen/.

8. Geographic or cultural location in the south will not necessarily furnish greater insight or licence either. Most readers of this book, even if southern-born, will have been educated in northern knowledge systems and hence will approach southern cultural resources from an objectifying perspective.

9. The violent colonial incursion and the European diseases it brought had a terrible impact on indigenous populations, in the south as well as the far north, while survivors faced various degrees of cultural and linguistic erosion. In Tierra del Fuego in 2021, a single octogenarian speaker of Yaghan or Yámana was rumoured to remain alive. Most Yaghan speakers had died before 1940. (Bernhard Schirg, personal communication, 'Southern Lives' workshop, Wolfson College, Oxford, 6 December 2021). However, in conversation with J. M. Coetzee at the 'Speaking from the South' conference, University of Adelaide (2 June 2024), the Argentine writer Fabián Martinez Siccardi disputed that there was only one speaker still alive. In Aotearoa, the estimated population of 100,000 to 160,000 Māori living there when *Endeavour* first dropped anchor had fallen by between a third and a half fifty years later. In Australia, of the 250 to 300 Indigenous languages that existed, today only about 145 are still spoken to some degree. In South Africa, most Khoikhoi speakers had died by the early twentieth century. Their words are now preserved in versions of Afrikaans and Afrikaaps, in the Nama language, and in ethnographic collections, such as the Bleek-Lloyd archive. Language learning was often also bound up in complicated ways with Christian outreach. Missionaries in southern Africa, Australia, and across the Pacific frequently worked as amateur ethnographers, harvesting indigenous linguistic knowledge, and creating inventories of words and concepts that they then compared negatively with European ones. Against this, for many decades after colonial arrival, places like the South Island of New Zealand or Tierra del Fuego continued to be predominantly Māori or Fuegan, as the case might be, with European populations remaining small. See Damon Ieremia Salesa, *Racial Crossings: Race, Intermarriage, and the Victorian British Empire* (Oxford: Oxford University Press, 2011), 54, 66, 88; Penelope Edmonds and Amanda Nettelbeck, eds., *Intimacies of Violence in*

the Settler Colony: Economies of Dispossession around the Pacific Rim (New York: Springer-Palgrave Macmillan, 2018).

10. Smith, *Decolonizing Methodologies*, 37, 59.

11. Araluen, 'Resisting', n.p.

12. Salmond, *Tears of Rangi*, 1–3, 7–9 (see chapter 1); Anna Knox, 'Towards Our Ancient Futures: An Interview with Witi Ihimaera', *Wasafiri* 115 (Autumn 2023): 88–93, especially 90.

13. Benjamin Whorf, *Language, Thought, and Reality: Selected Writings*, ed. John B. Carroll, Penny Lee, Stephen C. Levinson (1956; Boston MA: MIT Press, 2012). Whorf's views about tense in the Native American Hopi language have long been disputed, but his insight developed after Edward Sapir that 'human culture [was] . . . a mechanism for ordering reality', remains fruitful for understanding how referential meaning is mutually interactive with our world-view. See Madeleine Mathiot, *Ethnolinguistics: Boas, Sapir and Whorf Revisited* (The Hague: Mouton, 1979), 163.

14. See Julia Sedivy, *Memory Speaks* (Cambridge MA: Harvard University Press, 2021), on how the languages we learn first appear to have greater emotional colour, connected as they are to family and place. Language loss, therefore, not least of these first languages, can throw us into 'cultural limbo', especially when accompanied by other forms of dispossession, including territorial.

15. Evans, *Dying Words*, 19, 163, 169. See also Ann McGrath and Mary Anne Jebb, eds., *Long History, Deep Time: Deepening Histories of Place* (Canberra: ANU Press, 2015).

16. Smith, *Decolonizing Methodologies*, 57.

17. Song-lines or dreaming tracks work as a kind of memorised orientation that makes possible at once sensing and singing the land while moving through it. Though he did not use Indigenous knowledge responsibly, Bruce Chatwin's *The Songlines* (London: Jonathan Cape, 1987), remains evocative for western audiences for its treatment of the concept. See also Werner Herzog, dir., *Nomad: In the Footsteps of Bruce Chatwin* (with Elizabeth Chatwin and Nicholas Shakespeare, 28 April 2019, Tribeca); David Malouf, 'Born to be Nomads', review of *Songlines*, by Bruce Chatwin, *TLS*, no. 6106 (10 April 2020): 34. Against Chatwin's claims, Indigenous Australians believe that they have always lived in Australia; they did not migrate to the continent from Africa. If, following this theory, Australia, too, might be regarded as a cradle of humankind, like southern Africa, this gives us yet another provocative linkup across the Southern Hemisphere to consider.

18. See Archibald, Lee-Morgan, and De Santolo, *Decolonizing Research*.

19. See Elleke Boehmer, *Empire, the National, and the Postcolonial 1890–1920: Resistance in Interaction* (Oxford: Oxford University Press, 2002); 2–5; Néstor García Canclini, *Imagined Globalization*, trans. George Yúdice (Durham and London: Duke University Press, 2014).

20. Laura Peers and Alison K. Brown, *Visiting with the Ancestors: Blackfoot Shirts in Museum Spaces* (Athabasca: Athabasca University Press, 2016), explores how the descendants of those who made and used such crafted objects feel a sense of closeness with the ancestral spirits who are still believed to inhabit the objects they once handled as living people. Even for outsiders, observing the objects' contours, volume, and details of decoration gives a profound sense of how they were crafted and used. See also chapter 8 of this volume.

21. Tony Ballantyne, *Webs of Empire: Locating New Zealand's Colonial Past* (Wellington NZ: Bridget Williams Books, 2012), 20–1. Ballantyne is particularly interested in Indigenous agents

working within the colonial order who attempted 'to resist, reshape, or retreat' from it. See also Jonathan Dunk, 'Reading the Tracker: The Antimonies of Aboriginal Ventriloquism', *JASAL: Journal of the Association for the Study of Australian Literature* 17, no. 1 (2017): 3.

22. James McCracken, spreadsheet of southern words from the *OED*, private communication (20 September 2019). I am very grateful to James and to his colleague Emily Hoyland for generously sharing their findings on southern words with me. The spreadsheet showed the following numbers of southern borrowings into the *OED*: 293 Māori words, 209 from Aboriginal Australian languages, 358 from southern African or Bantu languages such as Zulu, and 324 from Afrikaans.

23. Peter Otto, 'Making, Mapping and Unmaking Worlds', in *Worlding the South*, ed. Sarah Comyn and Porscha Fermanis (Manchester: Manchester University Press, 2021), 39–57, especially 55.

24. Roberto Trotta, *Starborn* (London: Hachette, 2023), reminds us that the night sky has shaped human belief systems and structures of knowledge right around the world.

25. Tom Phillips, 'Refreshment Unit', *TLS*, no. 6115 (12 June 2020): 28; Clive Gamble, *Origins and Revolutions: Human Identity in Earliest Prehistory* (Cambridge: Cambridge University Press, 2007).

26. Doreen Massey, *For Space*, 6–9; Sarah Comyn and Porscha Fermanis, introduction to *Worlding the South*, 6.

27. On metaphoric thinking, see Barry Lopez, 'Love in a Time of Terror: On Natural Landscapes, Metaphorical Living, and Warlpiri Identity', *Lithub*, 7 August 2020, https://lithub.com/barry-lopez-love-in-a-time-of-terror/. Accessed 29 December 2020. See also Lopez, *Horizon*, 259, for the shaping effect that the archipelagic nature of the Galapagos Islands may have had on Darwin's theorizing about evolution and the creation of biological difference.

28. For an examination of the 'littoral condition' of the southern hemisphere, see Meg Samuelson and Charne Lavery, 'The Oceanic South', *English Language Notes* 57, no. 1 (2019): 37–50, https://doi.org/10.1215/00138282-7309666; Meg Samuelson, 'Rendering the Cape-as-Port: Sea-Mountain, Cape of Storms/Good Hope, Adamastor and Local-World Literary Formations', *Journal of Southern African Studies* 42, no. 3 (2016): 524.

29. Sanjeev Sanjal, *The Ocean of Churn* (Gurgaon: Penguin Random House, 2016); Tim Winton, *The Boy behind the Curtain* (Sydney: Penguin Random House Australia, 2016), 75.

30. Hau'ofa, *We Are the Ocean*, 31, 42.

31. Jonathan Pugh, 'Island Movements: Thinking with the Archipelago', *Island Studies Journal*, 8, no. 1 (2013): 9–24, especially 11–12. See also Elizabeth DeLoughrey, *Routes and Roots: Navigating Caribbean and Pacific Island Literatures* (Honolulu: University of Hawai'i Press, 2007).

32. Wright, *Carpentaria*, 378–80.

33. Knox, 'Towards', 92.

34. Naomi Arnold, *Southern Nights* (Auckland: HarperCollins, 2019), 104; King, *Penguin History of New Zealand*, 31.

35. See Antoinette Burton and Isabel Hofmeyr, introduction to *Ten Books That Shaped the British Empire: Creating an Imperial Commons* (Durham: Duke University Press, 2014), 2–3, on 'multiple singularities'. The mirroring of the stars in the archipelagic sea informs traditional Pacific funeral rituals, in which the dead are drifted to the horizon in canoes, thus, disappearing

into the reflection of the starry sky in the water. See Judith Binney, 'Tuki's Universe', *New Zealand Journal of History* 38, no. 2 (2004): 215–32. Herman Melville, *Moby-Dick; or, The Whale*, ed. Harold Beaver (1851; Penguin Classics, 1986), 589, also captures this reciprocal reflection of ocean and night sky in Polynesian funerals: 'after embalming a dead warrior, [they] stretched him out in his canoe, and so left him to be floated away to the starry archipelagoes; for not only do they believe that the stars are isles, but that far beyond all visible horizons, their own mild, uncontinented seas, interflow with the blue heavens; and so form the white breakers of the milky way'. The image recurs below. The same idea of interconnected diversity interestingly underpinned the agricultural system of the fifteenth-century Inca empire in present-day Peru, then the largest empire in the Southern Hemisphere. The system was organised on the principle of a vertical archipelago, involving cultivation at four distinct altitudes—an 'animated structure' of different but connected ecosystems. See John V. Murra, *The Economic Organization of the Inca State* (Chicago: University of Chicago Press, 1968); Cecilia Pardo and Jago Cooper, *Peru: A Journey in Time* (London: British Museum, 2021).

36. In the 'Song Cycle of the Moon-Bone', translated by Ronald M. Berndt, from Wonguri-Mandjigai, the term for a totem animal like a dugong is *bukalili*, or power-name.

37. *The Worlds of Ursula K. Le Guin*, directed by Arwen Curry (*Java Films*, 17 November 2019).

38. Caroline Nilson, 'A Journey Towards Cultural Competence: The Role of Research Reflexivity in Indigenous Research', *Journal of Transcultural Nursing* 28, no. 2 (2017): 119–27, https://doi.org/10.1177/1043659616642825.

39. The boomerang shape has been taken up in the design of aeroplane wings around the world, propagating the aerodynamics that the object itself describes when in motion. See Neale, 'On the Spot', 112.

40. Anonymous, 'Song Cycle'.

41. Ali Jimmy Drummond, 'Our Languages Are a Tool to Understanding Our Ways of Knowing and Being', *The Guardian*, 20 June 2019, https://www.theguardian.com/commentisfree/2019/jun/20/our-languages-are-a-tool-to-understanding-our-ways-of-knowing-and-being.

42. See David Malouf, 'Born to be Nomads', 34. Ideophones and onomatopoeia are also interesting for how they speak from the environment in a direct, sonic way. An example is the Khoi word *kama-kama*, or 'sort of', an equivocatory utterance made with a waving, horizontal hand gesture, which has lived on in some versions of Cape Afrikaans. Menán Du Plessis, Stellenbosch Institute for Advanced Study (STIAS), personal communication, 20 February 2020.

43. Wright, *Carpentaria*, 386.

44. On the embodied narratives of First Nations people in North America, see Debbie Lee, 'Listening to the Land: The Selway-Bitterroot Wilderness as Oral History', *The Oral History Review*, 37, no. 2 (2010): 235–48, www.jstor.org/stable/41440805.

45. Lopez, *Arctic Dreams*, 274–5, 277–8. Lopez writes: 'To learn the indigenous language, then, is to know what the speakers of the languages have made of the land' (278).

46. Mathiot, *Ethnolinguistics*; Whorf, *Language, Thought, and Reality*.

47. Wilfrid H. G. Haacke and Eliphas Eiseb, *A Khoekhoegowab Dictionary* (Windhoek: Gamsberg Macmillan, 2002).

48. W. H. I. Bleek and Lucy Lloyd, *Specimens of Bushman Folklore* (London: George Allen and Co., 1911), 2–15; Antjie Krog, *die sterre sê 'tsau'* (Cape Town: Kwela, 2004); Antjie Krog, *the*

stars say 'tsau': |xam poetry of Dia!kwain, Kweiten-ta-||ken, |a!kúnta, |han‡kass'o and ||kabbo (Cape Town: Kwela, 2004).

49. See Mattias Guenther, 'Dreams and Stories', in *Courage of ||kabbo*, ed. Janette Deacon and Pippa Skotnes (Cape Town: University of Cape Town Press, 2014), 194–210, especially 202.

50. Marnie Hughes-Warrington and Anne Martin, *Big and Little Histories: Sizing up Ethics in Historiography* (Abingdon: Taylor and Francis, 2021), 262. From the online Gamilaraay course I took with Tracey Cameron at the University of Sydney, March to May 2021, I gained a comparable sense of how space-time was designated in that language and how temporality was conceived. Gamilaraay uses the same suffix (*-ga*, or *-dha*) to denote nearby position: 'in', 'on', 'at', 'near', etc.

51. On outside names imposed on already densely named landscapes: In 1770, on the Cape York Peninsula, while the *Endeavour* was being repaired following its tearing on the Great Barrier Reef, James Cook recorded in his journal a list of about a hundred or so words in the local Guugu Yimidhirr language. He was engaged at the same time, as at every point on his journey, in naming geographical features using English proper names largely drawn from the British establishment. Yet he also began to express 'considerable uncertainty about which notable [person] was to be offered which' feature. It is worth asking whether his growing awareness of these local names might have been unsettling to his project. Was there a moment for Cook of self-estrangement when the activity of transferring names from very far away to an environment that evidently had no lack of them became suddenly ridiculous and unnerving? See Cook, *Journals*, 136; Moore, *Endeavour*, 175, 219–32.

52. Denver van Breda, Deidre Jantjies, and Menán du Plessis, '!Hub Di Gowab—'n Taal van ons Land', Woordfees festival discussion, Stellenbosch (11 March 2020). Van Breda noted that language relearning provided ways of healing a community and connecting to the ancestors. While colonial 'Hollander' forces had worked with destructive effect, inflicting '*kakapoesa*' or identity-erasure, Afrikaans and Griqua speakers had ('till 1875') kept Indigenous Khoi-San languages alive. In the western or 'trans-American' hemisphere, relatedly, as Edgar Garcia argues in *Signs of the Americas—A Poetics of Pictography, Hieroglyphs, and Khipu* (Chicago: Chicago University Press, 2020), Indigenous visual signs like petroglyphs can be seen to 'affect contemporary patterns of perception and imagination', as reflected, for example, in twentieth- and twenty-first-century poetry and the visual arts. Western capitalist time may in this way be 'constantly disrupted and challenged' by divergent indigenous temporalities (6).

53. Roseanne Kennedy, 'Indigenous Australian Arts of Return: Mediating Perverse Archives', in *Rites of Return: Diaspora Poetics and the Politics of Memory*, ed. Marianne Hirsch and Nancy K. Miller (New York: Columbia University Press, 2011), 88–104, https://doi.org/10.13140/RG.2.1.2416.5207. Kennedy argues that the 'challenge is to use such records—what I am calling *perverse* archives—to create an Indigenous cultural memory of dehumanization and survival' (90). On the third archive, see Neale, 'On the Spot', 112. See also Bruce Pascoe, *Dark Emu: Black Seeds: Agriculture or Accident?* (Broome: Magabala Books, 2013). Pascoe reads evidence of ancient Indigenous cultivation into settler accounts of weir-making and fishing and relates these to Dark Emu myths and stories of the southern night sky that marked the seasons of planting and harvest (see section 05). Against European claims that Indigenous Australians lacked agricultural knowledge (and hence that the continent was *tabula rasa*), Pascoe urges that the Australian landscape had long been shaped by certain distinctive husbanding practices, including seed harvesting and fire-stick farming.

54. See the website 'Australian Indigenous Astronomy', accessed 17 January 2022, http://www.aboriginalastronomy.com.au/content/topics/stars/.

55. See Anna Johnston, '"That's white fellow's talk you know, missis": Wordlists, Songs, and Knowledge Production on the Colonial Australian Frontier', in *Worlding the South*, 273–93. See also Jakelin Troy, 'The Sydney Language Notebooks and Responses to Language Contact in Early Colonial NSW', *Australian Journal of Linguistics* 12, no. 1 (1992), 145–70; Ross Gibson, *26 Views of the Starburst World: William Dawes at Sydney Cove 1788–91* (Crawley, WA: University of Western Australia Publishing, 2012). There is perhaps a dark irony to the fact that the observation of an astronomical event, the Transit of Venus, provided the incentive for the first voyage of James Cook, on the *'Endeavour'*, into the southern hemisphere.

56. William Beinart and Saul Dubow, *The Scientific Imagination in South Africa, 1700 to the Present* (Cambridge: Cambridge University Press, 2021), 40, 78–81; Hedley Twidle, 'Impossible Images: Radio Astronomy, the Square Kilometre Array and the Art of Seeing', *JSAS* 45, no. 4 (2019): 767–90. See also Twidle's website reflection on SKA: https://hedleytwidle.com/home/tag/SKA.

57. Where one of the observing astronomers was Charles Mason, who, with the surveyor Jeremiah Dixon, later plotted the Mason-Dixon line separating Maryland and Pennsylvania in the United States. See Nick Lomb, *Transit of Venus, 1631 to the Present* (New York: The Experiment, 2012); Cóilín Parsons, 'Planetary Parallax: *Ulysses*, the Stars, and South Africa', *Modernism/Modernity* 24, no. 1 (2017): 67–85. The necessary incompleteness of the planetary vision that fiction propagates, in Parsons's view, will reemerge as a consideration in later chapters.

58. Helize van Vuuren, 'A Song Sung by the Star !Gaunu', in *Courage of ||kabbo: Celebrating the 100th Anniversary of the Publication of Specimens of Bushman Folklore*, ed. Janette Deacon and Pippa Skotnes (Cape Town: University of Cape Town Press, 2014), 317–28.

59. In our time, the southern skies remain relatively dark. The hemisphere has less light pollution, and also deeper radio silence. Hence, the construction in the Karoo, in the Northern Cape, South Africa, and in the Western Australian desert, of the Square Kilometre Array (SKA) radio telescope that in effect builds and expands on these earlier south-south astronomical links. See Cherryl Walker, Davide Chinigò, and Saul Dubow, eds., 'Karoo Futures: Astronomy in Place and Space', special issue, *JSAS* 45, no. 4 (August 2019), especially the final three essays by, respectively, John Partington, David Morris and José M. de Prada-Samper, Davide Chinigò, and Hedley Twidle.

60. Nyunmiti Burton, *Kungkarangkalpa—Seven Sisters*, Art Gallery of South Australia, viewed at the 'Stars, Stardust and Story-Making in the South' workshop (7 November 2024). Many thanks to curator Nici Cumpston for explaining features of the painting to the workshop group, as well as to curator Gloria Strzelecki for her account of the starscapes and astral reckonings of Gulumbu Yunupingu and Gail Mabo, also in the AGSA. See Burton's painting and Yunupingu's *Ganyu-Stars* in this book's colour insert. See also note 82 to chapter 2, above.

61. Arnold, *Southern Nights*, 87, 93–4, 134.

62. Alejandro Martín López, 'Las Pléyades, el sol y el ciclo anual entre los mocovíes'/'The Pleaides, the Sun and the Annual Cycle Among the Mocovíes' (unpublished manuscript, 2019), trans. Cristóbal Pérez Barra and Elleke Boehmer, 2020. My thanks to Pablo Wainschenker for sharing the paper.

63. The mid-twentieth-century South African poet Guy Butler in his poem 'The Pleiades' records his delight at encountering stories and rituals of the 'friendly' constellation, 'feminine

as always', 'in the South', opening the poem with references to myths of the Seven Sisters from around the world, including Ancient Greece and China. The middle section records that Khoikhoi new year gatherings marked the constellation's reappearance, while new mothers displayed their babies to its 'friendly' light. The stars 'promise growth' also in Xhosa rites of passage, in which they are named the 'isilimela', derived from the Xhosa word for 'putting in seed'. Though Butler begins this evocation with citations from western anthropology, the *isilimela* reference is underpinned with 'the words of the great imbongi, S E K Mqhayi: "We bind ourselves together with the Pleiades—the stars we count our years by, the years of our manhood."' Chapter 6 will discuss the characteristic tendency of settler writing like Butler's to self-locate 'in the South' by invoking indigenous myth. But the poem is nonetheless interesting for its attention both to the rhythms of the southern skies and to local communities' responses. See Guy Butler, *Collected Poems* (Cape Town: David Philip, 1999), 248–50.

64. Arnold, *Southern Nights*, 110–19; Lopez, *Arctic Dreams*, 290, 294.

65. South African Astronomical Observatory, 'SALT and SAAO Telescopes Investigate the Origin of the First Detection of Gravitational Waves Produced by Two Colliding Neutron Starts', *SAOO*, 16 October 2017, https://www.saao.ac.za/2017/10/16/salt-and-saao-telescopes-investigate-the-origin-of-the-first-detection-of-gravitational-waves-produced-by-two-colliding-neutron-stars/. The collision produced 'a kilonova explosion of light', and gravitational waves that astronomers were able to detect for about a minute-and-a-half. Astronomer Stephen Potter commented: 'I knew that everyone with a working telescope in the Southern Hemisphere was scrambling to get data on it.' The spectrum that SALT—the Southern African Large Telescope—captured was the first to show significant 'anomalous behaviour'. SALT in the town of Sutherland was, during the period of writing this book, still the largest single optical telescope in the southern hemisphere and among the largest in the world, with a primary mirror array eleven metres across. With thanks to Christine Hobden for the weekend trip that we undertook to Sutherland while STIAS fellows, 22–23 February 2020, and to Thomas and Sam Matthews Boehmer for sending me links to the kilonova story. South African Chantal Stewart's novel *The Veil of Maya* (Cape Town: Minimal Press, 2022), is set in Sutherland and features a love affair between an astronomer and an ethnographer. The latter several times ponders the Khoikhoi story of the origin of the 'cloudy curtain' of the Milky Way (103) that also features in a number of other 2020s South African fictions and recurs in chapter 7.

66. Though neutron collision was first detected by gravitational wave observatories in the United States and Italy, radio and optical observatories in the southern hemisphere were able to rally quickly and provide further data. Chile produced the first visual imaging of the explosion's gravitational waves, while the South African Astronomical Observatory (SAAO) and SALT generated a spectrum analysis of the event.

67. 'SALT and SAAO Telescopes'. The exhaustive study of the event from several 'dark-sky' vantage points around the hemisphere confirmed the astronomical wisdom of founding SKA in the far south.

68. Steven Gulberg et al., 'A Comparison of Dark Constellations of the Milky Way', *Archaeological Reports* 23, no. 2 (July 2019): 390–404, https://doi.org/10.3724/SP.J.1440-2807.2020.02.10.

69. Chantal Conneller, Paul Pettitt, and Alistair Pike, 'Cave Art', *In Our Time*, hosted by Melvyn Bragg, BBC Radio 4, 24 September 2020, suggest that entoptic patterning might explain similarities in Paleolithic cave painting in Argentina and Australia. Provided we have shared

experiences, our brains appear to predispose us to discern similar outlines within similar patterns, whether within the contours of cave walls or in star shapes in the sky.

70. Robert S. Fuller, Michelle Trudgett, and Ray Norris, 'The Emu Sky Knowledge of the Kamilaroi and Euahlayi Peoples,' *Journal of Astronomical History and Heritage*, 17, no. 2 (2014): 4, https://doi.org/10.3724/SP.J.1440-2807.2014.02.04. See also Duane Hamacher, *The First Astronomers: How Indigenous Elders Read the Stars* (Sydney: Allen & Unwin, 2022), including 31, 120–24. I have used alternative indigenous terms to acknowledge the enormous linguistic diversity of Indigenous Australia in the past and up to today.

71. Noon and De Napoli, *Astronomy*, 37–42. From the perspective of other groups, the gash in the Milky Way is a scar marking the place where, at a 'critical moment during the Dreaming', the sky and the land were ripped apart. For Pascoe in *Dark Emu*, the dark emu shape in the sky 'inextricably' interlocks 'the wide grasslands of Australia' and its fauna with Aboriginal economies (2–5).

72. Alejandro Martin López and Sixto Benítez, 'The Milky Way and its Structuring Function in the Worldview of the Mocoví of Gran Chaco', *Archaeologica Baltica* 10 (2008): 21–24, https://e-journals.ku.lt/journal/AB/article/1243/info.

73. To this day, the Mocoví use the position of the Milky Way as a 'temporal marker', even despite present-day deforestation which means that they are less dependent on navigation by the stars. See López and Benítez, 'Milky Way', 22.

74. Menán du Plessis, *Kora: A Lost Khoisan Language of the Early Cape and the Gariep* (Pretoria: UNISA Press, 2019). See the entry for 'Stars'. See also Johnston, 'Wordlists', 285, on the sidereal wordlists developed by the colonial astronomer William Dawes and the Eora woman Patyegarang in the Sydney harbour area in the 1780s.

75. Personal notes, final panel, *Shared Sky* exhibition, Iziko/South African National Gallery, Cape Town, May 2015.

76. Thomas Bridges, *A Dictionary of the Speech of Tierra del Fuego*, ed. Ferdinand Hestermann and Martin Gusinde (Ushuaia, Argentina: Private publication, 1987), 81.

77. Connolly, 'Munda-gutta Kulliwari project'. The State Library of New South Wales' Rediscovering Indigenous Languages website is a free public resource based on data submitted by users. See https://indigenous.sl.nsw.gov.au/. At the time of writing, the website mod.org.au featured Dreaming stories of the skies told by Indigenous speakers.

78. See Arnold, *Southern Nights*, 87, 134

79. In the 21st century, the building of the SKA radio telescope has given new prominence to these interconnected cosmologies. Two major 2010s exhibitions made much of the intra- and intercontinental parallels that Indigenous people's celestial readings afford, as reflected in the catalogue titles: *Songlines: Tracking the Seven Sisters* (Canberra: Australian National Museum, 2017) and *Shared Sky* (Cape Town: Iziko/South African National Gallery, 2015). However, the SKA telescope was built on ancestral lands, sparking protest and critique. As Rebecca Charbonneau comments, the 'born global' SKA project was invested in promoting its pristine symbolic associations equally with the unspoiled Karoo, deep-time Indigenous myth systems, and its investigations of the birth of the universe, but not without social and cultural cost. Rebecca Charbonneau, presentation, 'Karoo Futures' Colloquium, Magdalene College, Cambridge, 25 October 2019 (personal notes). Beth and Willie Engelbrecht, *The Lost Tales of the Meerkat National Park: Karoo Farmlands and Their Stories* (Cape Town: Tourism Blueprint, 2023), and John

Parkington, David Morris, and Jose M. de Prada-Samper, *Karoo Cosmos: |xam-ka !au and the |xam* (Cape Town: South African Astronomical Observatory, 2021), also reflect on farm expropriations due to the SKA development, and the subsequent loss of local story traditions.

80. Meaghan Wilson Anastasios, *The Pacific in the Wake of Captain Cook* (Sydney: Harper Collins, 2018), 48–9.

81. Patrick Vinton Kirch, *On the Road of the Winds: An Archaeological History of the Pacific Islands before European Contact* (Berkeley: University of California Press, 2000); Jared Diamond, *Collapse: How Societies Choose to Fail or Succeed* (New York and London: Vintage, 2005), 86–7. See also Arnold, *Southern Nights*, 110; King, *Penguin History of New Zealand*, 33, 34, 36–37. 40. Diamond remarks that NASA consulted experts on Polynesian navigation for guidance on voyaging into the unknown.

82. Moore, *Endeavour*, 162, 195. Australian and Torres Strait Islander artist Gail Mabo's installation *Tagai* (2021), a wall-hanging in the Art Gallery of South Australia (viewed 16 October 2024), plays on the idea of the stick chart (that was also used to navigate the Torres Strait waters). Enlarging the traditional bamboo frame several times, Mabo's star markers take their shape from the sand grains of a beach in the region while at the same time picking out the shape of Tagai, an important constellation for Torres Strait navigation. The work is pregnant with cultural references, much like the star maps of old. Mabo's father was Eddie Koiki Mabo, who led the campaign against the colonial 'terra nullius' idea. The campaign culminated in the 1993 Native Title Act recognising Indigenous ownership of Australian and Torres Strait lands and waters.

83. Nienke Boer, *The Briny South: Displacement and Sentiment in the Indian Ocean World* (Durham, NC: Duke University Press, 2023), discusses identity construction through displacement within the networked theatre of the Indian Ocean.

84. Vicente M. Diaz and J. Kehaulani Kauanui, 'Native Pacific Cultural Studies on the Edge', *The Contemporary Pacific*, 13, no. 2 (2001): 317. Lopez, *Arctic Dreams*, 290, 294.

85. Epeli Hau'ofa, 'Our Sea of Islands', in *A New Oceania: Rediscovering Our Sea of Islands*, ed. Eric Waddell, Vijay Naidu, and Epeli Hau'ofa (Suva: University of the South Pacific, 1993), 6–7. See also Brunt and Thomas, *Oceania*.

86. Melville, *Moby-Dick*, 589.

87. Anne Salmond, 'Reimagining the Ocean', in *Oceania*, ed. Peter Brunt and Nicholas Thomas, 42–55, especially 47. Alfred Wendt is quoted in the Brunt and Thomas introduction, 25.

88. Arnold, *Southern Nights*, 113, 118–19. This fluid, memory-based knowledge worked in the precise opposite way to the stop-time of European navigation in which bearings were taken at set times of day perceived as static points on the clock. It assumed a view of the universe that was layered and curved, the islands sailing across the sea, and the stars the sky, like canoes. The knowledge extended to being able to plot where the canoe lay within a pattern of currents by listening to the sound of the water knocking against the hull. We can imagine that Tupaia's expertise showed Cook a more fluid and malleable understanding of the universe than the latter's own measurements allowed, yet one whose underlying patterns he could accept were viable. The continuing viability of Polynesian navigational techniques was demonstrated in 1976 when the Hōkūle'a, a specially designed double-hulled traditional vessel, successfully sailed from Hawai'i to Tahiti. On the Raiatean priest-assistant Mai, Tupaia's younger successor on English ships, see Kate Fullagar, *The Warrior, the Voyager, and the Artist: Three Lives in an Age of Empire*

(New Haven and London: Yale University Press, 2020); Vanessa Smith, *Intimate Strangers: Friendship, Exchange, and Pacific Encounters* (Cambridge: Cambridge University Press, 2010). Mai travelled to London on the *Adventure,* which sailed with Cook's second expedition, and returned to the Society Islands on the *Resolution* with Cook in 1776–7.

89. Anastasios, *Pacific,* 60–1, 413; Lopez, *Horizon,* 184, 217–18; Salmond, *Tears of Rangi,* 9; Moore, *Endeavour,* 183–6, 192–6, 210.

90. Moore, *Endeavour,* 195–6.

91. Cook, *Journals,* 70. See also 79, 84, 94.

92. Salmond, *Tears of Rangi,* 10, 17, 26–7.

93. Cook, *Journals,* 101, 274–5, 283.

94. Connell, *Southern Theory.*

Chapter Three

Note to epigraph: Captain Pringle Stokes, qtd. in Phillip Parker King and Robert FitzRoy, *Proceedings of the First Expedition, 1826–30, under the Command of Captain P. Parker King, R.N., F.R.S.* (London: Henry Colburn, 1839), 1:179. These lines are from the final paragraphs in Stokes's ship's notes, before his suicide in Puerto del Hambre, southern Chile, in 1828.

1. See Ricardo Padrón, *The Spacious Word: Cartography, Literature, and Empire in Early Modern Spain* (Chicago: University of Chicago Press, 2004), especially 31–63, for how changes in European cartography correlated with exploration and colonisation, making maps and geographical writings 'an important area' for the development of the imperial imagination. The reference to positive space is from page 54.

2. Commodore Byron, *An Account of the Voyages Undertaken by the order of His Present Majesty for Making Discoveries in the Southern Hemisphere,* ed. John Hawkesworth (1773; Cambridge: CUP, 2013), 1:30–31, 50, 100. Also referenced by Stokes, above, John Bulkeley was a noncommissioned seaman who helped to pilot a longboat to safety after the wreck of the HMS *Wager* in 1741. The *Wager* had been one of an expedition fleet of six ships under Commodore George Anson (who completed his planned circumnavigation on HMS *Centurion* in 1744). Bulkeley published with John Cummins *A Voyage to the South-Seas, in the Years 1740–1* (1743).

3. Cook, *Journals,* 23.

4. Cook, *Journals,* 117, 278. Cook's charts were first compiled and published by Alexander Dalrymple, the eighteenth-century armchair theorist of the southern continent.

5. Matthew Flinders, *A Voyage to Terra Australis,* 2 vols. (1814; Cambridge: Cambridge University Press, 2010), vii-viii. See also Gillian Dooley and Danielle Clode, eds., *The First Wave: Exploring Early Coastal Contact History in Australia* (Adelaide: The Wakefield Press, 2019).

6. Philip E. Steinberg, 'Of Other Seas: Metaphors and Materialities in Maritime Regions', *Atlantic Studies* 10, no. 2 (2013): 156–169, https://doi.org/10.1080/14788810.2013.785192. See also Philip E. Steinberg, *The Social Construction of the Ocean* (Cambridge: Cambridge University Press, 2001).

7. John Hawkesworth, 'General Introduction', in *An Account of the Voyages,* 1:7.

8. Elleke Boehmer, *Colonial and Postcolonial Literature: Migrant Metaphors,* 2nd ed. (1995; Oxford: Oxford University Press, 2005), 15.

9. Stefanie Massmann, 'Alonso de Ercilla's *La Araucana* and Pedro de Oña's *Arauco domado* in the National Imaginary', in *A History of Chilean Literature,* ed. Ignacio López-Calvo, trans.

Javiera Sepúlveda Salas (Cambridge: Cambridge University Press, 2021), 43–60. Raimund Schulz, *To the Ends of the Earth: How Ancient Conquerors, Explorers, Scientists, and Traders Conquered the World* (Oxford: Oxford University Press, 2024), considers the heroic self-image poised between their reading and their yearning that animated many explorers. For example, Columbus and Magellan were both inspired by chivalric tales, Vespucci by Dante and Petrarch.

10. As we will see again in chapter 4, Milton was a perennial resource for the English writers. On Darwin, see Nigel Leask, 'Darwin's Second Sun: Alexander von Humboldt and the Genesis of *The Voyage of the Beagle*', in *Literature, Science and Psychoanalysis, 1830–1970: Essays in Honour of Dame Gillian Beer*, ed. Helen Small and Trudi Tate (Oxford: Oxford University Press, 2003), 13–36. Coleridge also appears to filter into Darwin's thoughts, as when he writes of Tierra del Fuego: 'in these still solitudes, Death, instead of Life, seemed the predominant spirit' (*Voyage of the Beagle*, 222).

11. The intertextuality pertains to the novel's fabula as to its sujet. Captain Ahab follows the progress of the whale across the oceans by referring to 'piles of old log-books' that track the movement of sperm whales, so tracing 'courses over spaces that before were blank' (Melville, *Moby-Dick*, 298).

12. Hayot, *On Literary Worlds* (44) posits that a literary work 'worlds' by assembling a 'diegetic totality' that makes up and constitutes its imagined world. See also Pheng Cheah, *What Is a World? On Postcolonial Literature as World Literature* (Durham, NC: Duke University Press, 2016).

13. Harry Thompson, *This Thing of Darkness* (2005; London: Headline Review/Tinder Press, 2020), 205.

14. It remains proper to acknowledge here, as in chapter 1, the massively influential work of Edward Said, *Orientalism*, on the ideological construction of the east—in that the east was the prize that powered European exploration into the south.

15. The Pope's Treaty of Tordesillas in 1494 divided all present and future discoveries between the Peninsular powers with a line running from pole to pole around the globe. Spain claimed the American territories to the west of the line, leaving their rival Portugal's zone of influence to the east. With the Dutch and then the British following in the tracks of the Portuguese from a century or so later, one of the legacies of the Treaty was to establish the European language zones of the southern hemisphere that we retain to this day. The longitudinal line dividing the hemispheres still determines the western boundaries of the east-coast Australian states, and of Papua New Guinea and West Papua.

16. Ricardo Padrón, *The Indies of the Setting Sun: How Early Modern China Mapped the Far East as the Transpacific West* (Chicago: University of Chicago Press, 2020), especially 13–40.

17. Lowes, *Road to Xanadu*, 121.

18. See Josiah Blackmore, *Moorings: Portuguese Expansion and the Writing of Africa* (Minneapolis: Minnesota Press, 2009), 11, 34.

19. Alonso de Ercilla y Zúñiga, *La Araucana*, ed. Luis María Gómez Canseco (Madrid: Real Academia Española, 2022); and *The Araucaniad: A Version in English Poetry*, trans. Charles Maxwell Lancaster and Paul Manchester (1945; Nashville, TN: Vanderbilt University Press, 2014).

20. Eric Hobsbawm, *The Age of Capital 1848–1875* (London: Little, Brown, 1988); *The Age of Empire 1875–1914* (London: Cardinal, 1987).

21. Young, *Early Modern Global South*, 10, and see also 6–7, 13–14.

22. Anne M. Thell, *Minds in Motion: Imagining Empiricism in Eighteenth-Century British Travel Literature* (Lewisburg: Bucknell UP, 2017).

23. Young, *Early Modern Global South*, 10ff., 51; and Sandra Young, 'Charting English Global Presence and its Violent Effects in Early Modernity: Reading Strategies for an Ambivalent Archive,' *Jems* 12: 217–235, doi: http://dx. doi.org/10.36253/JEMS-2279-7149-14392. Young takes Martin Waldseemüller's *Cosmographiae Introductio* (1507) as a key text projecting a 'new world' discourse onto the amalgamated imaginary of a great 'elsewhere'. See also Richard Blome's 1682 edition of Bernhardus Varenius's *Geographia*, entitled *Cosmography and Geography*. I am grateful to Sandra Young for sharing this research with me.

24. Or, as in Boehmer, *Colonial and Postcolonial Literature*, 14ff., the wider world was made comprehensible using 'dependable textual conventions, both rhetorical and syntactic'.

25. Young, *Early Modern Global South*, 81.

26. Blackmore, *Moorings*, 53, defines the *roteiro* or rutter as 'a genre of nautical writing developed by Portuguese maritime travellers . . . a type of navigational guide. In this kind of text, coasts and coastal waters are described, and natural signs or markers (e.g., rivers, trees, or gulfs) are mentioned in order to help pilots navigate and recognize certain stretches of land'.

27. Phillip Allen, *The Atlas of Atlases* (London: Bounty Books, 2005).

28. Daniel Herwitz, 'History on White Linen', in *T'Kama-Adamastor: Inventions of Africa in a South African Painting*, ed. Ivan Vladislavic (Johannesburg: University of the Witwatersrand Press, 2000), 71–81.

29. Svetlana Alpers, *The Art of Describing: Dutch Art in the Seventeenth Century* (Chicago: University of Chicago Press, 1984); Herwitz, 'History', 78.

30. Dias turned back in the area of the Great Fish River mouth, in the present-day Eastern Cape, and, as if to defy later doubters and naysayers, planted three stone crosses on the southern African littoral, at Kwaaihoek, Cape Maclear, and on the Namibian coast. Each was an uncompromising 'we were here' sign, a Christian symbol set down in defiance of so-called heathen ground, a guide but also a caution to future travellers, equivalent to Camões's later dutiful notation of ports along the African seaboard that had been visited by the Portuguese (even though he also included a twist in the tale, as will become apparent). As for later colonisers, the names the early navigators gave to new shorelines drew from their national, professional, and personal histories and operated in a similar way to the crosses, turning till-then-uncharted space into land that could be possessed and penetrated.

31. Hawkesworth, dedication in *An Account of the Voyages*, n.p. and ix. Hawkesworth continues: 'By this narrative, it will be seen how far the existence or non-existence of a southern continent is already ascertained, and what land has in the course of these voyages been first discovered' (ix).

32. Katherine A. Parker, 'Contentious Waters: The Creation of Pacific Geographic Knowledge in Britain, 1669–1768' (PhD diss., University of Pittsburgh, 2016), v, 5.

33. Melville, *Moby-Dick*, 295.

34. Raoul McLaughlin, *Rome and the Distant East: Trade Routes to the Ancient Lands of Arabia, India and China* (London: Continuum, 2010).

35. Luís Vaz de Camões, *The Lusíads*, trans. Landeg White (1997; Oxford: Oxford University Press, 2001), 100 and note 243. See cantos 5.70; 8.71, 72; 5.13–15, respectively. Landeg White's 1997 translation has been valuable for loosely maintaining the ottava rima structure while introducing a far closer southern and east Africa focus than can be found in previous translations.

Further references to be cited in text with the abbreviation *L*, followed by the canto and stanza reference.

36. Richard L. Pflederer, *Catalogue of the Portolan Charts and Atlases in the Bodleian Library* (Oxford: Bodleian Library, 2008).

37. Marcel van den Broecke, *Ortelius Atlas Maps: An Illustrated Guide* (Houten: De Graaf Publishers, 2011); Peter C. J. van der Krogt, *Koeman's Atlantis Neerlandici*, new ed., vol. 3 (Leiden: Brill, 2003). Quotations from Cicero written onto the Ortelius map summon connotations of vastness at a verbal level also, as in, 'Who can consider human affairs to be great when he comprehends the eternity and vastness of the entire world'.

38. Anastasios, *Pacific* (Sydney: Harper Collins, 2018), 20.

39. Parker, 'Contentious Waters', 4.

40. John Thornton map, MS Bodl Add E 8 C-410 (1682).

41. See Pamila Gupta, Isabel Hofmeyr, and Michael Pearson, eds., *Eyes across the Water: Navigating the Indian Ocean* (Pretoria: UNISA Press, 2010), on the 'public sphere' of the colonial Indian Ocean. K. N. Chaudhuri, *Trade and Civilisation in the Indian Ocean: An Economic History from the Rise of Islam to 1750* (Cambridge: Cambridge University Press, 1985), is an early landmark study of the Indian Ocean as a space of commerce and exchange from at least the 11th century on that interconnected China, India, the Middle East, and the East African coast including port cities like Mombasa that figure in the *Lusíads*.

42. Thell, *Minds in Motion*, 7, 59, 217.

43. Steinberg, 'Of Other Seas', 161, 165.

44. See the influential account of how writing projected familiarity upon remoteness in Paul Carter, *The Road to Botany Bay* (London: Faber, 1987).

45. To draw on the phenomenologist Hans Robert Jauss's term, in *Toward an Aesthetic of Reception*, trans. Timothy Bahti (Minneapolis: U of Minnesota Press, 1982). See also Rita Felski, *The Limits of Critique* (Chicago: University of Chicago Press, 2015), 186–93.

46. This account is indebted to Dan Sperber and Deirdre Wilson, *Relevance: Communication and Cognition*, 2nd ed. (Oxford: Blackwell, 1995). For literary critical applications of relevance, see Terence Cave, *Thinking with Literature: Towards a Cognitive Criticism* (Oxford: Oxford University Press, 2016); Adrian Pilkington, *Poetic Effects* (Amsterdam: John Benjamins, 2000); Boehmer, *Postcolonial Poetics*.

47. Ivan Vladislavic, ed., introduction to *T'Kama—Adamastor: Inventions of Africa in a South African Painting* (Johannesburg: University of the Witwatersrand Press, 2000), 1–2.

48. William J. Burchell, *Travels in the Interior of Southern Africa* (London: Longman, Hurst, Tees, Orme, Brown and Green, 1822), 1; Susan Buchanan, *Burchell's Travels* (Cape Town: Penguin Random House, 2015), 11.

49. For an account of a similar process in Coleridge, see A. C. Swanepoel, 'Coleridge's Transcendental Imagination: The Seascape beyond the Senses in 'The Rime of the Ancient Mariner', *Journal of Literary Studies*, 26, no. 1 (2010): 191–214, https://doi.org/10.1080/02564710903495560.

50. Kohn, *How Forests Think*, 57–63, especially 63.

51. Steinberg, 'Of Other Seas', 161–5.

52. Blackmore, *Moorings*, 33–4. See also Richard Helgerson, *Forms of Nationhood* (Chicago: University of Chicago Press, 1994), especially ch. 4; Josiah Blackmore, 'The Shipwrecked

Swimmer: Camões's Maritime Subject', *Modern Philology* 109, no. 3 (February 2012), 312–325. https://www.jstor.org/stable/10.1086/663280.

53. White, introduction to *Lusíads*, ix.

54. Da Gama would repeat his near five-hundred-day voyage some years later, subsequently returning to India in 1524 as viceroy and dying in office in Cochin.

55. At certain points, Camões goes so far as to conflate da Gama's journey with his own, as when he represents the people of the Congo River as already Christianized.

56. Blackmore, *Moorings*, xiii-xvi, 86.

57. Blackmore, *Moorings*, 74.

58. See White, introduction to *Lusíads*, xvi-xvii; Blackmore, *Moorings*, xviii.

59. Helgerson, *Forms of Nationhood*, 163.

60. The Portuguese lacked the resources and manpower to maintain their African seaboard dominance, and from the mid-sixteenth century, British, French and Dutch ships increasingly threatened coastal states and cities under their control. In 1580, the year of Camões's death, the Portuguese crown passed to Phillip II of Spain.

61. White, introduction to *Lusíads*, xi.

62. Blackmore, *Moorings*, xxiii, 47.

63. In this guise, Adamastor has duly sparked South African rewritings and intertexts, as chapter 7 discusses.

64. Among the southern god's modern admirers was the South African novelist André P. Brink, whose fabulist *The First Life of Adamastor* reconstructs Adamastor as the Khoikhoi leader, T'kama. André P. Brink, 'A Myth of Origin', in *T'Kama—Adamastor*, 41–69. See chapter 7, where the figure resurfaces.

65. Vladislavic, *T'Kama*, 42, 45.

66. On the two Ethiopias of antiquity, see, in particular, Malvern van Wyk Smith, '"Waters flowing from darkness": The Two Ethiopias in the Early European Image of Africa', *Theoria: A Journal of Social and Political Theory* 68 (December 1986): 67–77.

67. Adamastor refers to Portuguese calamities in the Cape area in the years 1500, 1510, and 1552, that involved attacks and floundering, including that of Bartolomeu Dias. Four lines from of *L* 5.42 appear in the epigraph to the chapter, from which the title is also taken.

68. Blackmore, *Moorings*, xvi, 74, 83.

69. Lynn Festa, *Sentimental Figures of Empire in Eighteenth-Century Britain and France* (Baltimore: Johns Hopkins University Press, 2006), 56.

Chapter Four

1. Samuel Taylor Coleridge, *The Rime of the Ancient Mariner*, in *Coleridge's Poetry and Prose*, ed. Nicholas Halmi, Paul Magnuson, and Raimonda Modiano (New York: W.W. Norton, 2004), 58. Coleridge added this gloss in 1817, for the poem's publication in *Sybilline Leaves*. The poet revised the *Rime* many times from its first publication in 1798. While the Norton Critical Edition prints the 1798 and 1834 versions in parallel, my in-text references are to the 1834 version, using, where relevant, stanza numbers and line references. During the COVID-19 lockdown, I also consulted the online Poetry Society text, which is based on the 1834 edition. https://www.poetryfoundation.org/poems/43997/the-rime-of-the-ancient-mariner-text-of-1834. Accessed 4 November 2021.

2. Lowes, *Road to Xanadu*, 123–4. The curve around the 'tempestuous southern cape', Lowes echoes Coleridge in observing, brings the sun up 'on the opposite hand'.

3. Lowes, *Road to Xanadu*, 121–3.

4. Griffiths, *Slicing the Silence*, 54.

5. Melville, *Moby-Dick*, 294. Further page references will be cited in text, together with the abbreviation *MD*.

6. Charles Darwin, *The Origin of Species and The Voyage of the* Beagle (London: Vintage, 2009), 252–3. Further page references will be cited in text, together with the abbreviation *OSVB*. The word 'gloomy' recurs with some regularity across the *Voyage*.

7. This period coincides roughly with Richard Holmes's 'Age of Wonder', extending from Cook's first journey on the *Endeavour*, beginning in 1768, to Darwin embarking on the *Beagle* in 1831. For Holmes, notions of the quest and especially of 'the exploratory voyage, often lonely and perilsome' were central to Romantic science, part and parcel of the interest in expanding the borders of human knowledge. In a study of the south, however, the term 'wonder' is troubling, raising questions of who is doing the wondering and about whom. See Richard Holmes, *The Age of Wonder: How the Romantic Generation Discovered the Beauty and Terror of Science* (London: Harper Press, 2009), xvi, 15.

8. Alan Heimert, '*Moby-Dick* and American Political Symbolism', *American Quarterly* 15, no. 4 (Winter 1963): 498–534; Brian R. Pellar, *Moby-Dick and Melville's Anti-Slavery Allegory* (Chapel Hill, NC: Palgrave MacMillan, 2017).

9. On the imaginative anticipation that navigation drove, see Thell, *Minds in Motion*, 155, 157, 217.

10. Griffiths, *Slicing the Silence*, 35–6.

11. Ishmael describes his first sighting of an albatross—'a regal, feathery thing of unspotted whiteness'—in terms that echo Coleridge, who in turn may have had in mind the sightings that Cook records, as in the epigraph above (see *MD* 291). Shelley's Dr Frankenstein, meanwhile, parallels the overreaching of Christopher Marlowe's Dr Faustus. He is tempted by satanic ambition like his precursor to assume godlike powers of creation. See Harold Beaver, introduction to *Moby-Dick* (Penguin Classics, 1986), 20–42, here especially 26.

12. See Robert Fowke, *The Real Ancient Mariner: Pirates and Poesy on the South Sea* (Bishop's Castle: Travelbrief Publications, 2010), iii-iv. Shelvocke's *Voyage* told the story of the 'second captain' Simon Hatley who in 1719 shot a black albatross of 'ill omen'.

13. Three bestselling books about Cook's first voyage appeared in the decade from 1773 alone, spawning many spin-off publications and imitations. See Ruth Scobie, *Celebrity Culture and the Myth of Oceania in Britain* (Woodbridge: The Boydell Press, 2019), 9; Lowes, *Road to Xanadu*, 15–6, 140.

14. Aspects of Captain Ahab's obsession to find Moby Dick bear at least a cousinly relationship with Cook's overreaching aim of penetrating farther south than any master seaman had gone before.

15. Cook, *Journals*, 120, 131.

16. Cook, *Journals*, 241, 254, 276, 331. While at sea during the winter months, Cook tried to keep between 41° and 46°S.

17. Bernard Smith, 'Coleridge's Ancient Mariner and Cook's Second Voyage', *Journal of the Warburg and Courtauld Institutes* 19, no. 1–2 (1956): 117–154.

18. Charles Darwin, *The Origin of Species* (1859; London: Penguin, 1985), 301.

19. See again Lowes's extended commentary on Coleridge's sources, *Road to Xanadu*, 120, 128, 130–1. As he writes: 'the course of the Mariner's voyage was chartered long before Coleridge's century dawned'.

20. D'Arcy Wood, *Land of Wondrous Cold*; Leane, *Antarctica in Fiction*; McCann, *Wild Sea*.

21. Lowes, *Road to Xanadu*,128. During the global pandemic, the *Rime*'s insistence on the need for us to respect one another and act in ways that enhance life and support the commons understandably became pertinent for many people. The poem's salience was recognised in a project, the Ancient Mariner Big Read, based at the University of Plymouth in the United Kingdom in April 2020. The project involved performers, writers, and poets coming together to read the poem and to meditate on the Mariner's 'offence against nature' and the fatal consequences of the disconnect between human and natural worlds that it dramatises. See Philip Hoare, with Angela Cockayne and Sarah Chapman, 'Into the Deep', *The Guardian Review*, 25 April 2020, 20–21. In the article, Hoare talks evocatively about the poem's 'narcotic wildness' fuelling its modern-day resonances. See also Phillip Hoare, *Leviathan, or the Whale* (London: Fourth Estate, 2009).

22. His admirer, the writer Thomas De Quincey, suggestively wrote. See Frances Wilson, *Guilty Thing: A Life of Thomas De Quincey* (London: Bloomsbury, 2016), 29–31; Holmes, *Age of Wonder*, 111–12. See also the related recognition in Jorge Luis Borges, 'The Thousand and One Nights', trans. Eliot Weinberger, *The Georgia Review*, 38, no. 3 (Fall 1984): 564–74; Evelyn Fishburn, 'Traces of the *Thousand and One Nights* in Borges', *Middle Eastern Literatures* 7, no. 2 (2014): 213–22. Borges, a modern southern writer, highlights the sense of relationality that tales of the wide world can reveal, such as we find in the *Nights*: '[we] see how marvellous the world is and how interconnected things are' (573).

23. Lowes, 53–5, 120–26. His ideas for the *Rime* were perhaps honed, too, by the living model for the Mariner, the famed raconteur Walking Stewart, who De Quincey, for one, heard speak in both Bath and London, though several decades later. See Wilson, *Guilty*, 110 and 168.

24. Nicholas Halmi, Paul Magnuson, and Raimonda Modiano, eds., *Coleridge's Poetry and Prose* (New York: W.W. Norton, 2004), 59, note 1.

25. Fowke, *Mariner*, 84; Thompson, *This Thing*, 311: 'all of the elements are pluming forwards to the east'.

26. Swanepoel, '"Coleridge's Transcendental Imagination"', *Journal of Literary Studies* 26, no. 1 (2010): 191–214.

27. Thell, *Minds*, 155–7.

28. Derek Attridge, *Moving Words: Forms of English Poetry* (Oxford: Oxford University Press, 2013), 31, 43, 44, 48.

29. Elleke Boehmer, 'Wide Wide Sea: A Response to Terence Cave', Balzan Lecture Event, Occasional Papers, University of Bern (17 October 2014). Melville's *Moby-Dick*, too, repeatedly calls our attention to the 'aboriginal' 'awfulness' of the sea (as in the epigraph).

30. On beats and off-beats in poetry, especially in Coleridge, as well as Blake and Wordsworth, see Attridge, *Moving Words*, especially 31–49.

31. E. Janet Browne, *Charles Darwin: Voyaging* (Princeton: Princeton University Press, 1996), 212–14, 218, 227.

32. See Thompson, *This Thing*, 76. This remarkable historical novel explores the relationship between the captain of the *Beagle* and Charles Darwin from the depressive Fitzroy's point of

view. His morbid depressions are represented in many ways as of a piece with the south, as well as stimulated by being there, as were those of his predecessor, Captain Stokes (92).

33. Michael T. Ghiselin, *The Triumph of the Darwinian Method* (Berkeley: University of California Press, 1969). See also Thompson, *This Thing*, 165, on Darwin's speculations about an 'all-embracing hypothesis' to explain the earth's history.

34. George Levine, *Darwin and the Novelists: Patterns of Science in Victorian Fiction* (Cambridge, Mass.: Harvard University Press, 1988), 55, 57. Geology for him was, in a sense, 'mystic-marked', to draw in a suggestive phrase from Melville's archaeological description of the white whale (*MD* 405). See also Patience A. Schell, *The Sociable Sciences: Darwin and His Contemporaries in Chile* (Basingstoke: Palgrave Macmillan, 2013).

35. See also D'Arcy Wood, *Land of Wondrous Cold*, 238.

36. Browne, *Darwin*, 247.

37. To cite again the Argentine writer J. L. Borges, not inappropriately, as we are speaking of the south, and imaginative cognition. See Borges, 'Thousand and One Nights', 573–4.

38. D'Arcy Wood, *Land of Wondrous Cold*, 52–5; 148–152.

39. A formative moment in the making of Darwin's southern theory arose in relation to the African continent, specifically in the Cape Verde islands, close to the equator, where the *Beagle* first made landfall after leaving England. It was the harmattan season and the gauze covering the vane at the masthead had filtered the wind, depositing a layer of brown Saharan dust on deck. This, Darwin discovered, contained organic life—freshwater 'infusoria with siliceous shields' (*OSVB* 21–22). The transmission of the sand across the ocean by the wind, combined with the fact that this dust seemed originally to come not from Africa but South America, even farther away, prompted him to begin thinking about inter-relationality between regions and their animal inhabitants at a previously unimaginable scale.

40. James Weldon Long, 'Plunging into the Atlantic: The Oceanic Order of Herman Melville's *Moby-Dick*', *Atlantic Studies* 8, no. 1 (2001): 69–91, especially 71–2. In a reading shaped by his engagement with Carl Schmitt and Immanuel Wallerstein, Weldon Long suggests that Melville's philosophical analyses approach the world as incorporated into one system by capitalism. The ocean itself becomes an exploratory lens for a global analysis: 'Melville uses the ocean as a perspective from which to examine the world' (69). My reading expands upon this idea of the southern world as a lens onto the planet.

41. The novel's syntactic procedures also often work performatively, as when a preponderance of present participles is used to mimic the flensing process, for example. The crew is described as stripping the blubber off a whale in two ribbons or 'blanket-pieces' through a process of uncoiling (*MD* 425).

42. Weldon Long, 'Plunging into the Atlantic', 71–2. The image bears striking similarities with the 1942 Spilhaus projection of the earth seen as covered by a single body of water—the interconnected oceans of the world. Athelstan Spilhaus was a South African geophysicist.

43. 'And this excess of writing has in turn produced an array of critical writing—mythopoeic, psychoanalytic, postmodern' (Beaver, introduction to *Moby-Dick*, 25–26).

44. Later in the nineteenth century, encouraged by the south's distance-induced secrecy, whaling companies set up mechanised killing stations on sub-Antarctic islands like South Georgia and the South Shetlands. See María Ximena Senatore, 'Things in Antarctica. An Archaeological Perspective', *The Polar Journal* 10, no. 2 (2020): 397–419. This paper was presented

as a keynote address at the SCAR SC-HASS Biannual Conference, Ushuaia, Argentina, April 3–5, 2019. Senatore observes how the spread and range of the human ad animal remains on the sub-Antarctic islands testify to the extent of the destruction that took place. See also Andres Zarankin and Melisa A. Salerno, 'Antarctic Archaeology: Discussing the History of the Southernmost End of the World', in *The Oxford Handbook of Historical Archaeology*, ed. James Symonds and Vesa-Pekka Herva. https://doi.org/10.1093/oxfordhb/9780199562350.001.0001.

45. Melville through Ishmael also shows a keen awareness of the flow of raw materials and capital that draws the hemispheres into one world system (pace Wallerstein), noting that the 'brave houses and flowery gardens' of New England are filled with things and run on an energy that comes 'from the Atlantic, Pacific, and Indian oceans' (*MD* 126, 151, 157). Whaling had forged a complex new world-system of interconnecting hemispheres, through which the wealth of the south was channelled north, the dominant direction of resource-flow under empire (and subsequently). Or, as Queequeg observes, 'It's a mutual, joint-stock world, in all meridians' (*MD* 167, 169–70). See McCann, *Wild Sea*, 111. On south-to-north flow, see also Davies, 'Unwrapping', 837–856.

46. Lowes, 124–5.

47. In the great vastness of the Southern Ocean, not only remarkable meetings between explorers, but also excruciating near-misses sometimes occurred, as when explorers' letters left in maritime 'post-boxes' were picked up haphazardly by other passing ships, including whalers. In a particularly striking episode, the explorers Charles Wilkes and Dumont D'Urville approached the Adélie Coast of Antarctica on the afternoon of the same day in January 1840, sighting one another but without communicating. See D'Arcy Wood, *Land of Wondrous Cold*, 70, 186, 188.

48. For an expansion on this theme, see Elleke Boehmer, 'Fellowship and Aversion in the South: The Challenges of South-South Collaboration', in *Cosmopolitan Cultures and Oceanic Thought*, ed. Nishat Zaidi and Dilip Menon (London: Routledge, 2023), 37–46.

49. Mary Wollstonecraft Shelley, *Frankenstein: or The Modern Prometheus*, ed. Marilyn Butler (1818; Oxford World's Classics, 1998), 36. Page references will henceforth be cited in text, with the abbreviation *F*.

50. Mary Shelley would perhaps have attended Coleridge's memorable public recitations of the poem. Samuel Taylor Coleridge was a house guest in Shelley's father William Godwin's home in the days after her mother's death, when she was a tiny baby.

51. Mary Shelley's understanding of polar cold was profoundly affected by the extreme climatic conditions that pertained at the time she was writing *Frankenstein*, the decade of the so-called mini-Ice Age. Brought on by reduced solar activity and exacerbated by the 1815 Mount Tambora explosion in Indonesia, these years without a summer led Percy Shelley, her husband, to speculate about the earth freezing over. The unusual weather conditions will also, of course, have produced a strong sense, salient in Shelley's novel, of global interrelatedness. See E. J. Cleary, 'Vindicated: The Ongoing Relevance of Mary Wollstonecraft and her celebrated daughter', *TLS*, no. 6110 (8 May 2020): 24–5. See also Karen O'Brien, '*Frankenstein* by Mary Shelley'. https://www.english.ox.ac.uk/ten-minute-book-club/shelley-frankenstein. Accessed 14 October 2020.

52. Jules Verne's science fiction adventure stories like *Voyage au centre de la Terre/Journey to the Centre of the Earth* (1864, 1867), as well as *An Antarctic Mystery*, as in chapter 1, were modelled

on expeditions to locate the southern continent, and shared this perception of the interlinking of the world's peripheries with its better-known centres—for Verne via subterranean volcanic tubes and sweeping oceanic pathways. See also the twentieth-century response to Verne in Howard Phillips Lovecraft's meditations in *At the Mountains of Madness and Other Tales of Terror* (1936; New York: Del Rey, 2007) on the 'awfulness' of Antarctica.

Chapter Five

Note: The then Scott Polar Institute researcher Robert Law explains that 'the left of the equals sign are the new coordinates after time *t* has passed, and right of the equals sign is how you get to the next time-step', depending on the speed of the ice flow. Email communication (25 October 2022). Many thanks to Rob Law for his work on the calculation and for generously sharing it with me. See also Robert H. Thomas et al., 'The Ross Ice Shelf: Glaciology and Geophysics', *Antarctic Research Series* 42, no. 2 (1984): 21–53. The article notes that ice velocity increases as ice moves seawards.

1. See Tom Griffiths's eyewitness account in *Slicing the Silence*, especially, here, 43.

2. Peter Davidson, *The Idea of North* (London: Reaktion Books, 2005), 60. Bernd Brunner, *Extreme North: A Cultural History*, trans. Jefferson Chase (New York: W. W. Norton, 2022), reminds us that the characteristic representations of the north as a white canvas, and as more of a quality than a place, are prior to comparable southern ones. *Nilas*, *frazil* and *sastrugi* are all northern names for ice. See also Cal Flyn, 'Both Real and Imaginary', *TLS*, no. 6209, 1 April 2022: 19; Nancy Campbell, *The Library of Ice: Readings from a Cold Climate* (London: Scribner, 2019).

3. Jonathan Amos, 'Endurance: Shackleton's Lost Ship Is Found in Antarctic', 9 March 2022, https://www.bbc.com/news/science-environment-60662541. See Mensun Bound's own account, *The Ship Beneath the Ice: The Discovery of Shackleton's* Endurance (London: Macmillan, 2022). Darrel Bristow-Bovey, *Finding Endurance: Shackleton, My Father and a World Without End* (Johannesburg and Cape Town: Jonathan Ball, 2023), gives a quirky personal take on the Shackleton story and its moral for our time, which was sparked by the *Endurance* discovery. In contrast to Robert Law's calculation that opens this chapter, Bristow-Bovey quotes from a J. M. Barrie speech at the University of St Andrews in which he imagined Scott and his team reemerging from the ice 'as young as on the day they left' (162). Barrie was the author of *Peter Pan*. See also note 91 to this chapter.

4. Alfred Lansing, *Endurance: Shackleton's Incredible Voyage* (1959; London: Weidenfeld and Nicolson, 2000), 27, 37, 57.

5. Ernest Shackleton, *South: The* Endurance *Expedition* (1919; London: Penguin Random House, 2002), 70.

6. 'Endurance: "Finest wooden shipwreck I've ever seen"'. https://www.bbc.com/news/science-environment-60654016. Accessed 26 September 2022.

7. Bound, *Ship Beneath the Ice*, 43.

8. Worsley's memoir was also called *Endurance*. See Peggy Nelson, 'Shackleton: A Twitter novel', accessed 26 September 2022. https://eshackleton.com/2015/07/20/what-the-ice-gets-the-ice-keeps/.

9. See Bound, *Ship Beneath the Ice*, 361, 370–1.

10. On the complications of calculating the *Endurance*'s position, see Bound, *Ship Beneath the Ice*, 119–25, 201, 255, 283.

11. Pyne, *Ice*, 26, 40. See also the epigraph above.

12. McCann, *Wild Sea*, 97.

13. Leane, *Antarctica in Fiction*, 59.

14. McCann, *Wild Sea*, 23.

15. James Cook (1774), quoted in Pyne, *Ice*, 26.

16. Arnold, *Southern Nights*, 143–6. It is an evocation that immediately brings to mind the ending of Verne's *An Antarctic Mystery*.

17. For Barry Lopez, *Horizon*, it is both 'an old piece of Gondwana', yet 'Almost everything one sees here is new' (449).

18. Lisa E. Bloom, 'The New Aesthetics of Climate Change', Pennsylvania Academy of the Fine Arts lecture, online, 30 November 2020. Accessed 4 December 2020. See also Leane, *Antarctica in Fiction*, 55; Lize-Marié van der Watt and Sandra Swart, 'The Whiteness of Antarctica: Race and South Africa's Antarctic History', *Antarctica and the Humanities*, ed. Peder Roberts, Lize-Marié van der Watt, and Adrian Howkins (London: Palgrave Macmillan, 2016), 125–56.

19. Robert Falcon Scott, *Journals: Captain Scott's Last Expedition*, intro. Max Jones (1913; Oxford: Oxford University Press, 2006), 392.

20. D'Arcy Wood, *Land of Wondrous Cold*, 99.

21. Leane, *Antarctica in Fiction*, 14–15, 55, 155.

22. Human beings have now been born on the continent, in the Chilean segment.

23. McCann, *Wild Sea*, 67. See also Isabel Hofmeyr and Charne Lavery, 'Reading in Antarctica', *Wasafiri* 36, no. 2 (2021): 79–86, a magical account of the many ways of understanding Antarctica in and with books.

24. Jonathan Franzen, *The End of the End of the Earth* (New York: Farrar, Straus, Giroux, 2018).

25. Ursula Le Guin, *The Left Hand of Darkness* (1969; London: Gollancz, 2018), 220. This science fiction novel about interplanetary communication involves a memorable escape journey across a mile-thick, perpetually 'snapping' and 'jittering' ice sheet, the account of which is noticeably shaped by accounts of early Antarctic exploration (223, 225, 226, 247, 250–1). For a reading of Le Guin's short story 'Sur' about a successful South American women's expedition to the South Pole a few years before Amundsen and Scott, see Leane, *Antarctica in Fiction*, 1–21. The women name their base 'South South America' and leave no trace of their journey.

26. Lopez, *Horizon*, 446; Leane, *Antarctica*, 155ff.; Pyne, *Ice*, 150. See also Adrian Caesar, *The White: Last Days in the Antarctic Journeys of Scott and Mawson 1911–1913* (London: Macmillan, 2001); Sara Wheeler, *Cherry: A Life of Apsley Cherry-Garrard* (London: Vintage, 2001), 48.

27. From 1838, British, French, and American ships followed in Cook's wake in their attempt to reach and breach the 'barriers' of the southernmost continent and exploit its resources. See D'Arcy Wood, *Land of Wondrous Cold*, 9–10; Scott, *Journals*, xxv-xxvi; Lopez, *Horizon*, 471.

28. Klaus Dodds, *The Antarctic* (Oxford: Oxford University Press, 2012), 24; Lisa E. Bloom, *Climate Change and the New Polar Aesthetics* (Durham, NC: Duke University Press, 2022). To counter the whiteness of the Antarctic script, we could do worse than to remember the Māori Te Atu (John Sacs), who travelled with the United States Exploring Expedition in the 1840s. And, importantly, Captain Knowledge Bengu of the *Agulhas II*.

29. The 1895 Sixth International Geographical Congress resolved to officially encourage further research into the geological makeup of the southern continent. The 1901–4 Scott and 1907–8 expeditions led directly from this decision.

30. Leane, *Antarctica in Fiction*, 18.

31. See Susanna Maria Elizabeth van der Watt, 'Out in the Cold: Science and the Environment in South Africa's Involvement in the Sub-Antarctic and Antarctic in the Twentieth Century' (PhD diss., University of Stellenbosch, 2012). I am grateful to Lize-Marié van der Watt for sharing a copy of her thesis with me.

32. When Antarctica split off from Australia around 55 million years ago, cold ocean waters rushed into the gap, isolating and glaciating the continent, and so bringing about worldwide cooling.

33. See Peter Wadhams, *A Farewell to Ice: A Report from the Arctic* (London: Penguin, 2017), 11–12, on the latent heat through which ice forms a reserve for energy. Should the Antarctic ice cap melt, sea levels around the world will rise by sixty metres. Areas of the Antarctic are already among the most rapidly warming on the planet. See also D'Arcy Wood, *Land of Wondrous Cold*, 2–9, 13; Pyne, *Ice*, 40.

34. Griffiths, *Slicing the Silence*, 3–4.

35. Elizabeth Leane and Stephanie Pfennigwerth, 'Antarctica in the Australian Imagination', *Polar Record* 38, no. 207 (2002): 309–312.

36. Charne Lavery, 'Antarctica and Africa: Narrating Alternate Futures', *Polar Record* 55 (2019): 347–350, especially 348. These remarks are supported by my own observations at Wolwedans desert camp, Hardap Region, Namibia, 25 September 2022. See the image toward the end of chapter 8.

37. Pablo Wainschenker and Elizabeth Leane, 'The "Alien" Next Door: Antarctica in South American Fiction', *The Polar Journal* 9, no. 2 (2019): 324–39.

38. Leane, *Antarctica in Fiction*, 182. D'Arcy Wood, *Land of Wondrous Cold*, 1, concurs: 'Antarctica is remote from all human habitation, but not from human consciousness and endeavour'.

39. Davidson, *Idea of North*, 60.

40. 'Interview: Bill Manhire', *Flash Frontier: An Adventure in Short Fiction*, December 2018, https://flashfrontier.com/interview-bill-manhire. Accessed 8 February and 5 October 2022. See also Jennifer Levasseur and Kevin Rabalais, 'An Interview with Bill Manhire', *The Free Library*, accessed 4 October 2022, https://www.thefreelibrary.com/An+interview+with+Bill+Manhire.-a0114488300. Unsurprisingly, twentieth-century New Zealand poets repeatedly register Antarctica's proximity. The line-up begins with William Pember Reeves's 'A Storm in the Southern Ocean—The Albatross' at the century's turn (with its capitalisation of the 'White Unknown'), runs through Hubert Church on 'towering icebergs' thronging at the pole, in 'Spring in Maoriland' (1908), and Lucy Smith's cry 'To the South Wind' protesting its battering of her spring garden (1915), which is echoed by Ursula Bethell (1929), and then embraces Robin Hyde's image of 'lambent' ocean waves lapping 'the southernmost reach' in 'Thirsty Land' (1935). See Hubert Church, 'Spring in Maoriland', in *New Zealand Rhymes Old and New*, ed. Jessie Mackay (Christchurch: Whitcombe and Tombs, 1908), p. 100; L. E. Smith, *Daughters of Time and Other Poems* (Christchurch: Whitcombe and Tombs, 1952), 34; Robin Hyde, 'Thirsty Land', in *Houses by the Sea and the Later Poems of Robin Hyde*, ed. Gloria Rawlinson (Christchurch: Caxton Press, 1952), 148–9.

41. Jon McGregor, *Lean Fall Stand* (London: 4th Estate, 2021), 4. Page references will henceforth be cited in text together with the abbreviation *LFS*.

42. Jenny Diski, *Skating to Antarctica* (London: Granta, 1997), 124, 155. Page references will be cited in text together with the abbreviation *StA*.

43. Pyne, *Ice*, 153.

44. Griffiths, *Slicing the Silence*, 255.

45. Wainschenker and Leane, 'The "Alien"', 329–33.

46. Douglas Mawson, *The Home of the Blizzard* (London: Hodder & Stoughton, 1930). See also https://www.ebaumsworld.com/pictures/33-images-from-the-first-australian-antarctica-expedition/85658876/. Accessed 15 September 2022.

47. Lansing, *Endurance*, 9.

48. See also Joanne Price, *Scott's Hut: An Affective Biography* (forthcoming). My thanks to Joanne Price for her evocative presentations on the Scott hut, in Ushuaia in April 2019, and in Oxford in December 2021. See also Cian Duffy, *The Landscapes of the Sublime 1700–1830: Classic Ground* (Basingstoke: Palgrave Macmillan, 2013).

49. Lansing, *Endurance*, 38.

50. McCann, *Wild Sea*, 86.

51. Leane, *Antarctica in Fiction*, 1, 182.

52. I am grateful to Robert Freeman for our constructive exchanges on the poetic function of lines like the parabola and the asymptote.

53. Heather Lane, Naomi Boneham, Robert D. Smith, eds., *The Last Letters: The British Antarctic Expedition 1910–13* (Cambridge: Scott Polar Research Institute, 2012), 52. See also Scott, *Journals*, 415–22; John Turner, 'Reducing Down': D. H. Lawrence and Captain Scott', *Critical Survey* 14, no. 3 (2002): 14–27.

54. Scott, *Journals*, 411.

55. Alain Badiou, 'Down with Death!', *Verso Books* (blog), accessed 15 September 2022, https://www.versobooks.com/blogs/2176-badiou-down-with-death.

56. Scott, *Journals*, 410. See also Griffiths, *Slicing the Silence*, 13–14. Other sources have the lines in the form of the more self-consciously literary 'I am just going outside and I may be gone some time'.

57. Shackleton, *South*, 204. See also Johanna Grabouw, 'Haunting the Wide, White Page–Ghosts in Antarctica', in *Ghosts—or the (Nearly) Invisible: Spectral Phenomena in Literature and the Media*, ed. Maria Fleischhack and Elmar Schenkel (Frankfurt: Peter Lang, 2016), 125–36; McEwin, *Antarctic Affair*, 134. The experience famously inspired the line in T. S. Eliot's *The Waste Land* (1922): 'Who is the third who walks always beside you?'.

58. Apsley Cherry-Garrard, *The Worst Journey in the World* (London: Constable, 1922), chs. 7 and 13.

59. Charles Laseron, *South with Mawson: Reminiscences of the Australasian Antarctic Expedition, 1911–1914* (London: G. G. Harrap, 1947), 124.

60. McEwin, *Antarctic Affair*, 141. See also Lennard Bickel, *This Accursed Land* (London: Macmillan, 1977).

61. Kari Herbert, *Heart of the Hero: The Remarkable Women Who Inspired the Great Polar Explorers* (Glasgow: Saraband, 2013).

62. Le Guin, *Left Hand*, 255.

63. Jacques Derrida, 'Telepathy', trans. Nicholas Royle, *Oxford Literary Review* 19 (1988), 3–41, especially 3, 7. Thanks to Ankhi Mukherjee for this reference.

64. Chris Orsman, 'An Alien Continent' and 'The Photographer in the Antarctic', in *South* (1996: London: Faber and Faber, 1999), 32–3 and 40–42.

65. McEwin, *Antarctic Affair*, 174.

66. McCann, *Wild Sea*, 76, 89 and 102.

67. Nancy Robinson Flannery, ed., *This Everlasting Silence: The Love Letters of Paquita Delprat and Douglas Mawson* (Melbourne: Melbourne University Press, 2000).

68. Georg Seaver, *Edward Wilson of the Antarctic: Naturalist and Friend: Together with a Memoir of Oriana Wilson* (London: J. Murray, 1963), 219.

69. Beryl Bainbridge, *The Birthday Boys* (1991; London: Abacus, 2009), 179. Page references will henceforth be cited in text together with the abbreviation *BB*.

70. Lane, *Last Letters*, 58.

71. McEwin, *Antarctic Affair*, 57, 69. The bond of feeling held true till the end: Paquita travelled from Melbourne to Adelaide harbour on the exact day Douglas's *Aurora* returned. Reporters suspected secret communication by telegraph, but both denied this. It is more likely that the two had grown accustomed to synchronising their thoughts, and hence their plans. They both speak, in date-matched letters, of her arms wrapping around and warming him.

72. Chris Orsman, 'Kinematographing in the Pack', in *South*, 23.

73. Griffiths, *Slicing the Silence*, 3–4, 145: Klaus Dodds, 'Reflecting on the 60th Anniversary of the Antarctic Treaty', *Polar Record* 55 (2019): 311–316. Though the Antarctic Treaty sets aside arguments of sovereignty, it nonetheless protects sovereign interests, and hence has not prevented political manoeuvring, as illustrated by Chile's attempts to consolidate its Antarctic territory 'inside the limits of the sector between 53° W and 90° W', extending all the way to the pole. The Antarctic Treaty is up for review in 2048.

74. McCann, *Wild Sea*, 132–3; McEwin, *Antarctic Affair*, 1–3, 23–4. On glacial action, see Ernest Shackleton, *The Heart of the Antarctic*, with an account of the first journey to the South Magnetic Pole by T. W. Edgeworth David (Philadelphia: J. B. Lippincott Co., 1909), ch. 4.

75. Douglas Mawson Papers, Series 4 (geological notes, including correspondence and a paper about tillite formations across the Australian, Tasmanian and southern African landmasses), Special Collections, Barr Smith Library, University of Adelaide. Consulted 14 February 2017.

76. McEwin, *Antarctic Affair*, 37.

77. Lize-Marié van der Watt and Sandra Swart, 'Falling off the Map: South Africa, Antarctica and Empire, c. 1919–59', *Journal of Imperial and Commonwealth History* 43, no. 2 (2015): 267–291, especially 271 and 274. See also Beinart and Dubow, *Scientific Imagination*, 99–200.

78. Winton, *Island Home*, 16–18. Though Winton claims this endless sky for Western Australia, his observations would apply to any number of desert-edge vantage points across the south—the Atacama Desert, the Karoo, the Namib. His word *saltpan*, from Dutch through Afrikaans into English, neatly underlines the point.

79. Janet Frame, *Owls do Cry* (1957; Melbourne: Text Publishing, 2014), 173.

80. Bill Manhire, 'Cream Torpedoes: Recent Poetry in New Zealand', *World Literature Today* 85, no. 5 (Sept./Oct. 2011), 40–42. In the same article, Manhire reminds us that Rudyard Kipling called Invercargill 'the last lamppost in the world', an image redolent of antipodean farness—as seen from the north, of course.

81. Shackleton, *South*, 204.

82. Cherry-Garrard, *Worst Journey*, 304.

83. Orsman, *South*, 1–7, 105–6. Page references to *South* will henceforth be cited in text together with the abbreviation *S*. The opening memoir, 'Polar Raffle', recounts his grandfather's experience of briefly meeting Scott aboard the *Terra Nova* in Port Chalmers harbour as first prize in a raffle competition to raise funds for the trip. Significantly, the total number of poems

in *South* is fifty-two plus one, the number of weeks in a year, plus one, describing a round and then something more.

84. Scott, *Journals*, 57–8.

85. The two poems featuring longer stanzas capture moments of stasis—a group photograph; the experience of being becalmed.

86. On the interplanetary references that Orsman builds into the poem, see A. B. Jackson, 'The Polar Sublime in Contemporary Poetry of Arctic and Antarctic Exploration', (PhD diss., Sheffield Hallam University, 2015), https://www.proquest.com/dissertations-theses/polar-sublime-contemporary-poetry-arctic/docview/1973936945/se-2. Accessed 7 October 2022.

87. Scott, *Journals*, 391.

88. Bill Manhire, 'Antarctic Field Notes', in *Collected Poems* (Manchester: Carcanet, 2001), 251–87.

89. Levasseur and Rabalais, 'An Interview with Bill Manhire'. See also Bill Manhire, ed., *The Wide White Page: Writers Imagine Antarctica* (Wellington: Victoria University Press, 2004). The anthology includes Derek Mahon's villanelle referenced earlier. Page references to the poems will be cited in text together with the abbreviation *AFN*.

90. Leane, *Antarctica in Fiction*, 93–4.

91. These sentiments find an echo in J. M. Barrie's Peter Pan's famous line, 'To die will be an awfully big adventure'. In Scott's *Journals*, Peter Pan models his description of Oates' 'brave' end. See Scott, *Journals*, xxxvi, 410, 416. Barrie was one of Scott's closest friends and the recipient of one of his final letters. The letter closes with the asymptotic line, 'we have done the greatest march ever made and come very near to great success'.

92. Alexandra Harris, 'Disaster in the Antarctic', review of *Lean Fall Stand*, by Jon McGregor, *The Guardian Review*, 15 May 2021, 10–11.

93. On scale framing as a useful delimiting strategy in environmental fiction, see Clark, *Ecocriticism on the Edge*.

94. Meg Samuelson and Charne Lavery, 'The Oceanic South', *English Language Notes* 57, no. 1 (2019): 37–50; Charne Lavery, 'Thinking from the Southern Ocean', in *Sustaining Seas: Oceanic Space and the Politics of Care*, ed. Elspeth Probyn, Kate Johnston, and Nancy Lee (London: Rowman & Littlefield, 2020), 307–18.

95. Robyn Mundy, *The Nature of Ice* (Sydney: Allen and Unwin, 2009); Sophie Hardcastle, *Below Deck* (Sydney: Allen and Unwin, 2020).

96. Alicia Kopf, *Brother in Ice*, trans. Mara Faye Lethem (Sheffield: And Other Stories, 2018), 213. Similarly, Ilija Trojanow's *The Lamentations of Zeno*, trans. Philip Boehm (London: Verso, 2011), explores personal dissolution in the Antarctic region in the context of climate change and glacial melting. In parallel with the figure of the asymptote, Trojanow's title points to the logical impossibility of reaching a destination if, at each stage, target distances are halved.

97. Claire Keegan, *Antarctica* (London: Faber, 1999), 3–22.

Chapter Six

Note to first epigraph: Iva Davies, songwriter, 'Great Southern Land', Genius.com, track 1 on IceHouse, *Primitive Man*, Chrysalis, 1982, https://genius.com/Icehouse-great-southern-land-lyrics. The other epigraphs are taken from the case study texts and are referenced below. On far southern songs, it is also worth referencing Patti Smith's 'Under the Southern Cross' that takes the constellation in 'the inspired sky' as a symbol for the elsewhere, where 'gods get lost'. Thank you to Robert Freeman for reminding me.

1. Manhire, *Collected Poems*, 132.

2. Jorge Luis Borges, *Ficciones*, trans. various (New York: Grove, 1962).

3. Jorge Luis Borges, 'El Sur', in *Cuentos Completos* (Buenos Aires: Debolsillo, 2018), 222–8; 'The South', in *Collected Fictions*, trans. Andrew Hurley (New York: Penguin, 1998), 174–9.

4. Cynthia Lucy Stephens, *The Borges Enigma: Mirrors, Doubles and Intimate Puzzles* (Woodbridge: Tamesis, 2021); Borges, 'The Thousand and One Nights', 564–74.

5. In a companion story, 'El Fin', also in *Ficciones*, the phantasmic *llanura* seems to be always on the point of speaking yet never quite does. 'El Fin' plays out a possible end to the Hernández poem *Martín Fierro* in another knife-fight scene, set against a similar background of wide flatlands extending to infinity (*Cuentos Completos*, 214–17). See Mac J. Wilson, 'Scheherazade, Achilles, and Borges', *Confluencia* 34, no. 1 (Fall 2018): 47–60. Published a year after *Kangaroo*, D. H. Lawrence and his collaborator M. L. Skinner's novel *The Boy in the Bush*, ed. Paul Eggert (1924; Cambridge: Cambridge University Press, 2002), 95–6, relatedly describes the 'weird silent timelessness' of the Western Australian bush as withering to dust 'his father and his father's world and his father's gods'.

6. Alan Lester and Nikita Vanderbyl, 'The Restructuring of the British Empire and the Colonization of Australia, 1832–8', *History Workshop Journal* 90 (18 September 2020): 165–88; Peter J. Marshall, *The Making and Unmaking of Empires: Britain, India and America c. 1750–1783* (Oxford: Oxford University Press, 2005); Christopher A. Bayly, *Imperial Meridian: The British Empire and the World, 1780–1830* (London: Longman, 1989).

7. James Belich, *Replenishing the Earth: The Settler Revolution and the Rise of the Anglo-World, 1783–1939* (Oxford: Oxford University Press, 2009), 7.

8. Matthew Flinders, *A Voyage to Terra Australis*, vol. 1 (London: W Bulmer, 1814), xcv; Scobie, *Celebrity Culture*, 156.

9. See Keith Sinclair, *Imperial Federation: A Study of New Zealand Policy and Opinion, 1880–1914* (London: Athlone Press, 1955), 23. The term 'water hemisphere' is taken from Christina Stead, 'Sea People', *For Love Alone* (1945; London: Virago, 1978), 1.

10. Angela Smith, 'Landscape and the Foreigner Within: Katherine Mansfield and Emily Carr', in *Landscape and Empire, 1770–2000*, ed. Glenn Hooper (Aldershot: Ashgate, 2005), 143.

11. Blanche E. Baughan, 'Grandmother Speaks', *Brown Bread from a Colonial Oven* (London: Whitcombe and Tombs, 1912), 17.

12. J. M. Coetzee, 'Australia's Shame', *The New York Review of Books*, 26 September 2019, https://www.nybooks.com/articles/2019/09/26/australias-shame/.

13. Said, *Culture and Imperialism*, 7. On geographical specificity, see also Simonetta Moro, Mapping Practices and the Cartographic Imagination', *Subjectivity* 13, no. 4 (2020): 298–314.

14. Boehmer, *Colonial and Postcolonial Literature*, 59–71.

15. Jane Stafford and Mark Williams, *Maoriland: New Zealand Literature 1872–1914* (Wellington: Victoria University Press, 2006), 59, 204; J. M. Coetzee, *White Writing: On the Culture of Letters in South Africa* (New Haven, CT: Yale University Press, 1988), 2, 7–8, 11. Coetzee's perception of southern geographic victimhood has persisted from *White Writing* into the present day.

16. Judith Wright, *Half a Lifetime*, ed. Patricia Clarke (Melbourne: Text Publishing, 1999), 59–60.

17. Peter Read, *Belonging: Australians, Place and Aboriginal Ownership* (Melbourne: Cambridge University Press, 2000), 201. See also Michael Farrell, *Writing Australian Unsettlement: Modes of Poetic Invention 1796–1945* (New York: Palgrave Macmillan, 2015); Anna Snaith, *Modernist Voyages: Colonial Women Writers in London, 1890–1945* (Cambridge: Cambridge University Press, 2014), 1–35.

18. A. A. Phillips, 'The Cultural Cringe,' *Meanjin* 9, no. 5 (1950): 299.

19. Beinart and Dubow, *Scientific Imagination*, 9–10, 78. At the inauguration of the SALT telescope in the Karoo in 2005, it was similarly hailed as 'the most modern single optical-infrared telescope in the southern hemisphere'.

20. As my information leaflet instructed me on a visit to the Tasman Peninsula in December 2022.

21. Anthony Trollope, *Australia and New Zealand* (London: Chapman and Hall, 1873), 117.

22. On colonial sentiments of bifurcated belonging, see Boehmer, *Colonial and Postcolonial Literature*, 17, 204.

23. Jarad Zimbler, 'Guy Butler's Poetry and Poetics', *Wasafiri* 31, no. 2 (2016): 58–64.

24. Judith Wright, 'Old House', in *Collected Poems* (Sydney: Angus and Robertson, 1994), 81–2; *Half a Lifetime*, 1–2. Page references to the two works will henceforth appear in the text, along with the abbreviations *CP* and *HL*.

25. David Carter, *Dispossession, Dreams and Diversity: Issues in Australian Studies* (Frenchs Forest, Australia: Pearson Education, 2006), 10–11, 37. See also Gerardo Rodríguez-Salas, 'New Zealand or Nowheresville: Nation and Community in Janet Frame's *Living in the Maniototo*', *Antipodes* 30, no. 2 (December 2016): 280–293, especially 285; Graeme Turner, *Making it National: Nationalism and Popular Culture in Australia* (Sydney: Allen and Unwin, 1994). The standard source for any discussion of national imagining is the timeless Anderson, *Imagined Communities*.

26. Allen Curnow, 'New Zealand Literature: The Case for a Working Definition', in *Look Back Harder: Critical Writings, 1935–1984*, ed. Peter Simpson (Auckland: Auckland University Press, 1987), xx.

27. See Henry Lawson, *Stories and Sketches, 1888–1922*, vol. 1 of *Collected Prose*, ed. Colin Roderick (Sydney: Angus and Robertson, 1972), 104.

28. The Southern Cross also features in the flags of Samoa and Papua New Guinea.

29. Carter, *Dispossession*, 68.

30. In his poem 'Wild Iron', Curnow, for his part, writes about the warping, battering effects of Canterbury's wild winds.

31. Boehmer, *Colonial and Postcolonial Literature*, 210.

32. See Curnow, *Look Back Harder*. See also https://www.read-nz.org/writer/curnow-allen. Accessed 5 January 2023. Curnow's introduction talks about the unique 'pressures' of writing his country's 'isolation'.

33. William Pember Reeves, 'A Colonist in His Garden', in *The Passing of the Forest and Other Verse* (Sydney: Allen & Unwin, 1925); 'New Zealand', in *New Zealand and Other Poems* (London: Grant Richards, 1898), 1–3.

34. Fabián Martínez Siccardi, 'Feeling Southern: A Patagonian Story', *Granta* 146 (14 February 2019), https://granta.com/feeling-southern/. See also John Wylie, 'Landscape as

Not-Belonging: *The Plains*, Earth Writing, and the Impossibilities of Inhabitation', *Philological Quarterly* 97, no. 2 (Spring 2018): 177–196; Gerald Murnane, *The Plains* (Ringwood, Victoria: Penguin Books Australia, 1984), 33.

35. Robin Hyde, *The Godwits Fly* (1938; Auckland: Auckland University Press, 2001), xxxiii-xxxiv, xxxiii; and *Wednesday's Children* (1937; Auckland: New Women's Press, 1989), 139: 'This time of the year, the migratory birds shining cuckoo, godwit, golden plover, came back to New Zealand from the North'.

36. Charles Brasch, 'The Islands (2)', in *Disputed Ground: Poems 1939–45* (Christchurch: The Caxton Press, 1948).

37. Jed Esty, 'The Colonial Bildungsroman: *The Story of an African Farm* and the Ghost of Goethe', *Victorian Studies* 49, no. 3 (2007): 407–430. See also Graham Huggan, 'Greening White', *Journal of Postcolonial Writing* 58, no. 1 (2022): 21–35, on how contemporary environmental writing can establish at once a national and yet planetary relationship.

38. Katherine Mansfield, *The Aloe*, ed. Vincent O'Sullivan, intro. Kirsty Gunn (1982; London: Capuchin Classics, 2010), 54–5.

39. By the early twentieth century, *The Story of an African Farm* was widely regarded as an emblematic colonial novel. In Frank Sargeson's view in 'Olive Schreiner', in *Conversation in a Train and Other Critical Writing*, ed. Kevin Cunningham (Auckland: Auckland University Press, 1983), 99–112: 'I expect that everyone who knows anything about books, will at least have heard of Olive Schreiner, and her novel called "The Story of an African Farm"'. See also Cherry Clayton, 'Olive Schreiner and Katherine Mansfield: Artistic Tranformations of the Outcast Figure', *English Studies in Africa* 32, no. 2 (1989): 109–119.

40. Her 1903 and 1908 journeys to Europe were via Cape Horn, the ships travelling eastwards with the prevailing winds, as ocean-going vessels from New Zealand usually did.

41. Ursula Bethell, 'Catalogue', 'Pause', and 'Gale SWW', in *A Garden in the Antipodes*, in *Collected Poems*, ed. Vincent O'Sullivan (1929; Wellington: Victoria University Press, 1985), 3, 2. O'Sullivan's introduction (x-xxiii) quotes D'Arcy Cresswell's observation that 'New Zealand wasn't truly discovered, in fact, until Ursula Bethell, "very earnestly digging" [a quotation from her garden poems], raised her head to look at the mountains'.

42. Halford, 'Southern Conversations'. J. M. Coetzee, *The Childhood of Jesus*, *The Schooldays of Jesus*, *The Death of Jesus* (London: Secker, 2013, 2016, 2019), also offer reflections on southern modularity and derivativeness.

43. See Elena Fiddian-Qasmiyeh and Patricia Daley, eds, *Routledge Handbook of South-South Relations* (London: Routledge, 2020), for an extensive analysis of, specifically, Global South links and solidarities.

44. Stead, 'Sea People', in *For Love Alone*, 1–2. The same passage describes the Milky Way as 'broader and whiter than in the north', and day-time skies as 'crusted with suns and spirals'.

45. The poems are from *The Estate and Other Poems* (1957) and *Last Poems* (1974), respectively. In 'A View of Rangitoto', *Disputed Ground* (1948), New Zealand itself is pictured as a great 'long-limbed mountain / Dark on the waves', rising from 'far capes'. Robin Hyde in 'Young Knowledge' and 'Thirsty Land', *Houses by the Sea and the Later Poems of Robin Hyde*, ed. Gloria Rawlinson (Christchurch: The Caxton Press, 1952), similarly, speaks of 'thundering surf' and 'stars grown big as fists'.

46. Baughan, 'The Mountain Walk', in *Brown Bread*, 166–7.

47. Terri-ann White, *Finding Theodore and Brina* (Fremantle: Fremantle Arts Centre, 2001), 21–2.

48. Mia Couto, *Sleepwalking Land* (*Terra Sonambula*), trans. David Brookshaw (London: Serpent's Tale, 2006), 37, 83.

49. See Elleke Boehmer, ed., *Empire Writing: An Anthology of Colonial Literature 1870–1918* (Oxford: Oxford University Press, 1998), 177–189.

50. Dubow and Beinart, *Scientific Imagination*, 108–9, 197.

51. Snaith, *Modernist Voyages*, 40; Stafford and Williams, *Maoriland*, 235.

52. See Blanche Baughan, 'Young Hotspur', in *Reuben: and Other Poems* (Westminster: Archibald and Constable, 1903), 85–7.

53. Bruce Chatwin, *In Patagonia* (1977: London: Vintage, 2005), 92–5. Chatwin's Patagonian 'eddy' to 'the end of the world' crosses many transverse networks and pathways across the south, including the migratory journeys of Chiloé farmhands, penguin migrations, and albatross journeys (82, 119, 142).

54. Gerald Murnane, 'The Battle of Acosta Nu', in *Landscape with Landscape* (Melbourne: Norstrilia Press, 1985), 71.

55. Prichard, *Coonardoo*, 146, 172.

56. Halford, 'Southern Conversations', n. p.

57. W. A. Sewell, 'Why Our Authors Leave Home', *New Zealand Herald* (Supplement), 13 March 1937, 4. Campbell's poem 'Albatross' from *Adamastor* (London: Faber, 1930), 49–53, flies with the bird as 'the green foam-heaved antipodes / Capsize their thousand islands on the morn'. And in 'Tristan da Cunha' in the same volume, the poet identifies with the South Atlantic Ocean island's craggy isolation (72–5). Joseph Pearce, *Bloomsbury and Beyond: The Friends and Enemies of Roy Campbell* (London: Harper UK, 2001), 4, remarks that the young Campbell first perceived the 'pride and glory' of the Indian Ocean from his native Durban when he learned the Zulu word for the sea, *lwandhla*. Guy Butler, facing west from the Cape Peninsula, notices that 'the next land [is] Buenos Aires'. See his 'Hout Bay', in *Collected Poems*, 140–1.

58. James M. Bertram, *Capes of China Slide Away: A Memoir of Peace and War, 1910–1980* (Auckland: Auckland University Press, 1993), 27–28; and *Flight of the Phoenix: Critical Notes on New Zealand Writers* (1979; Wellington: Victoria University Press, 1985), 136. Many thanks to Joe Shaughnessy for helping to find these references.

59. Allen Curnow, 'An Abominable Temper', in *An Abominable Temper* (1973), in *Collected Poems, 1933–1973* (Wellington: A. H. & A. W. Reed, 1974), 252–62.

60. Read, *Belonging*, 20.

61. Winton, *Island Home*, 18–19.

62. Randolph Stow, *The Merry-Go-Round in the Sea* (1965; Camberwell, Victoria: Penguin, 2008), 3–23; Dan Sleigh, *Islands*, trans. André Brink (London: Secker, 2004), 309. Stow's work deserves a special mention here for its deep appreciation of the Western Australian country and its deep history. In *The Merry-Go-Round in the Sea*, Rob Coram grows up on a sheep station inland of Geraldton, surrounded by trees bent by the southerly, spiky aloes in the garden, and Easter or March lilies with their red stems—all features of this temperate strip of the far south that Zoë Wicomb in her stories interestingly observes also (see chapter 7). (The aloes and the March lilies are both natives of her Cape.) When the Coram family visits the 'Hand Cave' marked by Aboriginal handprints from long ago,

including a boy-sized handprint that fits his own, Rob feels keenly the age and 'desolation' of the land (24, 27, 72, 81–3).

63. Northrop Frye, *The Bush Garden: Essays on the Canadian Imagination* (Toronto: Anansi, 1971), 220.

64. Philip Steer, *Settler Colonialism in Victorian Literature: Economics and Political Identity in the Networks of Empire* (Cambridge: Cambridge University Press, 2020), 202.

65. Carter, *Road to Botany Bay*. See also Paul Carter, 'Australinda: The Geography of Imperial Desire', *Postcolonial Studies* 18 (2015): 222–33.

66. Allen Curnow, 'To Introduce the Landscape', in *Poems 1949–57* (1957); 'Landfall in Unknown Seas', in *Sailing or Drowning* (1943), both in *Collected Poems, 1933–1973* (Wellington: A. H. & A. W. Reed, 1974), 189, 136–7. For all Curnow's exacting cultural nationalism, his poetry is often suffused in a more pervasive, borderless element, like the 'deepest blue' air of 'Lone Kauri Road', or the exposed rock on the beach that asks the insistent question, 'I know you do you know me?', in 'A Sight for Sore Eyes'. See Allen Curnow, *Continuum: New and Later Poems 1972–1988* (Auckland: Auckland University Press, 1988), 52–53; 'Dialogue with Four Rocks', in *You Will Know When You Get There* (1982), in *Early Days Yet: New and Collected Poems, 1941–1997* (Auckland: Auckland University Press, 1997), 93–94. See also A. R. D. Fairburn's 'The Cave', in *Strange Rendezvous: Poems 1929–1941* (Dunedin: Renaissance Books, 1952).

67. The longer quotation reads: '*Maar wat ons nooit moet vergeet nie, is dat hierdie verandering van land en landskap as't ware aan die nuwe wordende taal geslyp, geknee, gebrei het . . . En so het Afrikaans in staat geword om hierdie nuwe land uit te sê*.' (But what we must never forget is that this change of land kneaded and knit a new language. . . . And so it became possible to give expression to the new country. [My translation]). Words carved onto the Taal Monument, Paarl, Western Cape, South Africa. Photographed on 19 February 2020. See also N. P. van Wyk Louw's epic *Raka* (1940; Pretoria: Nationale Boekhandel, 1964), for his use of Bantu-origin words like *kraal* and *knobkerrie*.

68. Curnow, 'House and Land' (1941), in *Collected Poems*, 91–2.

69. Boehmer, *Colonial and Postcolonial Literature*, chs. 1 and 2; Franco Moretti, *Atlas of the European Novel, 1800–1900* (London and New York: Verso, 1998), 47.

70. Gerald Murnane, *Velvet Waters* (South Yarra: McPhee Gribble, 1990), 108–109. I am grateful to Tom McLean for pointing this quotation out to me.

71. Carroll, *Empire of Air and Water*, 6; John Newton, *Hard Frost: Structures of Feeling in New Zealand Literature* (Wellington: Victoria University Press, 2018).

72. Alejandra Laera and Javier Villa, eds., *Una Historia de la Imaginación en la Argentina* (Buenos Aires: Museo de Arte Moderno, 2019), 23.

73. Lawson, 'The Bush Undertaker', in *Stories and Sketches*.

74. William Satchell, *The Land of the Lost*, ed. Kendrick Smithyman (1902; Auckland: Oxford University Press, 1985), 12.

75. Bertram, 'Charles Brasch: Last Landfall', in *Flight of the Phoenix*, 3–7.

76. A. D. Hope, 'Australia,' in *Collected Poems: 1930–1970* (1939; Sydney: Angus & Robertson, 1972), 13.

77. Belich, *Replenishing*, 59–60.

78. Stow's first novel *To the Islands* (1958; Melbourne: Text Publishing, 2015), ends with the aging missionary Stephen Heriot on a quest to find the mythic Aboriginal 'islands' of the dead.

79. See Esty, 'Colonial Bildungsroman', 407–430, on 'the historical tension between modernization processes that never sleep and national discourses that posit origins and ends'.

80. John Newton, 'Colonialism above the Snowline: Baughan, Ruskin and the South Island Myth', *Journal of Commonwealth Literature* 34, no. 2 (1999): 85–96; Paloma Fresno-Calleja and Janet M. Wilson, eds., *New Zealand and the Globalization of Culture*, Special Issue: *Journal of Postcolonial Writing* 56, no. 2 (2020).

81. Lydia Wevers, 'Speaking for Ourselves in 1945', *Journal of New Zealand Literature* 16 (1998): 97–111, especially, 104–5; Christopher Hilliard, '"Rough Architects": New Zealand Literature and Its Institutions from *Phoenix* to *Landfall*', in *A History of New Zealand Literature*, ed. Mark Williams (Cambridge: Cambridge University Press, 2016), 138–150.

82. Fairburn, quoted in Bertram, *Phoenix*, 57.

83. Erin Mercer, *Telling the Real Story: Genre and New Zealand Literature* (Wellington: Victoria University Press, 2017), 37, 64.

84. Jason R. Rudy, *Imagined Homelands: British Poetry in the Colonies* (Baltimore, ML: Johns Hopkins University Press, 2017), 62–5.

85. Quoted in Read, *Belonging*, 13–14.

86. Cynthia van den Driesen, *Writing the Nation: Patrick White and the Indigene* (Amsterdam: Brill, 2009).

87. Terry Goldie, *Fear and Temptation: The Image of the Indigene in Canadian, Australian, and New Zealand Literatures* (Montreal and Kingston: McGill-Queens University Press, 1989), 13; Stephen Turner, 'Settlement as Forgetting', in *Quicksands: Foundational Histories in Australia and Aotearoa New Zealand*, ed. Klaus Neumann, Nicholas Thomas and Hilary Ericksen (Sydney: UNSW Press, 1999), 20–38.

88. Carter, *Dispossession*, 174–8. In another example, Pauline Smith's idealised worlds of Boer pastoralists in *The Little Karoo* (1925; London: Everyman, 1930), occlude the presence of labouring Black Africans entirely.

89. Stafford and Williams, *Maoriland*, 11, 18, 110–133, 175; Stephen Turner, 'Being Colonial, Colonial Being', *Journal of New Zealand Literature* 20 (2000): 39–66, especially 41.

90. Baughan, 'Grandmother Speaks', in *Brown Bread*, 17.

91. Prichard, *Coonardoo*, 109.

92. King, *Penguin History of New Zealand*, 201–2.

93. Hedley Twidle, 'From *The Origin of Language* to a Language of Origin', in *Print, Text and Book Cultures in South Africa*, ed. Andrew van der Vlies (Johannesburg: University of Witwatersrand Press, 2012), 252–84; Donald Kerr, *Amassing Treasures for All Times: Sir George Grey, Colonial Bookman and Collector* (Dunedin: Otago University Press, 2006), 20. For poetic responses to Bleek and Lloyd, see Krog, *the stars say 'tsau'*, cited in both Afrikaans and English versions in chapter 2, and, curiously, from Aotearoa New Zealand, across the far south, Alistair Paterson's long poem *Africa: ||kabbo, Mantis and the Porcupine's Daughter* (Auckland: Puriri Press, 2008), which finds in the |xam beliefs a vision of interconnection between human, animal, and spiritual worlds.

94. Erin G. Carlston, Matthew Hayward, Brian M. Reed, 'Modernisms: Aotearoa New Zealand–Australia–Fiji, 1926–1986', *Modernist Cultures* 15, no. 3 (2020): 263–275.

95. Les Murray, 'The Buladelah-Taree Holiday Song Cycle', *Learning Human* (New York: Farrar, Straus, Giroux, 1998), 25–34; J. M Coetzee, *51 Poetas: Antología íntima*, ed. María Soledad Costantini (Buenos Aires: El Hilo de Ariadna, 2015), 528–84.

96. Olive Schreiner, *The Story of an African Farm* (1883; London: Virago, 1989), 1.

97. Olive Schreiner, *From Man to Man, or Perhaps, Only* (London: Fisher Unwin, 1926). I also used the UCT Press text edited by Dorothy Driver (2018). Page references are to the first edition, together with the abbreviation *FMtM*.

98. Joseph Furphy, *Such is Life: Being Certain Extracts from The Life of Tom Collins* (1903; Sydney: Angus and Robertson, 1956), ch. 1, punctuates descriptions of bullock-driving across the Riverina with reflections on its 'straight sky-line, broken here and there by a monumental clump or pine-ridge': 'And away beyond the horizon, southward still, the geodesic curve carries that monotony across the zone of salt-bush, myall, and swamp box'. Benito Lynch's novel *El Inglés de los Güesos* (1924; La Coruna: Ediciones del Viento, 2008) (about Darwin on the pampas), or the stories in *De los campos portenõs* (Buenos Aires: Ediciones Troquel, 1966), expose the damage and loss that the coming of refrigeration, the fencing of the pampas, and the incorporation of Argentina into the global economy of beef production, has wrought. See Pablo Ansolabehere, 'Cuentos de la Pampa: Los casos de Alberto Ghiraldo y Benito Lynch', *Anales de Literatura Hispanoamericana* 27 (1998): 89–109; Eunice Joiner Gates, 'Charles Darwin and Benito Lynch's "El Inglés de los Güesos"', *Hispania* 44, no. 2 (May 1961): 250–253.

99. See Snaith, *Modernist Voyages*, 36–66.

100. Coetzee, *White Writing*, 64–66. See also Anne McClintock, *Imperial Leather: Race, Gender and Sexuality in the Colonial Contest* (London: Routledge, 1995), 259.

101. Jeanne-Marie Jackson, *The African Novel of Ideas* (Princeton, 2021), 2–4, 20. David Johnson, *Dreaming of Freedom in South Africa* (Edinburgh: Edinburgh University Press, 2020), 13, suggests that the many alternative fictional forms with which Schreiner experimented allowed her to generate 'a vernacular language' with which 'to articulate . . . freedom'.

102. Dorothy Driver, 'Olive Schreiner's *From Man to Man* and "the Copy Within"', in *Changing the Victorian Subject*, ed. Maggie Tonkin, et al. (Adelaide: University of Adelaide, 2014). https://www.jstor.org/stable/10.20851/j.ctt1t305b6.10.

103. Coetzee, *White Writing*, 64–6.

104. See Peter Turchi, *Maps of the Imagination: The Writer as Cartographer* (San Antonio, TX: Trinity University Press, 2004), 64, 165.

105. Schreiner, *Story*, 1–4.

106. B. E. Baughan, *Shingle-Short and Other Verses* (Christchurch: Whitcombe and Tombs, 1908), and *Studies in New Zealand Scenery* (Auckland: Whitcombe and Tombs, 1917).

107. Baughan, 'The Old Place', in *Reuben*, 87–89. Stafford and Williams, *Maoriland*, explains that between 1909 and 1916, kahikatea forest in Aotearoa New Zealand was 'halved from 2,600 million superfeet to 1,117' (240).

108. Jane Stafford, 'B. E. Baughan, 1870–1958', *Kōtare*. 7, no. 3 (2008): 67–72; and 'Ineludible Envanishings', *New Zealand Review of Books* 112 (Summer 2015).

109. Carol Markwell, *Enough Horizon: The Life and Work of Blanche Baughan* (Wellington: The Cuba Press, 2021), 127, 156.

110. Baughan, 'Pipi on the Prowl', 'The Mountain Track', 'An Early Morning Walk', in *Brown Bread*, 2–14, 162–80, 114–124. The 'Pipi' quotation is from 2–3. For the quotations that follow, see 145, 181.

111. Baughan, 'Shingle-Short', in *Shingle-Short*, 11–40.

112. Baughan, 'A Bush Section', in *Shingle-Short*, 79–88. Curnow included the poem in his 1960 *Penguin Book of New Zealand Verse*, two years after Baughan's death. Stafford and Williams, *Maoriland*, 211–12, p. 221.

113. Baughan, 'Aboard a Coasting Schooner', in *Brown Bread*, 75.

114. Baughan, 'Spring in Autumn', in *Brown Bread*, 99.

115. The subtitle is from Katherine Mansfield, 'At the Bay', *Selected Stories*, ed. Angela Smith (Oxford: Oxford University Press, 2002), 281–314.

116. Conforming to that timeline to which Eric Hayot gives the name 'Eurochronology' (as in chapter 1).

117. On Mansfield's 'total identification' with her brother, see J. Lawrence Mitchell, '"Not the Kind to Die": Katherine Mansfield and the Unquiet Ghost of "Little Brother",' in *Katherine Mansfield and Virginia Woolf*, ed. Gerri Kimber, Todd Martin, and Christine Froula (Edinburgh: Edinburgh University Press, 2018), 179–196, especially 181; Claire Harman, *All Sorts of Lives: Katherine Mansfield and the Art of Risking Everything* (London: Chatto and Windus, 2023), 127–9. Andrew Dean in 'Nationalism, Modernism, and New Zealand', *Journal of New Zealand literature* 38, no. 1 (2020): 8–25, especially 22, writes insightfully about how Mansfield's 'notions of home' disrupt a strict critical nationalist agenda.

118. Harman, *All Sorts of Lives*, 35, 48. D. H. Lawrence gained insight into Mansfield's skill at forging parallel worlds when he visited the Antipodes himself, only then seeing 'how *very* Australian—or New Zealand' she was. Amongst the Bloomsbury circle, Mansfield always felt herself to be, as she said, 'an interloper and trespasser', 'the little colonial walking in the London garden patch'. Margaret Scott, ed., *The Katherine Mansfield Notebooks*, vol. 2 (Canterbury: Lincoln University Press, 1997), 32, 166; Snaith, *Modernist Voyages*, 110–132.

119. Kirsty Gunn, 'Stories That Simply Unfold', rev. of Claire Harman, *All Sorts of Lives*, *TLS* 6249 (6 January 2023): 3–4.

120. See Vincent O'Sullivan and Margaret Scott, eds, *The Collected Letters of Katherine Mansfield* (Oxford: Oxford University Press, 2008), 278; Harman, *All Sorts*, 4–5, 8.

121. See Schreiner, 'The Prelude—The Child's Play', in *From Man to Man*, 33–40, with its repeated references to burning heat; Mansfield quoted in Stafford and Williams, *Maoriland*, 161.

122. See Aarthi Vadde, *Chimeras of Form: Modernist Internationalism Beyond Europe, 1914–2016* (New York: Columbia University Press, 2017), on how crossovers between real and 'aberrant forms' give global modernists the scope to question 'the limits of imaginable community'. In my reading, it remains questionable whether Mansfield can be easily incorporated into the category of global modernism.

123. Mansfield, *Selected Stories*, 79–120, 281–314, 336–349.

124. Letter to Dorothy Brett, quoted in Harman, *All Sorts*, 19, 199–200.

125. James Bertram, 'Robin Hyde: A Reassessment', in *Phoenix*, 15–27.

126. Anthony Alpers, quoted in Bertram, in *Phoenix*, 84.

127. The quotation in the subheading pinpointing this self-division is from *HL* 158.

128. Read, *Belonging*, 38.

129. Judith Wright, 'The Granite Rocks of New England', in *The Nature of Love* (Sydney: Imprint Books, 1997), 188–92.

130. Judith Wright, 'Perspective', *Jindyworobak Review* (1948), quoted in Tony Hughes-D'Aeth, 'Judith Wright, an Activist Poet who was ahead of her time', *The Conversation*, 2 May 2022. https://theconversation.com/judith-wright-an-activist-poet-who-was-ahead-of-her-time-178422.

131. See Anne Collett and Dorothy Jones, 'Portrait of the Artist as a Young Colonial Girl: Emily Carr and Judith Wright', *The Journal of Commonwealth Literature* 44, no. 3 (2009): 51–67.

132. Frame, *Owls Do Cry; To the Is-land* (London: The Women's Press, 1983); *Towards Another Summer* (2007; London: Virago, 2008). Page references will be included in the text, along with the abbreviated titles *Owls, TtI*, and *TAS*.

133. Michael King, *Wrestling with the Angel: A Life of Janet Frame* (Auckland: Penguin Books, 2000), 79–80.

134. Andrew Dean, *Metafiction and the Postwar Novel* (Oxford: Oxford University Press, 2021), 88, 102–3; Mercer, *Telling*, 39.

135. King, *Wrestling*, 94, 96. On confinement in mental health institutions, the narrator of *Faces in the Water* (Auckland: George Braziller, 1982), observes that 'a great gap [had] opened in the ice floe between myself and the other people'.

136. King, *Wrestling*, 422; Dean, *Metafiction*, 102.

137. King, *Wrestling*, 487.

138. On the imbrication of the colonial and the indigenous, see Simon Gikandi, *Maps of Englishness: Writing Identity in the Culture of Colonialism* (New York: Columbia University Press, 1996), xviii.

Chapter Seven

Note to first epigraph: Kim Scott, *That Deadman Dance* (Sydney: Pan Macmillan Australia, 2010), 18, 26. Page references will be included in the text using the abbreviation *TDD*.

Note to second epigraph: Resoketswe Manenzhe, 'children of the first gods', in *Scatterlings* (Johannesburg: Jacana, 2020), 9. The story of 'the girl of the early race who made stars' is indebted to Bleek and Lloyd, *Specimens of Bushman Folklore*, in particular to the myth of the stars' creation, 'The girl of the early race who made stars', narrated by ||kabbo (72–79). |han‡kass'o, 'What the stars say, and a prayer to a star', 80–83 in the same volume, reflects on the cultural roles of stars. My thanks to Luan Staphorst for clarifying this reference.

Note to third epigraph: Wright, *Carpentaria*, 375–8. Page references to *Carpentaria* will be included in the text using the abbreviation *C*.

Note to fourth epigraph: Zoë Wicomb, 'A Trip to the Gifberge', in *You Can't Get Lost in Cape Town* (London: Virago, 1987), 181. Starry visions have replicated in several 2020s South African novels: in Basil Lawrence's *At the Edge of the Desert* (Johannesburg: Penguin, 2021), set on the Namibian coast, where the documentary-maker hero, stargazing, imagines tumbling up into the open sky and contemplating 'the glowing fires on the earth far below' (129, 191); in Chantal Stewart's *The Veil of Maya*, with its 'cloudy curtain' (see the 'Stars' section of chapter 2); and in David Ralph Viviers, *Mirage* (Cape Town: Umuzi, 2023), in which the constellation Corona Australis features as a clue in the unravelling of the plot (182–185). In the latter two, as in Manenzhe, the imprint of the ||kabbo story is unmistakable. See also Diana Ferrus's allusion to the

Southern Cross flickering above the watery tracks of Winnie Mandela's dreams in 'Winnie', in *Onskomvandaan* (Cape Town: Diana Ferrus Uitgewery, 2005), 14.

1. Jazz Money, 'bila, a river cycle', in *how to make a basket* (Brisbane: University of Queensland Press, 2021), 59–63. The poem was shortlisted for the 2021 Peter Porter prize. See 'The 2021 Peter Porter Prize', *Australian Review of Books*, accessed 10 January 2021, https://www.australianbookreview.com.au/component/k2/47-competitionsandprograms/6579-2021-peter-porter-poetry-prize. In *how to make a basket* the poem appears in a longer form, containing a further section about the delta region and the suburbs. See also Jazz Money, 'bila, a river cycle,' TEDxSydney, 30 August 2022, YouTube TEDx Talks video, 8:05, https://www.youtube.com/watch?v=8Z8eHNx8wKs.

2. Gabeba Baderoon, *The History of Intimacy* (Cape Town: Kwela, 2018); Toni Morrison, 'The Site of Memory', in *Inventing the Truth: The Art and Craft of Memoir*, ed. William Zinsser (Boston, New York: Houghton Mifflin, 1995), 83–102. Page references to *The History of Intimacy* will henceforth be cited in text, with the abbreviation *H*.

3. Money tells us that the model for her bila is the Murrumbidjee, a tributary of the Murray, with which the Wiradjuri, the people of the three rivers, have ancestral links.

4. Tara June Winch, *The Yield* (London: Harper Via, 2021), 5, 15, 104, 197. Page references will be included in text using the abbreviation *Y*. Money and Winch's sense of 'a world known as kin' harmonises with the late 2010s legal recognition in Aotearoa New Zealand of the personhood as 'an indivisible and living whole' of natural entities: the Whanganui River, Mount Taranaki or Taranaki Maunga, and the Urewera ranges. The Netherlands/New Zealand documentary *I Am the River, the River Is Me*, directed by Peter Lom (2024), reflects in depth on the personhood of the Whanganui River. See https://www.legislation.govt.nz/act/public/2017/0007/latest/whole.html. Accessed 17 April 2024.

5. Luke Patterson, 'Culture in the Making (a Walk and Talk)', review of *how to make a basket*, by Jazz Money, *Sydney Review of Books*, 8 February 2022, https://sydneyreviewofbooks.com/review/money-how-to-make-a-basket/. Accessed 13 June 2023. The 'bila' quotation is from A. Frances Johnson judge's citation, also excerpted in the *Australian Review of Books* article 'Bila, all bila, survive, even if degraded.'

6. See Gabeba Baderoon, *Regarding Muslims: From Slavery to Post-Apartheid* (Johannesburg: Wits University Press, 2014).

7. The quoted lines are from Gabeba Baderoon, 'This Is Where It Started', in *The Dream in the Next Body* (Cape Town: Kwela/Snailpress, 2005), 29. See also Meg Samuelson, 'Yvette Christiansë's Oceanic Genealogies', 27–38.

8. Nadia Davids, *An Imperfect Blessing* (Cape Town: Umuzi, 2014). Davids writes: 'She has heard the name District Six but has never thought to call this place, *right here*, this place that begins where her school ends, playground against rubble, by that name' (312). Diana Ferrus's 'My naam is Februarie' (2016) is a response to the 2015 discovery of the wrecked slave ship *Sao José* off the Cape Peninsula, in which a drowned slave, Februarie, is the speaker. See 'Afterword: My naam is Februarie', in *From No Return: The 221-Year Journey of the Slave Ship São José, 1794*, by Jaco Jacques Boshoff, et al. (Washington D. C.: National Museum of African American History and Culture, 2016); Charne Lavery, 'Diving into the Slave Wreck': The *São José Paquete d'Africa* and Yvette Christiansë's *Imprendehora*, *Eastern African Literary and Cultural Studies* 6, no. 4 (2020): 269–83. For the English translation of Ferrus's poem, see Diana Ferrus, 'My Name

is February', *New Agenda: South African Journal of Social and Economic Policy* 96, no. 1 (2025). https://doi.org/10.14426/na.v96i1.2785.

9. Baderoon, 'Plant Glossary', in *The Dream in the Next Body*, 62.

10. Gabeba Baderoon, Reading and Conversation, University of Cape Town campus, 11 March 2022.

11. The image recalls 'Klipgat' cave that also appears in Zakes Mda's *The Whale Caller* (Johannesburg: Penguin, 2005), and used to be 'the home, variously, of the Khoikhoi and San peoples long before the village came into being' (2, 6). Page references to the novel will henceforth be cited in text using the abbreviation *WC*.

12. The images of summer winds and hunters' pathways are from the epigraphs above, while *yurali* (eucaltypus blossom) and *ngurru-mirgang* (blue, as in the sky) are from 'The Dictionary of Albert Gondiwindi,' in Winch, *Yield*. *Ghoera* is the |xam name for a stringed musical instrument which appears in *the stars say 'tsau'*, first referenced in chapter 2. *Ghanna* is the Khoikhoi word for a grey, feathery bush, related to 'Khoikhoikooigoed', which is good for bedding. The bush is one of several medicinal plants that Mrs Shenton notices growing in the veld in the story 'A Trip to the Gifberge', quoted in the fourth epigraph, and further discussed below.

13. In de Sousa Santos' terms, the writing looks back from beyond the abyss that western thought-systems have sunk between the far south and the rest of the world. Boaventura de Sousa Santos, *Epistemologies of the South*, 121; Selina Tusitala Marsh and Jeanine Leane, 'A Trans-Indigenous Scholarly Dialogue', South Pacific ACLALS Speaker Series, online, 14 February 2021.

14. J. M. Coetzee, *White Writing*, reminds us: 'wherever Africa is named as antithesis, it is a negative and not Africa that is named'(169–70). See also David McDermott, *Whiteness in Zimbabwe: Race, Landscape and the Problem of Belonging* (New York, NY: Palgrave Macmillan, 2010).

15. Jeanine Leane, 'Gathering: The Politics of Memory and Contemporary Aboriginal Women's Writing', *Antipodes* 31, no. 2 (2017): 242–251; Jeanine Leane, 'Another Story', *Research Methodologies for Auto/biography Studies*, ed. Kate Douglas and Ashley Barnwell (New York and London: Routledge, 2019), 125–31, especially 129; *Purple Threads* (St. Lucia: University of Queensland Press, 2011); Danica Čerče, 'Jeanine Leane's Counter-Reading of Australian Historical and Cultural Memory Locally and Internationally', *Journal of Postcolonial Writing* 58, no. 1 (2022): 65–79, especially 66–7. See also Jan-Melissa Schramm, '"I feel I am a man and a free man too": Palawa voices and the Ethics of Representation in Contemporary Tasmanian Fiction', *Journal of Postcolonial Writing* 58, no. 1 (2022): 36–50.

16. Alexis Wright, 'On Writing *Carpentaria*', in *Indigenous Translationalism: Alexis Wright's Carpentaria*, ed. Lynda Ng (Sydney: Giramondo, 2018), 217–34, especially 224, 221. See also Quentin Deluermoz and Pierre Singaravélou, *A Past of Possibilities: A History of What Could Have Been* (New Haven: Yale University Press, 2021); Saidiya Hartman, *Lose Your Mother: A Journey Along the Atlantic Slave Route* (London: Serpent's Tail, 2021).

17. Wright, 'On Writing *Carpentaria*', 224.

18. To cite from two important readings of how poetry synthesises: Jahan Ramazani, *Poetry in a Global Age* (Chicago and London: University of Chicago Press, 2020), 4; George B. Handley, 'Derek Walcott's Poetics', 201–15, especially 201–2. Ramazani continues that a lyric poem 'folds within itself the heterogenous temporalities of words, forms, rhythms, tropes and genres' (8). In the view of Jennifer Wenzel, *The Disposition of Nature: Environmental Crisis and World*

Literature (New York: Fordham University Press, 2020), 15, writing can '[provide] the forms through which human understandings [of the environment] . . . are forged'. See also Maria Alonso and Maria Jesus Cabarcos Traseira, 'A Legacy of Waste', *Journal of Postcolonial Writing* 55, no. 2 (April 2019): 147–54; Elizabeth DeLoughrey, Jill Didur, and Anthony Carrigan, eds, *Global Ecologies and the Environmental Humanities: Postcolonial Approaches* (New York: Routledge, 2015); George B. Handley, *New World Poetics: Nature and the Adamic Imagination of Whitman, Neruda, and Walcott* (Atlanta: Georgia University Press, 2007); Puchner, *Literature for a Changing Planet.*

19. Even while 'acknowledging the profundity' of all that has been lost. Linda Tuhiwai Smith, *Decolonizing Methodologies*, 59; Schramm, 'Palawa Voices', 46.

20. Massey, *For Space*, 6–9.

21. Melissa Lukashenko, *Too Much Lip* (St Lucia: University of Queensland Press, 2018), 62, 98. 131. Further references will be cited in text using the abbreviation *TML*. Relatedly, the Black Australian writer Mudrooroo (a.k.a Colin Johnson), in *Doctor Wooreddy's Prescription for Enduring the Ending of the World* (Melbourne: Hyland House, 1998), uses tribal knowledge backprojected and revived from the colonial archive to disrupt the official linear narrative of the European invasion of Tasmania. See Clare Archer-Lean, 'Transnational Impulses as Simulation in Colin Johnson's (Mudrooroo's) Fiction', *Transnational Literature* 5, no. 2 (May 2013): 1–12. In an interesting parallel, Richard Flanagan's *Gould's Book of Fish* fictionalises the violent colonial history of Tasmania in even more extreme ways.

22. Geoffrey Rodoreda, *The Mabo Turn in Australian Fiction* (Oxford: Peter Lang, 2018), proposes that the 1992 Mabo decision of the Australian High Court and its recognition of Indigenous people's presence on the land, gave new impetus to both the Indigenous and wider Australian literary imaginary.

23. Boehmer, *Colonial and Postcolonial Literature*, 16.

24. Marcia Langton, 'Aboriginal Art and Film: The Politics of Representation', in *Blacklines: Contemporary Critical Writing by Indigenous Australians*, ed. Michèle Grossman (Melbourne: Melbourne University Press, 2003), 109–124, especially 119.

25. See Paula Morris, *Rangatira: A Novel* (Auckland: Penguin, 2011). Wicomb is discussed in Southscapes.

26. Nerida Blair, *Privileging Australian Indigenous Knowledge: Sweet Potatoes, Spiders, Waterlilys, and Brick Walls* (Champaign, IL: Common Ground publishing, 2015), 216. I am grateful to Katherine Collins for this reference.

27. Manenzhe, *Scatterlings*, 9–10.

28. Witi Ihimaera, *The Whale Rider* (1987; Rosedale: Penguin Group NZ, 2008), 13. Page references will be included in the text using the abbreviation *WR*.

29. Wright, 'On Writing *Carpentaria*', 219, 218, 222.

30. Lucy Rowland, 'Indigenous Temporality and Climate Change in Alexis Wright's *Carpentaria*', *Journal of Postcolonial Writing* 55, no. 4 (2019): 541–554, observes how Wright collapses and eliminates the 'psychological and physical distances between historical events'. See also Krim Benterrak, Stephen Muecke, and Paddy Roe, *Reading the Country: Introduction to Nomadology* (Fremantle W.A: Fremantle Arts Centre Press, 1996).

31. Wright, 'On Writing *Carpentaria*', 223. See also Peter Minter, 'Rubbish Places, Islands of Junk', and Nicholas Birns, 'The Notions of Permanence', in *Indigenous Transnationalism*, 185–6 and 67–8, respectively.

32. Rodoreda, *Mabo Turn*, 172–5.

33. Rodoreda, *Mabo Turn*, 182.

34. Wright, 'On Writing *Carpentaria*', 219–21.

35. Alexis Wright, *The Swan Book* (Sydney: Giramondo, 2013), 52, 42. With its epigraph from J. L. Borges, 'I am not even dust, I am a dream', Wright's novel after *The Swan Book*, *Praiseworthy* (Sydney: Giramondo, 2023), set in the titular town in the Gulf Country overrun by feral donkeys, develops further the end-of-days vision of the previous novels.

36. Araluen, 'Resisting the Institution'.

37. Bobby has several historical precursors, among them, most prominently, Boongaree, a Garigal man from the north of colonial Port Jackson, who in 1801–2 sailed with Matthew Flinders on HMS *Investigator*, becoming the first Aborigine to circumnavigate Australia, as far as is known. See Tiffany Shellam, 'Mediating Encounters through Bodies and Talk', in *Indigenous Intermediaries: New Perspectives on Exploration Archives*, ed. Shino Konishi, Maria Nugent, and Tiffany Shellam (Acton, ACT: Australian National University Press, 2015), 88. *That Deadman Dance* references Flinders's reports on the 'friendly frontier' (*TDD* 88). Bobby's story of communion with the whales can also be related to the culture of the Mirning people in the Australian Bight, who take the southern right whale as their totem. Their common whale ancestor is emblematised in the Milky Way constellation of the whale or Jeedara, who is believed to have come down from the stars together with the Seven Sisters (Pleiades). When the whales come to the Bight to calve, they are 'honouring Jeedara's great journey from the Milky Way'. See McCann, *Wild Sea*, 173–4.

38. Tuhiwai Smith, *Decolonizing Methodologies*, 8, 36, 37, 192. Ngugi wa Thiong'o's *Decolonising the Mind: The Politics of Language in African Literature* (London: Heinemann, 1986), and Abdul JanMohamed and David Lloyd's edited collection *The Nature and Context of Minority Discourse* (New York: Oxford University Press, 1990), have both long emphasised how using indigenous and vernacular languages counters the colonial redefinition of our world, and resists the creep of western hegemony.

39. Tuhiwai Smith, *Decolonizing Methodologies*, 57.

40. Relatedly, the Tasmanian novelist Rohan Wilson's *The Roving Party* (Sydney: Allen and Unwin, 2011), sets out to revive *palawa kani*, the language of the Tasmanian Aboriginal Community, by reconstructing wordlists retrieved from archival sources in ways that align symbiotically with Winch's project.

41. Tara June Winch, *The Yield* reading, 'Postcolonial Infrastructure', GAPS 2023 Annual Conference, University of Konstanz, Germany, 18 May 2023. See also Christopher Ehret, *History and the Testimony of Language* (Berkeley: University of California Press, 2011), 3.

42. Parkington, Morris, and De Prada-Samper, 'Elusive Identities', 729–47, especially 730–1; Luan Staphorst, '"van die oorspronklike lippe" ("from the original lips"): The 19th-Century Cape Colony, Holographic Archaeology and the Historicity of Gideon von Wielligh's |xam–Afrikaans Collection', *Journal of Southern African Studies* 48, no. 6 (2022): 993–1011, especially 999–1000. Khoikhoi bequeathed to Afrikaans interjections like '*eina!*' and '*sies!*', or *e-na* and *tsi*, the disappeared words resurfacing explosively to express pain and disgust, respectively; '*au*' for 'give' in some versions of Afrikaans may also be a |xam survival. See also Mike Nicol, 'The City I Live In', in *A City Imagined*, ed. Stephen Watson (Johannesburg: Penguin, 2005), 45–54, especially 47.

43. See Solomon T. Plaatje, *Mhudi* (1930; London: Heinemann, 1970). As in *Carpentaria*, the landscapes that Mhudi traverses form an environment in which the celestial bodies and all living beings are enmeshed with each other through the bonds of story. Parkington, Morris, and

De Prada-Samper relatedly observe in 'Elusive Identities' that the region of the Northern Cape where the SKA radio telescope is now located corresponds in significant ways to ||kabbo's nineteenth-century map in the Bleek and Lloyd archive. The descendants of the |xam in the area today speak Afrikaans. See also Julia Blackburn's personal reflections on the |xam sense of the landscape in *Dreaming the Karoo: A People Called the |Xam* (London: Jonathan Cape, 2022). Mhudi's views across the landscape from high koppies also correlate suggestively with Zulu poet H. I. E. Dhlomo's 1942 visions of the 'mazy slopes' of his hinterland in *Valley of a Thousand Hills*, ed. C. L. Brokensha (Durban: Daily News Press, 1962), as well as with Zoë Wicomb's view across Namaqualand in 'A Trip to the Gifberge'.

44. André Brink, *Die eerste lewe van Adamastor: 'n novelle* (1988; Cape Town: Human en Rousseau, 2003), in particular 36, 43, 44–5; and *The First Life of Adamastor* (London: Secker and Warburg, 1993). See also Jochen Petzold, 'André Brink's Magical History Tour: Postmodern and Postcolonial Influences in *The First Life of Adamastor*', *English in Africa* 27, no. 2 (2000): 45–58; Richard Samin, 'The Myth of Adamastor: The Ambivalent Metaphor of Otherness in South African Literature', *Commonwealth Essays and Studies* 29, no. 1 (2006): 59–69. For other engagements with Camões's Adamastor story, see Vladislavic, *T'Kama*. Adamastor returns in contemporary Cape literature, for example, as a 'geological' in the futuristic Jaco Adriaanse, *The Metronome: Adamastor City* (Cape Town: Burnt Toast, 2020), in which the sleeping giant of Table Mountain is at war with Spacebeasts and Afrobots. Fionuala Dowling's *Okay, Okay, Okay* (Cape Town: Kwela, 2019), features a University of Adamastor, while Antjie Krog's reflections on the menopause in *Body Bereft/Veweerskrif* (Cape Town: Umuzi, 2011), culminate in 'contemplations of Table Mountain' as a brooding presence that calls up associations of Adamastor.

45. Krog, *die sterre*, 10. Interestingly, too, in Brink's original Afrikaans version, the naming scene in which T'kama 'gives [his land] sound'—'I say lion, jackal, mocking-bird, partridge, *kiewiet*, I say *kombro*, I say *dagga*, I say *kierie* and *kaross*, I say *khuseti*, I say *t'gau*, I say *k'hrab*, I say *k'arakup*, I say beetle and fly and field-mouse'—does not italicise the Khoi words, several of which have now migrated into Afrikaans. There is also no glossary. From another southern vantage point, New Zealand-born writer Kirsty Gunn in *Going Bush* draws on Māori fauna names from the OED—'*kowhai* and *horoeka* and *kauri*'—to unsettle the local literary icon Katherine Mansfield's descriptions of 'the green places' of North Island. See Kirsty Gunn and Merran Gunn, *Going Bush* (Paris: The American University of Paris Press, 2016), 27.

46. Nathan Trantaal, *Chokers en Survivors* (Kaapstad: Kwela Boeke, 2013); *Alles Het Niet Kom Wôd* (Hatfield: Van Schaik Publishers, 2017); and the 'exaggerated' stories, *Wit issie 'n colour nie* (Cape Town: Kwela Boeke, 2018); Ronelda Kamfer, *Chinatown: Gedigte* (Cape Town: Kwela Boeke, 2019). The dynamic flow of Trantaal and Kamfer's Kaaps, its elisions, reversals, and deadpanning, powerfully enacts the 'confluences' made possible by poetry (see Ramazani, *Poetry in a Global Age*).

47. Or as Marlene van Niekerk, *Agaat*, trans. Michiel Heyns (Cape Town: Tafelberg/Jonathan Ball, 2006), writes, of being 'at the heart of the hearth . . . under the foundations' (249).

48. Wicomb, *You Can't Get Lost*, referenced above, and *The One That Got Away* (Cape Town: Umuzi, 2008). Page references appear in text along with the abbreviations *Can't* and *One*.

49. Zoë Wicomb, *Still Life* (Cape Town: Umuzi, 2020), p. 66.

50. Wicomb, 'Another Story', in *One That Got Away*, 189.

51. Derek Attridge, '"No Escape from Home": History, Affect and Art in Zoë Wicomb's Translocal Coincidences', in *Zoë Wicomb and the Translocal*, ed. Kai Easton and Derek Attridge (London: Routledge, 2017), 49–63, especially 51.

52. These are the same bright Northern Cape skies where the stars actually 'come out at night', according to Laverne in Terry-Ann Adams, those who live in cages (Johannesburg: Jacana, 2020), 82. Page references will appear in text along with the abbreviated title *Cages*.

53. *White Chalk* (Johannesburg: Jacana, 2022) is a follow-up collection of short stories and sketches that also curates voices and perspectives from Eldos, and, like *those who live in cages*, especially comes alive in the characters' conversational exchanges. In both works, Adams, as a writer of colour with albinism, confronts the stigma associated with the condition in her community. In *Cages*, Bertha's grandchild has albinism, and the parents 'agree on one thing: they don't want to raise their child' (89).

54. To cite from Jamil F. Khan's cover endorsement to *Cages*.

55. See Tim Winton, 'The Island Seen and Felt', in *Island Home: A Landscape Memoir* (Sydney: Penguin, 2016), 9–29, especially 25; Françoise Vergès (2001), cited in Charne Lavery, 'Diving', 270.

56. Yvette Christiansë, *Castaway* (Durham, NC: Duke University Press, 1999) and *Imprendehora* (Cape Town: Kwela Books/Snailpress, 2009); Charne Lavery, 'Diving', 269–72.

57. Samuelson, 'Yvette Christiansë', 27–38, especially 28–9.

58. Karen Jennings, *An Island* (Cape Town: Karavan Press, 2021), 10–11. Further south again, Nell Stevens's memoir *Bleaker House: Chasing My Novel to the End of the World* (London: Doubleday, 2017), describes the author's attempt to write a fiction in the solitary fastness of Bleaker Island in the Falklands. But the 'end of the world', far from creating fruitful conditions for her writing, instead haunts her with memories of people faraway.

59. Eleanor Catton, *The Luminaries* (London: Granta, 2013).

60. Or where 'the sun [slaps] the barren earth with an open palm', in Tara June Winch's description (*Y* 8). On the white light of the southern subtropics, see Elleke Boehmer, 'Migration and the South: J. M. Coetzee's *Jesus* Novels', *Journal of Modern Literature* 46, no. 2 (Winter 2023): 127–39. On mystery, see Winton, *Island Home*, 75–6, 85–7, 135–7. By day, the clear skies of the far south are crisscrossed with contrails, something Lukashenko, Alexis Wright, and Tim Winton all observe. By night, from the great western deserts of the three continental masses, the Atacama, the Karoo, and the Wajarri Yamaji lands in Western Australia, great telescopic eyes stare out, up into the dark zenith, probing back into the beginnings of time.

61. Avi Duckor-Jones, *Swim* (Sydney: Brio Books, 2018), 25, 47, 120.

62. Around the Great Australian Bight, and along the shorelines of the southwestern Cape and the Valdes Peninsula, Patagonia. See McCann, *Wild Sea*, xii, 154, 173–4.

63. Robert Sullivan, 'Hello Great North Road', *Poetry* (2018), accessed 29 July 2023, https://www.poetryfoundation.org/poetrymagazine/poems/89742/hello-great-north-road. Not unrelatedly, Sullivan's libretto *Captain Cook in the Underworld* (Auckland: Auckland University Press, 2002), pictures a bullish James Cook 'with Venus on the brain', guided westwards 'through the shades far / toward the southern land' (5, 13).

64. Meg Samuelson, '"Re-Enchanting the World" from Mozambique: The African Anthropocene and Mia Couto's Poetics of the Planet', in *Transcultural Ecocriticism: Global, Romantic*

and Decolonial Perspectives, ed. Stuart Cooke and Peter Denney (London: Bloomsbury Academic, 2021), 63–81.

65. Pablo Neruda, *Cuándo de Chile* (Santiago: Editorial Universitaria, 1952). It was also Neruda who, in his 1950 epic or 'general song' of Latin America, *Canto General*, wrote: 'I awaken suddenly in the night / thinking about the far south'. See Pablo Neruda, *Canto General*, 50th Anniversary Edition, trans. Jack Schmitt (Berkeley: University of California Press, 2000), 65. In the twenty-first century, the tradition of encyclopaedic poems of the continent continues, manifesting, for example, in Sergio Raimondi's alphabetically organised *Lexikón* (Buenos Aires: Mansalva, 2023). Like some of the other Latin American works cited in this chapter, the collection is keenly sensitive to what it is to write from a periphery, where the district schools are run down, yet pollution is as widespread as elsewhere. I am grateful to Elizabeth Chant and Ben Bollig for the Neruda and Raimondi references, respectively. See Ben Bollig, 'Here Comes Everybody', *TLS*, no. 6264 (21 April 2023): 19. Australian author Richard Flanagan's Second World War novel, *The Narrow Road to the Deep North*, reinforces the point about littoral tendencies in far south writing. The primary theatre of action is an Australian prisoner-of-war camp in Burma, but the love affair that shapes the hero Dorrigo Evans's life is south-tending. Formative scenes face the 'ceaseless and open' Southern Ocean, the element into which Dorrigo's lover Amy Mulvaney throws herself with an abandon that will impact them both: 'And when she burst back up, tasting salt, the sky an unbearable brilliance, all her confusion was gone and in its place she had the strange sensation that she had surfaced into some new centre of her life' (108, 121–2). Flanagan continues his thread of meditation on how eventuality, fatality, exclusion, and revolt converge in Tasmania, 'the scrag ends of an island at the end of the world, in its unhonoured and unknown wonder', in his memoir *Question 7* (London: Chatto and Windus, 2023), 43–44, 53.

66. *The Whale Caller* elongates the geography of the continent both towards the far south and beneath the surface of the sea, as Samuelson and Lavery, 'The Oceanic South', argue. The novel explicitly signals some of the remote proximities of the Southern Ocean in its references to histories of 'whale utilisation', and to a story 'from the Dreamtime' to describe how the whale got its blowholes (*WC* 139–41). It also shares explicit Jonah and Melville references with Kim Scott (*That Deadman Dance* 2, *WC* 8–9). The Whale Caller character has learned the songs of migrating whales during the many years he spent wandering along the coast of the Indian Ocean, down to Cape Agulhas, tracing in the reverse direction early European journeys around the Cape (as in chapter 3). For other intertextual and Southern Ocean expansions of whale-human relations, see Kim Kindersley's film *Whaledreamers* (2006), which appeared a year after Mda's novel, and establishes reciprocities between Indigenous Australian and whale efforts to avoid extinction in the southern waters of Western Australia.

67. Sarah Comyn and Porscha Fermanis, 'Rethinking Nineteenth-century Literary Culture: British Worlds, Southern Latitudes, and Hemispheric Methods', *The Journal of Commonwealth Literature* 58, no. 2 (2023): 409–26, especially 409.

68. Pablo Mukherjee, 'Consider the Whale', review of *Colonialism, Culture, Whales: The Cetacean Quartet* by Graham Huggan, *Journal of Postcolonial Writing* 58, no. 2 (2022): 265–268.

69. Amitav Ghosh, *The Great Derangement: Climate Change and the Unthinkable* (London: Allen Lane, 2016), 78–83. Or, in the likeminded phrasing of Bruno Latour, *Down to Earth: Politics in the New Climatic Regime* (Cambridge: Polity, 2019), 82–90, the reciprocal 'embedding' that distinguishes the life of all animate beings. Ghosh references *Down to Earth* on 82.

70. Beejay Silcox, 'Inner Space Odyssey', review of *In Ascension*, by Martin MacInnes, *TLS*, no. 6256 (24 February 2023): 16. See also Elizabeth DeLoughrey, 'Ordinary Futures', in *Global Ecologies and the Environmental Humanities*, 352–372.

Chapter Eight

1. Dipesh Chakrabarty, *The Climate of History in a Planetary Age* (Chicago: Chicago University Press, 2021), calls this 'facing the planetary' (90). His history of modernity, however, remains (perhaps necessarily) north-centred.

2. There is no through-traffic south, except to the icy continent, via the five Antarctic gateways: Ushuaia, Punta Arenas, Christchurch, Hobart, and Cape Town.

3. Tim Winton, 'The Island Seen and Felt', in *Island Home*, 9–27, speaks (plausibly to me) of feeling the Western Australian ground twitching underfoot: 'Even out in the shimmering distance where the horizon slips and crawls implausibly in the heat, the land twitches and ticks, forever threatening to foreground itself and take over the show' (26–7).

4. With hindsight, much of my writing, fiction and nonfiction, has been concerned with southern worlds. In brief—my short story collection *To the Volcano* (Brighton: Myriad Editions, 2019), tries to capture from a range of different viewpoints across the south moments of southern awareness and affinity. And in *The Shouting in the Dark* (Johannesburg: Jacana, 2015; Perth: UWA Press, 2019), the father character's yarning and storytelling takes place on a Kwazulu-Natal veranda, on the Berea in Durban, looking out to sea. Even 'Kaya', the very first short story I published, in 1989, though it is set in a single room that is not at first obviously northern or southern, still assumes a southern setting. Writing the story, I was aware the room was unusually shadowy, in the sense that such shadows are not generally found in interior southern spaces, unless, as here, there is a particular reason for that darkness. The room in the story was a servant's room in apartheid South Africa, called a *kaya* in Zulu, which meant the windows were small and high up, throwing the room into shadow. See Elleke Boehmer, 'Kaya', first published in *Kunapipi*, collected in *Sharmilla, and Other Portraits* (Johannesburg: Jacana, 2010), 3–6. See also 'The South in the World', *Worlding the South*, ed. Sarah Comyn and Porscha Fermanis (Manchester: Manchester UP, 2021), 378–91.

5. In the words of the South African artist Lola Frost. See Lola Frost, *Life-Force: Catalogue 2021, LolaFrostCatalogue_ForWeb.pdf*, 41. The phrase is from her account of her painting *Mairangi* (2019). I am grateful to Lola Frost for sharing her catalogues of recent work with me.

6. In other examples, Australian novelist M. L. Stedman's historical fiction *The Light between Oceans* (Melbourne. Vintage Australia, 2012), combines several trademark southern motifs—an isolated island south of Australia, a washed-up boat, buried secrets—to tell the story of the First World War veteran turned lighthouse keeper Tom Sherbourne. The Irish writer Paul Lynch's *Beyond the Sea* (London: OneWorld, 2019), explores ideas of physical and spiritual extremity by setting two South American fishermen, Bolivar and Hector, adrift on the far south Pacific Ocean, beyond the reach of radio and GPS. They feel increasingly split between 'there', where they left from, and 'here', the other world in which they find themselves now. Nick Mulgrew's *Hibiscus Coast* (Cape Town: Karavan Press, 2021), a comic novel concerned with white South African emigration to New Zealand, draws lines of tangled engagement between

these two southern spaces. The screen adaptation of the Stedman (2016) was filmed in Dunedin, Otago, as were Campion's *An Angel at My Table*, and *Top of the Lake*.

7. Corroborating these southern links, *An Angel at My Table* is the dramatisation of Janet Frame's autobiographical trilogy. Eleanor Catton's *Birnam Wood* (London: Granta, 2023) plays on the increasingly open secret of New Zealand's desirability to the world's most powerful elites as the place wherein to survive the apocalypse. In the novel, an activist collective called Birnam Wood collaborates (briefly) with the United States-based Autonomo project to mine rare earth minerals in the Southern Alps. Several of the characters, though of differing political persuasions, reflect with mixed feelings of anxiety and defiance on New Zealand's remoteness and position as 'automatic underdog' relative to the 'great power centres of the world'. See 31, 136, 160 for further references to remoteness and relative smallness.

8. This view of the south as qualifying how our humanness is currently defined, harmonises with Martha Nussbaum's considerations in *Justice for Animals: Our Contemporary Responsibility* (New York: Simon and Schuster, 2023), in which she contends that the anthropomorphic perspective that underpins most human philosophies, has now come to constrain our thriving as human beings.

9. J. M. Coetzee, *Elizabeth Costello* (London: Secker, 2003). As we saw before, J. M. Coetzee has famously translated the feeling of connectivity in his account of the 'one south' as being recognisable around the hemisphere yet difficult precisely to pinpoint, as his havering repetitions suggest: 'In this South the wind blows in a certain way and the leaves fall in a certain way and the sun beats down in a certain way that is instantly recognizable from one part of the South to another'. See J. M. Coetzee, 'Literatures of the South: Introductory Remarks', unpublished lecture, notes by Cristóbal Pérez Barra, San Martín National University, Buenos Aires (11 April 2016); Halford, 'Southern Conversations'. A sidenote: Coetzee observes that the leaves fall in a certain way right across the south. And so indeed they may, especially if we are talking about urban trees. As southern hemisphere cities all lie in a temperate band between the latitudes of approximately twenty-seven to thirty-four degrees south, the streetside trees do brown in the same way, and the light is similar at the same times of the year. To say nothing of the fact that many of the trees are either plane trees or jacarandas. On Coetzee's south as the setting for his post-2000s fictions, especially the *Jesus* novel trilogy, see Boehmer, 'Migration and the South', 127–139. See also Meg Samuelson, 'An "International Author, but in a Different Sense": J. M. Coetzee and "Literatures of the South"', *Thesis Eleven* 162, no. 1 (2021): 137–54; Derek Attridge, 'The South according to Coetzee', *Public Books*, 25 September 2019, https://www.publicbooks.org/the-south-according-to-coetzee/. On the Global South as providing a new 'matrix' for world history, see Isabel Hofmeyr, 'African History and Global Studies: A View from South Africa', *Journal of African History* 54, no. 3 (2013): 341–9. Against the possible charge that Coetzee's south is a-historical and has lost its specific African coordinates, the response might be that Coetzee is grappling to show that conversations grounded in the unique environments of the South can have global importance and impact. See also Lavery and Nuttall, *Reading from the South*; 'Speaking from the South' cultural event and conference website, University of Adelaide, Adelaide, South Australia (31 May–5 June 2024) https://www.adelaide.edu.au/newsroom/events/list/2024/05/speaking-from-the-south.

10. Today, right across the far south, whether in New Zealand, southern Africa, or Patagonia, decommissioned railways have been left to decay and peter into the sand, or turned into tourist

attractions, as in the (enjoyable and beautiful) Port Chalmers train journey on the Otago peninsula, among many others.

11. Ashley Ward, *Sensational: A New Story of Our Senses* (London: Profile, 2023), in particular, 3, 232–48.

12. See Boehmer, 'Time and Distance', 99–104.

13. Frost, 'Going South' exhibition, King's College London, 5–30 June 2015. https://www.lolafrost.net/going-south-exhibition.html. Frost's painting *The Edge of the Skirt of the World* is reproduced in this book's colour insert.

14. Tim Winton, *The Boy behind the Curtain* (Sydney: Penguin Random House Australia, 2016), 75. Human beings first recorded the Magellanic Clouds in drawings on rocks in Chile.

15. Schreiner, *From Man to Man*, ch. 9.

16. Conrad, *The Mirror of the Sea*, ch. 14.

17. Lawrence, *Kangaroo*, 18.

18. Samanta Schweblin, *Fever Dream* (*Distancia de Rescate*), trans. Megan McDowell (London: OneWorld, 2017), 103, and also 57, 142, 148. In Samanta Schweblin, *Mouthful of Birds* (*Pájaros en la boca*), trans. Megan McDowell (London: OneWorld, 2019), haunting, pollution and remoteness again predominate, while views from the world's outskirts also distinguish fellow Argentine writer Hebe Uhart's *A Question of Belonging: Crónicas*, trans. Anna Vilner (New York: Archipelago, 2024). See also César Aira, *An Episode in the Life of a Landscape Painter*, trans. Chris Andrews (2000; New York: New Directions, 2006), and *How I Became a Nun* (1993; New York: New Directions, 2007), which feature a lightning strike on the pampas, and contaminated strawberry ice cream in remote Coronel Pringles, respectively.

19. Eduardo Fernando Varela, *Patagonia, Route 203*, trans. Peter Bush (1988; London: Mountain Leopard Press, 2024), 1, 7.

20. British-born Walter Moody in Catton, *Luminaries*, finds the antipodean heavens 'upended and unformed' (342–3). Though Catton's novel is structured using Western astrological principles, it is the 'strange' southern night sky that watches over the action.

21. The same depths that the Square Kilometre Array (SKA) radio telescope in the Karoo in the Western Cape and Western Australia now probes and reads. As chapter 2 also noted, some of these patterns were beautifully picked out in the 2017 'Songlines: Tracking the Seven Sisters' exhibition at the National Museum of Australia, Canberra, 15 September 2017–28 February 2018, and the 'Shared Sky', at Iziko, the South African National Gallery, Cape Town, 13 February-31 May 2015. I was privileged to see both exhibitions, and first encountered the Yatjiki Vicki Cullinan painting a few weeks in advance of 'Songlines'. See the exhibition catalogue: Margo Neale, ed., *Songlines: Tracking the Seven Sisters* (Canberra: National Museum of Australia, 2017). Other visual artworks that have been inspiring to think with across the past seven years include Dorrit Black's *Cliffs at Second Valley* (1949), Nyunmiti Burton's *Kangkarangkalpa-Seven Sisters* (2020) (reproduced in this book's colour insert), Naminapu Maymuru-White's *Milngiyawuy/Milky Way* (2004), John D. Moore's *Clouds over Lord Howe Island* (1941), Sidney Nolan's frenetic *Antarctica* (1964), Mungurrawuy Yunupingu's *The Sea and the Sky* (1948), and (also found in the colour insert) Gulumbu Yunupingu's *Ganyu-Stars* (2006), all in the Art Gallery of South Australia; also, from southern Africa, Zimbabwean Barnabus Chiponza's *Tree Flowers* (1945), in which the stars in the background intersperse with floral branches, as well as Johannesburg artist Nolan Oswald Dennis's cartographically charged work representing the planet as freed from the hierarchy of a singular

north-south alignment (fortuitously exhibited in the Zeitz-MOCAA Gallery, Cape Town, October 2024). Thank you to Danielle Battigelli for sharing images of the last two.

22. Horacio Coppola, 'Buenos Aires Fervour', photographs from the Telefónica Collection. Museo Carmen Thyssen, Malaga, 28 March to 10 September 2023. See, for example, *Calle Florida* (1936).

23. Patricio Guzmán, dir., *Nostalgia de la Luz/Nostalgia for the Light* (Icarus Films, 2010). Set in the Atacama, the film oscillates between astronomers' probes of the southern heavens by night, and bereaved women searching through the desert sands by day, looking for the remains of loved ones killed under Pinochet's regime.

24. Davids, *Imperfect Blessing*, 325.

25. Lukashenko, *Too Much Lip*, 7.

26. Lawrence, *Kangaroo*, 93.

27. Christopher Hope, *The Garden of Bad Dreams* (London: Atlantic, 2008), 23.

28. Catton, *Birnam Wood*, 63. See also *The Luminaries* on Australasian light as having a 'thickened' brightness (449).

29. Bessie Head, *A Question of Power* (London: Heinemann, 1986), 30.

30. See my first foray into articulating this sensation in Elleke Boehmer, 'Tales of the Amazing Light Show of Life', *Sunday Times* (South Africa), 15 March 2020, https://www.timeslive.co.za/sunday-times/books/news/2020-03-15-tales--of-the-amazing-light-show-of-life/.

31. My thanks to Meg Samuelson for this observation, made at the 'Farther South' seminar at the University of Adelaide held on 15 February 2018, and further developed in her critical essays including 'An "International Author, but in a Different Sense"', cited above. See also Sidney I. Dobrin, *Blue Ecocriticism and the Oceanic Imperative* (London: Routledge, 2021).

32. Timothy Clark, *Ecocriticism on the Edge: The Anthropocene as a Threshold Concept* (New York: Bloomsbury, 2015), 78, 80.

33. For an expansion on these reflections on crafted objects, see Elleke Boehmer and Katherine Collins, eds, *Life Writing and the Southern Hemisphere* (London: Bloomsbury Academic, 2024), in particular, 13–24.

34. Peers and Brown, *Visiting with the Ancestors*, suggest that crafted indigenous objects offer ways of relating to the lifeways of their makers, even when the communities from which they came may have evanesced.

35. For a startlingly similar evocation, see Varela, *Patagonia*, 11.

36. Tracey Cameron, 'Reviving the Gamilaraay Language', https://slc-events.sydney.edu.au/calendar/reviving-gamilaraay-language-tracey-cameron/. Last accessed 1 October 2023. Huge thanks to Lynda Ng and Susan Poetsch for letting me know about Tracey's course and for putting us in touch, and, most of all, to Tracey for accepting me onto it. True, going online as a non-Indigenous person to learn a language spoken as a mother tongue by only about three hundred or so Indigenous people, continued not always to feel right. Something so precious, so fragile, I often thought, needed people in a room together talking. But Tracey was always very sure that as long as everyone in the group was open to finding out about Gamilaraay cultural ways alongside learning the language, it would be okay. Her certainty, combined with the enthusiasm and welcome of my classmates, who did eventually meet in person, convinced me to stay the distance.

37. The novelist Tara June Winch would agree. She observes that any language serves as a handbook of culture; it explains how kinship works; which feelings count; how to read the stars.

Personal notes, Tara June Winch, *The Yield* Reading and discussion, 'Postcolonial Infrastructure', GAPS 2023 Annual Conference, 18 May 2023. See https://theconversation.com/learning-language-is-part-of-rebuilding-our-nation-singing-the-world-alive-one-first-nations-word-at-a-time-243451. Tara June Winch, reading, 'Postcolonial Infrastructure', GAPS 2023 Annual Conference, University of Konstanz, Germany, 18 May 2023.

38. Hughes-Warrington and Martin, *Big and Little Histories*, 262.

39. D'Arcy Wood, *Land of Wondrous Cold*, 157, 257.

40. Bonnie Roos and Alex Hunt, *Postcolonial Green: Environmental Politics & World Narratives* (Charlottesville: University of Virginia Press, 2010), especially 'Afterword', 256–8. I am grateful to Martha Swift for pointing me to this work.

41. See McCann, *Wild Sea*, 190, 195, 200; Samuelson and Lavery, 'Oceanic South', 37–50, especially 38. The quotation is from Tony Press, a former director of the Australian Antarctic Division, cited by McCann. See also Elleke Boehmer, 'Faraway Close', *London Magazine* (Summer 2020): 32–36.

42. Darran Anderson, 'Apocalypse Now', review of *Notes from an Apocalypse*, by Mark O'Connell, and *The Great Flood*, by Edward Platt, *TLS*, no. 6116 (19 June 2020): 7–8.

43. See Lisa E. Bloom, *Climate Change and the New Polar Aesthetics* (Durham, NC: Duke University Press, 2022), on the sense of mutual responsibility that flows from these multi-scalar recognitions. See also Comyn and Fermanis, *Worlding the South*, on striving to see the world simultaneously from different perspectives, rather than in concentric ways; and Bruce Robbins, *Perpetual War: Cosmopolitanism from the Viewpoint of Violence* (Durham, NC: Duke University Press, 2012), 1–3, on cultivating a flexible commitment to 'varieties of multiple belonging'.

44. The character Anna Wetherell in Catton's *The Luminaries* encounters the same albatross colony on sailing into Otago harbour, watching them 'wheeling, turning, and catching the light' (626). My albatross photograph appears earlier in this book, at the start of chapter 4.

45. Mxolisi Nyezwa, *Bhlawa's Inconsolable Spirits* (Makhanda: Deep South, 2023), 8, 126–7, 148. The heartrending, at once ordinary and yet extraordinary visions of the earth and its oceans assembled in this Gqeberha or Port Elizabeth-set novel bear comparison with the perspective from the space shuttle that Samantha Harvey spotlights in her novel *Orbital* (London: Jonathan Cape, 2024), but they are pitched from hard-won and less privileged positions—namely, from the southern hemisphere. Or, as Nyezwa writes of his poet-protagonist: 'like a ship that has hauled with long ropes over a treacherous sea to a deserted bay, I have been moored to the singular harbour of a township that is inhabited by drowning men' (8). Harvey's 'ascending' and 'descending' views, startling though they are, assume the accepted image of the globe with the North Pole 'at the top'.

46. See again Clingman, *Grammar of Identity*, on fiction as transitive and hence as navigational. Witi Ihimaera speaks relatedly of 'underlying frameworks of knowledge' made up of mythologies, literatures, and history. See Knox, 'Towards our Ancient Futures', 88–93.

47. The quotations in this paragraph are, in order, from Money, 'how to weave a basket'; Hardy, 'Drummer Hodge', 257; and Joseph Conrad, *The Mirror of the Sea*, ch. 12.

48. See Tamson Pietsch and Frances Flanagan, 'Here We Stand: Temporal Thinking in Urgent Times', *Urgent Histories Forum* (11 June 2020): 252–71. Amitav Ghosh, *The Nutmeg's Curse: Parables for a Planet in Crisis* (London: John Murray, 2021), makes a similar argument for how we might conceive the widely ramifying impacts of mistreating the planet, in his case from the vantage point of the Indian Ocean.

BIBLIOGRAPHY

Abulafia, David. *The Boundless Sea: A Human History of the Oceans*. Oxford: Oxford University Press, 2019.

Adams, Terry-Ann. *Those who live in cages*. Johannesburg: Jacana, 2020.

———. *White Chalk*. Johannesburg. Jacana, 2022.

Adebayo, Mojisola. *Moj of the Antarctic: An African Odyssey*. London: Oberon Books, 2011.

Adriaanse, Jaco. *The Metronome: Adamastor City*. Cape Town: Burnt Toast, 2020.

Aira, César. *An Episode in the Life of a Landscape Painter*. Trans. Chris Andrews. New York: New Directions, 2006.

———. *How I Became a Nun*. 1993. Translated by Chris Andrews. New York: New Directions, 2007.

Allen, Phillip. *The Atlas of Atlases*. London: Bounty Books, 2005.

Alonso, Maria, and Maria Jesus Cabarcos Traseira. 'A Legacy of Waste'. *Journal of Postcolonial Writing* 55, no. 2 (April 2019): 147–54.

Alpers, Svetlana. *The Art of Describing: Dutch Art in the Seventeenth Century*. Chicago: University of Chicago Press, 1984.

Amos, Jonathan. 'Endurance: Shackleton's Lost Ship Is Found in Antarctic'. *BBC News*, 9 March 2022. https://www.bbc.com/news/science-environment-60662541.

Anastasios, Meaghan Wilson. *The Pacific in the Wake of Captain Cook*. Sydney: Harper Collins, 2018.

Anderson, Benedict. *Imagined Communities: Reflections on the Origin and Spread of Nationalism*. 1983. 2nd ed. London: Verso, 1991.

Anderson, Darran. 'Apocalypse Now'. Review of *Notes from an Apocalypse*, by Mark O'Connell, and *The Great Flood*, by Edward Platt. *TLS*, no. 6116 (19 June 2020).

Anderson, Warwick. *The Cultivation of Whiteness: Science, Health, and Racial Destiny in Australia*. Durham, NC: Duke University Press, 2006.

Ansolabehere, Pablo. 'Cuentos de la Pampa: Los casos de Alberto Ghiraldo y Benito Lynch', *Anales de Literatura Hispanoamericana* 27 (1998): 89–109.

Araluen, Evelyn. 'Resisting the Institution'. *Overland*, no. 227 (Winter 2017). https://overland.org.au/previous-issues/issue-227/feature-evelyn-araluen/.

Archer-Lean, Clare. 'Transnational Impulses as Simulation in Colin Johnson's (Mudrooroo's) Fiction'. *Transnational Literature* 5, no. 2 (May 2013): 1–12.

Archibald, Jo-Ann, Jenny Lee-Morgan, and Jason De Santolo, eds. *Decolonizing Research: Indigenous Storywork as Methodology*. London: Zed Books, 2019.

Ardener, Edwin. 'Remote Areas: Some Theoretical Considerations', *HAU: Journal of Ethnographic Theory* 2, no. 1 (Spring 2012): 519–33.

Arendt, Hannah. *The Origins of Totalitarianism*. 1951. Reprint. London: Penguin, 2017.

Armitage, David, Alison Bashford, and Sujit Sivasundaram. *Oceanic Histories*. Cambridge: Cambridge University Press, 2017.

Arnold, Naomi. *Southern Nights*. Auckland: HarperCollins, 2019.

Atkin, Lara, Sarah Comyn, Porscha Fermanis, and Nathan Garvey, eds. *Early Public Libraries and Colonial Citizenship in the British Southern Hemisphere*. London: Palgrave Pivot, 2019.

Attridge, Derek. *Moving Words: Forms of English Poetry*. Oxford: Oxford University Press, 2013.

———. '"No Escape from Home": History, Affect and Art in Zoë Wicomb's Translocal Coincidences'. In *Zoë Wicomb and the Translocal*, edited by Kai Easton and Derek Attridge, 49–63. London: Routledge, 2017.

———. 'The South According to Coetzee', *Public Books*, 25 September 2019. https://www.publicbooks.org/the-south-according-to-coetzee.

Attwell, David, and Derek Attridge, eds. *The Cambridge History of South African Literature*. Cambridge: Cambridge University Press, 2012.

Baderoon, Gabeba. *The Dream in the Next Body*. Cape Town: Kwela/Snailpress, 2005.

———. *The History of Intimacy*. Cape Town: Kwela Press, 2018.

———. *Regarding Muslims: From Slavery to Post-Apartheid*. Johannesburg: Wits University Press, 2014.

Badiou, Alain. 'Down with Death!' *Verso* (blog). https://www.versobooks.com/blogs/2176-badiou-down-with-death. Accessed 15 September 2022.

Bainbridge, Beryl. *The Birthday Boys*. London: Abacus, 2009.

Ballantyne, Tony. *Webs of Empire: Locating New Zealand's Colonial Past*. Wellington: Bridget Williams Books, 2012.

Banks, Joseph. *Joseph Banks Florilegium: Botanical Treasures from Cook's First Voyage*. London: Thames & Hudson, 2017.

Barlow, Harriott. 'Vocabulary of Aboriginal Dialects of Queensland'. *The Journal of the Anthropological Institute of Great Britain and Ireland* 2 (1873): 166–175.

Baughan, Blanche E. *Brown Bread from a Colonial Oven*. London: Whitcombe and Tombs, 1912.

———. *Reuben, and Other Poems*. Westminster: Archibald and Constable, 1903.

———. *Shingle-Short and Other Verses*. Christchurch, NZ: Whitcombe and Tombs, 1908.

———. *Studies in New Zealand Scenery*. Christchurch: Whitcombe and Tombs, 1916.

Bayly, Christopher A. *The Birth of the Modern World 1780–1914*. Oxford: Blackwell, 2004.

———. *Imperial Meridian: The British Empire and the World, 1780–1830*. London: Longman, 1989.

BBC Science and Environment. 'Endurance: "Finest Wooden Shipwreck I've Ever Seen"', *BBC News*, 9 March 2022. https://www.bbc.com/news/science-environment-60654016.

Beaver, Harold. Introduction to *Moby-Dick; or, The Whale*, by Herman Melville. Edited by Harold Beaver. London: Penguin Classics, 1986.

Beilharz, Peter. *Thinking the Antipodes: Australian Essays*. Clayton, Victoria: Monash University Publishing, 2015.

Beinart, William, and Saul Dubow. *The Scientific Imagination in South Africa, 1700 to the Present*. Cambridge: Cambridge University Press, 2021.

Belich, James. *Replenishing the Earth: The Settler Revolution and the Rise of the Anglo-World, 1783–1939*. Oxford: Oxford University Press, 2009.

Belich, James, John Darwin, Margret Frenz, and Chris Wickham. *The Prospect of Global History*. Oxford: Oxford University Press, 2016.

Benterrak, Krim, Stephen Muecke, and Paddy Roe. *Reading the Country: Introduction to Nomadology*. Fremantle, WA: Fremantle Arts Centre Press, 1996.

Berndt, Ronald, trans. 'Song Cycle of the Moon-Bone', *Oceania* 19, no. 1 (1948): 1–13.

Bertram, James M. *Capes of China Slide Away: A Memoir of Peace and War, 1910–1980*. Auckland: Auckland University Press, 1993.

———. *Flight of the Phoenix: Critical Notes on New Zealand Writers*. Wellington: Victoria University Press, 1985.

Bethell, Ursula. *Collected Poems*. Edited by Vincent O'Sullivan. Oxford: Oxford University Press, 1985.

Bhambra, Gurminder K., Lucy Mayblin, Kathryn Medien, and Mara Viveros-Vigoya, eds. *The Sage Handbook of Global Sociology*. Thousand Oaks, CA: Sage Publishing, 2024.

Bickel, Lennard. *This Accursed Land*. London: Macmillan, 1977.

Binney, Judith. 'Tuki's Universe'. *New Zealand Journal of History* 38, no. 2 (2004): 215–232.

Birns, Nicholas. 'The Notions of Permanence: Autochthony, Indigeneity, Locality in Alexis Wright's *Carpentaria*'. In *Indigenous Transnationalism*, edited by Lynda Ng, 201–217. Penrith: Giramondo Publishing, 2018.

Birns, Nicholas, and Louis Klee, eds. *The Cambridge Companion to the Australian Novel*. Cambridge: Cambridge University Press, 2023.

Blackburn, Julia. *Dreaming the Karoo: A People Called the |Xam*. London: Jonathan Cape, 2022.

Blackmore, Josiah. *Moorings: Portuguese Expansion and the Writing of Africa*. Minneapolis, MN: University of Minnesota Press, 2009.

———. 'The Shipwrecked Swimmer: Camões's Maritime Subject'. *Modern Philology* 109, no. 3 (2012): 312–25. https://www.jstor.org/stable/10.1086/663280.

Blair, Nerida. *Privileging Australian Indigenous Knowledge: Sweet Potatoes, Spiders, Waterlilys, and Brick Walls*. Champaign, IL: Common Ground Publishing, 2015.

Bleek, Wilhelm, and Lucy Lloyd. *Specimens of Bushman Folklore*. London: George Allen, 1911.

Bloom, Lisa E. *Climate Change and the New Polar Aesthetics*. Durham, NC: Duke University Press, 2022.

Blum, Hester. 'The Prospect of Oceanic Studies'. *Proceedings of the Modern Language Association* 125 (2010): 670–677.

Boehmer, Elleke. *Colonial and Postcolonial Literature: Migrant Metaphors*. 1995. 2nd ed. Oxford: Oxford University Press, 2005.

———. *Empire, the National, and the Postcolonial: Resistance in Interaction*. Oxford: Oxford University Press, 2002.

———, ed. *Empire Writing: An Anthology of Colonial Literature 1870–1918*. Oxford: Oxford University Press, 1998.

———. 'Faraway Close'. *London Magazine* (Summer 2020): 32–6.

———. 'Fellowship and Aversion in the South: The Challenges of South-South Collaboration'. In *Cosmopolitan Cultures and Oceanic Thought*, edited by Nishat Zaidi and Dilip Menon. London: Routledge, 2023.

———. *Indian Arrivals: Networks of British Empire 1870–1915*. Oxford: Oxford University Press, 2015.

———. 'Kaya', *Sharmilla, and Other Portraits*. Johannesburg: Jacana, 2010.

———. 'Migration and the South: J. M. Coetzee's *Jesus* Novels'. *Journal of Modern Literature* 46, no. 2 (Winter 2023): 127–39.

———. *Postcolonial Poetics: 21st-Century Critical Readings*. Basingstoke: Palgrave, 2018.

———. *The Shouting in the Dark*. Johannesburg: Jacana, 2015; Perth: UWA Press, 2019.

———. 'The South in the World'. In *Worlding the South*, edited by Sarah Comyn and Porscha Fermanis, 378–391. Manchester: Manchester University Press, 2021.

———. 'Tales of the Amazing Light Show of Life'. *Sunday Times* (South Africa), 15 March 2020. https://www.timeslive.co.za/sunday-times/books/news/2020-03-15-tales--of-the-amazing-light-show-of-life/.

———. 'Time and Distance'. *Agenda* 35, no. 4 (2021): 99–104.

———. *To the Volcano*. Brighton: Myriad Editions, 2019.

———. 'Wide Wide Sea: A Response to Terence Cave'. *Balzan Lecture Event, Occasional Papers*. University of Bern, 17 October 2014.

Boehmer, Elleke, and Katherine Collins, eds. *Life-Writing and the Southern Hemisphere*. London: Bloomsbury Academic, 2024.

Boer, Nienke. *The Briny South: Displacement and Sentiment in the Indian Ocean World*. Durham, NC and London: Duke University Press, 2023.

Bollig, Ben. 'Here Comes Everybody'. *TLS*, no. 6264 (21 April 2023): 19.

Bond, Sophie, and David Featherstone. 'The Possibilities of a Politics of Place Beyond Place? A Conversation with Doreen Massey'. *Scottish Geographical Journal* 124, nos. 3–4 (2009): 401–20.

Borges, Jorge Luis. *Collected Fictions*. Translated by Andrew Hurley. New York: Penguin, 1998.

———. *Cuentos Completos*. Buenos Aires: Debolsillo, 2018.

———. *Ficciones*. Translated by various. New York: Grove, 1962.

———. 'The Thousand and One Nights'. Translated by Eliot Weinberger. *The Georgia Review* 38, no. 3 (Fall 1984): 564–74.

Bose, Sugata. *A Hundred Horizons: The Indian Ocean in the Age of Global Empire*. Cambridge, MA: Harvard University Press, 2006.

Bound, Mensun. *The Ship Beneath the Ice: The Discovery of Shackleton's* Endurance. London: Macmillan, 2022.

Brandt, Willy. *North-South: A Programme for Survival; Report of the Independent Commission on International Development Issues*. Cambridge, MA: MIT Press, 1980.

Brasch, Charles. *Disputed Ground: Poems 1939–45*. Christchurch: The Caxton Press, 1948.

Bridges, Thomas. *A Dictionary of the Speech of Tierra del Fuego*. Edited by Ferdinand Hestermann and Martin Gusinde. Ushuaia, Argentina: private publication, 1987.

Brink, André P. *Die eerste lewe van Adamastor: 'n novelle*. 1988. Cape Town: Human en Rousseau, 2003.

———. *The First Life of Adamastor*. London: Secker and Warburg, 1993.

———. 'A Myth of Origin'. In *T'Kama—Adamastor: Inventions of Africa in a South African Painting*, edited by Ivan Vladislavic, 41–69. Johannesburg: University of the Witwatersrand Press, 2000.

Bristow-Bovey, Darrel. *Finding Endurance: Shackleton, My Father and a World without End*. Johannesburg and Cape Town: Jonathan Ball, 2023.

Browne, E. Janet. *Charles Darwin: Voyaging*. Princeton: Princeton University Press, 1996.

Brunner, Bernd. *Extreme North: A Cultural History*. Translated by Jefferson Chase. New York: W. W. Norton, 2022.

Brunt, Peter, and Nicholas Thomas, eds. *Oceania*. London: Royal Academy of Arts, 2018.

Buchanan, Susan. *Burchell's Travels*. Cape Town: Penguin Random House, 2015.

Budack, Kuno F. R. 'The ǂAonin or Topnaar of the Lower !Khuseib Valley and the Sea'. *Khoisan Linguistic Studies* 3 (1977): 1–42.

Buell, Lawrence. *The Future of Environmental Criticism: Environmental Crisis and the Literary Imagination*. Oxford: Blackwell, 2005.

Burchell, William John. *Travels in the Interior of Southern Africa*. 1822. 2 vols. London: Hurst, 2010, 2014.

Burton, Antoinette. '"The Sea's Watery Volume"'. In *Reading from the South: African Print Cultures and Oceanic Turns in Isabel Hofmeyr's Work*, edited by Charne Lavery and Sarah Nuttall, 148–158. Johannesburg: Wits University Press, 2023.

Burton, Antoinette, and Isabel Hofmeyr, eds. Introduction to *Ten Books That Shaped the British Empire: Creating an Imperial Commons*. Durham, NC: Duke University Press, 2014.

Butler, Guy. *Collected Poems*. Cape Town: David Philip, 1999.

Byron, Commodore John. *An Account of a Voyage around the World in the Years 1764–66*. 1773. Vol. 1 of *An Account of the Voyages undertaken by the Order of His Present Majesty for Making Discoveries in the Southern Hemisphere*. Edited by John Hawkesworth. Cambridge: Cambridge University Press, 2013.

Caesar, Adrian. *The White: Last Days in the Antarctic*. London: Macmillan, 2001.

Cameron, Tracey. 'Reviving the Gamilaraay Language'. https://slc-events.sydney.edu.au/calendar/reviving-gamilaraay-language-tracey-cameron/ (page no longer available).

Camões, Luíz Vaz de. *The Lusíads*. Translated by Landeg White. Oxford: Oxford University Press, 2008.

Campbell, Nancy. *The Library of Ice: Readings from a Cold Climate*. London: Scribner, 2018.

Campbell, Roy. *Adamastor*. London: Faber, 1930.

Canclini, Nestor Garcia. *Imagined Globalization*. Translated by George Yúdice. Durham, NC: Duke University Press, 2014.

Carey, Peter. *Theft*. London: Faber, 2006.

Carlston, Erin, Matthew Hayward, and Brian Reed. 'Modernisms: Aotearoa New Zealand-Australia-Fiji, 1926–1986'. *Modernist Cultures* 15, no. 3 (2020): 263–75.

Carter, David. *Dispossession, Dreams and Diversity: Issues in Australian Studies*. Frenchs Forest, Australia: Pearson Education, 2006.

Carter, Paul. 'Australinda: The Geography of Imperial Desire'. *Postcolonial Studies* 18 (2015): 222–33.

———. *The Road to Botany Bay*. London: Faber and Faber, 1987.

Carroll, Siobhan. *An Empire of Air and Water: Uncolonizable Space in the British Imagination, 1750–1850*. Philadelphia: University of Pennsylvania Press, 2015.

Casanova, Pascale. *The World Republic of Letters*. Translated M. B. Debevoise. Cambridge, MA: Harvard University Press, 2004.

Cassano, Franco. *Southern Thought and other Essays on the Mediterranean*. Ed. and trans. Norma Bouchard and Valerio Ferme. New York: Fordham University Press, 2012.

Castellanos, Bianet, Lourdes Gutiérrez Nájera, and Arturo Aldama, eds. *Comparative Indigeneities of the Américas: Toward a Hemispheric Approach*. Tucson: University of Arizona Press, 2012.

Catton, Eleanor. *Birnam Wood*. London: Granta, 2023.

———. *The Luminaries*. London: Granta, 2013.

Cave, Terence. *Thinking with Literature: Towards a Cognitive Criticism*. Oxford: Oxford University Press, 2016.

Cave, Terence, and Deirdre Wilson, eds. *Reading beyond the Code*. Oxford: Oxford University Press, 2018.

Čerče, Danica. 'Jeanine Leane's Counter-Reading of Australian Historical and Cultural Memory Locally and Internationally'. *Journal of Postcolonial Writing* 58, no. 1 (2022): 65–79.

Césaire, Aimé. *Discourse on Colonialism*. Translated by Joan Pinkham. 1950. New York: Monthly Review Press, 2000.

Chakrabarty, Dipesh. *The Climate of History in a Planetary Age*. Chicago: Chicago University Press, 2021.

———. *Provincializing Europe*. Princeton: Princeton University Press, 2000.

Chambers, Neil, ed. *The Letters of Sir Joseph Banks: A Selection, 1768–1820*. London: Imperial College Press, 2000.

Chatwin, Bruce. *In Patagonia*. London: Vintage, 2005.

———. *The Songlines*. London: Jonathan Cape, 1987.

Chaudhuri, K. N. *Trade and Civilisation in the Indian Ocean: An Economic History from the Rise of Islam to 1750*. Cambridge: Cambridge University Press, 1985.

Cheah, Pheng. *What is a World? On Postcolonial Literature as World Literature*. Durham, NC: Duke University Press, 2016.

Cherry-Garrard, Apsley. *The Worst Journey in the World*. London: Constable, 1922.

Child, Theodore. *A Peculiar People: The Australians in Paraguay*. Sydney: Sydney University Press, 1968.

———. *The South American Republics*. New York: Harper & Brothers, 1891.

Chomsky, Noam. *Hegemony or Survival: America's Quest for Global Dominance*. 2003; London: Penguin, 2023.

Christiansë, Yvette. *Castaway*. Durham, NC: Duke University Press, 1999.

———. *Imprendehora*. Cape Town: Kwela Books/Snailpress, 2009.

Church, Hubert. 'Spring in Maoriland'. In *New Zealand Rhymes Old and New*, edited by Jessie Mackay, 100. Christchurch, NZ: Whitcombe and Tombs, 1908.

Clark, Timothy. *The Cambridge Introduction to Literature and the Environment*. Cambridge: Cambridge University Press, 2011.

———. *Ecocriticism on the Edge: The Anthropocene as a Threshold*. Concept. New York: Bloomsbury, 2015.

———. 'Towards a Deconstructive Environmental Criticism'. *Oxford Literary Review* 30, no. 1 (2008): 45–68.

Cleary, E. J. 'Vindicated: The Ongoing Relevance of Mary Wollstonecraft and Her Celebrated Daughter'. *TLS*, no. 6110 (8 May 2020).

Clifford, James. 'The Others: Beyond the "Salvage" Paradigm', *Third Text* 3 (1989): 73–8.

———. *Returns: Becoming Indigenous in the Twenty-First Century*. Cambridge, MA: Harvard University Press, 2013.

Clingman, Stephen. *The Grammar of Identity*. Oxford: Oxford University Press, 2009.

Coetzee, J. M. 'Australia's Shame'. *The New York Review of Books*, 26 September 2019. https://www.nybooks.com/articles/2019/09/26/australias-shame/.

———. *The Childhood of Jesus*. London: Secker, 2013.

———. *The Death of Jesus*. London: Secker, 2019.

———. *Elizabeth Costello*. London: Secker, 2003.

———. *51 Poetas: Antología íntima*. Edited by María Soledad Costantini. Buenos Aires: El Hilo de Ariadna, 2015.

———. *The Schooldays of Jesus*. London: Secker, 2016.

———. *White Writing: On the Culture of Letters in South Africa*. New Haven, CT: Yale University Press, 1988.

Coleridge, Samuel Taylor. *The Rime of the Ancient Mariner*. In *Coleridge's Poetry and Prose*, edited by Nicholas Halmi, Paul Magnuson, and Raimonda Modiano. New York: W. W. Norton, 2004.

Collett, Anne, and Dorothy Jones. 'Portrait of the Artist as a Young Colonial Girl: Emily Carr and Judith Wright'. *The Journal of Commonwealth Literature* 44, no. 3 (2009): 51–67.

Comaroff, Jean, and John L. Comaroff. *Theory from the South: Or, How Euro-America Is Evolving Toward Africa*. Boulder: Paradigm Publishers, 2011.

Comyn, Sarah, and Fermanis, Porscha, eds. 'Rethinking Nineteenth-century Literary Culture: British Worlds, Southern Latitudes, and Hemispheric Methods'. *Journal of Commonwealth Literature* 58, no. 2 (2023): 409–26.

———. *Worlding the South: Nineteenth-Century Literary Culture and the Southern Settler Colonies*. Manchester: Manchester University Press, 2021.

Connell, Raewyn. *Southern Theory: The Global Dynamics of Knowledge in Social Science*. Sydney: Allen and Unwin, 2007.

Conneller, Chantal, Paul Pettitt, and Alistair Pike. 'Cave Art'. *In Our Time*. Hosted by Melvyn Bragg. BBC Radio 4, 24 September 2020.

Connolly, Michael. 'Munda-gutta Kulliwari Project'. *Yaraan-doo—Southern Cross* (2024). https://www.kullillaart.com.au/dreamtime-stories/The-Southern-Cross-Yaraan-doo-The-place-of-the-white-gum-tree.

Conrad, Joseph. *The Mirror of the Sea*. London: J. M. Dent and Sons, 1949.

———. *The N—of the 'Narcissus'*. 1897; London: Penguin, 1987.

Cook, James. *The Journals*. Ed. Philip Edwards, after J. C. Beaglehole. London: The Hakluyt Society and Penguin, 2003.

Cooper, Frederick, and A. Laura Stoler, eds. *Tensions of Empire: Colonial Cultures in a Bourgeois World*. Oakland: University of California Press, 1997.

Coppola, Horacio. 'Buenos Aires Fervour'. Photographs from the Telefónica Collection. Museo Carmen Thyssen, Malaga, 28 March to 10 September 2023.

Couto, Mia. *Sleepwalking Land* (*Terra Sonambula*). Translated David Brookshaw. London: Serpent's Tale, 2006.

Curnow, Allen. *Collected Poems, 1933–1973*. Wellington: A. H. & A. W. Reed, 1974.

———. *Continuum: New and Later Poems 1972–1988*. Auckland: Auckland University Press, 1988.

———. *Early Days Yet: New and Collected Poems, 1941–1997*. Auckland: Auckland University Press, 1997.

———. *Look Back Harder: Critical Writings 1935–1984*. Ed. Peter Simpson. Auckland: Auckland University Press, 1987.

Curry, Arwen, dir. *The Worlds of Ursula K. Le Guin*, Java Films. Aired 17 November 2019.

Dalrymple, Alexander. *Historical Collection of the Several Voyages and Discoveries in the South Pacific Ocean*. Cambridge: Cambridge University Press, 2015.

Damrosch, David. *What is World Literature?* Princeton: Princeton University Press, 2003.

Dana, Richard Henry. *Two Years Before the Mast*. New York: Harper and Brothers, 1840.

D'Arcy Wood, Gillen. *Land of Wondrous Cold: The Race to Discover Antarctica and Unlock the Secrets of Its Ice*. Princeton: Princeton University Press, 2020.

Darwin, Charles. *The Origin of Species*. 1859. London: Penguin, 1985.

———. *The Origin of Species and The Voyage of the* Beagle. London: Vintage, 2009.

Davids, Nadia. *An Imperfect Blessing*. Cape Town: Umuzi, 2014.

Davidson, Peter. *The Idea of North*. London: Reaktion Books, 2005.

Davies, Archie. 'Unwrapping the OXO Cube: Josué de Castro and the Intellectual History of Metabolism'. *Annals of the American Association of Geographers* 109 (2019): 837–56.

Davies, Iva, songwriter. 'Great Southern Land'. Genius.com, track 1 on IceHouse, *Primitive Man*. Chrysalis, 1982. https://genius.com/Icehouse-great-southern-land-lyrics.

Day, David. *Antarctica: A Biography*. Oxford: Oxford University Press, 2012.

Dean, Andrew. *Metafiction and the Postwar Novel*. Oxford: Oxford University Press, 2021.

———. 'Nationalism, Modernism, and New Zealand'. *Journal of New Zealand Literature* 38, no. 1 (2020): 8–25.

De Ercilla y Zúñiga, Alonso. *La Araucana*. Ed. Luis María Gómez Canseco. Madrid: Real Academia Española, 2022.

———. *The Araucaniad: A Version in English Poetry*. 1945. Translated Charles Maxwell Lancaster and Paul Manchester. Nashville, TN: Vanderbilt University Press, 2014.

Delgado, L. Elena, and Rolando J. Romero. 'Local Histories and Global Designs: An interview with Walter Mignolo'. *Imperial Discourses* 22, no. 3 (2000): 7–33.

DeLoughrey, Elizabeth, Jill Didur, and Anthony Carrigan, eds. *Global Ecologies and the Environmental Humanities: Postcolonial Approaches*. New York: Routledge, 2015.

———. *Routes and Roots: Navigating Caribbean and Pacific Island Literatures*. Honolulu: University of Hawaii Press, 2009.

DeLoughrey, Elizabeth, and Tatania Flores. 'Submerged Bodies: The Tidalectics of Representability and the Sea in Caribbean Art'. *Environmental Humanities* 12, no. 1 (2020): 132–166.

DeLoughrey, Elizabeth, and George B. Handley. *Postcolonial Ecologies: Literature of the Environment*. Oxford: Oxford University Press, 2011.

Deluermoz, Quentin, and Pierre Singaravélou. *A Past of Possibilities: A History of What Could Have Been*. New Haven: Yale University Press, 2021.

Derrida, Jacques. 'Telepathy'. Translated by Nicholas Royle. *Oxford Literary Review* 19 (1988).

De Sousa Santos, Boaventura, ed. *Another Knowledge Is Possible: Beyond Northern Epistemologies*. London: Verso, 2007.

———. *The End of the Cognitive Empire: The Coming of Age of Epistemologies of the South*. Durham: Duke University Press, 2018.

———. *Epistemologies of the South: Justice against Epistemicide*. London: Routledge, 2016.

Dening, Greg. *Mr Bligh's Bad Language: Passion, Power, and Theatre on the* ***Bounty***. Cambridge: Cambridge University Press, 1992.

Dhlomo, H. I. E. *Valley of a Thousand Hills*. Edited by C. L. Brokensha. Durban: Daily News Press, 1962.

Diamond, Jared. *Collapse: How Societies Choose to Fail or Succeed*. New York and London: Vintage, 2005.

———. *Guns, Germs, and Steel: The Fates of Human Society*. London: Vintage, 1998.

Diaz, Vicente M., and J. Kehaulani Kauanui. 'Native Pacific Cultural Studies on the Edge'. *The Contemporary Pacific* 13, no. 2 (2001): 315–42.

Dickens, Charles. *Dombey and Son*. London: Penguin, 2008.

Diski, Jenny. *Skating to Antarctica*. London: Granta, 1997.

Dobrin, Sidney I. *Blue Ecocriticism and the Oceanic Imperative*. London, Routledge 2021.

Dodds, Klaus. *The Antarctic*. VSI series. Oxford: Oxford University Press, 2012.

———. 'Awkward Antarctic Nationalism: Bodies, Ice Cores and Gateways in and beyond Australian Antarctic Territory/ East Antarctica'. *Polar Record* 53 (2017). 16–30.

———. 'Reflecting on the 60th Anniversary of the Antarctic Treaty'. *Polar Record* 55 (2019): 311–316.

Dodds, Klaus, and Mark Nuttall. *The Scramble for the Poles*. Cambridge: Polity, 1984.

Dooley, Gillian, and Danielle Clode, eds. *The First Wave: Exploring Early Coastal Contact History in Australia*. Adelaide: The Wakefield Press, 2019.

Dowdeswell, Julian, and Michael Hambrey. *The Continent of Antarctica*. Winterbourne, Berkshire: Papadakis, 2018.

Dowling, Fionuala. *Okay, Okay, Okay*. Cape Town: Kwela Press, 2019.

Driver, Dorothy. 'Olive Schreiner's *From Man to Man* and "the Copy Within"'. In *Changing the Victorian Subject*. Eds. Maggie Tonkin, Mandy Treagus, Madeleine Seys, and Sharon Crozier-De Rosa, 123–150. Adelaide: University of Adelaide, 2014. https://www.jstor.org/stable/10.20851/j.ctt1t305b6.10.

Drummond, Ali Jimmy. 'Our Languages Are a Tool to Understanding Our Ways of Knowing And Being'. *The Guardian*, 19 November 2019.

Dubow, Saul. 'How British was the British World? The Case of South Africa'. *The Journal of Imperial and Commonwealth History* 37 (2009): 1–27.

Duckor-Jones, Avi. *Swim*. Sydney: Brio Books, 2018.

Duffy, Cian. *The Landscapes of the Sublime 1700–1830: Classic Ground*. Basingstoke: Palgrave Macmillan, 2013.

Dunk, Jonathan. 'Reading the Tracker: The Antimonies of Aboriginal Ventriloquism'. *Journal of the Association for the Study of Australian Literature* 17 (2017): 1–12.

Du Plessis, Menán. *Kora: A Lost Khoisan Language of the Early Cape and the Gariep*. Pretoria: UNISA Press, 2019.

Edmonds, Penelope, and Amanda Nettelbeck, eds. *Intimacies of Violence in the Settler Colony: Economies of Dispossession around the Pacific Rim*. New York: Springer-Palgrave Macmillan, 2018.

Ehret, Christopher. *History and the Testimony of Language*. Berkeley: University of California Press, 2011.

Eisler, William. *The Furthest Shore: Images of Terra Australis from the Middle Ages to Captain Cook*. Cambridge: Cambridge University Press, 1995.

Engelbrecht, Beth and Willie. *The Lost Tales of the Meerkat National Park: Karoo Farmlands and Their Stories*. Cape Town: Tourism Blueprint, 2023.

Escallón, Eduardo. *El Cielo al Revés*. Bogotá: Ediciones Uniandes, 2019.

Esty, Jed. 'The Colonial Bildungsroman: *The Story of an African Farm* and the Ghost of Goethe'. *Victorian Studies* 49, no. 3 (2007): 407–430.

Evans, Nicholas. *Dying Words: Endangered Languages and What They Have to Tell Us*. Oxford: Blackwell, 2010.

Fabian, Johannes. *Time and the Other: How Anthropology Makes its Object*. New York: Columbia University Press, 1983.

Fairburn, A. R. D. *Strange Rendezvous: Poems 1929–1941*. Dunedin: Renaissance Books, 1952.

Fanon, Frantz. *Black Skin, White Masks*. 1952; London: Pluto Press, 1986.

Farrell, Michael, *Writing Australian Unsettlement: Modes of Poetic Invention 1796–1945*. New York: Palgrave Macmillan, 2015.

Felski, Rita. *The Limits of Critique*. Chicago: University of Chicago Press, 2015.

Ferrus, Diana. 'Afterword: My naam is Februarie'. In *From No Return: The 221-Year Journey of the Slave Ship São José, 1794*. By Jaco Jacques Boshoff, Stephen C. Lubkemann, Lonnie G. Bunch, and Paul Gardullo. Washington D.C.: National Museum of African American History and Culture, 2016.

———. *Onskomvandaan*. Cape Town: Diana Ferrus Uitgewery, 2005.

———. 'My Name is February'. *New Agenda: South African Journal of Social and Economic Policy* 96, no. 1 (2025). https://doi.org/10.14426/na.v96i1.2785.

Festa, Lynn. *Sentimental Figures of Empire in Eighteenth-Century Britain and France*. Baltimore: John Hopkins University Press, 2006.

Fiddian-Qasmiyeh, Elena, and Patricia Daley, eds. *Routledge Handbook of South-South Relations*. London: Routledge, 2020.

Field, Barron. *First Fruits of Australian Poetry*. Sydney: George Howe, 1819.

———. *Kangaroo and Other Poems*. Sydney: University of Sydney, 1998.

Fishburn, Evelyn. 'Traces of *The Thousand and One Nights* in Borges'. *Middle Eastern Literatures* 7, no. 2 (2014): 213–22.

Flanagan, Richard. *Gould's Book of Fish*. London: Atlantic, 2002.

———. *The Narrow Road to the Deep North*. London: Chatto and Windus, 2013.

———. *Question 7*. London: Chatto and Windus, 2023.

Flannery, Nancy Robinson, ed. *This Everlasting Silence: The Love Letters of Paquita Delprat and Douglas Mawson*. Melbourne: Melbourne University Press, 2000.

Flinders, Matthew. *Australia Circumnavigated: The Voyage of Matthew Flinders in HMS Investigator*. Ed. Kenneth Morgan. Abingdon-on-Thames: Routledge, 2015.

———. *A Voyage to Terra Australis*. 1814. 2 vols. Cambridge: Cambridge University Press, 2010.

Flint, Holly. 'White Talk, White Writing: New Contexts for Examining Genre and Identity in J. M. Coetzee's *Foe*', *Literature, Interpretation, Theory* 22, no. 4 (2011): 336–53.

Flyn, Cal. 'Both Real and Imaginary'. *TLS*, no. 6209 (1 April 2022).

Flynn, Eugenia. 'Beyond Cultural Difference: Australian Indigenous Literary and Creative Writing Practices As Sites of Knowledge Production', unpublished paper. Postcolonial and World literature seminar. English Faculty, Oxford. 29 November 2024.

Ford, Mark. *Thomas Hardy: Half a Londoner*. London: The Belknap Press of Harvard University Press, 2016.

Fowke, Robert. *The Real Ancient Mariner: Pirates and Poesy on the South Sea*. Bishop's Castle: Travelbrief Publications, 2010.

Frame, Janet. *Faces in the Water*. Auckland: George Braziller, 1982.

———. *Owls Do Cry*. Melbourne: Text Publishing, 2014.

———. *To the Is-land*. London: The Women's Press, 1983.

———. *Towards Another Summer*. 2007. London: Virago, 2008.

Franzen, Jonathan. *The End of the End of the Earth*. New York: Farrar, Straus, Giroux, 2018.

Fresno-Calleja, Paloma and Janet M. Wilson, eds. *New Zealand and the Globalization of Culture. Special Issue: Journal of Postcolonial Writing* 56, no. 2 (2020): 85–92.

Frost, Lola. 'Going South: Traversal and Attunement in Painting'. *GeoHumanities* 1, no. 2 (2015): 1–11.

———. *Life-Force: Catalogue 2021*. https://www.lolafrost.net/going-south-exhibition.html

Frye, Northrop. *The Bush Garden: Essays on the Canadian Imagination*. Toronto: Anansi, 1971.

Fullagar, Kate. *The Savage Visit: New World People and Popular Imperial Culture in Britain 1710–1795*. Berkeley: University of California Press, 2012.

———. *The Warrior, the Voyager and the Artist: Three Lives in an Age of Empire*. New Haven: Yale University Press, 2020.

Fuller, Robert, Michelle Trudgett, and Ray Norris. 'The Emu Sky Knowledge of the Kamilaroi and Euahlayi Peoples'. *Journal of Astronomical History and Heritage* 17, no. 2 (2014): 171–79. https://doi.org/10.3724/SP.J.1440-2807.2014.02.04.

Furphy, Joseph. *Such is Life: Being Certain Extracts from the Life of Tom Collins*. 1903. Sydney: Angus and Robertson, 1956.

Galeano, Eduardo, *Open Veins of Latin America: Five Centuries of the Pillage of a Continent*. Translated by Cedric Belfrage. New York: Monthly Review Press, 1997.

Gamble, Clive. *Origins and Revolutions: Human Identity in Earliest Prehistory*. Cambridge: Cambridge University Press, 2007.

Garcia, Edgar. *Signs of the Americas—A Poetics of Pictography, Hieroglyphs, and Khipu*. Chicago: Chicago University Press, 2020.

Garner, Helen. *The Feel of Steel*. London: Picador, 2001.

———. *Regions of Thick-Ribbed Ice*. Melbourne: Black Inc. Short Blacks, 2015.

Gascoigne, John. 'Cross-Cultural Knowledge Exchange in the Age of the Enlightenment'. *Indigenous Intermediaries: New Perspectives on Exploration Archives*. Edited by Shino Konishi, Maria Nugent and Tiffany Shellam, 131–146. Canberra: ANU Press, 2015.

Gates, Eunice Joiner. 'Charles Darwin and Benito Lynch's *El Inglés de los Güesos*'. *Hispania* 44, no. 2 (1961): 250–53.

Ghiselin, Michael T. *The Triumph of the Darwinian Method*. Berkeley: University of California Press, 1969.

Ghosh, Amitav, *The Great Derangement: Climate Change and the Unthinkable*. London: Allen Lane, 2016.

———. *The Nutmeg's Curse: Parables for a Planet in Crisis*. London: John Murray, 2021.

Gibson, Ross. *26 Views of the Starburst World: William Dawes at Sydney Cove 1788–91*. Crawley, WA: University of Western Australia Publishing, 2012.

Gikandi, Simon. *Maps of Englishness: Writing Identity in the Culture of Colonialism*. New York: Columbia University Press, 1996.

Gildea, Robert. *Empires of the Mind: The Colonial Past and the Politics of the Present*. Cambridge: Cambridge University Press, 2019.

Giles, Paul. *Antipodean America: Australasia and the Constitution of U. S. Literature*. Oxford: Oxford University Press, 2014.

Glissant, Édouard. *Poetics of Relation*. Translated by Betsy Wing. Ann Arbor, MI: Michigan University Press, 1997.

Godelier, Maurice. *The Imagined, the Imaginary and the Symbolic*. London: Verso, 2020.

Goldie, Matthew Boyd. *The Idea of the Antipodes: Place, People and Voices*. London and New York: Routledge, 2010.

Goldie, Terry. *Fear and Temptation: The Image of the Indigene in Canadian, Australian, and New Zealand Literatures*. Montreal and Kingston: McGill-Queens University Press, 1989.

Gorst, Harold E. *Farthest South: An Account of the Startling Discovery Made by the Wise Antarctic Expedition*. London: Greening & Co. Ltd., 1900.

Grabouw, Johanna. 'Haunting the Wide, White Page–Ghosts in Antarctica'. In *Ghosts—or the (Nearly) Invisible: Spectral Phenomena in Literature and the Media*, edited by Maria Fleischhack and Elmar Schenkel, 125–36. Frankfurt: Peter Lang, 2016.

Griffiths, Billy. *Deep Time Dreaming: Uncovering Ancient Australia*. Melbourne: Black Inc., 2018.

Griffiths, Tom. *Slicing the Silence: Voyaging to Antarctica*. Boston: Harvard University Press, 2007.

Guenther, Mattias. 'Dreams and Stories'. In *Courage of ||kabbo: Celebrating the 100th Anniversary of the Publication of* Specimens of Bushman Folklore, edited by Janette Deacon and Pippa Skotnes, 196–210. University of Cape Town Press, 2014.

Gulberg, Steven, Duane Hamacher, Alejandro Martin López, Javier Mejuto, Andrew Munro, and Wayne Orchiston. 'A Comparison of Dark Constellations of the Milky Way'. *Archaeological Reports* 23, no. 2 (July 2019): 390–404. https://doi.org/10.3724/SP.J.1440-2807.2020.02.10.

Gunn, Kirsty. 'Stories That Simply Unfold'. Review of *All Sorts of Lives: Katherine Mansfield and the Art of Risking Everything*, by Claire Harman. *TLS*, no. 6249 (6 January 2023).

Gunn, Kirsty, and Merran Gunn. *Going Bush*. Paris: The American University of Paris Press, 2016.

Gupta, Pamila, Isabel Hofmeyr, and Michael Pearson, eds. *Eyes across the Water: Navigating the Indian Ocean*. Pretoria: UNISA Press, 2010.

Guzmán, Patricio, dir. *Nostalgia de la Luz/Nostalgia for the Light*. Icarus Films, 2010.

Haacke, Wilfrid and Eliphas Eiseb. *A Khoekhoegowab Dictionary*. Windhoek: Gamsberg Macmillan, 2002.

Hadot, Pierre. *The Veil of Isis: An Essay on the History of the Idea*. Cambridge, MA: Harvard University Press, 2008.

Haggard, Henry Rider. *Mary of Marion Isle*. Oxford: Benediction Classics, 2010.

Halford, James. 'Southern Conversations: J. M. Coetzee in Buenos Aires'. *Sydney Review of Books*, 28 February 2017, https://sydneyreviewofbooks.com/essay/southern-conversations-j-m-coetzee-in-buenos-aires.

Halliday, Thomas. *Otherlands: A World in the Making*. London: Allen Lane, 2022.

Halmi, Nicholas, Paul Magnuson, and Raimonda Modiano, eds. *Coleridge's Poetry and Prose*. New York: W. W. Norton, 2004.

Hamacher, Duane. *The First Astronomers: How Indigenous Elders Read the Stars*. Sydney: Allen and Unwin, 2022.

Hamilton, James C. *Captain James Cook and the Search for Antarctica*. Huddersfield: Pen and Sword Books, 2020.

Handley, George B. 'Derek Walcott's Poetics of the Environment in *The Bounty*'. *Callaloo* 28, no. 1 (Winter 2005): 201–15.

———. *New World Poetics: Nature and the Adamic Imagination of Whitman, Neruda, and Walcott*. Atlanta: Georgia University Press, 2007.

Hardcastle, Sophie. *Below Deck*. Sydney: Allen and Unwin, 2020.

Hardy, Thomas. *A Pair of Blue Eyes*. Eds. Tim Dolin and Alan Manford. Oxford: Oxford University Press, 2009.

———. *Selected Poems*. Edited by David Wright. London: Penguin, 1978.

———. *Two on a Tower: A Romance*. London: Sampson Low, 1882.

Harman, Claire. *All Sorts of Lives: Katherine Mansfield and the Art of Risking Everything*. London: Chatto and Windus, 2023.

Harris, Alexandra. 'Disaster in the Antarctic'. Review of *Lean Fall Stand*, by Jon McGregor. *The Guardian Review*, 15 May 2021.

Hart, Jonathan. *Comparing Empires: European Colonialism from Portuguese Expansion to the Spanish-American War*. New York: Palgrave Macmillan, 2003.

Hartman, Saidiya. *Lose Your Mother: A Journey Along the Atlantic Slave Route*. London: Serpent's Tail, 2021.

Hau'ofa, Epeli. 'Epilogue: Pasts to Remember'. In *Remembrance of Pacific Pasts: An Invitation to Remake History*, edited by Robert Borofsky, 453–472. Honolulu: University of Hawai'i Press, 2000.

———. 'Our Sea of Islands'. In *A New Oceania: Rediscovering Our Sea of Islands*, edited by Eric Waddell, Vijay Naidu, and Epeli Hau'ofa, 2–16. Suva: University of the South Pacific, 1993.

———. *We Are the Ocean: Selected Works*. Honolulu: University of Hawai'i Press, 2008.

Hawkesworth, John, ed. *An Account of the Voyages Undertaken by the Order of His Present Majesty for Making Discoveries in the Southern Hemisphere*. 1773. Cambridge: Cambridge University Press, 2014.

Hayot, Eric. *On Literary Worlds*. Oxford: Oxford University Press, 2012.

Head, Bessie. *A Question of Power*. London: Heinemann, 1986.

Headland, Robert Keith. 'A Chronology of Antarctic Exploration: A Synopsis of Events and Activities from the Earliest Times until the International Polar Years 2007–09', *Polar Record* 46 (2010).

Heimert, Alan. '*Moby-Dick* and American Political Symbolism'. *American Quarterly* 15, no. 4 (1963): 498–534.

Helgerson, Richard. *Forms of Nationhood*. Chicago: University of Chicago Press, 1994.

Herbert, Kari. *Heart of the Hero: The Remarkable Women who Inspired the Great Polar Explorers*. Glasgow: Saraband, 2013.

Herwitz, Daniel. 'History on White Linen'. In *T'Kama—Adamastor: Inventions of Africa in a South African Painting*, edited by Ivan Vladislavic, 71–81. Johannesburg: University of the Witwatersrand Press, 2000.

Herzog, Werner, writer and director. *Nomad: In the Footsteps of Bruce Chatwin*. BBC documentary (2019).

Hessell, Nikki. *Romantic Literature and the Colonised World: Lessons from Indigenous Translations*. Basingstoke: Palgrave Macmillan, 2018.

Hiatt, Alfred. *Terra Incognita: Mapping the Antipodes Before 1600*. Chicago: University of Chicago Press, 2008.

Hilliard, Christopher. 'Rough Architects': New Zealand Literature and Its Institutions from *Phoenix* to *Landfall*'. In *A History of New Zealand Literature*, edited by Mark Williams, 138–152. Cambridge: Cambridge University Press, 2016.

Hitchcock, Peter. *The Long Space: Transnationalism and Postcolonial Form*. Stanford: Stanford University Press, 2010.

Hoare, Phillip. *Leviathan, or the Whale*. London: Fourth Estate, 2009.

Hoare, Philip, with Angela Cockayne and Sarah Chapman. 'Into the Deep'. *The Guardian Review*, 25 April 2020.

Hobsbawm, Eric. *The Age of Capital 1848–1875*. London: Little, Brown, 1988.

———. *The Age of Empire 1975–1914*. London: Cardinal, 1987.

Hobsbawm, Eric, and Terence Ranger, eds. *The Invention of Tradition*. Cambridge: Cambridge University Press, 2012.

Hofmeyr, Isabel. 'African History and Global Studies: A View from South Africa'. *Journal of African History* 54, no. 3 (2013): 341–9.

———. *Dockside Reading*. Johannesburg: Wits University Press, 2022.

———. *Gandhi's Printing Press: Experiments in Slow Reading*. Cambridge, MA: Harvard University Press, 2013.

———. 'Southern by Degrees: Islands and Empires in the South Atlantic, the Indian Ocean, and the Sub-Antarctic World'. In *The Global South Atlantic*, edited by Kerry Bystrom and Joseph R. Slaughter. New York: Fordham University Press, 2018.

Hofmeyr, Isabel, and Charne Lavery. 'Reading in Antarctica'. *Wasafiri* 36, no. 2 (2021): 79–86.

Holland, Robert. *The Warm South: How the Mediterranean Shaped the British Imagination.* New Haven: Yale University Press, 2018.

Holmes, Richard. *The Age of Wonder: How the Romantic Generation Discovered the Beauty and Terror of Science.* London: Harper Press, 2009.

Hope, A. D. *Collected Poems: 1930–1970.* 1939. Sydney: Angus & Robertson, 1972.

Hope, Christopher. *The Garden of Bad Dreams.* London: Atlantic, 2008.

Horrocks, Ingrid. 'A World of Waters: Imagining, Voyaging, Entanglement'. In *A History of New Zealand Literature*, edited by Mark Williams, 17–30. Cambridge: Cambridge University Press, 2016.

Hosking, Susan, Rick Hosking, Rebecca Pannell and Nena Bierbaum, eds. *Something Rich and Strange: Sea Changes, Beaches and the Littoral in the Antipodes.* Adelaide: Wakefield Press, 2009.

Huggan, Graham. 'Greening White'. *Journal of Postcolonial Writing* 58, no. 1 (2022): 21–35.

Hughes-D'Aeth, Tony. 'Judith Wright, an Activist Poet who was ahead of her time'. *The Conversation*, 2 May 2022.

Hughes-Warrington, Marnie, and Anne Martin. *Big and Little Histories: Sizing up Ethics in Historiography.* Abingdon: Taylor and Francis, 2021.

Hutcheson, John C. *The Wreck of the Nancy Bell; or, Cast Away on Kerguelen Land.* London: Black and Son, 1885.

Hyde, Robin. *The Godwits Fly.* 1928. Auckland: Auckland University Press, 2001.

———. *Houses by the Sea and the Later Poems of Robin Hyde.* Edited by Gloria Rawlinson. Christchurch: The Caxton Press, 1952.

———. *Wednesday's Children.* 1937. Auckland: New Women's Press, 1989.

Ihimaera, Witi. *The Whale Rider.* Rosedale: Penguin Group NZ, 2008.

Iqani, Mehita, and Fernando Resende. *Media and the Global South: Narrative Territorialities, Cross-Cultural Currents.* London: Routledge, 2019.

Jackson, A. B. 'The Polar Sublime in Contemporary Poetry of Arctic and Antarctic exploration'. PhD diss., Sheffield Hallam University (2015). https://www.proquest.com/dissertations-theses/polar-sublime-contemporary-poetry-arctic/docview/1973936945/se-2.

Jackson, Jeanne-Marie. *The African Novel of Ideas.* Princeton: Princeton University Press, 2021.

Jacob, Christian. *The Sovereign Map: Theoretical Approaches in Cartography throughout History.* Edited by Edward H. Dahl. Translated by Tom Conley. Chicago: University of Chicago Press, 2006.

James, C.L.R. *Mariners, Renegades and Castaways: The Story of Herman Melville and the World We Live In.* Lebanon, NH: Dartmouth College Press, 2001.

JanMohamed, Abdul, and David Lloyd, eds. *The Nature and Context of Minority Discourse.* New York: Oxford University Press, 1990.

Jauss, Hans Robert. *Toward an Aesthetic of Reception.* Translated by Timothy Bahti. Minneapolis: University of Minnesota Press, 1982.

Jennings, Karen, *An Island.* Cape Town: Karavan Press, 2021.

Johnson, David. *Dreaming of Freedom in South Africa.* Edinburgh: Edinburgh University Press, 2020.

———. *Imagining the Cape Colony.* Edinburgh: Edinburgh University Press, 2012.

Johnston, Anna. '"The Aboriginal Mother": Poetry and Politics', in *Remembering the Myall Creek Massacre.* Eds. Jane Lydon and Lyndall Ryan. Sydney: New South Publishing, 2018.

———. *Missionary Writing and Empire, 1800–1860*. Cambridge: Cambridge University Press, 2003.

———. '"That's white fellow's talk you know, missis": Wordlists, Songs, and Knowledge Production on the Colonial Australian Frontier'. In *Worlding the South*, edited by Sarah Comyn and Porscha Fermanis, 273–293. Manchester: Manchester University Press, 2021.

Jones, Gail. *Sorry*. Sydney: Vintage, 2007.

Jordan, Bobby. 'Island Mouse Plague', *Sunday Times (South Africa)*. *Insight* supplement (23 February 2020).

Jose, Nicholas. 'Alexis Wright in Conversation with Nicholas Jose'. *Signposts* 1 (2020).

Joseph, Confidence. 'The Representation of Water Spirits in Southern African Literature'. In *Life Writing and the Southern Hemisphere*, edited by Elleke Boehmer and Katherine Collins, 145–56. London: Bloomsbury Academic, 2024.

Kamfer, Ronelda. *Chinatown: Gedigte*. Cape Town: Kwela Boeke, 201.

Keegan, Claire. *Antarctica*. London: Faber, 1999.

Kennedy, Roseanne. 'Indigenous Australian Arts of Return: Mediating Perverse Archives', *Rites of Return: Diaspora Poetics and the Politics of Memory*. Edited by Marianne Hirsch and Nancy K. Miller. New York: Columbia University Press, 2011.

Kerr, Donald. *Amassing Treasures for All Times: Sir George Grey, Colonial Bookman and Collector*. Dunedin: Otago University Press, 2006.

King, Michael. *The Penguin History of New Zealand*. Auckland: Penguin, 2003.

———. *Wrestling with the Angel: A Life of Janet Frame*. Auckland: Penguin Books NZ, 2000.

King, Phillip Parker, and Robert FitzRoy. *Narrative of the Surveying Voyages of His Majesty's Ships* Adventure *and* Beagle *in between the Years 1826 and 1836, Describing Their Examination of the Southern Shores of South America, and the Beagle's Circumnavigation of the Globe*. Vol. 1 of *Proceedings of the First Expedition, 1826–30, under the Command of Captain P. Parker King, R.N., F.R.S.* London: Henry Colburn, 1839.

Kirch, Patrick Vinton. *On the Road of the Winds: An Archaeological History of the Pacific Islands before European Contact*. Berkeley: University of California Press, 2000.

Knox, Anna. 'Towards our Ancient Futures: An Interview with Witi Ihimaera'. *Wasafiri* 115 (Autumn 2023): 86–93.

Kohn, Eduardo. *How Forests Think: Toward an Anthropology Beyond the Human*. Berkeley: University of California Press, 2013.

Kopf, Alicia. *Brother in Ice*. Translated by Mara Faye Lethem. Sheffield: And Other Stories, 2018.

Koram, Kojo. *Uncommon Wealth: Britain and the Aftermath of Empire*. London: John Murray, 2022.

Krog, Antjie, *Body Bereft/Veweerskrif*. Cape Town: Umuzi Press, 2011.

———. *die sterre sê 'tsau'*. Cape Town: Kwela, 2004.

———. *the stars say 'tsau': /xam poetry of Dia!kwain, Kweiten-ta-//ken, /a!kúnta, /han‡kass'o and //kabbo*. Cape Town: Kwela Press, 2004.

Kuper, Simon. 'Is This New Zealand's Chance to Become the Place to Do Business?' *Financial Times* (30 April 2020). https://www.ft.com/content/24411500-8906-11ea-a01c-a28a3e3fbd33.

Laera, Alejandra, and Javier Villa, eds. *Una Historia de la Imaginación en la Argentina*. Buenos Aires: Museo de Arte Moderno, 2019.

Lane, Heather, Naomi Boneham, and Robert D. Smith, eds. *The Last Letters: The British Antarctic Expedition 1910–13*. Cambridge: Scott Polar Research Institute, 2012.

Langton, Marcia. 'Aboriginal Art and Film: The Politics of Representation'. In *Blacklines: Contemporary Critical Writing by Indigenous Australians*, edited by Michèle Grossman, 109–124. Melbourne: Melbourne University Press, 2003.

Lansing, Alfred. *Endurance: Shackleton's Incredible Voyage*. London: Weidenfeld and Nicolson, 2000.

Laseron, Charles. *South with Mawson: Reminiscences of the Australasian Antarctic Expedition, 1911–1914*. London: G. G. Harrap, 1947.

Latour, Bruno. *Down to Earth: Politics in the New Climatic Regime*. Cambridge: Polity, 2019.

Lavery, Charne. 'Antarctica and Africa: Narrating Alternate Futures'. *Polar Record* 42, no. 3 (2019): 217–27.

———. 'Diving into the Slave Wreck: The *São José Paquete d'Africa* and Yvette Christiansë's *Imprendehora*'. *Eastern African Literary and Cultural Studies* 6, no. 4 (2020): 269–83.

———. 'Thinking from the Southern Ocean'. In *Sustaining Seas: Oceanic Space and the Politics of Care*, edited by Elspeth Probyn, Kate Johnston, and Nancy Lee, 307–318. London: Rowman & Littlefield, 2020.

Lavery, Charne, and Nuttall, Sarah, eds. *Reading from the South: African Print Cultures and Oceanic Turns in Isabel Hofmeyr's Work*. Johannesburg: Wits University Press, 2023.

Lawrence, Basil. *At the Edge of the Desert*. Johannesburg: Penguin, 2021.

Lawrence, D. H. *Collected Letters*, vol. 4. Edited by Warren Roberts et al. Cambridge: Cambridge University Press, 2002.

———. *Kangaroo*. 1923. London: Penguin, 1950.

———. *Kangaroo*. Edited by Bruce Steele. London: Penguin, 1997.

Lawrence, D. H., and M. L. Skinner. *The Boy in the Bush*. Edited by Paul Eggert. Cambridge: Cambridge University Press, 2002.

Lawson, Henry. *Stories and Sketches*. Vol. 1 of *Collected Prose*, edited by Colin Roderick. Sydney: Angus and Robertson, 1972.

Leane, Elizabeth. *Antarctica in Fiction: Imaginative Narratives of the Far South*. Cambridge: Cambridge University Press, 2012.

Leane, Elizabeth, and Stephanie Pfennigwerth. 'Antarctica in the Australian Imagination'. *Polar Record* 38, no. 207 (2002): 309–12.

Leane, Jeanine. 'Another Story'. In *Research Methodologies for Auto/biography Studies*. Edited by Kate Douglas and Ashley Barnwell, 125–31. New York and London: Routledge, 2019.

———. 'Gathering: The Politics of Memory and Contemporary Aboriginal Women's Writing'. *Antipodes* 31, no. 2 (2017): 242–51.

———. *Purple Threads*. St. Lucia: University of Queensland Press, 2011.

Leask, Nigel. 'Darwin's Second Sun: Alexander von Humboldt and the Genesis of *The Voyage of the Beagle*'. In *Literature, Science and Psychoanalysis, 1830–1970: Essays in Honour of Dame Gillian Beer*, edited by Helen Small and Trudi Tait, 13–36. Oxford: Oxford University Press, 2003.

Lee, Debbie. 'Listening to the Land: The Selway-Bitterroot Wilderness as Oral History'. *The Oral History Review*, 37, no. 2 (2010): 235–48.

Le Guin, Ursula. *The Left Hand of Darkness*. 1969. London: Gollancz, 2018.

Lester, Alan, and David Lambert. *Colonial Lives across the British Empire*. Cambridge: Cambridge University Press, 2006.

Lester, Alan, and Nikita Vanderbyl. 'The Restructuring of the British Empire and the Colonization of Australia, 1832–8'. *History Workshop Journal* 90 (18 September 2020): 165–88.

Levasseur, Jennifer, and Kevin Rabalais. 'An Interview with Bill Manhire'. *The Free Library*, accessed 4 October 2022. https://www.thefreelibrary.com/An+interview+with+Bill+Manhire.-a0114488300.

Levine, George. *Darwin and the Novelists: Patterns of Science in Victorian Fiction*. Cambridge, MA: Harvard University Press, 1988.

Ley, Charles David, ed. *Portuguese Voyages, 1498–1663*. London: Phoenix Press, 2000.

Liboiron, Max. *Pollution is Colonialism*. Durham, NC: Duke University Press, 2021.

Lomb, Nick. *Transit of Venus, 1631 to the Present*. New York: The Experiment, 2012.

López, Alejandro Martin, and Sixto Benítez. 'The Milky Way and its Structuring Function in the Worldview of the Mocoví of Gran Chaco'. *Archaeologica Baltica* 10/*Astronomy and Cosmology in Folk Traditions and Cultural Heritage* 10 (2008): 21–24. https://e-journals.ku.lt/journal/AB/article/1243/info.

Lopez, Barry. *Arctic Dreams*. 1986. London: Vintage, 2014.

———. *Horizon*. London: The Bodley Head, 2019.

———. 'Love in a Time of Terror: On Natural Landscapes, Metaphorical Living, and Warlpiri Identity'. *Lithub* (7 August 2020).

Lovecraft, Howard Phillips. *At the Mountains of Madness and Other Tales of Terror*. 1936; New York: Del Rey, 2007.

Lowes, John Livingston. *The Road to Xanadu: A Study in the Ways of the Imagination*, 2nd rev. ed. 1927; London: John Constable, 1951.

Lukashenko, Melissa. *Too Much Lip*. St Lucia: University of Queensland Press, 2018.

Lynch, Benito. *De los campos portenõs*. Buenos Aires: Ediciones Troquel, 1966.

———. *El Inglés de los Güesos*. 1924. La Coruna: Ediciones del Viento, 2008.

Lynch, Paul, *Beyond the Sea*. London: OneWorld, 2019.

Mackay, Jessie, ed. *New Zealand Rhymes Old and New*. Christchurch: Whitcombe and Tombs, 1908.

Mac Sweeney, Naoise. *The West: A New History of an Old Idea*. London: W. H. Allen, 2023.

Malouf, David. 'Born to be Nomads'. Review of *Songlines*, by Bruce Chatwin. *TLS*, no. 6106 (10 April 2020).

Manenzhe, Resoketswe. *Scatterlings*. Johannesburg: Jacana, 2020.

Manhire, Bill. *Collected Poems*. Wellington: Victoria University Press, 2001.

———. 'Cream Torpedoes: Recent Poetry in New Zealand', *World Literature Today* 85, no. 5 (September/October 2011).

———. 'Interview: Bill Manhire', *Flash Frontier: An Adventure in Short Fiction*, December 2018. https://flashfrontier.com/interview-bill-manhire.

Manhire, Bill, ed. *The Wide White Page: Writers Imagine Antarctica*. Wellington: Victoria University Press, 2004.

Mansfield, Katherine. *The Aloe*. Edited by Vincent O'Sullivan. Introduction by Kirsty Gunn. London: Capuchin Classics, 2010.

———. *Collected Short Stories*. Edited by Gerri Kimber. Edinburgh: Edinburgh University Press, 2017.

———. *Selected Stories*. Oxford World's Classics. Edited by Angela Smith. Oxford: Oxford University Press, 2002.

Mar, Tracey Banivanua, and Nadia Rhook. 'Counter Networks of Empires: Reading Unexpected People in Unexpected Places'. *Journal of Colonialism and Colonial History* 19, no. 2 (2018).

Markwell, Carol. *Enough Horizon: The Life and Work of Blanche Baughan*. Wellington: Cuba Press, 2021.

Marsh, Selina Tusitala. 'Making It Niu': Blacking Out of Albert Wendt's *Pouliuli* the Tusitala Way'. In *Contemporary Revolutions: Turning Back to the Future in 21st-Century Literature and Art*, edited by Susan Stanford Friedman, 71–102. London: Bloomsbury Academic, 2018.

Marshall, Peter J. *The Making and Unmaking of Empires: Britain, India and America c. 1750–1783*. Oxford: Oxford University Press, 2005.

Marshall, Tim. *Prisoners of Geography*. London: Elliot and Thompson, 2015.

Martín López, Alejandro. 'Las Pléyades, el sol y el ciclo anual entre los mocovíes'/'The Pleaides, the Sun and the Annual Cycle Among the Mocovíes'. Translated by Cristóbal Pérez Barra and Elleke Boehmer. Unpublished paper (2019/2020).

Massey, Doreen. *For Space*. Los Angeles: SAGE Publications, 2005.

Massmann, Stefanie. 'Alonso de Ercilla's *La Araucana* and Pedro de Oña's *Arauco domado* in the National Imaginary'. In *A History of Chilean Literature*, edited by Ignacio López-Calvo, translated by Javiera Sepúlveda Salas, 43–60. Cambridge: Cambridge University Press, 2021.

Mathiot, Madeleine. *Ethnolinguistics: Boas, Sapir and Whorf Revisited*. The Hague: Mouton, 1979.

Mathur, Nayanika. *Paper Tiger: Law, Bureaucracy and the Developmental State in Himalayan India*. Cambridge: Cambridge University Press, 2015.

Mawson, Douglas. *The Home of the Blizzard: A True Story of Antarctic Survival*. New York: St. Martin's Press, 1999.

———. Mawson Papers, Series 4. Special Collections, Barr Smith Library, University of Adelaide.

Mbembe, Achille. *On the Postcolony*. Trans. Janet Roitman and Murray Last. Berkeley: University of California Press, 2001.

McCann, Joy. *Wild Sea: A History of the Southern Oceans*. Chicago: University of Chicago Press, 2019.

McClintock, Anne. *Imperial Leather: Race, Gender and Sexuality in the Colonial Contest*. New York: Routledge, 1995.

McDermott, David. *Whiteness in Zimbabwe: Race, Landscape and the Problem of Belonging*. New York: Palgrave Macmillan, 2010.

McEwin, Emma. *An Antarctic Affair*. Bowden SA: East Street Publications, 2008.

McGrath, Ann, and Mary Anne Jebb, eds. *Long History, Deep Time: Deepening Histories of Place*. Canberra: ANU Press, 2015.

McGrath, Ann, Laura Rademaker, and Jakeline Troy, eds. *Everywhen: Australia and the Language of Deep History*. Lincoln: University of Nebraska Press, 2023.

McGregor, Jon. *Lean Fall Stand*. London: 4th Estate, 2021.

McKittrick, Katherine. *Dear Science and Other Stories*. Durham, NC: Duke University Press, 2021, 17–19.

McLaughlin, Raoul. *Rome and the Distant East: Trade Routes to the Ancient Lands of Arabia, India and China*. London: Continuum, 2010.

McNamara, Nathan Scott. 'Emergency Lights Blinking'. *Los Angeles Review of Books*, 31 January 2019.

Mda, Zakes. *The Whale Caller*. Johannesburg: Penguin, 2006.

Melville, Herman. *Moby-Dick; or, The Whale*. Edited by Harold Beaver. 1851. London: Penguin Classics, 1986.

Menely, Tobias, and Jesse Oak Taylor, eds. *Anthropocene Reading: Literary History in Geologic Times*. University Park: Pennsylvania State University Press, 2017.

Menon, Dilip. *Changing Theory: Concepts from the Global South*. New York: Routledge, 2022.

Mercer, Erin. *Telling the Real Story: Genre and New Zealand Literature*. Wellington: Victoria University Press, 2017.

Mignolo, Walter D., and Catherine E. Walsh, *On Decoloniality: Concepts, Analytics, Praxis*. Durham and London: Duke University Press, 2018.

Minter, Peter. 'Rubbish Places, Islands of Junk'. In *Indigenous Transnationalism*, edited by Lynda Ng, 186–207. Penrith: Giramondo Publishing, 2018.

Mitchell, J. Lawrence. '"Not the Kind to Die": Katherine Mansfield and the Unquiet Ghost of "Little Brother"'. In *Katherine Mansfield and Virginia Woolf*, edited by Gerri Kimber, Todd Martin, and Christine Froula, 179–196. Edinburgh: Edinburgh University Press, 2018.

Money, Jazz. 'bila, a river cycle'. In *how to make a basket*. Brisbane: University of Queensland Press, 2021.

———. 'bila, a river cycle'. TEDxSydney. 30 August 2022. YouTube TEDx Talks video, 8:05. https://www.youtube.com/watch?v=8Z8eHNx8wKs.

———. *how to make a basket*. Brisbane: University of Queensland Press, 2021.

Monteiro, George. *The Presence of Camões: Influences on the Literature of England, America, and Southern Africa*. Lexington: University Press of Kentucky, 1996.

Moore, Peter. Endeavour: *The Ship and Attitude that Changed the World*. London: Penguin 2018.

Moretti, Franco. *Atlas of the European Novel, 1800–1900*. London and New York: Verso, 1998.

Moro, Simonetta. 'Mapping Practices and the Cartographic Imagination'. *Subjectivity* 13, no. 4 (2020): 298–314.

Morris, Paula. *Rangatira: A Novel*. Auckland: Penguin, 2011.

Morrison, Toni. 'The Site of Memory'. In *Inventing the Truth: The Art and Craft of Memoir*. Edited by William Zinsser, 83–102. Boston, NY: Houghton Mifflin, 1995.

Mudrooroo [Colin Johnson]. *Doctor Wooreddy's Prescription for Enduring the Ending of the World*. Melbourne: Hyland House, 1998.

Mukherjee, Pablo. 'Consider the Whale'. Review of *Colonialism, Culture, Whales: The Cetacean Quartet* by Graham Huggan. *Journal of Postcolonial Writing* 58, no. 2 (2002): 265–68.

Mulgrew, Nick. *Hibiscus Coast*. Cape Town: Karavan Press, 2021.

Mundy, Robyn. *The Nature of Ice*. Sydney: Allen and Unwin, 2009.

Murnane, Gerald. *The Plains*. Ringwood, Victoria: Penguin Books Australia, 1984.

———. 'The Battle of Acosta Nu'. In *Landscape with Landscape*, by Gerald Murnane, 71–122. Ringwood: Penguin, 1987.

———. *Velvet Waters*. South Yarra: McPhee Gribble, 1990.

Murra, John. *The Economic Organization of the Inca State*. Chicago: University of Chicago Press, 1968.

Murray, Les. 'The Buladelah-Taree Holiday Song Cycle'. *Learning Human*. New York: Farrar, Straus, Giroux, 1998.

Neale, Margo. 'First Knowledges: An Introduction'. In *Astronomy: Sky Country*, edited by Karlie Noon and Krystal De Napoli, 1–9. Melbourne: Thames and Hudson Australia, 2023.

———. 'On the Spot', *History Today*, November 2021.

———. *Songlines: Tracking the Seven Sisters*. Canberra: National Museum of Australia, 2017.

Nelson, Peggy. 'Shackleton: A Twitter Novel', accessed 26 September 2022. https://eshackleton.com/2015/07/20/what-the-ice-gets-the-ice-keeps/.

Neruda, Pablo. *Canto General*. 50th Anniversary Edition. Translated by Jack Schmitt. Berkeley: University of California Press, 2000.

———. *Cuándo de Chile*. Santiago: Editorial Universitaria, 1952.

———. *Veinte poemas de amor y una canción desesperada*. Santiago: Editorial Nascimento, 1924.

Newton, John. 'Colonialism above the Snowline: Baughan, Ruskin and the South Island Myth'. *The Journal of Commonwealth Literature* 34, no. 2 (1999): 85–96.

———. *Hard Frost: Structures of Feeling in New Zealand Literature*. Wellington: Victoria University Press, 2018.

Nicol, Mike. 'The City I Live In'. In *A City Imagined*, edited by Stephen Watson, 45–54. Johannesburg: Penguin, 2005.

Nilson, Caroline. 'A Journey Towards Cultural Competence: The Role of Research Reflexivity in Indigenous Research'. *Journal of Transcultural Nursing* 28, no. 2 (2017): 119–27. https://doi.org/10.1177/1043659616642825.

Noon, Karlie, and Krystal De Napoli. *Astronomy: Sky Country*. Melbourne: Thames and Hudson Australia, 2023.

Nussbaum, Martha. *Justice for Animals: Our Contemporary Responsibility*. New York: Simon and Schuster, 2023.

Nuttall, Sarah. *Entanglement: Literary and Cultural Reflections on Post-Apartheid*. Johannesburg: Wits University Press, 2008.

Nyezwa, Mxolisi. *Bhlawa's Inconsolable Spirits*. Makhanda: Deep South, 2023.

O'Brien, Karen. '*Frankenstein* by Mary Shelley'. *Ten-Minute Book Club*, accessed 14 October 2020. https://www.english.ox.ac.uk/ten-minute-book-club/shelley-frankenstein.

Orsman, Chris. *South*. London: Faber and Faber, 1999.

O'Sullivan, Vincent. Introduction to *Collected Poems*, by Ursula Bethell. Edited by Vincent O'Sullivan, x–xxiii. Wellington: Victoria University Press, 1985.

O'Sullivan, Vincent, and Margaret Scott, eds. *The Collected Letters of Katherine Mansfield*. Oxford: Oxford University Press, 2008.

Oswald, Alice, ed. *The Thunder Mutters—101 Poems for the Planet*. London: Faber, 2006.

Otto, Peter. 'Making, Mapping, and Unmaking Worlds'. In *Worlding the South*, edited by Sarah Comyn and Porscha Fermanis, 39–57. Manchester: Manchester University Press, 2021.

Padrón, Ricardo. *The Indies of the Setting Sun: How Early Modern China mapped the Far East as the Transpacific West*. Chicago: University of Chicago Press, 2020.

———. *The Spacious Word: Cartography, Literature, and Empire in Early Modern Spain*. Chicago: University of Chicago Press, 2004.

Pagden, Anthony. *Lords of All the World: Ideologies of Empire in Spain, Britain and France c. 1500–1800*. New Haven: Yale University Press, 1995.

Pardo, Cecilia, and Jago Cooper. *Peru: A Journey in Time*. London: British Museum, 2021.

Parker, Katherine A. 'Contentious Waters: The Creation of Pacific Geographic Knowledge in Britain, 1669–1768'. PhD diss., University of Pittsburgh, 2016.

Parkington, John, David Morris, and Jose M. de Prada-Samper. 'Elusive Identities: Karoo |xam Descendants and the Square Kilometre Array'. *JSAS* 45, no. 4 (2019): 729–47.

———. *Karoo Cosmos: |xam-ka !au and the |xam*. Cape Town: South African Astronomical Observatory, 2021.

Parkinson, Sydney. *A Journal of a Voyage to the South Seas, in His Majesty's Ship, the* Endeavour. London: Stansfield Parkinson, 1773.

Parsons, Cóilín. 'Planetary Parallax: *Ulysses*, the Stars, and South Africa'. *Modernism/Modernity* 24, no. 1 (2017): 67–85

Pascoe, Bruce. *Dark Emu: Black Seeds: Agriculture or Accident?* Broome: Magabala Books, 2013.

Paterson, Alistair. *Africa: ||kabbo, Mantis and the Porcupine's Daughter*. Auckland: Puriri Press, 2008.

Patterson, Luke. 'Culture in the Making (a Walk and Talk)'. Review of *how to make a basket*, by Jazz Money. *Sydney Review of Books*, 8 February 2022. https://sydneyreviewofbooks.com/review/money-how-to-make-a-basket/.

Pearce, Joseph. *Bloomsbury and Beyond: The Friends and Enemies of Roy Campbell*. London: Harper UK, 2001.

Peers, Laura, and Alison K. Brown. *Visiting with the Ancestors: Blackfoot Shirts in Museum Spaces*. Athabasca: Athabasca University Press, 2016.

Pellar, Brian R. Moby-Dick *and Melville's Anti-Slavery Allegory*. Chapel Hill, NC: Palgrave MacMillan, 2017.

Petzold, Jochen. 'André Brink's Magical History Tour: Postmodern and Postcolonial Influences in *The First Life of Adamastor*'. *English in Africa* 27, no. 2 (2000): 45–58.

Pflederer, Richard L. *Catalogue of the Portolan Charts and Atlases in the Bodleian Library*. Oxford: Bodleian Library, 2008.

Pietsch, Tamson, and Frances Flanagan. 'Here We Stand: Temporal Thinking in Urgent Times'. *Urgent Histories Forum* (11 June 2020): 252–71.

Pilkington, Adrian. *Poetic Effects*. Amsterdam: John Benjamins, 2000.

Phillips, A. A. 'The Cultural Cringe'. *Meanjin* 9, no. 5 (Summer 1950): 299–302.

Phillips, Tom. 'Refreshment Units'. *TLS*, no. 6115 (12 June 2020): 28.

Plaatje, Solomon T. *Mhudi*. 1930. London: Heinemann, 1970.

Poe, Edgar Allan. *The Narrative of Arthur Gordon Pym of Nantucket, and Related Tales*. Ed. J. Gerald Kennedy. 1893; Oxford: Oxford University Press, 2008.

Pothecary, Sarah, trans. *Strabo's Geography*. Princeton and Oxford: Princeton University Press, 2024.

Pratt, Mary Louise. *Imperial Eyes: Travel Writing and Transculturation*. London: Routledge, 1992.

Prebisch, Raúl. *Towards a Dynamic Development Policy for Latin America*. New York: United Nations, 1963.

Prentice, Chris. 'Grounding Postcolonial Fictions: Cultural Constituencies, Cultural Credentials and Uncanny Questions of Authority'. *SPAN* 36, no. 1–2 (1992): 100–112.

Prichard, Katharine Susannah. *Coonardoo*. Sydney: Angus and Robertson, 1956.

Priestley, Rebecca. *Dispatches from Continent Seven: An Anthology of Antarctic Science*. Wellington: Awa Press, 2016.

Ptolemy, Claudius, *Geographia*. New York: NY Public Library, 1932.

Puchner, Martin. *Literature for a Changing Planet*. Oxford and Princeton: Princeton University Press, 2022.

Pugh, Jonathan. 'Island Movements: Thinking with the Archipelago'. *Island Studies Journal* 8 (2013): 9–24.

Pynchon, Thomas. *Mason & Dixon*. New York: Vintage Classics, 1998.

Pyne, Stephen. *The Ice: A Journey to Antarctica*. London: Arlington Books, 1986.

Quint, David. *Epic and Empire: Politics and Generic Form from Virgil to Milton*. Princeton, NJ: Princeton University Press, 1993.

Radhakrishnan, R. *Theory in an Uneven World*. Malden, MA: Blackwell, 2003.

Raimondi, Sergio. *Lexikón*. Buenos Aires: Mansalva, 2023.

Ramazani, Jahan. *A Transnational Poetics*. Chicago: Chicago University Press, 2009.

———. *Poetry in a Global Age*. Chicago: Chicago University Press, 2020.

Rapoport, Amos. *The Meaning of the Built Environment: A Nonverbal Communication Approach*. London: Sage, 1982.

Read, Peter. *Belonging: Australians, Place and Aboriginal Ownership*. Melbourne: Cambridge University Press, 2000.

Reeder, Jessie. *The Forms of Informal Empire*. Baltimore: John Hopkins University, 2020.

Reeves, William Pember. *New Zealand and Other Poems*. London: Grant Richards, 1898.

———. *The Passing of the Forest and Other Verse*. Sydney: Allen and Unwin, 1925.

Rifkin, Mark. *Beyond Settler Time: Temporal Sovereignty and Indigenous Self-Determination*. Durham: Duke University Press, 2017.

Robbins, Bruce. *Perpetual War: Cosmopolitanism from the Viewpoint of Violence*. Durham: Duke University Press, 2012.

Roberts, Peder, Lize-Marié van der Watt and Adrian Howkins, eds. *Antarctica and the Humanities*. London: Palgrave Macmillan, 2016.

Robinson, Zandria F., ed. 'The Imaginary South'. Special issue: *Southern Cultures* 26, no. 4 (Winter 2020).

Rodoreda, Geoffrey. *The Mabo Turn in Australian Fiction*. Oxford: Peter Lang, 2018.

Rodríguez-Salas, Gerardo. 'New Zealand or Nowheresville: Nation and Community in Janet Frame's *Living in the Maniototo*'. *Antipodes* 30, no. 2 (December 2016): 280–293.

Roos, Bonnie, and Alex Hunt. *Postcolonial Green: Environmental Politics and World Narratives*. Charlottesville: University of Virginia Press, 2010.

Rose, Deborah Bird. *Nourishing Terrains: Australian Aboriginal Views of Landscape and Wilderness*. Canberra: Australian Heritage Commission, 1996.

Ross, Corey. *Liquid Empire: Water and Power in the Colonial World*. Princeton and Oxford: Princeton University Press, 2024.

Rowland, Lucy. 'Indigenous Temporality and Climate Change in Alexis Wright's *Carpentaria*'. *Journal of Postcolonial Writing* 55, no. 4 (2019): 541–554.

Rudy, Jason R. *Imagined Homelands: British Poetry in the Colonies*. Baltimore: John Hopkins University Press, 2017.

Rudy, Jason, Aaron Bartlett, Lindsey O'Neil, and Justin Thompson. 'Australia to Paraguay'. In *Worlding the South: Nineteenth-century Literary Culture and the Southern Settler Colonies*, edited by Sarah Comyn and Porscha Fermanis, 139–158. Manchester: Manchester University Press, 2021.

Russell-Wood, A. J. R. *The Portuguese Empire, 1415–1808: A World on the Move*. Baltimore: Johns Hopkins University Press, 1998.

Said, Edward. *Culture and Imperialism*. London: Jonathan Cape, 1993.

———. *Orientalism*. New York: Vintage, 1978.

Salesa, Damon Ieremia. *Racial Crossings: Race, Intermarriage, and the Victorian British Empire*. Oxford: Oxford University Press, 2011.

Salmond, Anne. 'Reimagining the Ocean'. In *Oceania*, edited by Peter Brunt and Nicholas Thomas, 42–55. London: Royal Academy of the Arts, 2018.

———. *Tears of Rangi: Experiments across Worlds*. Auckland: Auckland University Press, 2017.

———. *Two Worlds: First Meetings between Maori and Europeans, 1642–1772*. Auckland: Viking Press, 1991.

Samin, Richard. 'The Myth of Adamastor: The Ambivalent Metaphor of Otherness in South African Literature'. *Commonwealth Essays and Studies* 29, no. 1 (2006): 59–69.

Samuelson, Meg. 'An "International Author, but in a Different Sense": J. M. Coetzee and "Literatures of the South"'. *Thesis Eleven* 162, no. 1 (2021): 137–54.

———. '"Re-Enchanting the World" from Mozambique: The African Anthropocene and Mia Couto's Poetics of the Planet'. In *Transcultural Ecocriticism: Global, Romantic and Decolonial Perspectives*, edited by Stuart Cooke and Peter Denney, 63–81. London: Bloomsbury Academic, 2021.

———. 'Rendering the Cape-as-Port: Sea-Mountain, Cape of Storms/Good Hope, Adamastor and Local-World Literary Formations'. *Journal of Southern African Studies* 42, no. 3 (2016): 523–37.

———. 'Thinking the Anthropocene South'. *Contemporary Literature* 61, no. 4 (2020): 537–49.

———. 'Yvette Christiansë's Oceanic Genealogies and the Colonial Archive', *Eastern African Literary and Cultural Studies* 1, no. 1–2 (2014): 27–38. https://doi.org/10.1080/23277408.2014.941751.

Samuelson, Meg, and Charne Lavery. 'The Oceanic South'. *English Language Notes* 57, no. 1 (2019): 37–50.

Sanjal, Sanjeev. *The Ocean of Churn*. Gurgaon: Penguin Random House, 2016.

Sargeson, Frank. 'Olive Schreiner'. In *Conversation in a Train and Other Critical Writing*, edited by Kevin Cunningham, 99–112. Auckland: Auckland University Press, 1983.

Satchell, William. *The Land of the Lost*. 1902. Edited by Kendrick Smithyman. Auckland: Oxford University Press, 1985.

Schell, Patience A. *The Sociable Sciences: Darwin and His Contemporaries in Chile*. Basingstoke: Palgrave Macmillan, 2013.

Schramm, Jan-Melissa. '"I feel I am a man and a free man too": Palawa Voices and the Ethics of Representation in Contemporary Tasmanian Fiction'. *Journal of Postcolonial Writing* 58, no. 1 (2022): 36–50.

Schreiner, Olive. *From Man to Man, or Perhaps, Only*. London: Fisher Unwin, 1926.

———. *From Man to Man, or Perhaps, Only*. Edited by Dorothy Driver. Cape Town: UCT Press, 2018.

———. *The Story of an African Farm*. Oxford: Oxford University Press, 1986.

———. *Thoughts on South Africa*. New York: F. A. Stokes, 1923.

Schulz, Raimund. *To the Ends of the Earth: How Ancient Conquerors, Explorers, Scientists, and Traders Conquered the World.* Oxford: Oxford University Press, 2024.

Schweblin, Samanta. *Fever Dream* (*Distancia de rescate*). Translated by Megan McDowell. London: OneWorld, 2017.

———. *Mouthful of Birds* (*Pájaros en la boca*). Translated by Megan McDowell. London: OneWorld, 2019.

Scobie, Ruth. *Celebrity Culture and the Myth of Oceania in Britain.* Woodbridge: The Boydell Press, 2019.

Scott, Anne M., Alfred Hiatt, Claire McIlroy, and Christopher Wortham, eds. *European Perceptions of Terra Australis.* Abingdon: Routledge, 2017.

Scott, Kim. *That Deadman Dance.* Sydney: Picador, 2010.

Scott, Margaret, ed. *The Katherine Mansfield Notebooks.* Vol. 2. Canterbury: Lincoln University Press, 1997.

Scott, Robert Falcon. *Journals: Captain Scott's Last Expedition.* Oxford: Oxford University Press, 2006.

———. et al. *The Last Letters: The British Antarctic Expedition 1910–13.* Cambridge: Scott Polar Research Institute, 2012.

Seaver, Georg. *Edward Wilson of the Antarctic: Naturalist and Friend: Together with a Memoir of Oriana Wilson.* London: J. Murray, 1963.

Sedivy, Julia. *Memory Speaks.* Cambridge, MA: Harvard University Press, 2021.

Senatore, María Ximena. 'Antártida Como Narrativa'. *Vestigios: Revista Latino-Americana de Arqueologia Historica* 5, no. 2 (2011): 161–84.

———. 'Things in Antarctica. An Archaeological Perspective'. *The Polar Journal* 10, no. 2, (2020): 397–419.

Sewell, W. A. 'Why Our Authors Leave Home'. *New Zealand Herald* (Supplement), 13 March 1937.

Shackleton, Ernest, *South: The* Endurance *Expedition.* London: Penguin Random House, 2002.

———. *The Heart of the Antarctic.* Philadelphia: J. B. Lippincott Co., 1909.

Shaikh, Fariha. *Nineteenth-Century Settler Emigration in British Literature and Art.* Edinburgh: Edinburgh University Press, 2018.

Shakespeare, Nicholas. *In Tasmania.* New York: Overlook Press, 2004.

Shellam, Tiffany. 'Mediating Encounters through Bodies and Talk'. In *Indigenous Intermediaries: New Perspectives on Exploration Archives*, edited by Shino Konishi, Maria Nugent, and Tiffany Shellam, 85–102. Acton, ACT: Australian National University Press, 2015.

Shelley, Mary Wollstonecraft. *Frankenstein: or The Modern Prometheus.* 1818. Edited by Marilyn Butler. Oxford: Oxford World's Classics, 1998.

Shelton, Richard. 'Littorally Speaking: A Folk History of the West Coasts of Britain'. *TLS*, no. 6083 (1 November 2019).

Shipley, D. Graham J., and contributors. *Geographers of the Ancient Greek World.* Cambridge: Cambridge University Press, 2024.

Siccardi, Fabián Martínez. 'Feeling Southern: A Patagonian Story'. *Granta* 146 (14 February 2019). https://granta.com/feeling-southern/.

Sides, Hampton. *The Wide Wide Sea: Imperial Ambition, First Contact and the Fateful Final Voyage of Captain James Cook.* New York: Doubleday, 2024.

Silcox, Beejay. 'Inner Space Odyssey'. Review of *In Ascension*, by Martin MacInnes. *TLS*, no. 6256 (24 February 2023).

Silva, Tony Simões da. 'Raced Encounters, Sexed Transactions: 'Luso-tropicalism' and the Portuguese Colonial Empire.' *Pretexts: Literary and Cultural Studies* 11 (2002): 27–39.

Sinclair, Keith. *Imperial Federation: A Study of New Zealand Policy and Opinion, 1880–1914*. London: Athlone Press, 1955.

Sivasundaram, Sujit. *Waves Across the South: A New History of Revolution and Empire*. Chicago: University of Chicago Press, 2021.

Sleigh, Dan. *Islands*. Translated by André Brink. London: Secker, 2004.

Smith, Angela. 'Landscape and the Foreigner Within: Katherine Mansfield and Emily Carr'. In *Landscape and Empire, 1770–2000*, edited by Glenn Hooper, 141–57. Aldershot: Ashgate, 2005.

Smith, Bernard. 'Coleridge's Ancient Mariner and Cook's Second Voyage'. *Journal of the Warburg and Courtauld Institutes* 19, no. 1–2 (1956): 117–154.

———. *European Vision and the South Pacific, 1768–1850: A Study in the History of Art and Ideas*. New Haven: Yale University Press, 1985.

———. *Imagining the Pacific in the Wake of the Cook Voyages*. Carlton, Victoria: Melbourne University Press/Miegunyah Press, 1992.

Smith, L. E. *Daughters of Time and Other Poems*. Christchurch, NZ: Whitcombe and Tombs, 1952.

Smith, Linda Tuhiwai. *Decolonising Methodologies: Research and Indigenous Peoples*. Auckland: Zed, 1999.

Smith, Pauline. *The Little Karoo*. 1925. London: Everyman, 1930.

Smith, Vanessa. *Intimate Strangers: Friendship, Exchange, and Pacific Encounters*. Cambridge: Cambridge University Press, 2010.

———. 'Joseph Banks's Intermediaries: Rethinking Global Cultural Exchange'. In *Global Intellectual History*, edited by Samuel Moyn and Andrew Sartori, 81–109. New York: Columbia University Press, 2013.

Snaith, Anna. *Modernist Voyages: Colonial Women Writers in London, 1890–1945*. Cambridge: Cambridge University Press, 2014.

Solnit, Rebecca. *Whose Story Is This? Old Conflicts, New Chapters: Essays at the Intersection*. London: Granta, 2019.

Somerville, Alice Te Punga. *Once Were Pacific: Māori Connections to Oceania*. Minneapolis: University of Minnesota Press, 2012.

'The Song Cycle of the Moon-Bone'. In T*he Thunder Mutters—101 Poems for the Planet*, edited by Alice Oswald, translated by R. M. Berndt, 201-09. London: Faber, 2006.

South African Astronomical Observatory. 'SALT and SAAO Telescopes Investigate the Origin of the First Detection of Gravitational Waves Produced by Two Colliding Neutron Stars', *SAOO*, 16 October 2017, https://www.saao.ac.za/2017/10/16/salt-and-saao-telescopes-investigate-the-origin-of-the-first-detection-of-gravitational-waves-produced-by-two-colliding-neutron-stars/.

Sperber, Dan, and Deirdre Wilson. *Relevance: Communication and Cognition*. 2nd ed. Oxford: Blackwell, 1995.

Stafford, Jane. 'B. E. Baughan, 1870–1958'. *Kōtare* 7, no. 3 (2008): 67–72.

———. 'Ineludible Envanishings'. *New Zealand Review of Books* 112 (2015).

Stafford, Jane, and Mark Williams. *Maoriland: New Zealand Literature 1872–1914*. Wellington: Victoria University Press, 2006.

Stallard, Avan Judd. *Antipodes: In Search of the Southern Continent*. Melbourne: Monash University Publishing, 2016.

Staphorst, Luan. '"van die oorspronklike lippe" ("from the original lips"): The 19th-Century Cape Colony, Holographic Archaeology and the Historicity of Gideon von Wielligh's |xam–Afrikaans Collection'. *Journal of Southern African Studies* 48, no. 6 (2022): 993–1011.

Stead, Christina. *For Love Alone*. London: Virago, 1978.

Stedman, M. L. *The Light between Oceans*. Melbourne: Vintage Australia, 2012.

Steer, Philip. *Settler Colonialism in Victorian Literature: Economics and Political Identity in the Networks of Empire*. Cambridge: Cambridge University Press, 2019.

Steinberg, Philip E. 'Of Other Seas: Metaphors and Materialities in Maritime Regions', *Atlantic Studies* 10, no. 2 (2013): 156–69. https://doi.org/10.1080/14788810.2013.785192.

———. *The Social Construction of the Ocean*. Cambridge: Cambridge University Press, 2001.

Stephens, Cynthia Lucy. *The Borges Enigma: Mirrors, Doubles and Intimate Puzzles*. Woodbridge: Tamesis, 2021.

Stevens, Nell. *Bleaker House: Chasing My Novel to the End of the World*. London: Doubleday, 2017.

Stewart, Chantal. *The Veil of Maya*. Cape Town, Minimal Press, 2022.

Stiebel, Lindy, and Jane Carruthers, eds. *Thomas Baines: Exploring Tropical Australia, 1855 to 1857*. Canberra: National Museum of Australia, 2012.

Stow, Randolph, *To the Islands*. 1958. Melbourne: Text Publishing, 2015.

———. *The Merry-Go-Round in the Sea*. 1965. Camberwell, Victoria: Penguin, 2008.

Stratford, Elaine, Godfrey Baldacchino, Elizabeth McMahon. *Rethinking Island Methodologies*. Lanham, MD: Rowman and Littlefield, 2023.

Subrahmanyam, Sanjay. *The Career and Legend of Vasco da Gama*. Cambridge: Cambridge University Press, 1997.

Sullivan, Robert. *Captain Cook in the Underworld*. Auckland: Auckland University Press, 2002.

———. 'Hello Great North Road'. *Poetry*, 2018. https://www.poetryfoundation.org/poetrymagazine/poems/89742/hello-great-north-road.

Swanepoel, A. C. 'Coleridge's Transcendental Imagination: The Seascape beyond the Senses in "The Rime of the Ancient Mariner"'. *Journal of Literary Studies* 26, no.1 (2010): 191–214. https://doi.org/10.1080/02564710903495560.

Taylor, Peter. 'Poe's the *Narrative of Arthur Gordon Pym of Nantucket*'. *The Explicator* 59, no. 1 (2000): 17–19.

Teltscher, Kate. *Palace of Palms: Tropical Dreams and the Making of Kew*. London: Picador, 2020.

Thell, Anne M. *Minds in Motion: Imagining Empiricism in Eighteenth-Century British Travel*. Literature. Lewisburg, PA: Bucknell University Press, 2017.

Thiong'o, Ngugi wa. *Decolonising the Mind: The Politics of Language in African Literature*. London: Heinemann, 1986.

Thomas, Robert H., Douglas R. MacAyeal, David H. Eilers, and David R. Gaylord. 'The Ross Ice Shelf: Glaciology and Geophysics'. *Antarctic Research Series* 42, no. 2 (1984): 21–53.

Thompson, Christina. *Sea People: The Puzzle of Polynesia*. Glasgow: William Collins, 2019.

Thompson, Harry. *This Thing of Darkness*. 2005. Reprint. London: Headline Review/Tinder Press, 2020.

Tokarczuk, Olga. *Flights*. Translated by Jennifer Croft. London: Fitzcarraldo, 2017.

Trantaal, Nathan. *Alles Het Niet Kom Wôd*. Hatfield: Van Schaik Publishers, 2017.

———. *Chokers en Survivors*. Kaapstad: Kwela Boeke, 2013.

———. *Wit issie 'n colour nie*. Cape Town: Kwela Boeke, 2018.

Treagus, Mandy. *Empire Girls: The Colonial Heroine Comes of Age*. Adelaide: University of Adelaide Press, 2014.

Trisos, Christopher H., Jess Auerbach, and Madhusudan Katti. 'Decoloniality and Anti-Oppressive Practices'. *Nature Ecology & Evolution* 5 (2021): 1205–1212. https://doi.org/10.1038/s41559-021-01460-w.

Trojanow, Ilija. *The Lamentations of Zeno*. Translated by Philip Boehm. London: Verso, 2011.

Trollope, Anthony. *Australia and New Zealand*. London: Chapman and Hall, 1873.

Trotta, Roberto. *Starborn*. London: Hachette, 2023.

Troy, Jakelin. 'The Sydney Language Notebooks and Responses to Language Contact in Early Colonial NSW'. *Australian Journal of Linguistics* 12 (1992): 145–70.

Turchi, Peter. *Maps of the Imagination: The Writer as Cartographer*. San Antonio, TX: Trinity University Press, 2004.

Turner, Graham. *Making it National: Nationalism and Popular Culture in Australia*. Sydney: Allen and Unwin, 1994.

Turner, John. 'Reducing Down: D. H. Lawrence and Captain Scott'. *Critical Survey* 14, no. 3 (2002): 14–27.

Turner, Stephen. 'Being Colonial, Colonial Being'. *Journal of New Zealand Literature* 20 (2000): 39–66.

———. 'Settlement as Forgetting'. In *Quicksands: Foundational Histories in Australia and Aotearoa New Zealand*, edited by Klaus Neumann, Nicholas Thomas and Hilary Ericksen, 20–38. Sydney: UNSW Press, 1999.

Twidle, Hedley. 'From *The Origin of Language* to a Language of Origin'. In *The Cambridge History of South African Literature*, edited by Andrew van der Vlies, 252–84. Johannesburg: University of Witwatersrand Press, 2012.

———. 'Impossible Images: Radio Astronomy, the Square Kilometre Array and the Art of Seeing'. *JSAS* 45, no. 4 (2019): 767–90.

'The 2021 Peter Porter Prize', *Australian Review of Books*, https://www.australianbookreview.com.au/component/k2/47-competitionsandprograms/6579-2021-peter-porter-poetry-prize. Accessed 10 January 2021.

Uhart, Hebe. *A Question of Belonging: Crónicas*. Trans. Anna Vilner. New York: Archipelago, 2024.

Unaipon, David. *Legendary Tales of the Australian Aborigines*. 1930. Edited by Stephen Muecke and Adam Shoemaker. Melbourne: Miegunyah Press, 2006.

Ussher, Jane. *Still Life: Inside the Antarctic Huts of Scott and Shackleton*. Sydney: Murdoch Books, 2010.

Vadde, Aarthi. *Chimeras of Form: Modernist Internationalism Beyond Europe, 1914–2016*. New York: Columbia University Press, 2017.

Van Breda, Denver, Deidre Jantjies, Menán du Plessis. '!Hub Di Gowab—'n Taal van ons Land', Woordfees festival discussion, Stellenbosch, 11 March 2020, personal notes.

Van der Putten, Jan. 'Abdullah Munsyi and the Missionaries'. *Bijdragen tot de Taal-, Land en Volkenkunde (BKI)* 162 (2006): 407–40.

Van den Broecke, Marcel. *Ortelius Atlas Maps: An Illustrated Guide*. Houten: De Graaf Publishers, 2011.

van den Driesen, Cynthia. *Writing the Nation: Patrick White and the Indigene*. Amsterdam: Brill, 2009.

van der Krogt, Peter C. J. *Koeman's Atlantis Neerlandici*. New ed. Vol 3. Leiden: Brill, 2003.

van der Vlies, Andrew, ed. *Print, Text and Book Cultures in South Africa*. Johannesburg: University of Witwatersrand Press, 2012.

van der Watt, Lizé-Marie, and Sandra Swart. 'Falling off the Map: South Africa, Antarctica and Empire, c. 1919–59'. *Journal of Imperial and Commonwealth History* 43, no. 2 (2015): 267–91.

———. 'The Whiteness of Antarctica: Race and South Africa's Antarctic History'. In *Antarctica and the Humanities*, edited by Peder Roberts, Lize-Marié van der Watt, and Adrian Howkins, 125–56. London: Palgrave Macmillan, 2016.

van der Watt, Susanna Maria Elizabeth. 'Out in the Cold: Science and the Environment in South Africa's Involvement in the sub-Antarctic and Antarctic in the Twentieth Century'. PhD diss., University of Stellenbosch, 2012.

van Niekerk, Marlene. *Agaat*. Translated by Michiel Heyns. Cape Town: Tafelberg/Jonathan Ball, 2006.

Van Vuuren, Helize. 'A Song Sung by the Star !Gaunu'. In *Courage of ||kabbo: Celebrating the 100th Anniversary of the Publication of Specimens of Bushman Folklore*, edited by Janette Deacon and Pippa Skotnes, 317–28. Cape Town: University of Cape Town Press, 2014.

van Wyk Louw, N. P. *Raka*. Pretoria: Nationale Boekhandel, 1964.

Van Wyk Smith, Malvern, ed. *Shades of Adamastor: Africa and the Portuguese Connection: An Anthology of Poetry*. Grahamstown, South Africa: Institute for the Study of English in Africa, 1988.

Van Wyk Smith, Malvern. *The First Ethiopians: The Image of Africa and Africans in the Early Mediterranean World*. Johannesburg: Wits University Press, 2009.

———. 'Ptolemy, Paradise and Purgatory'. In *T'Kama—Adamastor: Inventions of Africa in a South African Painting*, edited by Ivan Vladislavic, 83–97. Johannesburg: University of the Witwatersrand Press, 2000.

———. '"Waters flowing from darkness": The Two Ethiopias in the Early European Image of Africa'. *Theoria: A Journal of Social and Political Theory* 68 (December 1986): 67–77.

Varela, Eduardo Fernando. *Patagonia, Route 203*. Translated by Peter Bush. 1988; London: Mountain Leopard Press, 2024.

Verne, Jules. *An Antarctic Mystery*. 1897. Translated by Cashel Hoey. Orinda, CA: Seawolf Press, 2020.

Viviers, David Ralph. *Mirage*. Cape Town: Umuzi, 2023.

Vladislavic, Ivan, ed. *T'Kama—Adamastor: Inventions of Africa in a South African Painting*. Johannesburg: University of the Witwatersrand Press, 2000.

Wadhams, Peter. *A Farewell to Ice: A Report from the Arctic*. London: Penguin, 2017.

Wainschenker, Pablo, and Elizabeth Leane. 'The "Alien" Next Door: Antarctica in South American fiction'. *The Polar Journal* 9, no. 2 (2019): 324–339.

Walker, Cherryl, Davide Chinigò, and Saul Dubow, eds. 'Karoo Futures: Astronomy in Place and Space'. Special issue: *JSAS* 45, no. 4 (August 2019).

Wallerstein, Immanuel. *Historical Capitalism with Capitalist Civilization*. London: Verso, 1996.

Ward, Ashley. *Sensational: A New Story of Our Senses*. London: Profile, 2023.

Weldon Long, James. 'Plunging into the Atlantic: The Oceanic Order of Herman Melville's *Moby-Dick*'. *Atlantic Studies* 8, no. 1 (2001): 69–91.

Wenzel, Jennifer. *The Disposition of Nature: Environmental Crisis and World Literature*. New York: Fordham University Press, 2020.

West-Pavlov, Russell, ed. *The Global South and Literature*. Cambridge: Cambridge University Press, 2018.

Wevers, Lydia. 'Speaking for Ourselves in 1945'. *Journal of New Zealand Literature* 16 (1998): 97–111.

Wheeler, Sara. *Cherry: A Life of Apsley Cherry-Garrard*. New York: Vintage Books, 1997.

———. *Terra Incognita: Travels in Antarctica*. London: Vintage, 2001.

White, Landeg. Introduction to *The Lusíads*, translated by Landeg White, 1997. Oxford: Oxford University Press, 2001.

White, Patrick. *Voss*. Ed. William Walsh. London: Edward Arnold, 1976.

White, Ross, Sumeet Jain, and Catalina Giurgi-Oncu, eds. *Counterflows for Mental Well-being: What High-income Countries Can Learn from Low and Middle-Income Countries*. London: Informa Healthcare, 2014.

White, Terri-ann. *Finding Theodore and Brina*. Fremantle: Fremantle Arts Centre, 2001.

Whorf, Benjamin. *Language, Thought, and Reality: Selected Writings*. Edited by John B. Carroll, Penny Lee, Stephen C. Levinson. Boston, MA: MIT Press, 2012.

Wicomb, Zoë. *Still Life*. Cape Town: Umuzi, 2020.

———. *The One That Got Away*. Cape Town: Umuzi, 2008.

———. *You Can't Get Lost in Cape Town*. London: Virago, 1987.

Williams, Elizabeth Lewis, 'Remote Imag(in)ing the Antarctic: Life-writing and the Resonant Page'. In *Life Writing and the Southern Hemisphere*, edited by Elleke Boehmer and Katherine Collins, 215–236. London: Bloomsbury, 2024.

Williams, Mark, ed. *A History of New Zealand Literature*. Cambridge: Cambridge University Press, 2016.

Wilson, Eric. *The Spiritual History of Ice: Romanticism, Science and the Imagination*. New York: Palgrave Macmillan, 2003.

Wilson, Frances. *Guilty Thing: A Life of Thomas De Quincey*. London: Bloomsbury, 2016.

Wilson, Mac J. 'Scheherazade, Achilles, and Borges'. *Confluencia* 34, no. 1 (2018): 47–60.

Wilson, Rohan. *The Roving Party*. Sydney: Allen and Unwin, 2011.

Winch, Tara June. *The Yield*. London: Harper Via, 2021.

———. Reading. GAPS 2023 Annual Conference, University of Konstanz, Germany, 18 May 2023.

Winton, Tim. *The Boy behind the Curtain*. Sydney: Penguin Random House Australia, 2016.

———. *Island Home: A Landscape Memoir*. Sydney: Penguin Random House Australia, 2015.

———. *Land's Edge*. Sydney: Penguin Random House Australia, 2010.

Wright, Alexis. *Carpentaria*. Sydney: Giramondo, 2006.

———. 'Introduction'. In *The Thunder Mutters—101 Poems for the Planet*, edited by Alice Oswald. London: Faber, 2006.

———. *Praiseworthy*. Sydney: Giramondo, 2023.

———. 'On Writing *Carpentaria*'. In *Indigenous Translationalism: Alexis Wright's Carpentaria*, edited by Lynda Ng, 217–234. Sydney: Giramondo, 2018.

———. *The Swan Book*. Sydney: Giramondo 2013.

Wright, Judith. *Collected Poems*. Sydney: Angus and Robertson, 1994.

———. 'The Granite Rocks of New England'. In *The Nature of Love*, by Judith Wright, 188–92. Sydney: Imprint Books, 1997.

———. *Half a Lifetime*. Edited by Patricia Clarke. Melbourne: Text Publishing, 1999.

Wylie, John, 'Landscape as Not-Belonging: *The Plains*, Earth Writing, and the Impossibilities of Inhabitation'. *Philological Quarterly* 97, no. 2 (2018): 177–196.

Yap, Melanie, and Dianne Leong Man. *Colour, Confusion and Concessions: The History of the Chinese in South Africa*. Hong Kong: Hong Kong University Press, 1996.

Young, Sandra. 'Charting English Global Presence and its Violent Effects in Early Modernity: Reading Strategies for an Ambivalent Archive'. *Jems* 12 (2023): 217–235.

———. *The Early Modern Global South in Print: Textual Form and the Production of Human Difference as Knowledge*. Farnham, Surrey: Ashgate, 2015.

Zarankin, Andres and Salerno, Melisa A. 'Antarctic Archaeology: Discussing the History of the Southernmost End of the World'. In *The Oxford Handbook of Historical Archaeology*. Edited by James Symonds and Vesa-Pekka Herva. Oxford: Oxford University Press, 2014. https://doi.org/10.1093/oxfordhb/9780199562350.001.0001.

Zimbler, Jarad. 'Guy Butler's Poetry and Poetics'. *Wasafiri* 31, no. 2 (2016): 58–64.

INDEX

Abulafia, David, 217n18
Adamastor, xxiv, 20, 65, 69, 70, 75, 84, 95, 112, 238n67, 262n44. *See also* Camões, Luís de
Adams, Terry-Ann, 21, 170, 177, 179–80, 182, 184; *those who live in cages*, 182–84, 263n52
Africa, 6, 7, 21, 27, 107, 118; as 'backward', 13, 90–91; navigating around, 55–63, 65–74, 173; flora and fauna of, 148–49, 181
Afrikaans, 36, 39, 150, 160, 171, 178–79, 180–81, 183, 225n9, 262n43, 253n67; monument to, 142; as a creole language, 171, 179, 143
aiagata, 36, 37
albatross, 77, 78, 83–85, 97, 100, 210, 239n11. *See also* Coleridge, Samuel Taylor
Alpha Centauri, 41, 45, 197, 199
Amundsen, Roald, 107, 110, 111, 120, 123, 216n10
Anglo-Boer War, 2, 123, 140
Antarctic, the, 73, 85, 100, 108–9, 114, 125, 128, 139; Antarctic circle, 82, 120; Antarctic seas, 79; Antarctic skies, 96; Antarctic waters, 84; Antarctic writing, 110
Antarctica, xx, 6, 9, 19, 20, 22, 100, 101–3, 106–110, 114, 121–22, 126, 131, 133, 159, 201, 210, 212; photograph of, xi; Ross expedition, 89; remoteness of, 104, 119, 125, 127–28; and the sublime, 105, 112; whiteness of, 107; as a southern reference point, 116–19; light from, 158
Aotearoa New Zealand, 11, 18, 21, 119, 130–31, 136, 145, 146, 151–54, 158, 160, 171; photograph of, xii, xv; Cook voyage to, 9, 48–49, 52, 82; Darwin voyage to, 91; Polynesian journeys to, 47; writing on, 109, 118, 125; British colonisation of, 117
Arabian Nights, The, 54, 84, 131–32
Araucana, The (Alonso de Ercilla), 20, 54, 56, 66, 234–35
archipelago, 34, 35, 89, 93; archipelagic ocean, 96, 106; starscapes, 96; archipelagic thinking, 32, 35; archipelagic worlds, 48
Argentina, 45, 91, 108–109, 111, 116, 128, 143, 210
astrolabe, 12, 53, 66, 138
asymptote, 5, 22, 23, 109, 111, 112; asymptotic association, 110, 114; asymptotic feature, 118; asymptotic thinking, 107
Aurora Australis, 214
Australia, 3, 4, 6, 21, 27, 42, 53, 92, 108, 133, 136, 144, 156–57, 161, 199; photograph of, xi, xiii, xv; Cook expedition to, 2; Indigenous, 5, 28, 39–40, 44–45, 164, 176, 184, 200, 206; colonisation of, 11, 53, 59, 82, 91, 157; colonial, 145–46, 156; postcolonial, 185–86

Baderoon, Gabeba, 164–71, 185–86, 208
Badiou, Alain, 113, 123
Baiame, 26
Bainbridge, Beryl, 21, 109–110, 118, 122, 123
basket, 91, 203–5
Baughan, Blanche Edith, 21, 133, 135–40, 145–47, 151–53, 156, 161
Baynton, Barbara, 139

Bethell, Ursula, 138, 245n40
Bhambra, Gurminder, 16
billabong, 31, 37
biltong, 31
birds, xviii, 6, 11, 44, 47, 77, 103, 115, 117, 137. *See also* albatross
Blombos carving, 33, 41, 47
blue hemisphere, 34
Boehmer, Elleke, 265n4
boomerang, 2, 22–23, 24, 31, 36, 37, 91, 219n44, 228n39
boomeranging, 49
Borges, Jorge Luis, 131–32, 138, 161
Bougainville, Louis-Antoine de, xviii, 9, 61
Brasch, Charles, 137, 139, 142–44, 146, 158, 160
Brathwaite, Kamau, 15
Brazil, 6, 45, 67, 91, 136
Breda, Denver van, 39
Bristow-Bovey, Darrel, 243n3
Browning, Robert, 104
buchu, 31
Butler, Guy, 144, 230n63, 252n57
Byron, John, 52, 57, 61

Camões, Luís de, 20, 55–56, 59, 62–70, 73–78, 82–85, 95, 236n30; *Os Lusíades (The Lusíads)*, 20, 56–68, 71, 73–74, 78, 93, 16
Campbell, Roy, 141, 144, 252n67
Cape Horn, 7, 9, 23, 52, 59, 77–78, 81, 86, 92, 93, 95, 210
Cape of Good Hope, 7, 8, 23, 41, 55, 59, 61, 67, 82, 91, 92, 94
carbon dioxide, 12
Carter, Paul, 142
Casanova, Pascale, 17
Catton, Eleanor, 185, 193, 201, 266n7, 267n20, 269n44
Chatwin, Bruce, 140, 226n17
Chile, xxvi, 54, 56, 88, 91–92, 108–9, 111, 128, 131, 141, 186, 200, 210
Christiansë, Yvette, 185
climate change, xx, 176, 207
Clingman, Stephen, 221n60
coastline, 34, 47, 53, 127, 139; of southern hemisphere, 5–6, 34, 127, 185, 211; African, 55, 57, 61, 66–68, 117, 188; Antarctic, 103, 111, 113
Coetzee, J. M., 133, 134, 138, 141, 147, 150, 194, 266n9
Coleridge, Samuel Taylor, 5, 10, 14, 20, 23, 54, 56, 63, 74, 77–87, 94–96, 98, 100, 120, 160, 194, 208; *The Rime of the Ancient Mariner*, 20, 23, 54, 56, 77–80, 84–86, 92, 94, 96, 98–99, 119, 160, 194, 240n21
colonial history, 19, 54, 107
Comaroff, Jean and John, 16
compass, 32, 53, 182
Connell, Raewyn, 16
Conrad, Joseph, 5, 8, 10, 23, 197
convex lens, 191
Cook, James, xviii, 2, 5, 9, 14, 20, 24, 41, 43, 48, 52–62, 79–83, 98, 100, 106, 218n37, 220n53, 229n51
Couto, Mia, 139, 186
Crux, 45, 175, 197, 197–200
Curnow, Allen, 136–37, 140, 142–43, 158, 250n30, 253n66, 256n112

D'Arcy Wood, Gillen, 217n21
da Gama, Vasco, 4, 8, 54, 56–57, 60, 62–63, 65–68, 70–73, 75, 79, 84
Dalrymple, Alexander, 215n2
Dark Emu (constellation), 44, 198, 229n53, 232n71
Darwin, Charles, 14, 20, 75, 79, 80, 81–84, 89–92, 96, 100, 134, 149, 207, 210, 241n39; library of, 54; *The Voyage of the* Beagle, 56, 80–81, 87–90, 98
Davids, Nadia, 167, 201
Davies, Iva, 129
deixis, 112
Diamond, Jared, 223n76
Dias, Bartolomeu, 4, 55, 57, 58, 73, 94, 236n30
Diski, Jenny, 21, 110, 114, 118–19, 123, 125, 126
Drake, Francis, xviii, 9, 52, 79
Durban, 7, 103, 192, 209, 252n57, 265n4

D'Urville, Jules Dumont, 10, 62, 100

eina, 31
Elephant Island, 104
empire, 19, 28–29, 62, 68, 136, 194
emu, 44, 198. *See also* Dark Emu
Endurance, 21, 103–5, 113
equator, 5
etak, 47

Ferrus, Diana, 167
Flanagan, Richard, 215n5, 219n46
Flinders, Matthew, 53, 133, 261n37
Flynn, Eugenia, 223n85
Frame, Janet, 21, 24, 118, 133, 136–37, 147, 151, 157–61, 191, 201–2, 209
Frost, Lola, 195, 265n5
Frye, Northrop, 142
Furphy, Joseph, 255n98

Gamilaraay, 44, 205–6
Gilmore, Mary, 145
Glissant, Édouard, 15
Global South, 9, 16, 18
Godelier, Maurice, 216n3
gogga, 36, 37
Gondwanaland, xx, 6, 41, 108, 117
Grey, Sir George, 145

haecceity, xix, 14, 28, 49, 112, 133, 195, 213
haka, 31
Hancock, W. K., 136
Hangklip (cliff), 168, 169, 173
Hardy, Thomas, 2, 149, 221n63
Hau'ofa, Epeli, 15, 34, 35, 108
Hayot, Eric, 220n49
HMS *Beagle*, 52, 54, 79, 83, 87, 91, 98
HMS *Endeavour*, 2, 41, 48–49, 62, 82, 91, 113, 229n51
Hofmeyr, Isabel, 15, 222n65, 227n35
Hooker, Joseph, 6, 11, 89–90, 217n21
Hope, A. D., 143, 156
Hurley, Frank, 104
Hyde, Robin, 133, 137, 155

ice, 101–3, 105, 107, 111–12, 116, 120–21, 124, 191
Ihimaera, Witi, 24, 35, 172–73, 179, 186–87, 188, 194, 208, 269n46; *The Whale Rider*, 172–73, 185–88
indigenous language, xxvi, 29, 31, 36, 167, 177, 206, 224n1
indigenous words, 20, 36, 41
islands, 19, 82, 130, 159, 161, 172, 186–87; of the Southern Ocean, xx; of the south, 5–6, 13, 24, 116, 140, 166, 185, 200–201; of Aotearoa New Zealand, 18, 58, 133; and the stars, 34, 40, 49; of the Pacific, 46–48

jacaranda trees, xx
Justo, Liborio, 111, 114, 128

||kabbo, 6, 38–39, 146, 229n48, 230n58, 254n93, 257
kangaroo, 2, 3, 4, 26, 31, 45
Karoo, 43–45, 138, 147–50
Keats, John, 8, 118
Keegan, Claire, 128
Kennedy, Roseanne, 229n53
Kerguelen-Trémarec, Yves-Joseph de, xviii, 10
Khoekhoegowab, 38
Kipling, Rudyard, 139, 247n80
Krog, Antjie, 6, 39, 179
kupu, 30

Lane, William, 140
Lavery, Charne, 128, 264n66
Law, Robert, 243
Lawrence, D. H., xviii, 2, 198, 201
Lawson, Henry, 136, 139–40, 147
Le Guin, Ursula, xviii, 18, 36, 106, 114, 244n25; *The Left Hand of Darkness*, 18, 106, 114, 244n25
Lessing, Doris, 137, 141
Liboiron, Max, 220n51
light, xx
Linnaean system, 9, 218n36
Lopez, Barry, 12
Lukashenko, Melissa, 170, 176, 177, 201

Lusíads, The. See Camões, Luís de
Lynch, Benito, 133, 148

Mabo decision (1992), 233n82, 260n22
Mabo, Gail, 233n82
Magellan, Ferdinand, xviii, 4, 8, 60, 73, 79
Magellanic clouds, xx, 41, 45, 196
Malouf, David, 38
Manenzhe, Resoketswe, 172
manhang, 172
Manhire, Bill, 21, 109–10, 118, 121–22, 130–32, 138, 143
Mansfield, Katherine, 21, 133, 135–38, 140, 144, 147, 152, 154–55, 201, 213
maps, 51, 53, 55, 57–58, 61, 62, 218n37
Marshall, Tim, 7, 217n25
Massey, Doreen, 15, 170
Mawson, Douglas, 113–15, 117, 128
McCracken, James, 227n22
McGregor, Jon, 21, 109–10, 114, 118, 124–25
McKitterick, Katherine, 224n91
Mda, Zakes, 128, 187, 188, 208, 213, 264n66
Melville, Herman, 10, 20, 48, 54, 56, 77, 81–84, 87, 93, 95–97, 100, 126, 134, 194–95, 208, 213, 228n35, 240n29, 242n45; *Moby-Dick*, 23, 54, 56, 75, 77, 80, 81, 91–98, 228n35, 241n29
Menon, Dilip, 16
mia-mia, 31
Mignolo, Walter, 15
Milky Way, xx, 2, 40, 44–46, 164, 166, 173, 196, 224, 231n65; photograph of, xii; curve of, 23; mirror of, 35; mythology of, 46; as Tsoab, 179; brightness of, 198
Milton, John, 51, 54, 88
modes of navigation, 31
Money, Jazz, 164–69, 171, 185–86, 191, 194, 204, 205, 208, 213, 258n3
Morris, Paula, 171
Mqhayi, S.E.K., 231n63
Muller, C.F.J., 136
Murnane, Gerald, 133, 141, 143
Murray, Les, 146–47

Nama, xxvi, 27, 29, 35, 150, 179, 186
Narrative of Arthur Gordon Pym of Nantucket, The, 23. *See also* Poe, Edgar Allen
navigational writing, 64
Neruda, Pablo, 6, 141, 186, 264n65
Newton, John, 143–44
Nussbaum, Martha, 266n8
nyamilay, 36, 37
Nyezwa, Mxolisi, 212, 269n45

ocean, 19–20, 29, 32, 34–35, 48, 71, 72; Southern, xx, 5, 8, 11, 20, 57, 59, 80, 92, 95, 108, 109, 128, 137, 143, 168, 169, 202, 207–8, 212; Atlantic, 6, 55, 59, 64, 65, 73, 74, 80, 93, 124, 185, 212; Indian, 6, 8, 55–56, 63, 66, 69–70, 90, 92, 93, 140, 209; Pacific, 6, 10, 17, 33, 46–47, 48, 52, 55, 59, 60–62, 77, 83, 85, 91, 92–98, 130–31, 141, 151, 152, 154–56, 186–87, 225n9, 227n35, 242n45
Oliver, W. H., 136
Orion, 42, 45, 46
Orsman, Chris, 21, 109–10, 116, 118–22, 126, 212
ostrich, 44, 45, 90

parabola, 5, 20, 22–23, 70–71, 77, 80, 85, 110–11; parabolic disposition, 53; figure, 107; parabolic journey, 110, 171; parabolic pathway, 72, 85; parabolic rhythm, 147; parabolic route, 74, 80
pareidolia, 44
Pascoe, Bruce, 229n53
Patagonia, 44, 87–92, 114, 140, 161, 199
Paterson, Banjo, 140, 144, 254n93
Plaatje, Solomon, 261n43
planet, xviii, 189; south of, xix, xxi, 5, 22, 98, 131–32, 207; climate change and the, xxi, 47, 214; Antarctica and the, 100, 102, 107, 108
Pleiades, 42, 44–45, 47, 60, 192
Poe, Edgar Allen, 4, 24, 216n13
polar continent, 133
polar darkness, 120
polar night, 112
polar speculation, 99

Pole Star, 55, 60, 118, 197, 199
Polynesian navigators, 35, 43, 64
Ponting, Herbert, 110, 114, 119, 120, 125
Portuguese, xx, 6, 9, 66, 68
Prichard, Katharine Susannah, 3–4, 133, 141, 145
Ptolemy, Claudius, xviii, 8, 9
purakau, 35

Read, Peter, 141
Reeves, William Pember, 138, 245n40
remote proximate (faraway close), 192, 207–8
rhea, 44, 90
Richardson, Henry Handel, 137
Rime of the Ancient Mariner, The. See Coleridge, Samuel Taylor
Rodoreda, Geoffrey, 260n22
Ross, James Clark, 10

Said, Edward, 13, 134
St Helena (island), 63, 140, 185
Samuelson, Meg, 128, 185, 219n48
Santos, Boaventura de Sousa, 15, 215n4, 222n65, 259n13
Sapir, Edward, 30, 226n13
scale framing, 109, 125, 201–2, 248n93
Schouten, Willem Corneliszoon, 4, 60, 61
Schreiner, Olive, 5, 14, 21, 24, 133, 135, 138, 140–41, 147–55, 158, 168, 197; *From Man to Man*, 148–50; *The Story of An African Farm*, 138, 148–50
Scott, Kim, 170, 176, 185–86
Scott, Robert Falcon, 103, 106, 110–11, 113, 115, 119, 120, 122–24, 128
sea country, 35
sea, 15, 19, 32, 34, 37, 41, 48, 68, 73, 81, 93
Sedivy, Julia, 226n14
settler literature, 19
Shackleton, Ernest, 21, 103–5, 110–14, 117–18, 121, 123
Shelley, Mary, 20, 54, 81, 98–100; *Frankenstein*, 56, 79, 80, 82, 98–100, 119, 242n51
Siccardi, Fabián Martinez, 137, 225n9
Sivasundaram, Sujit, 17
sky, 28, 33, 34, 37, 44, 46, 117, 130, 141–42, 147, 163, 164, 209; southern, xviii, 8, 18–19, 26, 118, 192, 196–99, 201, 206; spirit of, 26–27; night, 2, 24, 32, 34, 40, 41, 43–44, 46, 48, 60, 96, 153, 192, 199, 200; open, 132; African, 150; sea and, 165–69, 172–73, 186
Smith, Linda Tuhiwai, 14, 29, 30, 177
Smith, Patti, 248
Smuts, Jan, 118
South Africa, 107–8, 116–17, 132, 140, 146, 174, 180–81, 184, 192, 200, 202, 212
South America, 6, 7, 45, 61, 66, 79, 89, 92, 108, 133, 200
South Celestial Pole, 41
South Magnetic Pole, 117
South Pole, 5, 23, 24, 60, 77, 83, 96, 111, 116, 159; as the centre, xix, xx, 131, 197; voyaging to, 19, 103, 106–7, 113, 119, 123
south, the (including 'far south'), 5, 7, 15, 20, 109, 112, 119, 145, 171, 205; as at the centre, xviii, xxiv–xxv, xx, xxi, 21, 24, 27–28, 30, 32, 49, 170, 189, 192, 199–201, 214; as peripheral or remote, 11, 20, 23, 57, 63, 75, 77, 84, 104, 135, 207; defying comprehension, 1, 7–8, 18, 54, 59, 82, 132–34, 161; as knowing otherwise, 2, 5, 13, 34, 36, 70, 74, 87, 92, 96, 128, 138, 160, 186, 212; reach of, 4, 8, 89, 199; across, 88–91, 109, 117, 146, 188; physical features of, 6, 9, 19, 155; northern views of, 9–12, 17, 24, 53, 66, 71, 81, 83, 93, 194; and 'global south', 16; indigenous ideas of, 22, 29, 144–45; languages of, 35–46, 169; Antarctica and, 100, 118; as entrapping, 159
southerly vision, 100
southern affinity, 213
southern awareness, 192
Southern Cross, 27, 44, 60, 85, 106, 136, 161, 164, 169, 182, 192, 197–200
southern disposition, 213
southern environments, 24
southern farness, 205
southern haecceity, 14, 28

Southern hemisphere, xix, xx, 43, 53, 59, 72, 89, 94, 114, 191, 205, 212
southern heuristic, 109, 207–8
southern histories, 18
southern imagining, xviii, xix, xx, 2, 57, 98, 102, 107, 108, 213
southern inclination, 182
southern journeying, 79
southern knowledge, 29, 31
southern landmass, 6, 108, 116, 202, 208, 217n23
southern lands, xviii, xx, 7, 10, 12–13, 18, 21, 23, 30, 32, 34, 43, 54, 58, 81, 92, 106, 108, 116, 133–34, 140, 169, 191, 194
southern latitudes, 8, 12
southern light, xxviii, 181, 201–2, 185, 214
southern ontologies, 19
southern optic, 191; and perception, 21, 27, 54, 192, 201
southern orientation, 132
southern practice, 205
southern realities, 34
southern skies, xviii, 17, 20, 154, 192, 199
southern space, 14, 18, 21, 22, 205
southern theory, 49
southern words, 35, 40
southern writing, 133, 139
southerners, xviii
starry skies, xx, 35, 133
stars, 20, 34, 37, 43, 46–48, 130, 163–64, 182, 196, 200, 206
Stead, Christina, 137, 139, 251n44
stick-map, 47, 56
stone, 33, 34, 46
Stow, Randolph, 102, 118, 133, 142, 144, 161, 252n62
Strabo, xviii
sublime, the, 105, 112
Sun, xviii
sunlight, xx

Tasman, Abel Janszoon, 18, 52, 53, 58–59, 61
Tasman Peninsula, 250n20
Tasman Sea, 17, 140
Te Ranhikaheke, Wiremu, 146
Tennyson, Alfred, 107
Thell, Ann, 220n58
Tokarczuk, Olga, 18, 221n63
Trojanow, Ilija, 248n213
Trollope, Anthony, 135
Tropic of Capricorn, xviii
Tupaia, 48, 49, 62

van Wyk Louw, N. P., 142
van Wyk Smith, Malvern, 218n35, 238n66
verbal artefacts, 31, 37
Verne, Jules, 4, 10, 23–24, 59, 103, 202, 242n52
vlei, 31
Voyage of the Beagle, *The*, 56, 80, 81, 87–90

Wallerstein, Immanuel, 219n47
Wallis, Samuel, 9, 52, 57, 60–61
Ward, Ashley, 194
Warlpiri, 30
watery south, 63
Weddell Sea, 21, 103, 105
Wegener, Alfred, 217n20
whale, 12, 26, 36–37, 74, 92–100, 127–28, 163, 172, 177, 186–88, 235n11, 261n37, 264n66
whaling, 7, 10, 12–13, 80, 94, 185
white, 107, 121, 131
White, Patrick, 137, 145
Whorf, Benjamin, 30, 226n13
Wicomb, Zoë, 14, 170–71, 177, 179, 180, 181
Wilkes, Charles, 10
Wilson, Bill and Oriana, 115
Wilson, Rohan, 261n40
Winch, Tara June, 177, 186, 197, 268n37
Winton, Tim, 118, 141, 247n78
Worsley, Frank, 104
Wright, Alexis, 14, 21, 35, 164, 165, 167, 170, 173, 184, 186, 189; *Carpentaria*, 28, 172, 174, 175, 189
Wright, Judith, 14, 21, 133–35, 137, 147, 156, 157, 161

Yámana, 46, 62, 225n9

A NOTE ON THE TYPE

This book has been composed in Arno, an Old-style serif typeface in the classic Venetian tradition, designed by Robert Slimbach at Adobe.